# Teaching Literacy to Learners with

# Dyslexia

# Education at SAGE

**SAGE** is a leading international publisher of journals, books, and electronic media for academic, educational, and professional markets.

Our education publishing includes:

- accessible and comprehensive texts for aspiring education professionals and practitioners looking to further their careers through continuing professional development

- inspirational advice and guidance for the classroom

- authoritative state of the art reference from the leading authors in the field

Find out more at: **www.sagepub.co.uk/education**

# Teaching Literacy to Learners with
# Dyslexia
## A Multisensory Approach

Kathleen Kelly &
Sylvia Phillips

Los Angeles | London | New Delhi
Singapore | Washington DC

KH

SAGE Publications Ltd
1 Oliver's Yard
55 City Road
London EC1Y 1SP

SAGE Publications Inc.
2455 Teller Road
Thousand Oaks, California 91320

SAGE Publications India Pvt Ltd
B 1/I 1 Mohan Cooperative Industrial Area
Mathura Road
New Delhi 110 044

SAGE Publications Asia-Pacific Pte Ltd
33 Pekin Street #02-01
Far East Square
Singapore 048763

**Library of Congress Control Number: 2011923361**

**British Library Cataloguing in Publication data**

A catalogue record for this book is available from the British Library

ISBN 978-0-85702-534-0
ISBN 978-0-85702-535-7 (pbk)

Typeset by C&M Digitals (P) Ltd, Chennai, India
Printed by MPG Books Group, Bodmin, Cornwall
Printed on paper from sustainable resources

7/18/12

# ENDORSEMENT

'*Teaching Literacy to Learners with Dyslexia* has it all – a feast of practice offering a prescription for success. All teachers will be eager to get their hands on this book! Grounded in solid and up to date research, it combines best practice in teaching literacy with insights into the cognitive and practical skills essential for literacy learning. Part II on Conquering Literacy is a complete multisensory teaching programme and one that echoes the spirit of recent government initiatives that purport to effectively deal with dyslexia and their desire to boost the training of teachers in this area. This book shows exactly how to achieve this! Steeped in the long established tradition of the most appropriate and successful approaches for teaching children with dyslexia Kathleen Kelly and Sylvia Phillips, using their vast knowledge base and unquestionable experience, have utilised, what is considered by most, to be best practice in teaching literacy and incorporated this into a 'user-friendly' teaching manual. By providing a clear rationale and practical explanations of literacy concepts and conventions they will simplify the task of dealing with the literacy challenges for many teachers. Every school needs to have access to this book.'

*Dr. Gavin Reid, Educational Psychologist, International Consultant and Author*

# CONTENTS

# ABOUT THE AUTHORS

**Dr Kathleen Kelly**

Dr Kathleen Kelly PhD, MA (SEN), Dip TESL, AMBDA, is a senior lecturer at Manchester Metropolitan University in the Centre for Inclusion and Special Educational Needs. She is Programme Leader for the MA in Specific Learning Difficulties and has presented papers at a number of international conferences in this area. For several years she has taught courses on specific learning difficulties (dyslexia) to undergraduates as part of the initial teacher training programme in addition to postgraduate awards. She has considerable experience in delivering courses to meet the criteria set out by the British Dyslexia Association for Approved Teacher Status (ATS) and is Associate Member of the British Dyslexia Association (AMBDA).

Kathleen has taught a wide range of learners with dyslexia, from children as young as four years to those at Key Stage 5. She has worked in both mainstream and special schools, for language support and learning support services, as a SENCO in a primary school, and as Head of Sixth Form in a special school. She has many years' experience of supporting multilingual children with special educational needs (including specific learning difficulties). Multilingualism and dyslexia is a particular area of interest and her doctorate was also in this area.

**Sylvia Phillips**

Sylvia Phillips, BA, DASE, MEd (SEN), AMBDA, began her career as a teacher of English in secondary schools where she first became interested in why some learners had severe literacy difficulties. She later joined Manchester Metropolitan University where she was a Principal Lecturer, Head of SEN, and then Head of Continuing Professional Development. At MMU she developed the first courses for specialist dyslexia teachers at both undergraduate and postgraduate levels. During her time there, she also continued to work in primary, secondary and special schools both with teachers and directly with pupils. She developed and taught on SEN courses for teachers in the UK and was the UK partner (with Italy, Belgium and Spain) developing and teaching EU courses on 'Inclusion and SEN' for European educationalists. She has served on the Accreditation Board of the British Dyslexia Association and has also been involved in several dyslexia research projects. She is currently course leader of the specialist dyslexia teachers' course at Glyndwr University, Wales.

She has co-authored *Putting the Code to Work* (Primary and Secondary editions, 1998, MMU – MET Publications), *Inspection and Beyond* (1997, Pearson), *Management Skills for SEN co-ordinators* (1999, Falmer Press), and *A Multi-sensory Teaching System for Reading* (1998, MMU Publishing), a fully scripted set of materials for teaching small groups of pupils with dyslexia.

Sylvia's other main areas of interest lie in 'learner voice', pupils' social, emotional and behavioural difficulties, and supporting teachers undertaking enquires into their practice.

# ACKNOWLEDGEMENTS

The authors would like to thank the following:

The DfE for permission to include 'The Simple View of Reading', from Rose, J. (2006) *Independent Review of the Teaching of Reading, Final Review*, Appendix I, p. 77, para. 17. London: HMSO.

Wiley-Blackwell for permission to reproduce the diagram of the Dual-Route Cascaded Model from Coltheart, M. (2005) 'Modelling Reading: the Dual-Route Approach', in Snowling, M.J. and Hulme, C. (eds), *The Science of Reading: A Handbook*. Oxford: Blackwell, p.12.

CCW resources @ www.cursivewriting.org for permission to use the Joinit cursive writing font.

Margaret Taylor Smith, who has allowed us to use and adapt some of the Concept Cards from her multisensory teaching scheme used in Texas, USA.

We would also like to acknowledge some of the many people who have contributed to our professional development as tutors on courses training specialist dyslexia teachers. These include:

Suzanne Briggs and the late Jean Augur, who supported the introduction of the specialist courses at Manchester Metropolitan University (MMU), and whose edition of 'The Hickey Multisensory Language course' was a major resource for teachers on our courses for many years;

Judy Capener and Liz Symes, who as colleagues at MMU have shared many ideas and discussions about teaching strategies and the learning needs of practitioners;

The many learners with dyslexia we have taught who have helped us to improve our practice and understanding of dyslexia;

The practitioners we have trained as 'specialists in dyslexia' who have provided feedback on the methods we have advocated and on their experiences of using other multisensory schemes and who have also made numerous suggestions for amending and updating programmes building on successful practice and current thinking.

We hope this book shows that we have valued their comments.

Finally, we would like to thank our partners, Derek and Mike, for their patience and support during the period we have been writing this book.

# LIST OF FIGURES AND TABLES

# DOWNLOADABLE MATERIALS

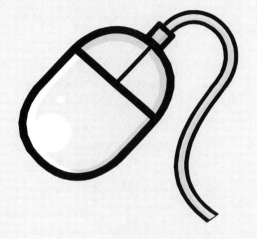

This book is supported by a wealth of resources that can be downloaded from www.sagepub.co.uk/kelly&phillips for use in your setting. A full list of the resources is available below:

Figure 9.1: Model for Lesson Plan Lasting One Hour

Table IV.1: Accelerated Programme Structure Table

Table IV.2: The Accelerated Programme: Record Sheet

Conquering Literacy: Accelerated Programme Placement Test

Conquering Literacy Accelerated Programme Skills Assessment Procedure (CLAPSAP)

Table V.1: Main Programme Record Sheet

Figure V.1 Concept Cards 1–8 Front

Figure V.2 Concept Cards 1–8 Reverse

Figure V.3 Concept Cards 9–16 Front

Figure V.4 Concept Cards 9–16 Reverse

Figure V.5 Concept Cards 17–24 Front

Figure V.6 Concept Cards 17–24 Reverse

Figure V.7 Concept Cards 25–32 Front

# INTRODUCTION

This book provides a text which explores theories and research into the nature and causes of dyslexia and presents a teaching programme – Conquering Literacy (for learners with dyslexia aged 4–16) – based on that research together with relevant theories about the acquisition of literacy. It is designed for those practitioners, including teachers, who wish to specialise in teaching learners with dyslexia and is particularly appropriate for those undertaking courses leading to Approved Teacher Status (ATS) and Associate Member of the British Dyslexia Association (AMBDA). The book may be of use to non-specialists who nevertheless wish to find out more about dyslexia and how to teach literacy to learners with dyslexia (e.g., SENCOs, Learning Support Teachers, Teaching Assistants and students on Initial Teacher Training courses wishing to develop a specialism in this area). Existing specialist teachers may find that some of the thinking reflected within it can add a new dimension to their teaching.

In the UK the recent emphasis on making schools 'dyslexia-friendly' (see, *inter alia*, McKay, 2006) has led to more inclusive teaching and helped learners with dyslexia (and many without) access a wider curriculum. However, this does not necessarily assist those learners in acquiring good literacy skills and there is still a need for specific intervention, particularly for those with more severe dyslexia. This has been acknowledged in the Rose Report (2009). Brooks (2007) and Singleton (2009) have pointed to successful intervention using structured, sequential, multi-sensory programmes based on phonics-teaching (whilst also acknowledging that not all learners with dyslexia do make good progress on these or other programmes). Most of these programmes use methods developed in the USA by Gillingham and Stillman (1956) and Cox (1972). One of the most commonly used programmes in England is the Hickey Multisensory Language Course (Hickey, 1977), which closely follows the structure laid down by Cox. Indeed, the work of Cox and Hickey has influenced the programme set out in Part III of this book.

Why, then, have we developed a new programme? Both of us have experience of teaching children and young people with severe reading difficulties, including those with dyslexia, and have used a variety of published teaching programmes as well as devising our own approaches. For more than twenty years, we have been involved in teaching qualified teachers on courses accredited by the British Dyslexia Association (BDA) at ATS and AMBDA levels. Evaluation from those teachers has often indicated the need for a greater explanation of the principles and rationale underpinning structured, multisensory programmes. Moreover, during this time developments in research into dyslexia have given more prominence to the roles of speed of processing, automaticity and working memory than is currently evident in existing schemes. We believe these areas need to be more explicitly addressed in teaching. Similarly, we place greater emphasis on helping learners become more aware of how to distinguish phonemes in their speech than is the case with most programmes.

A further concern of specialist teachers working with learners with dyslexia is 'where to start' teaching when using a structured programme with older learners and/or those who have some basic reading skills. Very often the recommendation in most structured programmes is that teaching should start at the beginning of the programme (to ensure that there are no 'gaps' in knowledge that have been overlooked) but at a pace that will match the individual learner's needs. In developing Conquering Literacy we have introduced an accelerated version and a Placement Test to address this area of concern. We also suggest ways in which the programme can be adapted for use both with very young children and with groups of learners.

We would hold that it is particularly important that specialist teachers should be able to 'personalise' their teaching to meet individual needs and that this can only be achieved if they are confident in their knowledge and understanding of the theories and research underpinning any programme they use. This book therefore seeks to engage teachers with relevant, accessible, literature while also acknowledging they will have to keep up-to-date with and be able to reflect on contemporary and future research as it is published.

## References

Brooks, G. (2007) *What Works for Pupils with Literacy Difficulties?* London: DCSF.
Cox, A.R. (1972) *Structures and Techniques: Multisensory Teaching of Basic Language Skills*. Cambridge, MA: Educators Publishing Service, Inc.

Gillingham, A. and Stillman, B. (1956) *Remedial Training for Children with Specific Difficulty in Reading, Spelling and Penmanship.* Cambridge, MA: Educators Publishing Service, Inc.

Hickey, K. (1977) *The Hickey Multisensory Language Course.* London: Kathleen Hickey.

McKay, N. (2006) *Removing Dyslexia as a Barrier to Achievement: the Dyslexia Friendly Schools Toolkit* (2nd edition). Wakefield: SEN Marketing.

Rose, J. (2009) *Identifying and Teaching Children and Young People with Dyslexia and Literacy Difficulties.* London: DFCS.

Singleton, C. (2009) *Intervention for Dyslexia.* Hull, UK: University of Hull.

# PART 1

# TEACHING LEARNERS WITH DYSLEXIA: THEORY AND CONTEXT

The first part of the book provides an overview of some of the main research and theories explaining the causation and characteristics of dyslexia with particular reference to literacy difficulties. It therefore seeks to provide a rationale for developing a cumulative, structured, multisensory programme for teaching literacy to learners with dyslexia. Because this book is intended to be a core text for practitioners wishing to become specialists in the field of dyslexia, an appreciation of underlying theoretical explanations is necessary. It serves to provide an introduction to current thinking and research, although at times there are references to older studies. This is because at the beginning of a course (or in the case of other practitioners who are not wishing to specialise) readers may need to read a book or article which outlines basic principles or seminal research which have given rise to more recent research into specific aspects. The earlier research therefore establishes a knowledge base which serves as a context for later studies. Practitioners can then read more recent research, including articles in peer reviewed journals, with greater understanding.

In all chapters explicit links are made to the implications for practice, and to the ways in which the chapter content is related to the development of the Conquering Literacy programme in this book.

Part I, however, can be seen as complete in itself in providing background knowledge which can inform the critical use of any literacy interventions for learners with dyslexia.

# CHAPTER 1

# THE CONTRIBUTION OF THEORIES OF CAUSATION TO THE DEVELOPMENT OF A MULTISENSORY TEACHING PROGRAMME

## Chapter Overview

At the time of writing there is a general acceptance that dyslexia exists (Rose, 2009), but while there have been significant advances in research into dyslexia in the last twenty-five years there is still no universally-accepted definition and no agreed explanation of its causation. In considering some of the main definitions and areas of research this chapter will show that there are, however, many areas of agreement as well as some unresolved and contentious issues. Three main theories of causation will be explored, both as explanations of the literacy difficulties of learners with dyslexia and as the sources of a rationale for a multisensory programme.

# Definitions of Dyslexia

Reid (2009) has categorised definitions of dyslexia as:

- descriptive;
- discrepancy-based;
- working and operational.

**Descriptive definitions** concentrate on describing a set of characteristics presented by learners with dyslexia. These would include that which has been proposed most recently by the British Dyslexia Association (BDA), namely that dyslexia is:

> … a specific learning difficulty which mainly affects the development of literacy and language related skills. It is likely to be present at birth and to be lifelong in its effects. It is characterised by difficulties with phonological processing, rapid naming, working memory, processing speed, and the automatic development of skills that may not match up to an individual's other cognitive abilities. It tends to be resistant to conventional teaching methods, but its effects can be mitigated by appropriately specific intervention, including the application of information technology and supportive counselling. (BDA, 2010)

This definition is particularly useful because it is based on recent research (discussed later in this chapter) and also supports the need for intervention over and above that which is conventionally used in good first teaching of literacy.

An earlier definition from the BDA referred to further possible 'accompanying weaknesses' in motor skills and to difficulties in 'mastering and using written language, which may include alphabetic, numeric and musical notation' (Peer, 2001: 67). This is also interesting because it indicates other areas of the curriculum which may be affected in addition to literacy.

Current definitions of dyslexia provide descriptions of the difficulties whereas some earlier definitions attempted to distinguish dyslexia from other forms of reading difficulty by 'ruling out' reasons which might otherwise account for those difficulties, such as sensory impairments, second or additional language learning, and the lack of good, conventional and consistent teaching. The definition proposed by the World Federation of Neurology in 1968 provides a well-known example, stating that dyslexia is:

> A disorder manifested by difficulties in learning to read, despite conventional instruction, adequate intelligence and socio-cultural opportunity.

Whilst this definition might now seem outdated it serves to remind us of the need to explore a range of possible causes when we identify literacy difficulties.

# Discrepancy-based Definitions

In the 1970s and 1980s several definitions emerged which again sought to distinguish between learners with 'general learning difficulties' and those with dyslexia. Rutter and Yule (1975) distinguished between children with 'specific reading retardation' and 'generally backward readers', based on a discrepancy between the general ability scores and predicted reading level for those with a 'specific' difficulty. The discrepancy definition was used extensively to identify dyslexia/a specific learning difficulty from the 1970s and an example is given by Selikovitz who defined a specific learning difficulty as:

> an unexpected and unexplained condition, occurring in a child of average or above intelligence, characterised by a significant delay in one or more areas of learning. (1994: 4)

Stanovich (1988, 1996) has been highly critical of the discrepancy theory, arguing that there is no qualitative difference in the pattern of reading errors between learners with high and low IQs. Badian (1994: 45) continued the IQ and discrepancy debate in a study of 110 children aged 6–10 consisting of a group of poor readers with dyslexia, 'garden-variety poor readers', and good readers. She concluded that it *is* possible to distinguish 'garden-variety poor readers' from those with dyslexia but not on the basis of IQ, because dyslexia can be identified at all verbal IQ levels. Phonological difficulties were found in both types of poor readers (although more severe in those with dyslexia), but those with dyslexia also had 'unique' deficits in both 'automatic visual recognition and phonological recoding of graphic stimuli'. The term 'garden-variety' to describe non-specific general reading difficulties not associated with dyslexia was used by Gough and Tunmer (1986) and Stanovich (1988) and is still prevalent in research, although we would consider it a very negative term.

Controversy continues and there are many who believe that rather than use a discrepancy definition based on IQ, it is still worth considering whether learners whose literacy skills are very poor when compared with their oral contributions in lessons should be assessed to see whether or not they are dyslexic. (Another way of expressing this would be to say that poor literacy is 'unexpected'.)

## Working/operational definitions

A working definition is one which can be used to identify learners with dyslexia and provide a basis for intervention. It should also reflect research evidence. The Rose Report (2009) suggests the following Working Definition:

- Dyslexia is a learning difficulty that primarily affects the skills involved in accurate and fluent word reading and spelling.

- Characteristic features of dyslexia are difficulties in phonological awareness, verbal memory, and verbal processing speed.
- Dyslexia occurs across a range of intellectual abilities.
- It is best thought of as a continuum and not as a distinct category and there are no clear cut-off points.
- Co-occurring difficulties may be seen in aspects of language, motor co-ordination, mental calculation, concentration and personal organisation, but they are not, by themselves, markers of dyslexia.
- A good indication of the severity and persistence of dyslexic difficulties can be gained by examining how the individual responds or has responded to well-founded intervention.

Research into the nature, causation and prevalence of dyslexia varies according to the preferred definition and conceptual framework used by the researchers.

## Prevalence

Prevalence figures can provide valuable information for policy makers, schools, and local authorities when planning teaching and resource allocation. However, as the definitions and criteria from which the figures are derived vary, any statistics about prevalence should be examined carefully. Figures differ according to the definition used, the assessment procedures involved, and the cut-off points in relation to severity. As dyslexia is considered to be a continuum, it is important to note exactly which methods and criteria have been used in any study of prevalence. One consequence of adopting exclusionary criteria in defining dyslexia, for example, was that researchers often eliminated learners who were of below average ability or from socially disadvantaged backgrounds. Another issue to consider is whether in some cases learners who may have more than one co-morbid specific difficulty have been included or excluded from a study. It is only in recent years that researchers have started to move away from exclusionary criteria to include a wider sample that will be more representative of the population as a whole. Nevertheless, any research is likely to reflect the conceptual model held by the researchers involved.

Prevalence figures vary from country to country and even within a country. Rutter and Yule (1975), for example, reported a figure of 3.9 per cent with specific reading difficulties in the Isle of Wight, but using the same methods and psychological characteristics found 9.9 per cent in London. More recently, Chan et al. (2008) described two studies in China, where one suggested that dyslexia was found in less than 1 per cent of the population whereas the other suggested about 10 per cent. However, different criteria were employed in the two studies. The BDA (2010) suggests that about 10 per cent of the UK population may be dyslexic with about 4 per cent severely affected. This implies that there could be one learner with severe dyslexia and about three with moderate dyslexia in any class of 25. Recent studies to investigate reading difficulties in both England and the USA do not always specify whether the children studied have been identified as having dyslexia. Screening undertaken as part of the 'No to Failure' Project in England (Dyslexia–SpLD Trust, 2009) found that 21 per cent of children of primary school age may have literacy difficulties which could be described as dyslexia. This is similar to the figures reported in the USA (Shaywitz et al., 2008), although these may include other 'poor readers'.

Snowling (2008) points out that dyslexia incidence figures may vary according to the age of learners because they might present different patterns of problems at different ages. She also suggests that while word-decoding problems do predominate at primary school age, during adolescence and adulthood many people with dyslexia will have learned to read but will still have problems with spelling and/or writing. This is another factor to consider when evaluating incidence studies.

Where literacy difficulties are taken as major indicators of dyslexia, international studies often reflect that the transparency of the orthography of a language can affect learners' ease or difficulty in acquiring literacy (see Chapters 3 and 7).

There also appear to be gender differences, as more boys than girls (about 4:1 according to the BDA) are identified as having dyslexia. This difference may be due to genetic factors but could be related to the process of referral. Shaywitz et al. (2008), reporting on an earlier study, suggest that schools may refer more boys for assessment because of disruptive classroom behaviour, whereas if girls are less disruptive they may not be referred. They point to their own studies and those of Flynn and Rahbar in 1994 which show that significant numbers of girls do experience reading difficulties. Their hypothesis may be supported by Singleton (1999) who reported that although more boys than girls were identified as dyslexic when at school, in higher education more female students than males are identified as dyslexic for the first time. Pennington and Olson (2005: 472), summarising genetic research, concluded that genetic influences on dyslexia 'operate similarly in both males and females'.

## Implications for Practice

- Early identification and assessment of literacy difficulties is important in view of the incidence of dyslexia.
- Referrals should not be made on the basis of disruptive behaviours.
- It is important not to assume that dyslexia is more commonly found in males.
- A 'checklist' for screening is a useful first step and it is worthwhile remembering that characteristics/observable behaviours may be different at different ages.

Definitions of dyslexia reflect both observed behaviours and research into the causes of those behaviours. Research into the causation of dyslexia provides insights into understanding the difficulties of learners with dyslexia and also provides bases for devising appropriate intervention strategies.

# Theories of Causation

Morton and Frith (1995) suggested that using a causal modelling framework is helpful when analysing theories of psychological and learning behaviours such as dyslexia. This involves a consideration of three levels of description:

- biological;
- cognitive;
- behavioural.

All of these are influenced/affected by the environment which includes physical, social, cultural, and dietary factors. Interaction with the environment is a significant aspect for teachers because it not only suggests ways in which a learner's experiences in their home may contribute to (or compensate for) their dyslexia, but also how their school and learning experiences may affect the development of their learning and achievements. School factors will include not only the nature of the tasks that are presented to them but also their interactions with peers, teachers, and other adults. Environmental aspects will add a further dimension – that of social and emotional development, particularly of self-concept and self-esteem, which in turn can affect cognitive processing and behaviours (see Burden, 2008).

The causal modelling framework is a useful tool for examining research and theories about dyslexia. A report from the British Psychological Society (BPS, 1999) used it to present ten different theoretical explanations of dyslexia so that similarities and differences could be identified. We have adopted the framework to structure an overview of the three main theories and from this have produced a model to show where and how we believe they may be inter-related rather than distinct approaches. This forms the basis for the teaching programme in Part III. The three theories are those of:

- phonological deficit;
- magnocellular deficit;
- cerebellar deficit/automaticity deficit.

All three offer explanations as to why literacy – particularly reading – is affected. We also include an overview of genetic theories and hemispheric influence.

Currently the dominant theory about dyslexia is that it is caused by a core phonological deficit (Snowling, 2000; Ramus et al., 2003). A vast body of research shows that the majority of people with dyslexia have difficulties in phonological processing, particularly in English-speaking countries. This hypothesis assumes a difference at brain level which could relate to an impairment in the perisylvian region (suggested by Frith, 1997) or may be related to magnocellular disorders or a direct genetic link or combination of any or all of these. We discuss the phonological deficit hypothesis when considering cognitive processing.

# Discussion of Theories of Causation in Relation to Morton and Frith's Framework

## Biological Level

### (A) Genetic factors

Long-held theories that dyslexia is largely inherited have been substantiated as a result of medical and technical advances. Pennington and Gilger (1996) have claimed that up to 65 per cent of the children with dyslexic parents and 40 per cent of the siblings of a child with dyslexia will also have the condition. Debate in the last decade has focused on which genes are involved and associated phenotypes. There is general agreement that dyslexia is unlikely to be related to only one gene and also that the genetic loci may not influence dyslexia per se but affect skills which underpin dyslexic characteristics (Pennington and Olson, 2005).

Research has identified that chromosomes 1, 2, 3, 6, 11, 15, and 18 show a genetic linkage to dyslexia with the possible main site being on chromosome 6 (Grigorenko, 2005; Schumacher et al., 2007) where genes have been linked to particular types of phonological processing difficulties, with the site 6p being linked to phonological decoding (Grigorenko et al., 2000; Francks et al., 2004) and oral reading of non-words (Kaplan et al., 2002) and site 6q to phonological awareness (Petryshen et al., 2001). Schumacher et al. (2007) also discuss three studies linking chromosome 1 to phonological aspects of dyslexia. Gilger (2008), in an overview of genetic research and dyslexia, refers to work by Francks and colleagues in 2002 – who found an association between chromosome 2 and phonological awareness and single word reading – and that of Olson in 2006 – linking a gene on chromosome 15 to disrupted auditory processing. Gilger also cites work by Taipale et al. in 2003, suggesting a link between 15q and spelling, and research by Chapman et al. in 2004 showing a link between 15 and single word reading, although the findings about chromosome 15 have not always been replicated. A number of other studies have found links to other, less-well-researched chromosomes and a genetic link to dyslexia is no longer disputed.

There is a general consensus that a polygenetic view should be taken and that the genetic loci for dyslexia should be conceptualised as 'susceptibility loci'. (For discussion, see Pennington and Olson, 2005.) This is because it is also acknowledged that environmental factors may affect the foetus (as well as the post-natal environment). Olson and Byrne (2005) suggest that at least 50 per cent of the variance can be explained by genetic factors and the remainder by environmental factors. Reid (2009) points out that 'dyslexic genes' on chromosome 6 are in the same region as the genes implicated in auto-immune diseases that also show a high level of association with dyslexia. Stein (2008), referring to his work in 2001, suggests that the Major Histocompatibility Complex (MHC) system is responsible for producing antibodies and seems to control the development of magnocells which are particularly vulnerable to environmental factors such as drugs and disease, noting the high incidence of auto-immune problems such as asthma, eczema, and hay fever in 'poor readers'. This offers one explanation for a magnocellular deficit, which is discussed below.

The wide range of difficulties experienced by learners with dyslexia, together with the range of degree of severity, can be explained by the genetic make-up of an individual together with the antenatal influence of environmental factors. The characteristics presented in schools will further reflect the effects of environmental factors since birth, both at home and at school.

It is important to recognise that having parents with dyslexia does not necessarily mean that children will have dyslexia. Moreover, while dyslexia is highly heritable Snowling et al. (2007) point out, on the basis of a longitudinal study, that some parents with dyslexia may specifically foster their children's reading skills and some learners with dyslexia may actively choose to read more, thereby improving their literacy skills.

---

## Implications for Practice

- Children who have a parent/sibling who is dyslexic may be considered 'at risk' and observed carefully for early signs of phonological/reading difficulties and other signs of dyslexia.
- Teachers should be aware that a number of compensatory factors (including those in a child's social environment) might mean that a child who has inherited the gene(s) does not necessarily develop literacy difficulties.
- There is also a need to consider the school/learning context in relation to home factors, as the learning context may present unfamiliar challenges to children and young people and therefore be a source of 'barriers to learning' for those with dyslexia.

---

### (B) Neurobiological factors

Technological developments – in particular, positron emission topography (PET) and magnetic resonance imaging (MRI) – have advanced research into brain-based neurobiological theories of causation.

### (i) Hemispheric differences

Several studies have investigated difficulties in processing information in relation to differences between the left and right hemispheres. Galaburda and Rosen

(2001) noted differences in the visual and auditory systems and proposed these provided a neurological explanation for some difficulties associated with dyslexia. Breznitz (2008) has paid particular attention to fluency in reading (including fluency in word decoding) and claims that speed of processing (SOP) is a highly significant factor in explaining dyslexia. She and her colleagues considered that the visuo-graphic system (right hemisphere) processes information holistically whereas the auditory-phonological system (left hemisphere) processes information sequentially and these differences will affect speed and fluency. Breznitz claims that learners with dyslexia have difficulties transferring information from one hemisphere to the other and proposes the 'Asynchrony Phenomenon' as an explanation of dyslexia. She refers to research which investigated information transfer between the left and right hemispheres among dyslexics compared with normal readers. This showed that information arrived in the right hemisphere first for students with dyslexia and was then transferred to the left, whereas for normal readers information arrived in the left hemisphere first and was then transferred to the right and in about half the time (measured in milliseconds) that the transfer took for readers with dyslexia. This theory is supported by the fact that brain imaging showed more activity among dyslexic learners in the right temporal and perisylvian areas than in normal readers during word decoding tasks.

Breznitz's work supports that of others (e.g. Wolf and Bowers, 1999) in claiming that speed of processing is a fundamental cause of dyslexia. This theory is not incompatible with the three main theories discussed below and speed of processing is incorporated into the model we propose.

### (ii) Magnocellular deficit

Stein (2001a) suggested that dyslexia is largely the result of abnormalities in the neural pathways of the visual system which is divided into two areas – the parvocellular and magnocellular systems. Magnocells form a direct link between the lateral geniculate nucleus (LGN) of the thalamus and the retina and are very sensitive to rapidly changing visual stimuli. Stein (2001a) argued that the visual system is the most crucial to reading and therefore impairment in the visual magnocellular system is the major cause of dyslexia. This view has been strongly challenged by those who consider that it is phonological processing that is the major cause (e.g., Vellutino et al., 2004).

The magnocellular deficit hypothesis also proposes that problems in the visual magnocellular system result in binocular instability and visual perceptual instability (Stein, 2001a, 2001b) due to a reduced ability to detect rapidly changing visual stimuli as the eye scans print (Evans, 2001; Stein, 2003). This can result in visual stress and sensory integration problems (see Everatt, 2002; White et al., 2006) where letters appear to blur or move about when trying to read, creating difficulty in determining the order of letters in words and hence a lack of reading fluency. (See earlier work by Pavlides (1990) and Irlen (1991).) Signs of visual stress may include headaches, eye strain, poor concentration, tracking difficulties, words or lines omitted when reading or copying text, difficulty remembering what has been read, and poor concentration (Jordan, 2006). Rose (2009), however, points out that many non-dyslexic people also experience visual stress and this should not in itself be seen as a characteristic of dyslexia.

The magnocellular pathway in the auditory system is not as clearly defined but has a set of large auditory neurons that detect changes in the frequency and amplitude of sounds. Reading requires fast and accurate processing of both visual and auditory stimuli and the magnocellular deficit theory proposes that readers with dyslexia have lower sensitivity to both visual and auditory stimuli than normal readers due to impaired development of the large neurons (Stein and Talcott, 1999). This claim was supported by post-mortem research (e.g., Livingstone et al., 1991) and by brain imaging studies (Stein et al., 2001) which found magnocells in the deep layers of the visual thalamic nucleus (Lateral Geniculate Nucleus) were disordered and overall smaller than their normal size. Impairments in magnocellular systems could be due to genetic factors but may also be the result of possible deficiencies in Omega 3 and Omega 6 fatty acids, as magnocells need these to maintain flexibility in the membrane surrounding the cells and to function efficiently (Stein, 2008).

The magnocellular deficit hypothesis suggests that phonological deficits could be a result of poor temporal processing in the magnocellular system. Stein et al. (2001) point out that phonemic awareness seems to depend on the ability to track changes in both sound frequency and amplitude. Difficulty in processing rapidly changing stimuli in the auditory pathways of the magnocellular system can compromise phonological awareness and memory storage and result in a slower work rate (Tallal, 2007; Valeo, 2008).

At a behavioural level this suggests why many phonemes (speech sounds) (e.g., /b/, /t/, /k/, /d/) may not be distinguished, thereby affecting both reading and spelling. Similarly, poor visual perceptual processing may cause letters to be mis-sequenced, transposed, or blurred.

Stein (2008) argues that the differences in the visual, auditory, phonological, kinaesthetic, sequencing, motor and memory difficulties found in learners with dyslexia are the result of differences in the particular magnocellular systems they have inherited.

## Implications for Practice

- This theory points to the need to consider *all* behavioural characteristics and sensory processing systems when assessing and teaching learners with dyslexia.
- It offers an explanation for the differences in the individual profiles of learners.
- It provides a justification for using a multisensory approach, particularly one involving auditory and visual approaches.
- It points to the need to make grapheme-phoneme linkages clear, using overlearning to ensure they can be rapidly distinguished (e.g., through the use of structured routines).

### (iii) Cerebellar deficit theory

Fawcett and Nicolson (2008) consider that the cerebellar deficit theory may provide a more useful hypothesis to explain the literacy difficulties found in dyslexia although they do not claim that *only* the cerebellum is affected in dyslexia. Their research in the early 1990s challenged the phonological deficit theory by identifying a range of non-phonological deficits in dyslexia. Their early experiments suggested that when engaged in balancing tasks learners with dyslexia could balance as well as those without dyslexia, but when asked to undertake two tasks simultaneously (e.g., count and balance at the same time) they would have difficulty balancing because they could not concentrate sufficiently. Fawcett and Nicolson suggested that poor skill automatisation could result in difficulty in learning to read and problems in multi-tasking and poor motor planning – and might also lead to handwriting difficulties and appearing clumsy and unco-ordinated. (This theory has been challenged by those who would argue that these are indicators of dyspraxia (or developmental co-ordination difficulties) and other co-morbid difficulties.)

Since the 1990s, their research has concentrated less on the theory related to balance and motor skills and more on automaticity deficit (which can be seen as a cognitive processing deficit). The automaticity deficit hypothesis suggests that a dysfunction of the cerebellum leads to a lack of fluency in skills that should be automatic, such as letter-sound knowledge and the motor co-ordination needed for articulation, balance, and handwriting (Nicolson and Fawcett, 2008). They also argue that the cerebellum is central for 'language dexterity' and speech, including verbal memory. Differences in the size and structure of the cerebellum have been found in people with dyslexia compared with non-dyslexics using magnetic resonance spectroscopy (Rae, 2001). Rae suggests that the larger left cerebellum found in people with dyslexia leads to slower information processing (and slower reading). The volume of the left cerebellum is larger but the number of neurones is less and more spread out in people with dyslexia resulting in greater difficulties in making connections. A functional deficit in the right cerebellum has also been found when adults with dyslexia engage in motor tasks (Nicolson et al., 1999).

Nicolson and Fawcett (2000) proposed a 'square root rule' to indicate the number of repetitions needed for a child with dyslexia to learn a complex task compared with one without dyslexia. This suggested that if acquiring a skill normally requires, say, 900 repetitions, a child with dyslexia might take 30 (the square root of 900) times as many (i.e., 27,000). Whilst we would advise that this 'rule' should not be applied rigidly (bearing in mind the range of individual differences in learners with dyslexia), it does remind us of the extraordinary difficulties faced by many learners with dyslexia in developing complex skills such as reading. There are clear implications for intervention strategies, in that repetition and overlearning are essential (without 'boring' the learner) and breaking complex tasks down into simpler tasks will aid automaticity. The importance of repetition has also been stressed by Dehaene (2004) who suggested that drills in lessons should be repeated until the optimal level has been achieved. This helps develop and strengthen neurological pathways. These tasks can be presented in a cumulative, sequential manner to build more complex skills.

## Implications for Practice

- Strategies must be used to foster automaticity in all tasks through 'overlearning' and the use of routines and repetition.
- When accuracy is established, learners should be encouraged to respond 'automatically' and speedily e.g., to letter-sound correspondence.
- Complex skills should be broken down into sub-skills so each is more readily achieved.
- Kinaesthetic strategies should be used to integrate skills and develop motor co-ordination.
- Teaching should include handwriting activities even where 'poor handwriting' has not been identified as a difficulty.

## Cognitive Processing Level

### (A) General comments

It is sometimes difficult to determine whether some of the cognitive processes (such as speed of processing and automaticity) should be considered from a cognitive or neurobiological perspective when describing theories of causation. We have already considered some cognitive processes such as automaticity and visual/auditory processing (when discussing the magnocellular deficit hypothesis) and speed of processing (in relation to brain functioning and hemispheric factors).

The role of memory, and in particular, short-term memory/working memory, is very significant for understanding the learning processes of learners with dyslexia and Chapter 2 explores this further. Another area of significance is that of metacognition because several studies (e.g., Tunmer and Chapman, 1996) have suggested that learners with dyslexia have poor metacognitive awareness (i.e., awareness of how they learn and think), leading them to adopt inappropriate strategies in reading and spelling. Metacognition is an important aspect of the Conquering Literacy programme.

## Implications for Practice

- Intervention should build up speed of processing and automaticity using 'routine'/ drill, rapid responses and sequencing skills.
- Metacognition strategies should be taught to help learners understand how they learn and problem-solve and also to aid them in feeling 'in control' of their learning.

## (B) Phonological deficit

For the last twenty years, the most widely accepted causal theory has been the phonological deficit hypothesis. Much research has shown that difficulties in phonological processing can distinguish those who have dyslexia from those who do not and that phonological awareness difficulties at an early age can predict later reading difficulties (Bryant and Bradley, 1990; Snowling, 2000; Lundberg, 2002) because of difficulties in learning the alphabetic principle that letters (graphemes) represent sounds (phonemes). Phonological difficulties have also been found in studies of adults with dyslexia. Ramus et al. (2003), in a case study of 16 dyslexic (and 16 non-dyslexic) university students, found all 16 had a phonological deficit, ten also had an auditory deficit, four a motor difficulty, and two a visual deficit. Five of them had a phonological deficit *only*. (An auditory deficit aggravates a phonological deficit.)

Most researchers recognise difficulties in phonological processing as a core deficit although they may disagree as to its cause (e.g., Nicolson and Fawcett, 2008). The phonological deficit hypothesis assumes a difference at brain level (possibly in the perisylvian region). Snowling has suggested that the 'causal status' of brain differences in dyslexia is 'debatable because brain development shows considerable plasticity: both its structure and function are shaped by use' (2008:5). Research into genetics described earlier indicates a direct genetic link, whereas the magnocellular hypothesis suggests temporal processing and disordered auditory systems may give rise to it. The cerebellar deficit theory links automaticity and possibly motor control to the phonological deficit and also claims a direct language link to the cerebellum. Snowling (2008) maintains that there is a direct phonological deficit, although she has also suggested that future research should consider whether there might be low-level impairments in the pre-school years that may be 'developmental antecedents'/indicators of the phonological deficit. In earlier studies (e.g., Snowling, 1992) she proposed that difficulty in the retrieval of phonological codes stored in long-term memory was a cause of reading difficulties and suggested that phonological coding deficits were responsible for short-term memory difficulties. This offers an explanation for difficulties in remembering long or complex instructions, relaying messages incorrectly, and recalling names or events out of sequence. Snowling has argued that rather than indicating a limited memory capacity these behaviours may be a result of inefficient verbal rehearsal strategies, resulting in information loss during the transfer from short- to long-term memory. She continues to claim that although most of the research leading to the phonological deficit theory was undertaken in the 1980s and 1990s it is still the most likely cause of dyslexia (Snowling, 2009). The 2009 Rose Report on dyslexia accepted the view of dyslexia as primarily affecting reading and spelling development due to impairments of phonological processing, verbal processing speed, and verbal short-term memory.

Wolf and Bowers (1999) found that some learners with dyslexia have a particular difficulty in rapid naming speed (rapid naming processing) because of impaired timing rather than impaired phonological processing. They identified three types of dyslexic learners: those with phonological awareness difficulties, those with a rapid naming speed deficit, and those who experienced both and therefore had a 'double deficit'. The latter type of learners will be particularly disadvantaged. Their studies brought together the automaticity and phonological deficits theories.

A further aspect to be considered is that English orthography is less regular/consistent in its grapheme-phoneme correspondence than many other alphabetic languages such as Spanish and Italian (i.e., it has a less transparent orthography). This may explain why many learners have particular difficulty with decoding and spelling in English and in turn has implications for assessment and teaching. It could also explain some differences in research into dyslexia in different countries.

Pavlides (2004), for example, claimed that visual processing difficulties are found in 80 per cent of Greek learners with dyslexia compared with only 20 per cent with phonological difficulties because the grapheme-phoneme correspondence in Greek is more consistent than in English.

## Implications for Practice

- Assessment of phonological awareness will provide a useful baseline for identifying children who may be dyslexic (see Chapter 3).
- Assessing a learner's ability to name letters and provide even a single 'sound' correspondence will indicate their knowledge of the alphabetic principle.
- Teaching should involve work based on the alphabetic principle and *systematically* teach phoneme-grapheme correspondence in order to establish that auditory, visual, and articulation skills are integrated.
- Learners should be encouraged to adopt verbal rehearsal strategies, using routines where they say aloud the phoneme-grapheme correspondence, name letters on presentation, and say each letter name as they write it during spelling.

## Behavioural Level

This level describes the observed literacy difficulties of learners with dyslexia (although we would acknowledge that while dyslexia affects other areas of school and everyday life, literacy is the focus of this book). These are the 'signs' or 'indicators' of dyslexia – some learners with dyslexia may present all of them, some may only present a few, and each of these may vary in severity. Such behaviours will be influenced by a range of environmental factors, including the teaching learners have had, the emotional support they receive, and a range of social and cultural factors which may exacerbate, alleviate, overcome, or prevent some of the difficulties. These characteristics can provide useful guidance to teachers and parents for identifying those learners who 'may' have dyslexia and therefore further assessment will be required.

The main characteristics *in literacy* may be summarised as:

- difficulty following instructions;
- a slow processing speed;
- a poor standard of written work (compared with oral work);
- confusion of letters/directionality problems (e.g., b/d, p/q, u/n, etc.);
- many reversals of letters;
- transposition of letters e.g. beard (for bread), saw (for was);
- phonetic and/or bizarre spellings;
- sequencing difficulties (letters and numbers);
- loses place in reading;
- a poor grapheme–phoneme correspondence in reading;
- omits/inserts words when reading;
- hesitant in reading aloud;
- no or inappropriate expression in reading;
- first letter guessing.

It is important to relate these to a learner's chronological and developmental age as some of the characteristics may be of a temporary nature (e.g., children of 6 or 7 years will often reverse 'b' and 'd' in their early stages of writing).

Similarly, if the learner's first language is not English this should be taken into account (see Chapter 7 for a consideration of this area).

## Implications for Practice

- Clusters of characteristics may indicate that further assessment is required for learners who *may* have dyslexia (see the BDA website for checklists at preschool, primary, secondary, and adult levels). Note that checklists should not be seen as a means of identifying dyslexia but they may point to areas which require further investigation.
- Consider cognitive processes which may result in these behaviours as they can inform teaching strategies.

Table I.1   *Characteristics of Dyslexia at Different Ages*

| Characteristics of Dyslexia at Different Ages | |
| --- | --- |
| An understanding of theories of causation of dyslexia helps us to appreciate how dyslexia may be manifested at different ages. This is summarised below. | |
| **Age** | **Behaviours** |
| Pre-school 0–5 | <ul><li>Delayed speech</li><li>Articulation difficulties</li><li>Poor ability to detect rhyme</li><li>Poor self-help skills e.g., dressing</li></ul> |
| Primary school years 5–11 | <ul><li>Poor letter–sound knowledge</li><li>Transposition of letters in spelling/poor orientation (beyond the age of 7–8)</li><li>Omitting letters or syllables in spelling and reading</li><li>Poor decoding skills</li><li>Frequently losing place in reading</li><li>Poor copying skills</li><li>Difficulty following long or complex instructions</li><li>Slow recall of facts</li></ul> |
| Secondary 11–16 | <ul><li>Many of the above may persist</li><li>Slow reading speed</li><li>Phonetic approximations in spelling</li><li>Difficulty organising/structuring written work</li><li>Poor/slow handwriting</li><li>Difficulty in decoding unfamiliar/polysyllabic words</li><li>Poor automatic recall of facts</li><li>Poor skimming/scanning skills</li></ul> |
| Adult Post-16 | <ul><li>Many of those under 'secondary' persist</li><li>Poor organisation of study skills</li><li>Difficulties in structuring arguments in assignments</li><li>Spelling difficulties</li><li>Difficulty multi-tasking (e.g., listening and writing at the same time)</li></ul> |

N.B. Not all of these will necessarily be displayed. More detailed examples of characteristics of learners with dyslexia may be found in age-related checklists on the BDA website at http://www.bdadyslexia.org.uk

# Interaction with Environmental Factors

The Morton and Frith (1995) model emphasises not only that there are relationships between the levels but also that all levels are affected by and interact with the environment. In developing a holistic model to integrate the three main theories of causation, we consider the levels should be depicted as encompassed by the environment. This is important because we do not view 'dyslexia' and a learner's manifestations of dyslexia as a 'within child' or 'medical' model. At a biological level, learners may be affected by birth trauma or pre-natal experiences, including their parents' diet, and at the cognitive and behavioural levels their family and school contexts will affect how they achieve as well as their motivation, learning styles, and compensating strategies.

## An Integrated Causal Model

Whilst the British Psychological Society Working Party (BPS, 1999) showed how the causal modelling framework could be used to show similarities and differences in theories by mapping each separately, we have found it useful to develop an integrated model (Fig. 1.1) pointing to the possible relationships between the theories. We have included a polygenetic element at the 'top' of a triangular model to draw attention to the way that a different genetic make-up can also offer an explanation for the variety of difficulties experienced by learners with dyslexia, together with other factors.

We consider that the three main theories (outlined in bold) are inter-related. The model demonstrates that because the cerebellum does not normally act alone, but in conjunction with other parts of the brain, it will take in and organise information from the auditory and visual pathways of the magnocellular system. If the magnocellular deficit results in faulty information being received by the cerebellum (indicated by a bold dotted line in the model), then organisation, storage, and retrieval may be affected.

Nicolson and Fawcett (2008) claim that because the cerebellum is implicated in eye movement, the visual processing difficulties described by Stein (2001a) could be the result of a cerebellar dysfunction rather than a magnocellular deficit. We have represented this as an indirect link (a dotted line) because further evidence is needed in order to establish it as a direct cause. The model gives prominence to the core phonological deficit and shows not only a direct link to the genetic component, but also a relationship to the magnocellular deficit and cerebellar theories.

The inter-relationship between these theories is most evident at the cognitive processing levels, where there are links between speed of processing, automaticity, visual and auditory processing, motor skills, and phonological processing difficulties.

The model also gives significance to interactions with the environment *at all levels*. Earlier we suggested that diet and allergies might affect genetic and neurobiological factors. At the cognitive and behavioural levels diet may also be significant as well as language and other social factors in the home, such as a child's early experiences of literacy. In addition it is important to consider the school learning context where the amount, nature, and speed of presentation of information may negatively affect the learning of those with dyslexia. The orthography of the language of the school may also affect the behaviours presented by learners. In addition, the nature and level of support and social interactions will affect learning.

## Subtypes or Dyslexic Profiles?

Attempts to establish the existence of subtypes of dyslexia have largely been based on reading processes e.g., dyseidetic/visual dyslexia and dysphonetic/auditory dyslexia

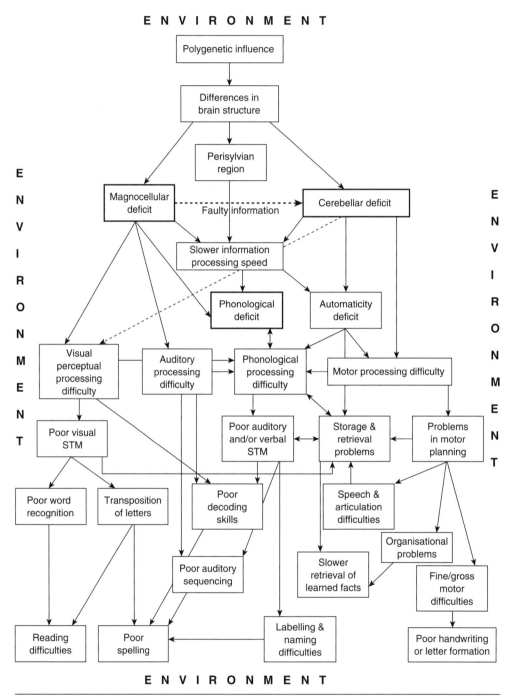

Figure 1.1  *A Model that Integrates the Three Main Theories of Causation*

(see Coltheart's 2005 model of reading discussed in Chapter 4). However, subtypes are not very useful for describing or explaining the range of different behaviours of learners with dyslexia which may not only vary in severity but also occur in different combinations. If a rigid view of subtypes of dyslexic behaviours and their underlying cognitive processes is adopted the forms of assessment may be restricted, resulting in not identifying (or wrongly identifying) difficulties. An example here would be if teachers only assess phonological processing skills to screen for dyslexia they may overlook difficulties in visual processing or speed of processing or short-term memory.

A more useful approach is to consider an individual's 'profile' and to look closely at a range of strategies rather than adopting a more crude approach. For example, teaching based on 'sub-types' might suggest that a learner with a visual perceptual difficulty should be presented with a programme based on auditory processing (an assumed 'strength') whereas further investigation may show it is possible to use some visual methods (e.g., with the use of coloured overlays). Profiling should enable teachers to 'personalise' their teaching within a structured programme to meet individual needs.

## Developing the Teaching Programme

Although there remain some controversies about causation, there is agreement that 'dyslexia' is a continuum and also that many aspects of dyslexia – such as poor organisational skills, automaticity and speed of processing, poor memory and sequencing skills – can affect everyday life and not just literacy. However, literacy remains a major concern internationally and improving the literacy skills of learners with dyslexia has become a national priority in England (Rose, 2009).

The research discussed in this chapter suggests that any intervention should be phonics-based, with a structure that enables overlearning, and should involve multisensory teaching. Reading and spelling require an ability to make linkages, for example, between sounds and letter names forming a relationship between auditory (phonological) and visual stimuli and output. If these links are taught in a multisensory way – using visual, auditory, kinaesthetic (speaking/writing) and tactile channels – then neural pathways can be developed (or strengthened) within the brain, in particular making better connections between the left and right hemispheres.

Using a multisensory approach, employing as many senses as possible, *simultaneously*, will aid automaticity and speed of retrieval by enabling each mode of information to be stored in its specific location in the brain, while establishing linkages between them. Multisensory teaching, therefore, aids the transfer from short-term to long-term memory (as discussed in the following chapter).

Summaries of the implications for teaching derived from the main theories have been given at the end of each section above. These implications form the basis for the Conquering Literacy programme and the teaching strategies recommended in this book. It is interesting to reflect on the fact that the research into the nature and causation of dyslexia since the 1980s reinforces a justification for the approach used by Gillingham and Stillman (1956) and Cox (1972) on whose work most current programmes are based. However, whereas those early programmes promoted the view that learners with dyslexia should only use such approaches and not be required 'to read' other books/sources while on the intervention programme we prefer a more balanced approach. Specialist lessons, therefore, whilst based on a structured programme, should also include some 'real reading' – even if this means the teacher reading to and/or with the learner in order to help them become familiar with 'literary' language and develop comprehension skills. Study skills should also be included from basic to more advanced levels. We suggest that it is not necessary for *all* learners to start at the beginning of a structured intervention programme in order to ensure that they do not have 'gaps' in their literacy learning. Many programmes and specialist teachers strongly endorse the view that it is essential to do this. In our experience this practice, even when 'adjusting the pace appropriately', will be disliked by many learners who will either be bored or feel their 'failure' is being reinforced. We have, therefore, provided an 'accelerated' version of the programme, with an associated assessment procedure that may be used with older learners or with those who already have several basic decoding skills.

## Summary

We considered that the needs of learners with dyslexia who present moderate to severe literacy difficulties can best be met through the use of a programme based on the results of research into the behaviours and causes of dyslexia discussed above. Such a programme will be structured, sequential, multisensory, and phonics-based, and will build up automaticity. The success of this type of approach has been reported in reviews by Singleton (2009), Torgeson et al. (2006), and Brooks (2007), and is endorsed in the Rose Report (2009). The Conquering Literacy programme contained in this book embraces these principles.

## References

Badian, N.A. (1994) 'Do dyslexic and other poor readers differ in reading-related cognitive skills?', *Reading and Writing*, 6 (1): 45–63.

Breznitz, Z. (2008) 'The origin of dyslexia: the asynchrony phenomenon'. In Reid, G., Fawcett, A.J., Manis, F. and Siegel, L.S. (eds), *The Sage Handbook of Dyslexia*. London: Sage. pp. 12–29.

British Dyslexia Association (BDA) (2010) http://www.bdadyslexia.org.uk/

British Psychological Society (BPS) (1999) *Dyslexia, Literacy and Psychological Assessment*. Leicester: British Psychological Society.

Brooks, G. (2007) *What Works for Pupils with Literacy Difficulties?* London: DCSF.

Bryant, P. and Bradley, L. (1990) *Children's Reading Problems*. Oxford: Blackwell.

Burden, R. (2008) 'Dyslexia and self-concept: a review of past research with implications for future action'. In Reid, G., Fawcett, A.J., Manis, F. and Siegel, L.S. (eds), *The Sage Handbook of Dyslexia*. London: Sage. pp. 395–410.

Chan, D.W., Ho, C.S., Tsang, S., Lee, S. and Chung, K.K.H (2008) 'Estimating incidence of developmental dyslexia in Hong Kong: what differences do different criteria make?', *Australian Journal of Learning Difficulties*, 13 (1): 1–16.

Cox, A.R. (1972) *Structures and Techniques: Multisensory Teaching of Basic Language Skills*. Cambridge, MA: Educators Publishing Service, Inc.

Dehaene, S. (2004) 'The biological basis of number processing and developmental dyscalculia'. Paper presented at 55th International Dyslexia Association (IDA) Conference, Philadelphia.

Dyslexia-SpLD Trust (2009) *No to Failure Final Report 2009*. Available at www.the-dyselxia-spldtrust.org.uk.

Evans, J.W. (2001) *Dyslexia and Vision*. London: Whurr.

Everatt, J. (2002) 'Visual processes'. In Reid, G. and Wearmouth, J. (eds), *Dyslexia and Literacy: Theory and Practice*. Chichester: Wiley. pp. 85–98.

Fawcett, A.J. and Nicolson, R.I. (2008) 'Dyslexia and the cerebellum'. In Reid, G., Fawcett, A.J., Manis, F. and Siegel, L.S. (eds), *The Sage Handbook of Dyslexia*. London: Sage. pp. 77–98.

Francks, C., Parrachini, S., Smith, S.D., Richardson, A.J. et al. (2004) 'A 77-kilobase region of chromosome 6p22.2 is associated with dyslexia in families from the United Kingdom and the United States', *American Journal of Human Genetics*, 75 (6): 1046–1058.

Frith, U. (1997) 'Brain, mind and behaviour in dyslexia'. In Hulme, C. and Snowling, M.J. (eds), *Dyslexia: Biology, Cognition and Intervention*. London: Whurr. pp. 1–19.

Galaburda, A.M. and Rosen, G.D. (2001) 'Neural plasticity in dyslexia: a window to mechanisms of learning disabilities'. In McLelland, J.L. and Siegler, R.S. (eds), *Mechanisms of Cognitive Development: Behavioural and Neural Perspectives*. Mahwah, NJ: Erlbaum. pp. 307–323.

Gilger, J.W. (2008) 'Some special issues concerning the genetics of dyslexia: revisiting multivariate profiles, co-morbidities and genetic correlations'. In Reid, G., Fawcett, A.J., Manis, F. and Siegel, L.S. (eds), *The Sage Handbook of Dyslexia*. London: Sage. pp. 30–52.

Gillingham, A. and Stillman, B. (1956) *Remedial Training for Children with Specific Difficulty in Reading, Spelling and Penmanship*. Cambridge, MA: Educators Publishing Service, Inc.

Gough, P.B. and Tunmer, W.E. (1986) 'Decoding, reading and reading disability', *Remedial and Special Education*, 7: 6–10.

Grigorenko, E.L. (2005) 'A conservative meta-analysis of linkage and linkage-association studies of developmental dyslexia', *Scientific Studies of Reading*, 9: 285–316.

Grigorenko, E.L., Wood, F.B., Meyer, M.S. and Pauls, D.L. (2000) 'Chromosome 6 influences on different dyslexia-related cognitive processes: further confirmation', *American Journal of Human Genetics*, 66: 715–723.

Irlen, H. (1991) *Reading by the Colours*. New York: Avery.

Jordan, I. (2006) *How a Teacher can Recognise, Assess and Screen for Visual Dyslexia, Visual Dyspraxia and other Vision linked Stress*. Available from IanJordan@visual-dyslexia.com

Kaplan, D.E., Gayan, J., Ahn, J., Won, T.W., Pauls, D., Olson, R.K. et al. (2002) 'Evidence for linkage and association with reading disability on 6p21.3–22', *American Journal of Human genetics*, 70: 1287–1298.

Livingstone, M.S., Rosen, G.D., Drislane, F.W. and Galaburda, A.M. (1991) 'Physiological and anatomical evidence of magnocellular defect in developmental dyslexia', *Proceedings of the National Academy of Science of the USA*, 88: 7943–7947.

Lundberg, L. (2002) 'The child's route into reading and what can go wrong', *Dyslexia*, 8 (1): 1–13.

Morton, J. and Frith, U. (1995) 'Causal modelling: a structural approach to developmental psychopathology'. In Cicchetti, D. and Cohen, D.J. (eds), *Manual of Developmental Psychopathology*. New York: Wiley. pp. 357–390.

Nicolson, R.I. and Fawcett, A.J. (2000) 'Long-term learning in dyslexic children', *European Journal of Cognitive Psychology*, 12: 357–393.

Nicolson, R.I. and Fawcett, A.J. (2008) 'Learning, cognition and dyslexia'. In Reid, G., Fawcett, A.J., Manis, F. and Siegel, L.S. (eds), *The Sage Handbook of Dyslexia*. London: Sage. pp. 192–211.

Nicolson, R.I., Fawcett, A.J., Berry, E.L., Jenkins, I.H., Dean, P. and Brooks, D.J. (1999) 'Association of abnormal cerebellar activation with motor learning difficulties in dyslexic adults', *Lancet*, 353: 1662–1667.

Olson, R. (2006) 'Genes, environment and dyslexia: the 2005 Norman Gerschwind Memorial Lecture', *Annals of Dyslexia: An Interdisciplinary Journal of the International Dyslexia Association*, 56 (2): 214–232.

Olson, R. and Byrne, B. (2005) 'Genetic and environmental influences on reading and language ability and disability'. In Catts, H. and Kamhi, A. (eds), *The Connections between Language and Reading Disability*. Hilldale, NJ: Erlbaum. pp. 173–200.

Pavlides, G.Th. (1990) *Perspectives on Dyslexia: Neurology, Neuropsychology and Genetics* (Vol.1). Chichester: Wiley.

Pavlides, G. Th. (2004) 'Prognosis and Diagnosis of Dyslexia and ADHD Internationally', 3rd International Multilingualism and Dyslexia Conference, EDA, Cyprus, July.

Peer, L. (2001) 'What is dyslexia?' In Smythe, I. (ed.), *The Dyslexia Handbook 2001*. Reading: British Dyslexia Association.

Pennington, B.F. and Gilger, J. (1996) *How is Dyslexia Transmitted?* Baltimore, MD: York.

Pennington, B.F. and Olson, R.K. (2005) 'Genetics of dyslexia'. In Snowling, M.J. and Hulme, C. (eds), *The Science of Reading: A Handbook*. Oxford: Blackwell.

Petryshen, T.L., Kaplan, B.J., Fu Liu, M., de French, N.S., Tobias, R., Hughes, M.L. and Field, L.L. (2001) 'Evidence for a susceptibility locus on chromosome 6q influencing phonological coding in dyslexia', *American Journal of Medical Genetics,* 105: 507–517.

Rae, C. (2001) 'Evidence for magnetic resonance studies for cerebellar involvement in dyslexic dysfunction'. Paper presented at the 5th BDA International Conference, York, April.

Ramus, F., Rosen, S., Dakin, S.C., Day, B.L., Castellote, J.M., White, S. and Frith, U. (2003) 'Theories of developmental dyslexia: insights from a multiple case study of dyslexic adults', *Brain,* 126: 841–865.

Reid, G. (2009) *Dyslexia: A Practitioner's Handbook* (4th edn). Oxford: Wiley-Blackwell.

Rose, J. (2009) *Identifying and Teaching Children and Young People with Dyslexia and Literacy Difficulties*. London: DFCS.

Rutter, M. and Yule, W. (1975) 'The concept of specific reading retardation', *Journal of Child Psychology and Psychiatry*, 16: 181–197.

Schumacher, J., Hoffmann, P., Schmal, C., Schulte-Korne, G. and Nothen, M.M. (2007) 'Genetics of dyslexia: the evolving landscape', *Journal of Medical Genetics,* 44: 289–297.

Selikovitz, M. (1994) *Dyslexia and Other Learning Difficulties*. Oxford: Oxford University Press.

Shaywitz, S.E., Morris, R. and Shaywitz, B.A. (2008) 'The education of dyslexic children from childhood to young adulthood', *Annual Review of Psychology*, 59: 451–475.

Singleton, C. (1999) *Dyslexia in Higher Education: Policy, Provision and Practice: Report of the National Working Party on Dyslexia in Higher Education*. Hull, UK: University of Hull.

Singleton, C. (2009) *Intervention for Dyslexia*. Hull, UK: University of Hull.

Snowling, M.J. (1992) Dyslexia – *A Cognitive Developmental Perspective*. Oxford: Blackwell.

Snowling, M.J. (2000) *Dyslexia* (2nd edn). Chichester: Wiley-Blackwell.

Snowling, M.J. (2008) *State-of-Science Review: SR-D2: Dyslexia for the Government Office for Science*. London: Government Office for Science.

Snowling, M.J. (2009) 'Changing concepts of dyslexia: nature, treatment and co-morbidity', *Journal of Child Psychology and Psychiatry,* published online 4/11/0, DOI 10.1111/j.1469-7610.2009.02197.

Snowling, M.J., Muter, V. and Carroll, J. (2007) 'Outcomes in adolescence of children at family-risk of dyslexia', *Journal of Child Psychology and Psychiatry,* 48: 609–618.

Stanovich, K.E. (1988) 'Explaining the difference between dyslexic and the garden-variety poor readers: the phonological core model', *Journal of Learning Disabilities,* 21 (10): 590–604.

Stanovich, K.E. (1996) 'Towards a more inclusive definition of dyslexia'. *Dyslexia, 2* (3): 154–166.

Stein, J. (2001a) 'The magnocellular theory of developmental dyslexia', *Dyslexia, 7* (1): 12–36.

Stein, J. (2001b) 'The sensory basis of reading problems', *Developmental Neuropsychology,* 20: 509–534.

Stein, J. (2003) 'Visual motion sensitivity and reading', *Neuropsychologia,* 41: 1785–1793.

Stein, J. (2008) 'The neurobiological basis of dyslexia'. In Reid, G., Fawcett, A.J., Manis, F. and Siegel, L. (eds), *The Sage Handbook of Dyslexia.* London: Sage. pp. 53–76.

Stein, J. and Talcott, J. (1999) 'Impaired neuronal timing in developmental dyslexia – the magnocellular hypothesis', *Dyslexia,* 5 (2).

Stein, J., Talcott, J. and Witton, C. (2001) 'The sensorimotor basis of developmental dyslexia'. In Fawcett, A. (ed.), *Dyslexia, Theory and Good Practice.* London: Whurr.

Tallal, P. (2007) *Experimental Studies of Language Impairments: From Research to Remediation.* Available at http://en.scientificcommons.org

Torgeson, C., Brooks, G. and Hall, J. (2006) *A Systematic Review of the Research Literature on the Use of Phonics in the Teaching of Reading and Spelling.* London: DfES. Research Report RR711.

Tunmer, W.E. and Chapman, J. (1996) 'A developmental model of dyslexia. Can the construct be served?', *Dyslexia,* 2 (3): 179–189.

Valeo, T. (2008) *Dyslexia Studies Catch Neuroplasticity at Work.* The Dana Foundation, www.dana.org

Vellutino, F.R., Fletcher, J.M., Snowling, M.J. and Scanlon, D.M. (2004) 'Specific reading disability (dyslexia): what have we learned in the past four decades?', *Journal of Child Psychology and Psychiatry,* 45: 2–40.

White, S., Milne, E., Rosen, S., Hansen, P., Swettenham, J., Frith, U. and Ramus, F. (2006) 'The role of sensorimotor impairments in dyslexia: a multiple case study of dyslexic children', *Developmental Science,* 9 (3): 237–269.

Wolf, M. and Bowers, P.G. (1999) 'The double-deficit hypothesis for developmental dyslexia', *Journal of Educational Psychology,* 91: 415–438.

# CHAPTER 2

# THE ROLE OF MEMORY IN ACQUIRING LITERACY SKILLS

## Chapter Overview

In Chapter 1, we considered an integrated model of causation showing links between the three main causation theories. Subsumed into these theories is difficulty at the cognitive level with the storage and retrieval of information, particularly in relation to phonological representations. A consequence of this is that the role of short-term working memory in dyslexia is not always given the attention it deserves. Indeed, the relevance of memory to learning is often overlooked in planning intervention programmes for learners with dyslexia. This chapter, therefore, focuses on the discussion surrounding the impact of dyslexia on the sub-components of working memory, both as an explanation for literacy difficulties and for the strategies incorporated into the teaching programme in Part III.

# What is Memory?

'Memory' is a blanket term that has often been used to describe the activities of acquiring, retaining, and recalling information. Memory can be divided into short term (recent memory) and long term. The term *'short-term memory'* refers to information presented verbally or visually that is stored for only a very short period of time (seconds). Where a learner needs to hold on to information long enough to use it, as in following an instruction, or needs to manipulate information, as in performing a mental calculation, then it is stored in short-term *working memory*. Learners with dyslexia will usually exhibit working memory deficits as they tend to have very few strategies available to them to keep information in working memory for long enough. If information decays too quickly then it is not transferred to *long-term memory* for permanent storage. Similarly, if information retrieved from the long-term memory cannot be kept in the working memory long enough for it to be organised and communicated (through speech, drawing, writing, etc.) then it may become jumbled (mis-sequenced) or lost from working memory, leaving the feeling that you know something but cannot produce/recall it (the tip of the tongue phenomena). Later on you may perhaps suddenly think of the information because you have been able to retrieve it from your long-term memory. Working memory, then, is seen as having a vital role in holding information in our short-term memory long enough to act on it and in both the storage and retrieval of information from our long-term memory. This is demonstrated in the input-output model (see Figure 2.1).

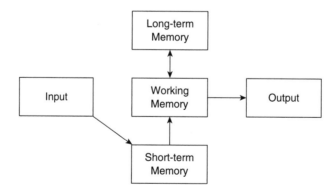

Figure 2.1    *Input Output Model of Memory (Kelly and Phillips, 2011)*

# Models of Working Memory

Working memory is made up of several components, each with its own role. Gathercole and Packiam-Alloway (2008) produced a simplified model of this (see Figure 2.2), showing how the different components interact.

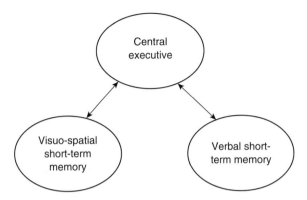

Figure 2.2    *Model of Working Memory (Gathercole, and Packiam-Alloway, 2008)*

In this model information flows two ways from the central executive to both the visual-spatial short-term memory store and the verbal short-term memory store, but there is no direct link between verbal and visual memory. The central executive is described as controlling attention and being involved in higher level mental processes.

It is useful to examine this model in relation to causal theory. Magnocellular deficit theory suggests that problems in processing rapidly presented visual information may result in difficulty in taking in information accurately into visuo-spatial short-term memory and so faulty information may be passed to the central executive for long-term storage. This could result in the letters in words being stored in the wrong sequence (e.g., 'siad' for said), confusion in the orientation of a letter (e.g., b/d/p), or confusion between words with similar shapes (e.g., 'shop' and 'stop'), thereby affecting whole word recognition. The same theory suggests that problems in the auditory pathway (temporal processing difficulties) may result in difficulty taking in information accurately into verbal short-term memory and again faulty information may be sent to the central executive to be organised and stored in long-term memory. This could result in sounds being mis-sequenced within words or confusion between similar sounding letters, making sound-symbol correspondence more difficult to establish and retrieval of letter names and sounds more effortful or even inaccurate.

In the integrated model of causation (Figure 1.1) in the previous chapter, we demonstrated a link between the magnocellular system and the cerebellum, in that it is possible that in learners with dyslexia faulty information is passed from the visual and/or auditory pathways to the cerebellum in the same way that Figure 2.2 shows visual and/or auditory memory sending information to the central executive for organisation and storage. The cerebellar/automaticity deficit theory argues that the cerebellum has a role in developing automaticity. This involves a speedy retrieval of information from long-term store into working memory via the central executive, which requires the cerebellum to interact with other parts of the brain (e.g., the frontal cortex) – a role for which it is particularly suited. The theory suggests that in learners with dyslexia disorganised neurons within the cerebellum cause speed of processing difficulties, as it interacts less efficiently with other parts of the brain and so more processing time is required. However, problems in motor processing/planning in the cerebellum could also cause faulty storage and retrieval of information resulting in: reversal of letters or words (as a learned sequence of motor movements must be recalled); the grapheme-phoneme relationship becoming more difficult to establish; poorly formed letters; difficulty in organising thoughts on paper for essay writing; and sequencing difficulties (e.g., in recalling a spelling).

If information is stored incorrectly in long-term memory then faulty information will be retrieved by the central executive. In learning to spell children will move through several stages of spelling development (see Chapter 5) as they become mature spellers, but learners with dyslexia will usually take longer to move through these stages and might also use phonetic spelling such as 'sed' for a much longer period before learning the correct spelling, building up two or more memory traces for the word 'said' (through repeated incorrect motor movements). It is possible, therefore, for a learner to retrieve an incorrect spelling even after they have been taught the correct one. This may be seen as carelessness on the learner's part by some teachers but is actually a consequence of a working memory deficit.

The phonological deficit theory discussed in Chapter 1 argues that it is not a visual processing difficulty that leads to letter reversals but a naming difficulty (Snowling, 1992). The theory proposes that correct visual images are stored but the learner is unable to retrieve the correct label for each image. It also maintains that it is phonological processing difficulties that lead to problems in rehearsal in the phonological loop component of short-term verbal memory. Auditory information that is received and recognised as meaningful speech is sent via the phonological loop to the central executive for storage. However, information that requires verbal coding (particularly if it is sequential information such as a telephone number) often needs to be kept in short-term verbal memory through a process called rehearsal if it is to be successfully transferred to long-term memory. The phonological loop is involved in the rehearsal process. Learners with dyslexia will often not use strategies such as rehearsal (repeating information silently or through sub-vocalisation) and a memory may therefore decay before it reaches the long-term store. Verbal repetition is a strategy that can be used to help learners with dyslexia to keep information in their working memory for a greater length of time.

## Working Memory Deficits

An alternative explanation for phonological deficits was presented by Gathercole and Baddeley (1993) who argued that reading difficulty is the result of a slower articulation speed causing a dysfunction of the phonological loop and that this difficulty partly lies in a more limited capacity phonological store. This accounts for the comprehension difficulties that are sometimes experienced when long and complex sentences are being read. They found that comprehension was not affected when short simple sentences were used. It may, therefore, be the length of the memory string that causes information to be lost. Learners with dyslexia will usually have a smaller than average working memory capacity (as tested by a digit span test) and may only be able to remember three or four units of information (letters, numbers, words) at a time. A digit span test normally asks the learner to listen to a list of between three and seven numbers and then recall them in the sequence in which they were dictated. This tests immediate recall. However, if a list of numbers is given and the learner is asked to recall them in reverse order this tests working memory as information must be held on to whilst the sequence is reversed. Assessment of short-term working memory capacity can inform the planning and delivery of lessons, as learners with dyslexia may need information to be broken down into smaller chunks (e.g., shorter verbal instructions, shorter sentences for dictation or reading). A digit span test (forwards and/or reverse) is included in most dyslexia screening tests.

Learners with working memory deficits are also more vulnerable to memory 'interference' or 'distraction'. Information can be interfered with at the input stage (see Figure 2.1) if the learner cannot pay sufficient attention to the stimuli. This can happen, for example, in a noisy classroom where the learner has to filter out a lot of background noise in order to focus their attention on the relevant information. Learners with dyslexia can often find this difficult to do and so faulty or incomplete information will arrive in their short-term memory. To achieve a successful filtering-out of irrelevant background noise they will have to concentrate much harder than their non-dyslexic peers and as a result, they can sometimes appear to be ignoring a person speaking to them as they are concentrating intently on the task in hand. A quiet learning environment then needs to be a feature of a dyslexia-friendly classroom. This is supported by a study undertaken by Bastien-Toniazzo et al. (2009) who explored the audio-vision integration of speech in native French-speaking children and found that learners with dyslexia had more difficulty processing visual cues (where they had to guess what was being said by watching lip movements) than their non-dyslexic peers. They also found that the hindrance of background noise led children to rely more on visual information than auditory information, suggesting that learners with dyslexia are more disadvantaged in noisy learning environments.

Information can also be interfered with once it has reached working memory due to it being crowded out by more incoming information. If working memory capacity is smaller than average and speed of information processing is slower, then information may not have been transferred to long-term memory before further information is received that exceeds memory capacity and therefore 'pushes out' some of the previous information – which is then lost. Gathercole and Packiam-Alloway (2008) explain this in relation to what is called the 'primacy effect' and the 'recency effect'. If a list of items is presented verbally to a learner which they are then asked to recall, those that are best remembered will be the first in the list (because they have been transferred to long-term memory), which is the primacy effect, and the last in the list (because they are still in working memory), which is the recency effect. The middle items on the list will be the least well remembered and often 'lost', as memory capacity was not great enough to hold all the items in working memory and so the most recent ones push out those already in place. This effect can be seen in all learners but in those with dyslexia a smaller working memory capacity means that it happens more frequently and in situations where their peers can cope (e.g., when given a series of instructions as in a science experiment).

Learners with dyslexia do not usually have a general memory difficulty, however, and may excel in areas of the curriculum that have fewer language demands, such as Information Technology, Engineering, Architecture, Business or Mathematics. The uneven academic profile usually presented by learners with dyslexia is evidence that they can learn and remember certain types of information quite well. To explain this we need to look at a model of working memory that shows how it interacts with long-term memory.

## Baddeley's Three-component Model of Working Memory

Gathercole and Packiam-Alloway's (2008) model is based on an earlier model of working memory developed by Baddeley (1986), in which the visuospatial sketchpad (visual short-term memory) and the articulatory/phonological loop (verbal short-term memory) are both controlled by the central executive. He later added a third component to his model – the episodic buffer – to explain how episodic memory (our memory for experiences) is stored (see Figure 2.3). In this model of working memory the episodic buffer integrates visual, spatial, and verbal information with time sequencing (such as the memory of a story).

The episodic buffer allows us to remember events that we have experienced as it is assumed to have links to long-term memory and semantic meaning (Baddeley, 2000). It can hold much more information than could be held in the phonological loop and it is believed to act as a temporary long-term store, enabling us, for example, to remember what we had for lunch for several days previously. A routine event – such as what we ate for lunch or what we wore yesterday – will normally only be remembered for a few days, but where an experience has a particular relevance or produces a particular emotion (for example, what we wore on our wedding day) it is stored in a more permanent form in long-term memory. Personal experiences such as these are referred to as autobiographical memories (see Gathercole and Packiam-Alloway, 2008). They point out that personal experiences also allow us to acquire a wide range of factual knowledge about the world around us that is stored in semantic memory.

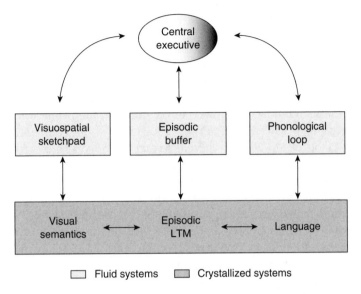

*Figure 2.3   Baddeley's Three-component Model of Working Memory*

*Source*: Baddeley, A. (2003) 'Working memory and language: an overview', *Journal of Communication* Disorders, 36 (3): 189–203.

It is this part of long-term memory that enables us to store the meaning of words and the knowledge of how different concepts are related to each other. When we recall information, if it is automatic recall of a fact such as the colour 'blue', then it is likely that we are retrieving it from semantic memory as it is a fact that we have met so many times that we feel that we 'know' it rather than remember it. If on the other hand we recall a fact such as 'the sand in the Sahara desert is hot' because we have been there, then it is likely that this has been recalled from our episodic memory. Episodic memory and semantic memory are both types of *declarative memory* (or memory of facts) which is believed to be unimpaired in learners with dyslexia. Rather the problem seems to lie in *procedural memory* – skills that have been practised and become automatic (such as riding a bicycle). Nicolson and Fawcett (2008) suggest that it may be possible to distinguish between general and specific learning difficulties by finding out if both declarative and procedural memory are affected or if only procedural memory has been impaired.

Baddeley's (2003) model distinguishes between the features of long-term and short-term memory by depicting long-term memory as a crystallised system that we are unable to change but short-term memory as a fluid system that can be altered in terms of capacity and the length of time material is held. The lessons described in Part II of the book aim to improve both storage and retrieval and short-term working memory in two ways:

- through structure and routines;
- through direct memory training (see Chapter 12).

Multisensory teaching is a key strategy in both types of activity. The theory suggests that when information is received through several senses *at the same time* the central executive organises and then stores this information in several places in the brain. Tactile memory is believed to be stored in the primary somotosensory cortex of the parietal lobe (Harris et al., 2002) and auditory memory in the left parietal lobe (Scott et al., 2000), whereas visual memory appears to be stored in several different locations in the right hemisphere depending on the type of information: memory for objects, spatial position or faces (Salmon et al., 1996). To facilitate the transfer of information from short-term memory to long-term memory storage, the multisensory teaching approach recommended in this book involves the use of *as many* of the senses as possible (simultaneously) in any given activity. Using verbalisation is particularly recommended as it is an important technique for keeping information in working memory long enough for it to be stored in long-term memory. Presenting information through a multisensory approach also makes its retrieval easier as connections are made between the right hemisphere, the primary somotosensory cortex of the parietal lobe, and the left parietal lobe.

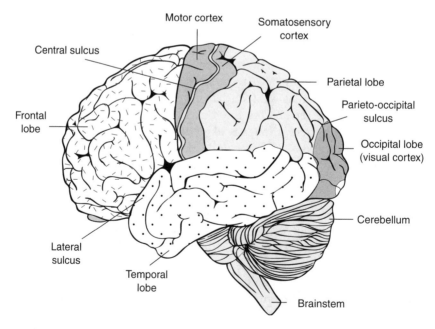

Figure 2.4   *Sketch of the Brain and its Structures*

# Involving Parents

Teachers could encourage parents to provide educational experiences for their children, learning through doing, so that they can make use of episodic and autobiographical memory in storing information from activities outside school. Other approaches might involve playing memory games and devising strategies to support the recall and retention of information. Teachers will need to explain to parents how these experiences and activities relate to developing memory.

There is a range of published memory games that parents can play with their children to develop memory skills (e.g., pairs games where they have to remember the position of a picture or symbol to turn over two matching cards from several rows of cards – computerised versions of the kind of game can also be used – or oral memory games such as 'I went to market' where the learner remembers a sequence by saying aloud "I went to market and I bought ... ", gradually adding on more items as the learner and parent take turns to create the longest string of objects possible). Parents might link the items to be remembered to their child's hobbies or interests in order to personalise their learning.

Learners with dyslexia may need support from parents in developing good organisational skills. By checking their homework diary parents can help their child to plan their time more effectively to make sure they meet homework deadlines. It is useful to check coat pockets on a regular basis for school letters as often learners with dyslexia forget to pass these on and thus parents may not receive information about school events, parents evenings, etc. (Teachers could perhaps also check that important letters are not still lurking in coat pockets several days after they have been sent home, or use phone or text messages instead of sending out letters). At home, a copy of their school diary could be prominently displayed so that support can be given in organising the relevant equipment for example, for sport or food technology. Learners should also be encouraged to make their own checklists (e.g., items to be packed when going on holiday or a school trip) and to jot down reminders, even if they are the only people who can read these back.

## Implications for Practice

- A slower rate of presentation will be needed. School staff should avoid speaking too quickly when giving explanations or instructions.
- Strategies for remembering need to be taught.
- There should be a regular review of learned facts.

*(Continued)*

*(Continued)*

- Instructions should be kept short and be clearly phrased.
- Understanding of a task should be checked by asking a learner to repeat what they have to do.
- Accuracy should be the first aim in reading and spelling and then speed should be improved.
- Time should be allowed for thinking and planning.
- The importance of a quiet learning environment should be taken into account.
- Instructions and explanations may need to be repeated.
- Correct memory traces can be strengthened through overlearning.
- Activities should be *fully* multisensory and include verbalisation.
- Learning should be personalised to help to create autobiographical memories.

## Summary

This chapter has provided a rationale for giving significance to the place of strategies for developing short-term working memory in planning a literacy intervention programme for learners with dyslexia. Activities should be broken down into small steps so that they are within an individual's working memory capacity, but teaching should also draw on other types of memory such as episodic, semantic, and autobiographical (which are often strengths for learners with dyslexia) by personalising learning and ensuring that students are actively engaged in the learning process.

## References

Baddeley, A.D. (1986) *Working Memory.* Oxford: Clarendon.

Baddeley, A.D. (2000) 'The episodic buffer: a new component in working memory?', *Trends in Cognitive Science,* 4 (11): 417–423.

Baddeley, A.D. (2003) 'Working memory and language: an overview', *Journal of Communication Disorders,* 36 (3): 189–203.

Bastien-Toniazzo, M., Stroumza, A. and Cavé, C. (2009) 'Audio-visual perception and integration in developmental dyslexia: an exploratory study using the Mcgurk Effect', *Current Psychology Letters: Behaviour, Brain and Cognition,* 25 (3).

Gathercole, S.E. and Baddeley, A.D. (1993) *Working Memory and Language.* Oxford: Clarendon.

Gathercole, S.E. and Packiam-Alloway, T. (2008) *Working Memory and Learning*. London: Sage.

Harris, J.A., Miniussi, C., Harris, I.M. and Diamond, M.E. (2002) 'Transient storage of a tactile memory trace in Primary Somatosensory Cortex', *The Journal of Neuroscience*, 22 (19): 8720–8725.

Nicholson, R.I. and Fawcett, A.J. (2008) *Dyslexia, Learning, and the Brain*. London: The MIT Press.

Salmon, E., Van de Linden, M., Collette, F., Delfiore, G., Maquet, P., Degueldre, C. and Frank, G. (1996) 'Regional brain activity during working memory tasks', *Brain*, 119 (5): 1617–1625.

Scott, S.K., Blank, C.C., Rosen, S. and Wise, R.J.S. (2000) 'Identification of a pathway for intelligible speech in the left temporal lobe', *Brain*, 123 (12): 2400–2406.

Snowling, M.J. (1992) *Dyslexia – A Cognitive Developmental Perspective*. Oxford: Blackwell.

# CHAPTER 3

# PHONOLOGICAL SKILLS, LITERACY AND DYSLEXIA

## Chapter Overview

This chapter considers the relationship between phonological processing skills and literacy acquisition with particular reference to learners with dyslexia. The types of phonological processing skills subsumed under the term of 'phonological awareness' are described and some of the relevant research into the relationship between these skills and literacy acquisition are discussed in relation both to young 'beginning readers' and learners with dyslexia. A brief summary of the terms used to categorise and analyse speech sounds is provided to help practitioners appreciate the emphasis given to articulation/pronunciation of phonemes in the Conquering Literacy programme.

Learning to read and spell in an alphabetic language relies heavily on an ability to establish phoneme-grapheme correspondence. Good phonological processing skills (the ability to process the 'sound' system of language, e.g., spoken words) are crucial to this. There is general agreement, however, as stated in the first chapter of this book that: 'the vast majority of cases of developmental dyslexia are attributable to a phonological deficit that may vary in severity' (Snowling and Hulme, 2005: 400).

This specific deficit disadvantages learners with dyslexia whose other language skills (syntax, vocabulary/semantics and pragmatics) are normal, or even areas of strength, as indicated in the next chapter.

Many writers (e.g., Swan and Goswami, 1997; Reid, 2009) describe people with dyslexia as having difficulties in 'phonological representations', a term which Hatcher and Snowling (2002) point out is not always easily understood. They explain that 'representation' is an abstract concept to describe 'a kind of brain "image" or memory trace that captures the individual's knowledge or experience' of speech sounds (2002: 69). The term could simply be interpreted as having difficulties processing (perceiving, coding, retrieving, and producing) speech sounds. The phonology of a language is knowledge of the 'sound' of a spoken language and comprises two aspects:

- non-segmental (or suprasegmental) – concerning control and understanding of volume, stress, and intonation (all of which may affect understanding as well as expressive language);
- segmental – concerning breaking speech and words into smaller units including individual single sounds (phonemes) e.g., the three phonemes in dog are /d/ /ŏ/ /g/ and the syllables in fascination are fas-cin-a-tion.

Hatcher and Snowling suggest that 'the most consistently reported phonological difficulties found in dyslexia' (2002: 70) relate to problems in short-term verbal memory. Manifestations of this in the classroom include following instructions and 'keeping up' with dictation. They cite a review of relevant research by Hulme and Roodenrys in 1995 supporting the theory that the storage of verbal information in short-term memory depends on speech-based codes (Chapter 2 of this book has already shown the importance of short-term memory in any study of dyslexia). A phonological deficit also affects rapid naming (the ability to name or label object, letters, numbers, symbols at speed), word-finding (the ability to retrieve an appropriate word quickly), and phonological awareness, and research into reading and spelling reflects all of these.

The aspect of phonology most researched in relation to literacy, particularly reading, is that of phonological awareness. This refers to sensitivity to the sounds of spoken language and the ability to process and analyse speech and words into smaller units and synthesise sounds into words. It incorporates phonemic awareness, which is the ability to retrieve and manipulate individual sounds. A phoneme is a single unit of sound in a language and it is generally accepted that there are 44 sounds in the English language.

A relationship between phonological awareness and reading difficulties was established by Bryant and Bradley (1990) who found that poor phonological awareness at age 4 predicted possible reading difficulties at age 8. Their research and that of others showed that some phonological processing skills are more significantly related to literacy that others. Muter (1996) summarises several research studies which show that different types of phonological skills may exert a stronger influence than others at different stages of learning to read and spell (see below). Anthony and Francis (2005) also suggest that there is now strong evidence that different phonological skills develop/emerge in a predictable sequence for 'normal' children speaking English as a first language.

# Phonological Processing Skills ('Awareness' Skills)

Adams (1990), in a review of the research, identified five levels of 'difficulty' of phonological skills. Most of the research was undertaken when children were 3–7 years old and reflected their abilities when set a range of tasks requiring phonological processing. She produced a typology according to 'normal' development, although it is important to note that as children develop the later skills, they continue to use and 'refine' those already acquired.

## Phonological Awareness/Processing Skills (After Adams, 1990)

- *Knowledge of nursery rhymes* – she regards this as a primitive skill involving only 'an ear for sound of words'.
- *Knowledge of rhyme and alliteration* – the ability to produce words that rhyme or to spot 'oddities' which do not rhyme or those which begin with a different sound e.g. cat, can, cot, hen, car. This requires an ability to focus on particular sounds.
- *Blending phonemes and syllable segmentation/spelling* – an awareness that words can be broken into smaller units e.g. rab-bit, snow-man, cl-ue.
- *Phonemic segmentation* – understanding that words can be broken down into a series of single sounds (phonemes) and the ability to produce these phonemes when asked to do so.
- *Phoneme manipulation* – an ability not only to understand the phonemic structure of words, but also to 'manipulate' phonemes by adding, deleting, or transposing a phoneme in order to produce a new word or non-word. For example, when given the word 'cot', if you remove the /k/ sound and put /d/ in its place, what word do you make? This task also places a heavier load on memory.

---

**Note**

Throughout this book, including in the Conquering Literacy programme, we have not used phonetic transcriptions for either the reader or the learner, as these require additional knowledge. However, we have differentiated a sound (by using / /) from a letter name (where we use ' ' round the letter). Thus /k/ represents the sound 'c' makes in the word 'cot', whereas /s/ represents the sound 'c' makes in the word 'centre'.

---

In the 1990s both Adams (1990) and Muter (1996) made important contributions to our understanding of the pre-requisites for progress in learning to read. Each pointed out that some of these skills (particularly phoneme segmentation and manipulation) are stronger predictors of progress in learning to read than the earlier acquired skills of rhyme and syllable segmentation, although they develop later. It is the phonemic levels which are so essential to the act of attaching a label (name) and a grapheme (symbol) to a sound. A lack of, or difficulty in, these skills is likely to lead to difficulties during the early stages of reading tuition.

The implication for all young children learning to read, because these phonological skills are still developing, is that there should be explicit teaching of phonological awareness skills and particularly of those emphasising phonemic awareness. This is particularly true for children with (or at risk of) dyslexia and the significant number of other children who also have phonological representation difficulties. Muter suggested that there is a reciprocal relationship between phonological processing skills and learning to read, and that perhaps the stage of phonological segmentation is not reached until 'the child has received formal instruction in letter-sound knowledge' (1996: 34). Most writers would agree with the finding of Hatcher et al. (1994) that phonological training alone is not as effective in improving literacy as training using reading and phonological awareness.

Goswami and Bryant (1990) suggested that rhyming tasks do not require a sensitivity to individual phonemes, but to distinguishing onset-rime units (where *onset* refers to initial consonant/consonant blends and *rime* refers to the vowel(s) and rest of the word). Their work supports the notion that rhyming ability and phoneme segmentation are distinct phonological skills. They found that onset-rime awareness enables learners to use analogy in reading and spelling. Muter et al. (1994) found that segmentation made a significant contribution to reading and spelling development at the very early stages of reading but rhyming did not. However, they also found that when children in their study were 6 (in their second year at primary school) rhyming as well as phonemic segmentation skills contributed to literacy acquisition and in particular contributed to their use of analogy in spelling. An example would be to consider the word 'tame' where 't' is the onset and 'ame' is the rime. A family of words can be generated by changing the onset e.g., frame, game, same, blame. In addition Muter (1996) also found (as have others) that for children to make progress in reading they need to make explicit links between sounds and their knowledge of letters (name and graphic representation). Teaching using synthetic phonics aids the development of phonemic segmentation and the method adopted in most structured multisensory programmes, where sounds and letters are introduced at the same time, is based on theories of a two-way interactive process as described by Muter. The aim is to develop and strengthen phonological processing and the rapid retrieval of letter sounds and names. A recent study by Blomert and Willems (2010) of children aged 4–6 years at familial risk of dyslexia (40 per cent did present reading difficulties when aged 6) has shed further light on early reading development and dyslexia. They found no support for the claim that poor letter knowledge is related to later reading difficulties and suggested that letter knowledge learning and the ability to integrate letters and sounds (as in learning grapheme-phoneme correspondence) were two distinct processes. This study has yet to be replicated but was concerned with reading difficulties only. The approach used in the Conquering Literacy programme explicitly fosters the integrative process but reinforces it by also introducing letter names as these are particularly useful in spelling.

The linguistic complexity of a language can affect phonological development and processing. The sounds occurring in a word are influenced by their adjacent sounds and words are influenced by syntax and morphology (how meaningful units are put together to form words). Anthony and Francis (2005) claim that children who speak Greek, Turkish or Italian, for example, attain syllable awareness earlier than children speaking English because the languages have better-marked syllables and fewer consonant clusters. Articulation and hearing skills can also affect phonological representation, but difficulty with phonemic segmentation should not be seen as being the same as auditory discrimination. Articulation, however, can be seen as speech sound accuracy which has been linked to phonological awareness (McDowell et al., 2007).

The phonological complexity of a language should be distinguished from its orthographic complexity. The orthography of a language concerns the written representation (i.e., the spelling of sounds/words). There is likely to be a greater problem in making links between phonemes and graphemes where there is an 'opaque' or 'deep' orthography, that is, where a sound can be represented in several ways e.g., /k/ can be 'c', 'k', or 'ck'. Similarly when reading the graphemes may represent varying sounds e.g., 'ough' in cough, through, bough, dough, thorough, rough, thought. The lack of 'transparency' or consistency in English spelling has sometimes been identified as one reason for a high incidence of early literacy difficulties, even leading one writer to raise the question 'Is English a dyslexic language?' (Spencer, 2000). While it is possible to enumerate the way in which the 26 letters of the English alphabet are combined to make the 44 sounds, by listing, for example, that there are 28 initial blends, 48 final blends and so on, one implication for teaching must be to teach what *is* consistent and where 'rules' can be applied rather than to emphasise irregularities while also dealing with these when they arise.

Because articulation can affect phonological representations it is considered important when teaching learners both phonemic segmentation in words, and how to isolate sounds when teaching grapheme-phoneme correspondence for reading and spelling, for the teacher not to add a 'schwa' to a sound. This is the /uh/ sound that is heard in 'about' (the sound made by 'a') and in words such as 'heaven' (the second 'e' unless this is omitted). Presenting 'single' sounds often involves the involuntary addition of a schwa (e.g., a teacher may present 'm' for 'mat' by saying 'muh-a–tuh'). Practice is needed to prevent this, which could otherwise lead to confusion in spelling. (Note that it is relatively easy to say some sounds such as /m/ and /n/ without the schwa, but more difficult with others e.g., /b/, /k/, /t/.) The teacher will need to model consonant sounds without opening their mouth at the end to avoid releasing a vowel sound (the schwa) where possible.

## Phonology and Articulation

This section explains some of the main terms used to describe how the 44 sounds (phonemes) of English are produced. These terms can be used to describe speech production/the sounds of *all* languages, although the actual sounds of different languages may be different just as the written forms to represent those sounds may vary. Readers interested in this area may wish to refer to the International Phonetics Alphabet (IPA) where a set of internationally agreed symbols (phonetic symbols) has been established so that the standard ('regular') sounds of any language can be put into a written form that will be accessible to anyone knowing how to 'read' (interpret) the symbols. In this book and programme we have not introduced phonetic symbols, with one exception (the symbol /ə/ for the schwa sound /uh/ which was described earlier). We have done this because while sometimes it is the sound of a vowel (as in the 'a' in 'about') it is often an 'additional' sound 'escaping' as a result of uttering a particular phoneme such as a plosive 'p'/p/, which often results in a /puh/ or /pə/ sound.

As stated earlier, we do not use phonetic symbols which could impose a further memory load on both practitioners and learners. Nevertheless we have indicated pronunciation by using the symbol / / to surround common letters with diacritical marks and clue words e.g., / ō / as in 'bone' and / o͞o / as in 'moon'. It is also acknowledged that regional accents may affect 'Standard'/Received Pronunciation and therefore teachers may have to exercise their professional judgement in cases where a learner's pronunciation is at variance with the examples provided and consider the relationship between speaking and spelling in order to adapt their teaching.

Practitioners involved in teaching literacy – particularly phonics-based teaching – will find a knowledge and understanding of certain aspects of speech production useful. These are, with examples from English:

- distinguishing between vowels and consonants
  - o vowel: a sound produced with an open vocal tract so that air can escape directly, with nothing blocking the air (e.g. / ǎ/, /ě/, /ǐ/, /ǒ/, /ǔ/ and 'y' as a semi-vowel when pronounced as /ǐ/);
  - o consonant: a sound where there is some blocking of the air (partial or complete) at some point;
- distinguishing between 'voiced' and 'unvoiced' sounds e.g. /<u>th</u>/ as in 'this' (voiced) and '/th/' as in 'with' (unvoiced). Voicing describes whether the vocal cords or folds are vibrating during articulation. (In teaching, learners will be encouraged to place a hand under the chin, on the vocal cords or folds, to 'feel' this vibration.)

It is possible to classify consonant sounds according to:

- manner of articulation (how breath is used);
- place of articulation (where/how the sound is produced.

## Classifying English Consonants According to Manner of Articulation

| Category | Description and consonants | |
|---|---|---|
| Stops/ plosives | The airflow from the lungs is completely blocked at some point and then released: | |
| | /p/, /t/, /k/ | *unvoiced* |
| | /b/, /d/, /g/ | *voiced* |
| Fricatives | The airflow is constricted or partially (but not completely) blocked: | |
| | /f/, /th/, /s/, /sh/, /h/ | *unvoiced* |
| | /v/, /<u>th</u>/, /z/ | *voiced* |
| Affricatives | Begin with a complete blockage (like plosives) but then have a partly restricted flow of air (like fricatives): | |
| | /ch/ as in <u>church</u>/ | *unvoiced* |
| | /j/ as in ju<u>dg</u>e | *voiced* |
| Nasals | The air passes through the nose: | |
| | /m/, /n/ and the /ng/ sounds | *voiced* |

| Glides | Where articulators are close to each other: | |
| | /y/, /w/, /wh/ | *voiced* |
| Liquid | Air escapes at the side of the tongue: | |
| | /l/, /r/ | *voiced* |

While the above provides a useful classification for the teacher and facilitates an understanding of texts on phonology, being able to identify and distinguish sounds according to an awareness of the position of tongue, teeth, and lips is of more use.

## Classifying English Consonants According to Place of Articulation

| **Category** | **Description and consonants** |
|---|---|
| Bilabial | Both lips together: /p/, /b/, /m/, /w/ |
| Labiodental | Lower lip in contact with upper teeth: /f/, /v/ |
| Dental | The tongue is behind/touching teeth: /t/, /d/, /th/, /<u>th</u>/ |
| Alveolar | The tongue contacts the upper alveolar ridge behind the teeth: /s/, /z/, /n/, /l/, /r/ (and sometimes /t/, /d/) |
| Palatal | Roof of the mouth: /j/ |
| Velar | The soft palate (velum) at the back of the mouth: /k/, /g/, /ng/ |
| Glottal | Throat: space between the vocal chords: /h/ |

## Vowels

Vowel sounds are all voiced and tend to be classified according to whether lips are rounded (O-shaped) or flat/spread when making the sound /r/ whether the muscles round the mouth are tense (as in /ē/ in 'bee') or lax (as in most short vowels such as /ĕ/ in 'bet'). They are also classified in relation to the height of the tongue and whether the tongue is at the front or back of the mouth. When asking learners about how they 'make' a vowel sound, therefore, practitioners should ask about what their lips/lip-shape looks like and where their tongue is – high or low in their mouth and whether it is at the back or the front. If they place their hands or fingers at the sides of the mouth (just on to their cheeks) they will also discover muscle tension.

## Using the Classification of Vowels and Consonants

Of course there is no expectation that these terms should be learned by pupils, but this framework should help teachers when asking learners to describe how they make sounds and, in particular, when working out the position of the tongue.

In Chapter 11 we indicate where and how learners can be encouraged to consider consciously and describe overtly how they form sounds in order to distinguish them before relating them to written symbols.

# Phonological Awareness and Literacy Development in the Conquering Literacy Programme

At the heart of the first part of the programme lies the aim of teaching sound-symbol (phoneme-grapheme) correspondence to facilitate good literacy development for learners who are presenting specific difficulties in reading and/or spelling. Multisensory strategies are used to maximise learners' strengths and to establish and develop neural pathways using repetition and routines to establish automaticity. Ramus and Szenkovits (2008) propose the theory that the phonological deficit in developmental dyslexia is a deficit in the accessing of phonological representations rather than a deficit in phonological representations per se. They point to difficulties particularly in short-term memory when learners are faced with tasks that make demands on their phonological awareness. (As stated earlier, Hatcher and Snowling (2002) also point to the significance of verbal short-term memory.) In practice, however, we believe that work on both memory and phonological awareness does benefit learners.

The programme reinforces phonemic segmentation skills by asking learners to listen to and detect a particular sound and note the position (beginning, middle, end) of a word and to produce the sound. The learner is asked to describe *how* they make the sound and to consider the physical aspects of that sound (the position of their tongue, teeth, lips, and the vibrations for 'voiced' and 'unvoiced' sounds – e.g., /th/ in /this/ and /th/ in /thing/). Using small mirrors so they can 'see' their mouth while saying a sound and word is also recommended. Opinions still vary as to what sort of 'feedback' we experience when producing sounds, but these methods at the very least reinforce learners' knowledge of sounds.

What is also clear from a study of phonological development is that while the majority of learners with dyslexia will have phonological difficulties, so too will a large number of non-dyslexic learners with literacy difficulties. The Conquering Literacy programme is therefore also appropriate for them. However, if they have other associated learning difficulties the programme may need to be adapted to their pace and experiences. We have found that what we have recommended for a one hour lesson will take much longer with learners with more general learning difficulties. In particular they may take longer to acquire concepts, requiring far more examples and practice. More attention has to be paid to language comprehension, to ensure learners' understanding of what they decode. They will also often require more practice in phonological awareness training. Nevertheless, they will benefit from a multisensory, structured, cumulative programme with lots of opportunities for overlearning.

## Implications for Practice

- Reading and spelling can be improved by intervention which links reading with phonological awareness training.
- It is important to recognise that learners with dyslexia need systematic teaching to establish sound-symbol relationships (phoneme-grapheme) and this will require practice and overlearning.
- Strategies should aim to develop learners' short-term memory as in Chapters 2 and 12.

## Summary

This chapter reviewed some of the research showing how a phonological deficit can affect the acquisition of literacy. Whilst pointing to problems in short-term verbal memory it particularly draws attention to the significance of phonological awareness. This research has suggested that some types of phonological processing skills have greater impact on learning to read and spell than others. It is acknowledged that there are many learners presenting poor phonological processing skills who do not have dyslexia and that some of the same teaching approaches could be used with them. Similarly it is clear that phonological processing difficulties are more evident in languages which have a 'deep' or 'opaque' orthography (such as English) and not so prominent in speakers of languages which are 'more transparent'. Aspects of speech production were considered to provide background information for practitioners that could facilitate their understanding of the intervention strategies introduced in the Conquering Literacy programme.

The chapter concluded that it is important to teach sound-symbol (phoneme-grapheme) correspondence to facilitate good literacy development and supported the view that learners with phonological difficulties, particularly those with dyslexia, will benefit from a multisensory, synthetic phonics-based, structured, cumulative programme which includes memory training and many opportunities for overlearning.

## References

Adams, M.J. (1990) *Beginning to Read: Thinking and Learning about Print*. Cambridge, MA: MIT Press.

Anthony, J.L. and Francis, D.J. (2005) 'Development of phonological awareness', *Current Directions in Psychological Science,* 14 (5): 255–259.

Blomert, L. and Willems, G. (2010) 'Is there a causal link from a phonological awareness deficit to reading failure in children at familial risk of dyslexia?', *Dyslexia, Special Issue: Part 2: Investigating the Links between Neurocognitive Functions and Dyslexia,* 16 (4): 300–317.

Bryant, P. and Bradley, L. (1990) *Children's Reading Problems.* Oxford: Blackwell.

Goswami, U. and Bryant, P.E. (1990) *Phonological Skills and Learning to Read.* Hove: Erlbaum.

Hatcher, J. and Snowling, M.J. (2002) 'The phonological representation of dyslexia: from theory to practice'. In Reid, G. and Wearmouth, J. (eds), *Dyslexia and Literacy: Theory and Practice.* London: Wiley. pp. 69–83.

Hatcher, P.J., Hulme, C. and Ellis, A.W. (1994) 'Ameliorating early reading failure by integrating the teaching of reading and phonological skills: the phonological linkage hypothesis', *Child Development,* 65: 41–57.

McDowell, K.D., Longian, C.J. and Goldstein, H. (2007) 'Relations among socioeconomic status, age and predictors of phonological awareness', *Journal of Speech, Language and Hearing Research,* 50: 1079–1092.

Muter, V. (1996) 'Predicting children's reading and spelling difficulties'. In Snowling, M. and Stackhouse, J. (eds), *Dyslexia, Speech and Language: A Practitioner's Handbook.* London: Whurr. pp. 31–44.

Muter, V., Snowling, M. and Taylor, S. (1994) 'Orthographic analogies and phonological awareness: their role and significance in early reading development', *Journal of Child Psychology and Psychiatry,* 35: 293–310.

Ramus, F. and Szenkovits, G. (2008) 'What phonological deficit?' *The Quarterly Journal of Experimental Psychology,* 61 (1): 129–141.

Reid, G. (2009) *Dyslexia: A Practitioners Handbook* (4th edn). Chichester: Wiley-Blackwell.

Snowling, M.J. and Hulme, C. (2005) 'Learning to read with a language impairment'. In Snowling, M.D. and Hulme, C. (eds), *The Science of Reading: A Handbook.* Oxford: Blackwell: pp. 397–412.

Spencer, K. (2000) 'Is English a dyslexic language?', *Dyslexia,* 6: 152–162.

Swan, D. and Goswami, U. (1997) 'Phonological awareness deficits and phonological representations hypothesis', *Journal of Experimental Child Psychology,* 60: 334–353.

## Further Reading

Teachers interested in learning more about phonology and phonetics will find the following texts useful:

Odden, D.A. (2005) *Introducing Phonology.* Cambridge: Cambridge University Press.

Roach, P. (2009) *English Phonetics and Phonology: A Practical Course* (4th edn). Cambridge: Cambridge University Press.

# CHAPTER 4

# THE DEVELOPMENT OF READING SKILLS

## Chapter Overview

This chapter examines models of reading and the processes involved, particularly in decoding print, as this is the aspect of reading that poses the greatest difficulties for learners with dyslexia. Appreciation of models of the reading processes supports teachers' ability to develop, select, and use appropriate intervention methods. The models discussed below have been used as a basis for the structured literacy programme in this book and this programme will therefore be used more confidently if practitioners understand the underpinning theories.

Teachers have long recognised that reading involves two main skills:

- the ability to decode – translating printed symbols (graphemes) into sounds (phonemes) and forming words;
- the ability to comprehend – extracting meaning from those words.

However, in many cases these were considered sequential skills, i.e. it was thought that children had to learn to identify words first and then develop their comprehension of a text.

A somewhat different approach is taken in the Simple View of Reading model (Gough and Tunmer, 1986). This model was adopted by the National Primary Strategy in England in 2007 following the *Independent Review of the Teaching of Early Reading* (Rose, 2006) and provides a useful framework for considering the assessment and teaching of all children. It also enables us to distinguish learners with dyslexic-type difficulties from those with more general reading difficulties (the 'garden-variety' referred to by Gough and Tunmer), thereby helping teachers to select appropriate strategies and resources.

Gough and Tunmer (1986) claimed that reading was a product of both decoding (D) and language comprehension (C) and that both aspects were necessary for skilled reading by which they meant reading with understanding (R). They represented this as $R = D \times C$. By decoding they meant recognising/pronouncing words out of context (i.e., having a knowledge of grapheme-phoneme correspondence) and by comprehension they meant language (linguistic) comprehension. This is the ability to access meanings and combine words into sentences and passages (semantic and syntactic knowledge), thereby being able to interpret at both a sentence and discourse level. Language comprehension is the skill and knowledge of language which a reader brings to the text and this will vary according to previous experiences. It is different

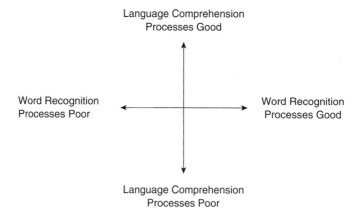

Figure 4.1    *The Simple View of Reading (Rose, 2006)*

from *reading* comprehension but essential to it (see the reference to Goodman, 1976, later in this chapter). The Simple View of Reading model is represented above. Rose (2006), among others, has substituted 'Word-Recognition' for 'decoding' in order to emphasise that letters have to be combined into words.

This model is useful for assessment and teaching because it reflects the fact that learners may have differing strengths and difficulties, making progress along one dimension but not necessarily in the other.

It is, of course, important to acknowledge that other psychological factors (e.g., motivation, interest, self-esteem, preferred learning styles) and environmental factors (e.g., whether the learner has previously received good teaching in reading, the literacy environment in the home, parental support, peer influence, and whether English is an additional language) will affect both dimensions. However, we can use the model to establish a basic framework for teaching. Catts et al. (2005) found that children's ability to read words (decoding) and understand spoken passages (language comprehension) accounted for more than 70 per cent of the reading comprehension of children aged 8–14. (As might be expected over this age range, word recognition was a more significant factor for the younger children, with the value of listening (language) comprehension playing an increasing role as they became more proficient in fluent/automatic word reading. Evidence that the two dimensions are separate has also been found in other studies, e.g., Nation and Snowling, 1997.)

Using this model we can locate learners with dyslexia (who will usually have strengths in linguistic comprehension but difficulties in word recognition) in the top left quadrant, whereas learners with reading difficulties attributed to poor word recognition skills and also poor language comprehension would be located in the bottom left quadrant. (The latter represent the group identified as 'garden-variety'.) The model also explains why, when learners with dyslexia improve their word recognition skills through intensive systematic teaching, they can 'read to learn' because they have good language comprehension skills whereas learners with poor language comprehension skills may still struggle to read with understanding even when their word recognition skills improve.

From the many models of the cognitive processes involved in reading we have identified two which have been particularly influential in studying the difficulties in decoding experienced by learners with dyslexia. These are the connectionist 'triangle' model proposed by Seidenberg and McClelland in 1989 and the Dual-Route Cascaded model (DRC) developed by Coltheart in the 1970s.

Adams (1990) used the triangle model when writing about the process of learning to read. Her account is valuable in both assessing and teaching learners with dyslexia because of her emphasis on the importance of phonological awareness and acquisition of the alphabetic principle in word recognition.

The connectionist (triangle) model emphasises interactions between *meaning* (semantics) *orthography* (print) and *phonology* (speech) and suggests they form an interactive network of processing elements which can be represented as the three 'points' of a triangle.

A two-way connection between the Orthographic and Phonological Processors indicates that as a visual image (of letters) is processed in the Orthographic Processor it activates corresponding units in the Phonological Processor which, in turn, sends feedback and pronounces the 'word'. These processors also have two-way connections to the Meaning Processor.

The Meaning Processor interprets the reader's knowledge of word meanings and stimulates both a visual image and the phonological units/phonemes involved in its pronunciation. This connectivity ensures that all three processors are working on the same stimulus simultaneously, thereby facilitating word reading. The model accepts the fact that the first stimulus in reading is visual. Adams argues, however, that the Phonological Processor is not just involved in reading aloud but that it also provides 'an alphabetic back-up system' (1990: 159) which is critical for developing fluency – it maintains speed and accuracy and helps to store words in the memory by relating a spelling (orthographic) pattern to pronunciation. The Meaning Processor is also linked in both directions to a Context Processor, as the context will aid a learner's comprehension of the meaning of individual words just as the meaning of individual words in turn affects their understanding of the context. (For a more detailed account, see Adams, 1990, and Seidenberg, 2005.) What is, perhaps, missing from the model is the wider link between Meaning and Context to language comprehension (which includes syntactic knowledge), which the Simple View of Reading model suggests is crucial to reading. One of the characteristics of many learners with dyslexia is that they may rely heavily on their linguistic competence to predict words. This can be a strength when teaching them that reading is about extracting meaning from a text and it reflects Goodman's (1976) proposal that reading is a 'psycholinguistic guessing game'. His model of reading involved an integrated process of the 'cues' contained in written language which relate to a linguistic knowledge of:

- syntax – the grammar of a language: how words are related to each other and how words are formed from phonemes and morphemes (meaningful units of phonemes);
- semantics – the meanings of words;
- grapheme/phoneme correspondence.

Skilled reading, he argued, involves integrating all three forms of knowledge. However, there are often times where reliance on context (particularly syntax and meanings) will lead to learners 'guessing' a word because they lack knowledge of the alphabetic principle (e.g., the sentence, 'The bird flew up into the *sky*' may be read as 'The bird flew up into the *tree*'). This substitution is syntactically appropriate and reflects some contextual understanding, but shows no use of grapheme-phoneme correspondence.

Adams argues, as do many others, that there is a need for explicit teaching of phonemic awareness and the alphabetic principle in order to develop word recognition skills. The connectionist model suggests that where there is a weakness in one (or more) of the processors it is likely that the reading process will be impaired because there will be no speedy explicit connections. The implication for teaching therefore is to devise activities using all three main processors, thus strengthening the neural pathways in order to develop speed/automaticity of response. This will lead to greater fluency in reading, whether reading aloud or silently, and therefore aid a learner's understanding of the text.

Although Adams applies this model to reading single words as well as words in context (as does Plaut, 2005), Coltheart (2005) considers that the connectionist model fails to address the acquisition of the decoding skills needed to pronounce 'non-words' (e.g., 'napt', 'grib') which have no meaning in English. Rack et al. (1992) and other researchers have shown that poor non-word reading (which requires a good knowledge of grapheme-phoneme correspondence) is one of the main characteristics of dyslexia.

Coltheart (2005) argues that the Dual-Route Cascaded (DRC) model continues to offer a more comprehensive explanation of both reading aloud and reading comprehension and can account for the pronunciation of non-words. He points out that while connectionist models also suggest dual routes, computational research studies reveal that the DRC model alone addresses all aspects of reading including non-words. He suggests that the Meaning (Semantics) Processor in the connectionist model interferes with or impairs the ability to read non-words. When only the orthography-phonology route is used then non-words can be read.

Coltheart's model represents a lexical (whole word) and non-lexical route to word recognition. In fact the model suggests two possible lexical routes, each of which generates the pronunciation of a word which exists in the reader's lexicon (word/vocabulary bank). In the case of the lexical-semantic route the reading process passes from identifying letters to the orthographic lexical system (the store of visual images), making links with known meanings in the semantic system, and from there to the phonological output system so that relevant phonemes are then automatically produced. This route is used for familiar words and can be seen as a 'fast' route. A more direct (and faster) lexical route passes directly from the orthographic lexicon to the phonological system and through to the phoneme output system. This route could explain how some words are 'read' (pronounced/recalled) but not necessarily understood. Non-words cannot be read through the lexical route because they are not recognised visually (are not stored in the orthographic lexicon) and they have no meaning attached to them (and cannot be stored in the semantic lexicon). It could be argued that a non-word may activate an orthographically similar word leading to activation of the phonological output. This could explain the 'analogy' process (e.g., the non-word *'fode'* may activate *pod, code, food, fodder*) often noted in readers' responses to non-word reading tests. It could also explain the use of analogy and 'regularisation' in some reading errors of real words (e.g., mispronouncing 'lose' by an analogy with 'rose').

The non-lexical route is usually slower because the process goes from identifying letters to the grapheme-phoneme rule system. This route facilitates the pronunciation of unfamiliar and non-words (e.g., kanlopt) in a serial fashion. It does not deal well

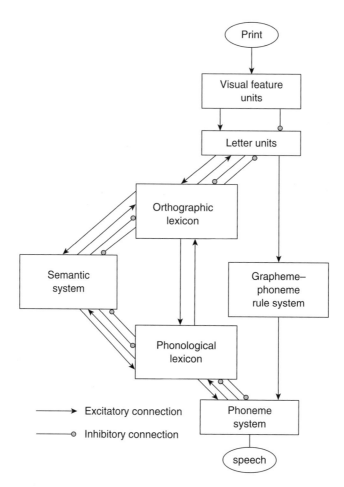

Figure 4.2 *The Dual-Route Cascaded Model (Coltheart, 2005)*

with irregular words because it applies 'normal' grapheme-phoneme rules. The lexical route relies more heavily on a visual store and 'whole-word' approach, whereas the non-lexical route relies on making grapheme-phoneme correspondences. Both routes show a 'cascaded' process as information passes down through the different channels.

This model has often been used to distinguish 'sub-types' of dyslexia, in particular between learners with 'phonological dyslexia' (sometimes described as 'dysphonetic') because they have phonological difficulties and therefore have difficulty accessing the non-lexical route, and those with 'surface dyslexia' (sometimes called 'dyseidetic') who have difficulties with the visual-orthographic system (see Castles and Coltheart, 1993). Those with phonological difficulties have greater difficulty learning to 'decode' words and read non-words, although they may be successful reading irregular words particularly if these are high-frequency words. Those with 'surface dyslexia' however, because they use the non-lexical route, are better able to read non-words.

Much research in the 1970s and 1980s was based on attempting to distinguish sub-types. Boder and Jarrico (1982) developed a diagnostic test of reading and spelling to identify learners as dyseidetic or dysphonetic, whereas Bakker (1979) distinguished between 'P-type' (perceptual) learners who read very slowly and are particularly influenced by the perceptual features of text and 'L-type' (linguistic) readers who are heavily influenced by their use of language and do not necessarily attend carefully to perceptual features. We have not discussed these here as there have been no significant recent studies following up their work. It is interesting to note, however, that Milne (2005) chooses to use a sub-type model to underpin approaches to teaching reading both to those first 'learning-to-read' ('beginning readers') and those experiencing difficulties, particularly those with dyslexia. His approach clearly relates to Coltheart's model and he uses the terms 'dyseidetic' and 'dysphonetic' when describing dyslexia. Milne also suggests that brain-imaging studies show that 'Reading involves visually perceiving the word in the back of the brain and then mapping this perception to sound in the front of the brain' (2005: 33). Two circuits can be used, an upper and lower circuit. The upper circuit is equivalent to the non-lexical route described by Coltheart in that it starts by analysing visual components (at the back of the brain) and then maps each letter onto its corresponding phoneme/sound component (in what he describes as the auditory module at the front of the brain) so that the word can be pronounced. The lower circuit is equivalent to Coltheart's direct lexical route, connecting a word recognition component in the visual module to the communication/ speech output at the front of the brain. In the same way Milne suggests that where the upper circuit has been used (e.g., through phonics teaching) a 'snapshot' will have been taken to allow the visual form to be stored in the lower circuit, thereby building up a word-bank/lexicon particularly for familiar and high frequency irregular words. Milne's book has proved useful to specialist teachers in providing simple explanations of the reading process and dyslexic-type difficulties to parents and others.

Vellutino and Fletcher (2005) support the view that 'phonological dyslexia' is a valid sub-type but also state there is more conflicting evidence regarding the separate existence of surface dyslexia, as most children with dyslexia will have difficulties with both the phonological and orthographic levels of word recognition. They refer to studies by Stanovich in 1977 and 1985 (substantiated by many later writers) showing that phonological processing difficulties form the core of all reading difficulties.

In the first chapter of this book, we stated our view that it is more useful for teachers to consider individual profiles than search for distinct sub-types. However, we have included the above summary of sub-types to explain the terminology which can be found in other texts.

The models of reading discussed above provide useful conceptual frameworks for devising teaching strategies when examining the nature of the characteristics presented by particular learners with dyslexia. Together with the research into dyslexia and literacy difficulties cited in earlier chapters they point to the adoption of a synthetic phonics approach to teaching reading (i.e., explicit teaching of the grapheme(s) representing particular sounds and how to build these into words). 'Jolly Phonics' (Wernham and Lloyd, 1993) is a current example of a popular scheme to teach beginning readers in primary schools that is based on a synthetic phonics approach. However, it is not sufficiently detailed and structured to meet the needs of learners with dyslexia.

In addition to synthetic phonics, children learning to read (and spell) will often apply analytical skills both visually and aurally when they have acquired some grapheme-phoneme correspondence (see Goswami, 1990) and these can be developed by explicit teaching of both how to analyse words into graphemes and phonemes and how to use onset and rime, e.g. analyse the word 'clock' into 'cl' (onset) and 'ock' (rime) in order to work out how to read (and spell) flock, stock, block, etc. It follows from the Simple View of Reading that word recognition can also be helped by building on a learner's lexical and syntactic knowledge which, as stated earlier, is often a strength in learners with dyslexia. This includes their knowledge of morphology – how meaningful units (which may be a single phoneme, a group of phonemes, or a whole word) combine to affect a word and, in turn, sentence structure and meaning. Examples include how adding 's' to a noun (e.g., 'house') forms a plural, but adding it to a verb (e.g., 'hop') indicates the third person singular, present tense.

Learners with dyslexia vary in their understanding of morphology, but for some, morphological processing (a significant component of language comprehension) appears to be a strength, although its use and development can often be hindered in the early stages of learning to read because of phonological difficulties and a lack of knowledge of grapheme-phoneme correspondence. A discussion of the significance of morphology in reading may be found in Marlen-Wilson et al. (1994) and recent texts by Nunes and Bryant (2006, 2009) suggest useful approaches for teachers of literacy. We have introduced morphological approaches in Conquering Literacy at an early stage after establishing basic routines using synthetic phonics, because these can build on the language knowledge of learners and also facilitate reading sentences, making 'reading' within a structure more varied. This is in line with much of the research. Bowers et al. (2010), in a review of 22 studies of morphological interventions for literacy skills for learners aged 5–14, found that morphological instruction benefited learners of all ages (particularly those who were poor readers) and that it was most effective when combined with other aspects of literacy teaching.

Deacon et al. (2008) claim that research suggests that morphological processing may be independent of phonological processing, although phonological difficulties may affect learners' ability to recognise morphemes in reading and spelling. There also appears to be a link with orthographic processing. They conclude that this area requires further research. In our experience many learners with dyslexia have enjoyed using and extending their morphological knowledge which can aid speed of word recognition, help spelling, and develop vocabulary. It is particularly valuable for older learners in helping them read and spell polysyllabic words, when they can also feel 'in control' of learning because they understand how words are formed.

Reading skills develop not only as a result of instruction but also through practice i.e., the activity of reading itself. However, children with poor word recognition skills are not able to access reading independently (and in many cases actively avoid engaging in it) so that at an early age they will start to fall behind their peers who have acquired good decoding skills. This is often the case for learners with dyslexia who may have a good understanding of a text when it is read *to* them because of good language comprehension and vocabulary but are unable to 'read' (decode) it. They are, therefore, disadvantaged in areas where they need to 'read to learn' and the gap between them and 'skilled readers' will widen unless there is early intervention. Stanovich (1986) described this as the 'Matthew effect', which is based on a quotation from the parable of the talents in St. Mathew's gospel (25 v29). Stanovich used this to draw attention to the fact that children who can read will become better readers (by reading) whilst those who are poor readers will become poorer (by comparison with the good readers).

## Fluency in Word Recognition

Fluency – the ability to read words accurately and quickly – is considered important for reading comprehension in that it should enable words to 'flow' rapidly and meaningfully into sentences, thereby aiding ability to interpret meaning. Fluency is likely to be affected, therefore, not only by knowledge of grapheme-phoneme correspondence but also by skills in rapid naming, speed of processing, and verbal short-term memory. All of these represent areas of weakness for many learners with dyslexia. Most intervention programmes concentrate on decoding skills because inaccuracy will clearly impair reading comprehension. Repetition and overlearning can help to establish or improve automaticity and speed of processing and recall. However, many learners with dyslexia remain slow 'dysfluent' readers, even when their word recognition skills have improved (and many will be allowed extra time in examinations to compensate for this). Shaywitz et al. (2008) call for more research into effective teaching to improve fluency. They point out that some programmes concentrate on fluent reading of connected text while others focus more on improving word recognition, building on semantic knowledge and orthographic patterns to build up fluency in word recognition. They cite a review by Kuhn and Stale in 2003 of fluency-oriented instruction approaches which shows that repeated reading of a text, with scaffolding by a teacher or peer, can produce gains in fluency (although this does not necessarily improve comprehension).

## Reading Comprehension

Although this chapter has focused on models of word recognition processes because that is a prime area of difficulty for learners with dyslexia, any teaching strategy must ensure that learners understand that word recognition is not 'what reading is' and also grasp that the purposes of reading for enjoyment and information involve extracting meaning from print. The Simple View of Reading model emphasises this. Gough et al. (1996) suggest that the relationship between listening comprehension and reading comprehension grows stronger with age whereas word recognition becomes less significant. This applies particularly to readers who have developed good word recognition skills at an early age. (It is clear that during the early stages of learning to read, a reader's comprehension of a text will be severely impaired by inaccurate word reading.)

The relationship between rate of reading and reading comprehension is less clear. Johnston and Kirby (2006), among others, have found that measures of rapid naming skills in young children are related to later reading comprehension. However, although rate of reading connected prose has often been considered a measure of fluency which will affect comprehension, Cain cites a study by Goff, Pratt and Ong in 2005 which suggests that rate of reading is *not* related to reading comprehension 'after the influence of general ability has been taken into account' (Cain, 2010: 98). Nevertheless, we consider it vital within a structured programme to foster fluency (accuracy and speed of reading) because learners on that programme are at an early stage of learning to read and fluency will help them cope with the demands of school.

Certainly one distinction between the reading development of learners with dyslexia and those with 'common or garden variety' reading difficulties lies in the fact that when both groups have acquired sufficient word recognition skills to read appropriate texts independently the language comprehension (and lexical) skills of the learners with dyslexia appear to 'compensate' for and help their reading comprehension (in spite of dysfluent reading), whereas the non-dyslexic group with poor language comprehension will still have reading comprehension difficulties. (We pointed out earlier that relying on language knowledge can lead to 'errors' and misunderstandings if a reader cannot decode accurately, so accurate word recognition is essential at the beginning stages.)

Reading comprehension at discourse level requires not only good linguistic knowledge but also an ability to follow (and recall) sequences – as in stories and factual texts – and this will also be affected by the general knowledge and experiences a learner brings to the text. This is a vast area beyond the scope of this book and so we have not included strategies for developing language comprehension within the Conquering Literacy programme which is directly aimed at teaching word recognition strategies. However, the programme does emphasise the need to build/blend words from graphemes as soon as possible by using morphological structures and combining words into sentences from an early stage both for reading *and* writing. We also reinforce learners' understanding of literary language and the purposes of reading for enjoyment (through shared reading and reading *to* the learner) and 'reading for learning' through the teaching of study skills, including applying alphabet work to dictionary skills and proof reading passages. Follow-up activities should also include items that will foster comprehension.

# Reading Development

We have considered models of the reading process to be more useful in informing intervention strategies for learners with dyslexia than adopting a developmental model showing normal readers' progression in relation to word recognition. Frith (1985) proposed three developmental stages in the acquisition of early literacy which can be applied both to reading and spelling (and suggested how the two are related for young learners). These are considered in the next chapter. Her model has limitations, however, because children do not all go through the same stages in similar ways and, as other models of reading indicate, some routes to word recognition may not involve an alphabetic 'stage'/approach.

## Implications for Practice

- It is more useful to consider individual profiles than to try to 'categorise' learners with dyslexia into sub-types.
- The Simple View of Reading should help teachers to identify strengths and weaknesses in the two dimensions.
- Learners with dyslexia need explicit teaching in word recognition skills, particularly when acquiring the alphabetic principle involved in grapheme-phoneme correspondence.
- Teachers should identify the strategies learners are using to read in order to replace any ineffective or inefficient strategies with more appropriate methods – for example:

  o  sometimes predicting words through a reliance on context or language knowledge can lead to inaccuracy in word reading;
  o  learners may be using some grapheme-phoneme decoding skills but at a very basic level;
  o  learners may be decoding but without trying to make meaning from those words;
  o  learners may be first-letter guessing;
  o  they may not be attending to the letters sequentially;
  o  they may be using analogy to read unknown words which can be a strength or lead to confusions (see Goswami, 1990);
  o  they may be showing good 'instant' recognition, particularly of high frequency words (which should be built on and may reflect good memory skills), but may still need help with decoding and using grapheme-phoneme correspondence.

*(Continued)*

*(Continued)*

- Teachers should continue to read to and with learners in order to familiarise them with literary language and should *discuss* this reading to encourage comprehension skills.
- Teachers need to recognise that word recognition skills have not been acquired by these learners despite good teaching and that progress will be slow.
- Teaching must be consistent and contain overlearning, yet must also maintain learners' interest and be conducted in ways which will enhance their independence and self-esteem.
- Teaching should emphasise the need for automaticity and fluency (accuracy and an appropriate rate of reading).
- Learners' language comprehension should be *built on* in order to develop *reading comprehension* e.g., using prediction exercises in reading passages, cloze procedure and extending vocabulary.

(Parts II and III provide examples of the above.)

## Summary

The models of the reading processes described in this chapter point to a need for intervention to target decoding skills with a particular emphasis on phonological processes to teach grapheme-phoneme correspondence using systematic phonics teaching. Clearly, this involves developing what for most learners are deficit areas – automaticity and phonological awareness! In order to build up neural pathways to facilitate the automaticity of processing (indicated by those models of reading) there must be repetition and the use of other channels of learning to support development and aid memory (i.e., visual and kinaesthetic methods as well as auditory/phonological).

## References

Adams, M.J. (1990) *Beginning to Read: Thinking and Learning about Print.* Cambridge, MA: MIT Press.

Bakker, D.J. (1979) 'Hemispheric differences and reading strategies: two dyslexias?', *Bulletin of the Orton Society,* 29: 84–100.

Boder, E. and Jarrico, S. (1982) *Boder Test of Reading – Spelling Patterns*. New York: Grune and Stratton.

Bowers, P.N., Kirby, J. and Deacon, S.H. (2010) 'The effects of morphological instruction on literacy skills: a systematic review of the literature', *Review of Educational Research,* 80: 144–179.

Cain, K. (2010) *Reading Development and Difficulties*. Oxford: Blackwell.

Castles, A. and Coltheart, M. (1993) 'Varieties of developmental dyslexia', *Cognition,* 47: 149–180.

Catts, H.W., Hogan, T.P. and Adolf, S.M. (2005) 'Developmental changes in reading and reading disabilities'. In Catts, H. and Kamhi, A. (eds), *The Connection between Language and Reading Disabilities*. Mahwah, NJ: Erlbaum. pp. 23–36.

Coltheart, M. (2005) 'Modeling reading: the dual-route approach'. In Snowling, M.J. and Hulme, C. (eds), *The Science of Reading: A Handbook*. Oxford: Blackwell. pp. 6–23.

Deacon, S.H., Parrila, R. and Kirby, J.R. (2008) 'A review of the evidence on morphological processing in dyslexics and poor readers: a strength or weakness?'. In Reid, G., Fawcett, A.J., Manis, F. and Siegel, L.S. (eds), *The Sage Handbook of Dyslexia*. London: Sage. pp. 212–237.

Frith, U. (1985) 'Beneath the surface of developmental dyslexia'. In Patterson, K.E., Marshall, J.C. and Coltheart, M. (eds), *Surface Dyslexia: Neurological and Cognitive Studies of Phonological Reading*. London: Erlbaum. pp. 301–330.

Goodman, K. (1976) 'Reading: a psycholinguistic guessing game'. In Singer, H. and Ruddell, R.B. (eds), *Theoretical Models and Processes of Reading* (2nd edn). Newark, NJ: International Reading Association. pp. 497–508.

Goswami, U. (1990) 'A special link between rhyming skills and the use of orthographic analogies by beginning readers', *Journal of Child Psychology and Psychiatry,* 31: 301–311.

Gough, P.B. and Tunmer, W.E. (1986) 'Decoding, reading and reading disability', *Remedial and Special Education,* 7: 6–10.

Gough, P.B., Hoover, W.A. and Peterson, C.L. (1996) 'Some observations on a simple view of reading'. In Cornoldi, C. and Oakhill, J. (eds), *Reading Comprehension Difficulties: Processes and Interventions*. Mahwah, NJ: Erlbaum. pp. 1–13.

Johnston, T.C. and Kirby, J.R. (2006) 'The contribution of naming speed to the simple view of reading', *Reading and Writing,* 19: 339–361.

Marlen-Wilson, W.D., Tyler, L.K., Waksler, R. and Older, L. (1994) 'Morphology and meaning in the English mental lexicon', *Psychological Review,* 101: 3–33.

Milne, D. (2005) *Teaching the Brain to Read*. Hungerford: SK Publishing.

Nation, K. and Snowling, M.J. (1997) 'Assessing reading difficulties: the validity and utility of current measures of reading skill', *British Journal of Educational Psychology,* 67: 359–370.

Nunes, T. and Bryant, P. (2006) *Improving Literacy by Teaching Morphemes*. London: Routledge.

Nunes, T. and Bryant, P. (2009) *Children's Reading and Spelling: Beyond the First Steps*. Oxford: Blackwell.

Plaut, D.C. (2005) 'Connectionist approaches to reading'. In Snowling M.J. and Hulme, C. (eds), *The Science of Reading: A Handbook*. Oxford: Blackwell. pp. 24–38.

Rack, J.P., Snowling, M.J. and Olson, R.K. (1992) 'The non-word reading deficit in dyslexia: a review', *Reading Research Quarterly,* 27: 29–53.

Rose, J. (2006) *An Independent Review of the Teaching of Early Reading*. London: DfES.

Shaywitz, S.E., Morris, R. and Shaywitz, B.A. (2008) 'The education of dyslexic children from childhood to early adulthood', *Annual Review of Psychology,* 59: 451–475.

Seidenberg, M.S. (2005) 'Connectionist models of word reading', *Current Directions in Psychological Science*, 14: 238–242.

Stanovich, K.E. (1986) 'Matthew effects in reading: some consequences of individual differences in the acquisition of literacy', *Reading Research Quarterly*, 26: 7–29.

Vellutino, F.R. and Fletcher, J.M. (2005) 'Developmental dyslexia'. In Snowling, M.J. and Hulme, C. (eds), *The Science of Reading: A Handbook*. Oxford: Blackwell. pp. 362–378.

Wernham, S. and Lloyd, S. (1993) *Jolly Phonics*. Chigwell, Essex: Jolly Learning.

# CHAPTER 5

# SPELLING DEVELOPMENT AND DYSLEXIA

## Chapter Overview

Treiman and Kessler (2005) point out that writing is a form of representing the language and requires an ability to spell – i.e., represent the language in a graphic form. Learners with dyslexia often experience greater difficulties in spelling than reading, and these difficulties often persist into adulthood. This chapter considers some theories which may offer relevant explanations. Particular attention is paid to the relationships between reading and spelling processes, the significance of phonological and visual difficulties in spelling, and the link between spelling and handwriting, although the latter is discussed in greater detail in the next chapter.

Snowling (2000) suggested that children are not able to use 'compensatory strategies' as successfully in spelling as they are in reading. She claimed that exposure to print through reading does not necessarily lead to good spelling, whilst not disputing that there is a close relationship between reading and spelling as proposed by Frith (1985) and Ehri (2002). Spelling, like reading, relies heavily on a knowledge of phoneme-grapheme correspondence (and related rules), morphological knowledge, and auditory and visual memory.

There is general agreement that difficulties with phonological representations underpin the spelling difficulties of learners with dyslexia. Snowling (1994) found the spelling of children with dyslexia showed more 'phonetically acceptable' errors than those in a control group of non-dyslexic children with spelling difficulties. She has proposed that poor phonological representations mean there is no framework for developing spelling (Snowling, 2000). Other research supports this link between phonological difficulties and spelling (see Reid, 2009, and Treiman and Kessler, 2005). While Treiman and Kessler emphasise the significance of phonological skills and the alphabetic principle in spelling, they also acknowledge the importance of visual processing. Much of the earlier research into spelling also pointed to visual processing difficulties. Seymour and McGregor (1984), for example, pointed to difficulties in visual sequencing and Romani et al. (1999) suggested that poor visual sequential memory might affect a learner's ability to learn letter sequences. Peters (1985) identified two major factors affecting spelling: visual processing and speed of handwriting. Cripps (1998) developed spelling schemes based on Peters' research, linking visual and handwriting training. Although these schemes helped some learners the style of joined handwriting used is not fully cursive and our view is that it will not aid speed as much as a script that uses approach and joining strokes such as is advocated in the next chapter. Cursive writing develops fluency and speed which then frees up working memory capacity, enabling the learner to pay more attention to how a word has been spelt. Treiman and Kessler (2005) suggest that a 'motivated' approach to introducing letter shapes may help learners to memorise letter-sound relationships, citing using a 'snake' drawing to depict 's'. (This is often known as 'animating' letters, as in Letterland (http://www.letterland.com), and has been useful with young children.) The Conquering Literacy programme prefers introducing letter names and sounds by linking them with clue-words (to support memory) so that learners are presented with a correctly-formed letter.

Frameworks for understanding the processes involved in spelling have largely been based on developmental models. One of the most influential has been that of Frith (1985) who provided a model of literacy development showing the relationship between reading and spelling. This identified three stages:

1  *Logographic* – a learner recognises a word as a unit (not necessarily spelling it correctly) but can read the whole word.
2  *Alphabetic* – as a child learns to read and write they will learn phoneme-grapheme correspondence – how letters represent sounds in conventional spelling – and they

begin to store these in their memory. In this stage, recognising an alphabetic principle, they often 'invent' spellings because they will try to represent the sounds they hear in a word by using the letters they know (and the sounds *they* associate with them). Just as reading helps children to appreciate grapheme-phoneme correspondence which is important for spelling, at this stage learning to write and spell aids their ability to decode.

3   *Orthographic* – the learner reaches this stage when they have a good knowledge of letter-sound relationships and conventional spelling rules. They may be able to recall whole words or morphemes, but will not be operating on single phonemes.

Frith emphasises the interaction between reading and spelling at all stages and suggests the major literacy hurdle for learners with dyslexia lies at the alphabetic stage. She points to the low incidence in Japan (which does not use an alphabetic script) and much research referred to elsewhere in this book shows that phonological difficulties are not reported so much in learners in countries where there is a more consistent orthography and therefore reduced complexity in acquiring the alphabetic principle.

Another model of spelling development found useful by teachers is that of Gentry (1987) who proposed five stages:

1   *Pre-communicative* – scribble writing and drawing (this may be a commentary on what they are doing). However some studies of children's early writing have suggested there can be a communicative intention even at this stage.

2   *Semi-phonetic* – a single letter or group of letters is used to represent a word or group of words. This can also include 'invented' spellings. Vowels will often be omitted.

3   *Phonetic* – represents the 'surface sound' features of words (Gentry, 1987: 23) – 'Spelling as it sounds'.

4   *Transitional* – the spellings begin to be influenced by some spelling rules (they may begin to rely also on visual memory or knowledge of phoneme-grapheme rules).

5   *Correct* – standard spelling including irregular words.

Gentry's model is compatible with that of Frith, but both could be open to the criticism that they reflect traditional approaches to teaching literacy, current at their time of writing, where whole word recognition of some words (key sight vocabulary) was taught before introducing phonics. In addition, they assume that all children pass through all these stages in the same order and this may not be the case, particularly for learners with dyslexia. However, they provide a useful framework for analysing children's spelling and monitoring progress although they are over twenty years old.

Both draw attention to the significance of phonological skills and there are implications also for teaching using a morphological approach and teaching spelling rules.

Developmental models suggest what sort of processing may be dominant as literacy is acquired but focus on behaviours, whereas it is also useful to understand the spelling process at a cognitive level. Spelling has sometimes been considered a 'reverse' process of the reading process, involving the same skills but starting from different stimuli, in that reading starts from a visual representation (print) whereas spelling starts from an auditory (or 'internalised' sound) stimulus. We propose the model below (Figure 5.1) based on a dual-route model of reading.

When we need to spell a word it is usually because we are in the act of composing (a story/assignment/letter) and therefore we are 'generating' the word in our head. It may be that internally we 'hear' the word. In education and certain work situations we may be required to spell words we hear (i.e., they are dictated to us or we are making notes about what someone is saying). We have represented these two situations by 'think/hear', in the model below.

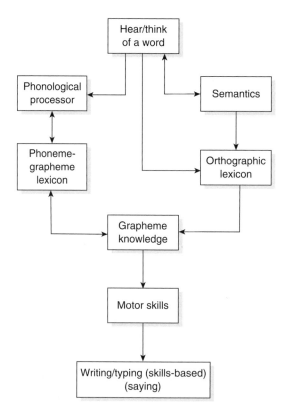

Figure 5.1   *Application of a Dual-Route Model to Spelling*

The lexical route reflects that, as they experience how words are spelled (through reading and spelling practice), learners begin to memorise the spelling of words and store these in an orthographic lexicon. This route may be triggered directly from the sound of a word or pass through a semantic (meaning) processor to the orthographic lexicon and through a grapheme knowledge buffer into writing the word or saying the letter name. Reliance on this 'visual' route may partly explain the use of analogy (Goswami, 1993, 2003) and some of the 'typical spelling errors' of learners with dyslexia, such as the omission of a letter or writing the correct letters but in the wrong sequence.

In the non-lexical (or sub-lexical) route, the sounds of the word are analysed and these are 'translated' into the related graphemes (grapheme-phoneme correspondence), passing through the grapheme buffer before producing the spelling. This route relies more heavily on phonological skills and a good knowledge of the alphabetic system whereas the lexical route relies more heavily on visual memory. Spelling requires greater use of the non-lexical route. Poor phonological representations, therefore, can result in 'phonetic approximations' or 'plausible' spellings where a learner will try to represent the sounds of a word.

Frequently-used words may well become stored in the orthographic lexicon and this route may also be used for irregular words. However, as in the dual-routes models of reading the significance of the indirect route – using the phonological processor and then making sound-symbol relationships – is that it takes more time and is adversely affected by phonological difficulties and working memory as discussed in Chapter 2. It is particularly affected by difficulties in phonological segmentation as argued in Chapter 3 and this is compounded if there is poor knowledge of phoneme-grapheme correspondence. This route can be developed by the systematic teaching of synthetic phonics and then reinforced by the use of analogy (based on analytic phonics and using onset-rime techniques) as discussed in Chapter 4. Goswami (1993) pointed to young children's use of analogy, suggesting that onset-rime strategies should be used even with beginning readers (and spellers). Others (e.g., Muter, 1996) suggest this is more appropriate in the second year of learning to read. Houghton and Zorzi (2003), exploring the use of a dual-route connectionist model of spelling in normal readers, suggest that multiple routes are active in parallel to produce spelling. This does not, however, gainsay the theory that impairment in either pathway adversely affects spelling.

Use of the letter name is important in spelling as the name is consistent even if that letter makes several sounds (e.g., the letter 'a' says /ă/ in cat but /ā/ in acorn and /ŏ/ in wan): on the other hand a single sound can be represented by many different spellings (e.g., /ā/ can be spelled 'a' as in acorn, 'ai' as in paid, 'a-e' as in made, 'ay' as in say, 'ei' as in rein, 'eigh' as in sleigh, 'ey' as in grey). It is particularly important in view of this that in spelling learners are encouraged to think of the letter names that represent these sounds. In addition, as Treiman and Kessler (2005) point out, in English the name of the letter normally incorporates its 'common' sound (e.g., 'b' and /b/) and this also supports teaching learners to 'say the name of a letter as you write it' when spelling words, as suggested in Chapter 11. Naming speed is also important, as Wolf et al. (2000) have indicated for reading, and the ability to name letters readily in order to write them quickly would seem significant in spelling. A study of young French children (Plaza and Cohen, 2006) suggested that syllable awareness and visual attention were the most significant predictors of both reading and spelling in the first grades, but that naming speed and phoneme awareness were also very significant.

## What Works in Teaching Spelling?

Brooks and Weeks (1999) studied a range of methods for teaching spelling to learners with spelling difficulties (not necessarily with dyslexia) and concluded that children's rate of acquiring spellings could be improved by using 'individual' learning strategies which could be readily used within normal English/spelling teaching. Another useful source for teaching spelling is Ott (2007). The range of methods suggested in both these sources tends to reflect the need to combine phonological, visual, and kinaesthetic (by speaking and writing) strategies.

We would suggest that if a teacher has concerns about a learner's spelling, but other aspects of their literacy are well-developed, it would be appropriate to use one of their recommended approaches. Where there are severe literacy difficulties, however, a more comprehensive programme such as the one in this book is necessary.

## Spelling in English: Implications for Teaching

It is very easy to point to inconsistencies in English spelling and pronunciation (e.g., the different ways of pronouncing 'ough' in though, enough, through and bough and the fact that 'wind' can be pronounced in two ways). There are also inconsistencies in spelling particular sounds (e.g., /ā/ in acorn, maid, bake and pay). Teaching strategies should therefore teach rules which apply consistently and also indicate where there are 'alternative' spellings (as for /ā/ above) what 'choices' are available to learners, what 'rules' they can apply (where there *are* some), and how to choose a particular spelling in relation to frequency of occurrence. Kohnen et al. (2008) report a single case study of a girl with developmental dysgraphia who had poor sound-letter knowledge, but after training based on applying spelling rules was able to spell both regular and non-words and generalise the rule to include unfamiliar words. This strengthens the case for the significance of a non-lexical (or sub-lexical) route.

It is important in teaching spelling, whatever the methods used, to remember that an incorrect spelling may have been stored in phonological, visual, and motor memories and therefore any intervention strategy must build up *new* patterns to establish automaticity. One option we have found effective is to implement the same approach that is used in teaching irregular words (Johnson et al., 1997a). The learner is asked to look at the correct spelling of the word presenting a difficulty and highlight the 'bits' they find hard (got wrong), but noting what they got right. The teacher then talks the learner through the rule/correction (to provide a meta-cognitive strategy) and the correct word is then written and checked, using the Simultaneous Oral Spelling strategy described in Part III. This strategy is useful where a learner frequently misspells a particular word. Where it appears clear that the learner needs to learn a particular rule and generalise it (e.g., the doubling rule for 'hop'/'hopping' and the 'drop-e' rule in 'hoping') the above 'correction' strategy is *not* useful because they need to learn the rule. Whatever approach is used, practice is essential in order to develop automaticity.

Teaching phoneme-grapheme correspondence facilitates acquisition for both reading and spelling, and synthetic phonics particularly aids spelling because it helps with phonemic segmentation and the ability to acquire knowledge of how to 'write' (spell) a sound. It is interesting to note that while researching the impact of a synthetic phonics-based programme to teach reading to children with dyslexic-type difficulties (Johnson et al., 1997b) children's spelling improved (as well as their reading) although the programme did not aim to 'teach spelling' (Johnson et al., 1997a; see also, Johnson 2001).

Morphological approaches are also relevant so that learners can recognise and learn meaningful units as 'chunks'. This draws on (and extends) their knowledge and understanding of the meaning of words and should be used in teaching both reading and spelling, as appreciating the morphology of a language helps readers to 'decode' polysyllabic words and also memorise 'groups' of words according to their meaning and spelling/orthography. One approach is to teach syllabification and how to recognise base words with prefixes and suffixes. Word meanings can be explored particularly through teaching the meanings and origins of prefixes. An example of this is to teach 'peri' in perimeter, peripheral, to mean 'around'; 'post' as in postscript, postpone, postnatal, to mean 'after'. Many learners enjoy discovering the linguistic and historical derivation of words using both the base word and affixes (prefix or suffix). For example, knowing that 'anti' is Greek meaning opposed to or against but 'ante' is Latin meaning before aids the correct spelling of words like antecedent and anticlockwise. This in turn facilitates recall by strengthening a link between the semantic processor and orthographic output lexicon. Siegel (2008) has suggested that some learners with dyslexia show poorer morphological awareness than non-dyslexic peers and supports the view that learners with dyslexia need training in this area. A study of 7–9 year-old children (Deacon, 2008) showed that children often recognise 'root' words in spelling, particularly when these occur at the beginning of words. This suggests a skill that can be built on by more explicit teaching of prefixes and suffixes.

Drawing on earlier chapters and theories of spelling development, Conquering Literacy therefore teaches reading and spelling together based on the systematic teaching of synthetic phonics – including rules about grapheme-phoneme correspondence and the development of morphological approaches. The programme integrates handwriting into teaching because of the significance of handwriting to success in spelling.

---

## Implications for Practice

- Spelling can be improved by teaching using synthetic phonics to aid the development of phoneme-grapheme correspondence and the development of phonemic segmentation skills.
- Handwriting speed will affect spelling.
- Teaching rules and 'spelling choices' should be part of teaching spelling as should morphological approaches.
- Use letter names when teaching spelling as they are more consistent.
- When spelling improves, learners may concentrate more freely on developing their compositional skills.

---

## Summary

The research discussed both in this and the preceding chapter suggests that processors of reading and spelling draw on and reinforce the same systems. This implies that reading and spelling should be taught together. It also points to the use of a systematic phonic-based approach, initially using synthetic phonics to establish phoneme-grapheme correspondence (i.e., knowledge of the alphabetic principle essential to both reading and spelling). The value of morphology in teaching spelling has been recognised and this chapter also indicates the importance of handwriting and speed to success in spelling. The approaches described in this chapter have been incorporated into the Conquering Literacy programme.

## References

Brooks, P. and Weeks, S. (1999) *Individual Styles in Learning to Spell: Improving Spelling in Children with Literacy Difficulties and All Children in Mainstream Schools*. London: Department for Education and Employment.

Cripps, C. (1998) *A Hand for Spelling*. Wisbech: LDA.

Deacon, H. (2008) 'The metric matters: determining the extent of children's knowledge of morphological spelling irregularities', *Developmental Science*, 11 (3): 396–406.

Ehri, L.C. (2002) 'Reading processes, acquisition and instructional applications'. In Reid, G. and Wearmouth, J. (eds), *Dyslexia and Literacy: Theory and Practice.* Chichester: Wiley. pp. 167–185.

Frith, U. (1985) 'Beneath the surface of developmental dyslexia'. In Marshall, J.C., Patterson, K.E. and Coltheart, M. (eds), *Surface Dyslexia in Adults and Children.* London: Routledge and Kegan Paul. pp. 301–330.

Gentry, J.R. (1987) *Spel... is a Four Letter Word.* Leamington Spa: Scholastic.

Goswami, U. (1993) 'Phonological skills and learning to read', *Annals of the New York Academy of Sciences*, 682: 296–311.

Goswami, U. (2003) 'Phonology, learning to read and dyslexia: a cross-linguistic analysis'. In Csépe, V. (ed.), *Dyslexia: Different Brain, Different Behaviour.* New York: Kluver Academic/Plenum. pp. 1–40.

Houghton, G. and Zorzi, M. (2003) 'Normal and impaired spelling in a connectionist dual-route architecture', *Cognitive Psychology*, 20 (2): 115–162.

Johnson, M. (2001) *Results of Monitoring of Introduction of Multisensory Teaching System for Reading into Four Schools in Ireland: Report to Irish Ministry of Education, Dublin.* Manchester: MMU.

Johnson, M., Bryan, K., Phillips, S. and Peer, L. (1997a) *Effective Mainstream Identification and Intervention Strategies for Pupils at Risk of Developing Mild to Moderate Literacy Difficulties: Report to DfEE.* Manchester: MMU.

Johnson, M.C., Phillips, S. and Peer, L. (1997b) *A Multi-sensory Teaching System for Reading.* Manchester: MMU.

Kohnen, S., Nickels, L., Brunsdon, R. and Coltheart, M. (2008) 'Patterns of generalisation after treating sub-lexical deficits in a child with mixed dysgraphia', *Journal of Research in Reading*, 31 (1): 157–177.

Muter, V. (1996) 'Predicting children's reading and spelling difficulties'. In Snowling, M. and Stackhouse, J. (eds), *Dyslexia, Speech and Language: A Practitioner's Handbook.* London: Whurr. pp. 31–44.

Ott, P. (2007) *How to Manage Spelling Successfully.* Abingdon: Routledge.

Peters, M.L. (1985) *Spelling: Caught or Taught?* London: Routledge and Kegan Paul.

Plaza, M. and Cohen, H. (2006) 'The contribution of phonological awareness and visual attention in early reading and spelling', *Dyslexia,* 13: 67–76.

Reid, G. (2009) *Dyslexia: A Practitioner's Handbook.* Chichester: Wiley.

Romani, C., Ward, J. and Olson, A. (1999) 'Developmental surface dysgraphia: what is the underlying cognitive impairment?', *Quarterly Journal of Experimental Psychology*, Section A, 52: 97–128.

Seymour, P.H.K. and McGregor, C.J. (1984) 'Developmental dyslexia: experimental analysis of phonological, morphemic and visual impairments', *Cognitive Neurophysiology*, 1: 43–82.

Siegel, L.S. (2008) 'Morphological awareness skills of English language learners and children with dyslexia', *Topics in Language Disorders*, 28 (1): 15–27.

Snowling, M.J. (1994) 'Towards a model of spelling acquisition: the development of some component skills'. In Brown, D.A. and Ellis, N.C. (eds), *Handbook of Spelling: Theory, Process and Intervention*. Chichester: Wiley. pp. 111–128.

Snowling, M.J. (2000) *Dyslexia* (2nd edn). Oxford: Blackwell.

Treiman, R. and Kessler, B. (2005) 'Writing systems and spelling development'. In Snowling, M.J. and Hulme, C. (eds), *The Science of Reading: A Handbook*. Oxford: Blackwell. pp. 120–134.

Wolf, M., Bowers, P.G. and Biddle, K. (2000) 'Naming-speed processes, timing and reading: a conceptual overview', *Journal of Reading Disabilities,* 33: 387–407.

# CHAPTER 6

# TEACHING HANDWRITING

## Chapter Overview

This chapter is concerned with the mechanics of handwriting (sometimes called 'penmanship' in the USA) and not with teaching compositional aspects of writing such as form, content, style and genre. It is important to recognise, however, that dyslexia also affects writing style and composition because of organisational and sequencing difficulties. There is a consideration of the debate about whether handwriting should still be taught to learners with handwriting difficulties or whether writing should be replaced by word processing skills or even the use of 'talking computers' (i.e., voice activated software).

In many texts about dyslexia, handwriting and spelling are considered jointly (e.g., Reid, 2009), largely because early research (see Peters, 1985) found a strong relationship between speed of handwriting and spelling attainment. It follows from earlier chapters that speed of handwriting not only depends on motor skills but also on the ability to select, name, and write letters quickly. Poor working memory may also affect writing speed if a learner loses their train of thought during the activity. Graham et al. (2000) suggested that speed of handwriting in young children is closely related to their ability to compose. Automaticity in handwriting implies that a learner can then concentrate on ideas, spelling, grammar, maintaining arguments, and style. Several studies reported by Montgomery (2007) show that even in secondary schools many learners will write significantly more slowly than their peers. Her research of learners who have followed the National Literacy Strategy for seven years suggested that not only was the cohort studied writing significantly more slowly than expected for their age and experience, but nearly 20 per cent were writing at 40 per cent below the mean speed – and 'appear to have SEN in this area' (Montgomery, 2007:46).

Assessment of handwriting speed is often used to determine whether or not learners could benefit from extra time when sitting examinations and it is important to distinguish between 'copying' speed and speed in free writing (e.g., stories and assignments), as the latter will also be affected by difficulties in memory and organisation of ideas. This distinction should be borne in mind not only when assessing handwriting but also when reading and interpreting research in this area. Detailed Assessment of Speed of Handwriting, known as DASH (Barnett et al., 2007), a procedure for learners aged 9–16 years, suggests that a minimum speed of 19 words per minute is required in free writing at age 16 to access formal external examinations.

Learners who do not develop a legible script are also disadvantaged in school and external examinations, where there is a tendency to judge content by appearance. Studies in the 1970s showed that poorly written scripts (in terms of letter formation and legibility) gained lower marks that those which were neatly written even when the content was the same (Briggs, 1980).

In teaching handwriting in schools an emphasis has been given to legibility and, in our experience, very little attention has been paid to speed and fluency. Learners with dyslexia often display handwriting difficulties with poor and inconsistent letter formation, compounded by spelling difficulties which may also result in words crossed out and very untidy presentation. In addition, they may produce very little written work – possibly as a result of a combination of factors:

- Poor speed of writing.
- Insecurity about spelling.
- Difficulties 'ordering' and organising ideas (teaching how to plan assignments will improve this).
- Low self-esteem as a writer leading to a reluctance to write.
- Embarrassment about the appearance of their written work.

There is general agreement in the literature on dyslexia, and in structured programmes such as Cox (1972) and Hickey as in Combley (2001), that cursive writing helps *all* learners to write more quickly than printing, but that it is particularly appropriate for those with dyslexia. Cursive script leads to speed in writing because the pen/pencil does not have to be lifted after each letter (there are a few exceptions in some styles (e.g., 'x' and letters such as 'i' and 't' where there is a crossing stroke or a dot to be added after writing the word, requiring a 'pen lift'). It is also easier to maintain consistency of form and spacing. Jarman (1979) reminds readers that 'print' was introduced early in the twentieth century because it was believed to be 'easier' for young children. Many of today's cursive writing schemes are based on a 'joining' of rounded, print letters, assuming that primary school children will first be taught a print script. In part, this follows the guidelines of the National Literacy Strategy (DfEE, 2001) which recommended that schools could choose their own handwriting style, but it should be one which could lead easily to 'joining' so that a cursive style could then be introduced. Apart from the 'tradition' of teaching print first, teachers have argued that print is what children see in books and the environment, and therefore it provides a visible and comprehensible link between reading and writing.

In the Conquering Literacy programme, learners are taught how to form letters using a cursive script as part of the technique of introducing a new phonogram. The technique used is based on over-writing, developing the letter from its printed form. This assumes that the learner has previously been taught to print and also makes a link to the printed form which has just been written on a Reading Card (see Chapter 9). Teachers should use their discretion as to whether this approach is appropriate or whether to introduce only the cursive form. We are aware that many schools have now introduced cursive writing in the Foundation Stage or early in Key Stage 1. Similarly, although in this chapter we recommend a particular form of cursive script, there are many variations available and teachers are advised to use the style adopted by the learner's school. However, if the school's style does not lend itself to fluency, or a learner has particular difficulties using it, then it may be useful to negotiate the use of a different style.

## Handwriting, Motor Skills and the Brain

Alston (1993) and Alston and Taylor (1993) point out that seating position, posture, grip and position of paper are all relevant factors in handwriting. Fine motor skills are required and motor-skill planning and practice are essential to build up graphic-motor memory. This will require a lot of practice to establish fluency and speed. A multisensory approach will help to establish motor-control, from 'sky-writing' (forming large letters in the air using a finger), 'writing' a large letter on the back of a learner (subject to the school's policy on 'touch'), and reducing in size from writing in a sand/salt tray, using a marker on a whiteboard, and then pen on paper, in order to establish the form of a letter. The letter name should be said aloud whilst writing/tracing. Part of this motor-skills training should involve using a 'tripod' grip pencil hold and sometimes this may be helped by using a pre-shaped rubber 'penhold' grip: this is available commercially.

The motor cortex (in the frontal lobes) and the cerebellum are responsible for motor learning, establishing the actions involved and making them more automatic. Impairment to the cerebellum, therefore, may adversely affect the development of automaticity in handwriting as will problems in the pathways between the left and right hemispheres: the causation theories summarised in Chapter 1 offer possible explanations as to why so many learners with dyslexia have poor handwriting skills.

## Do We Still Need to Teach Handwriting?

Many people argue, as Dixon and Addy (2004) point out, that technological advances may have reduced the need to write by hand. Certainly most professional, business, and personal communication is conducted electronically. Learners will text each other or communicate through social networking sites. The British Dyslexia Association (BDA) website recommends a range of technological aids to facilitate curriculum access. Foremost amongst these is the computer, particularly when used for word-processing so that work will be presented legibly and judged for its content rather than 'neat presentation'. Assignments at secondary school and college are often submitted 'word-processed' and increasingly this is becoming an official requirement. Digital recorders/dictaphones can be used to replace note-taking during lessons/lectures or when reading. Crivelli et al. (2004) provide a good overview of how ICT can be used for learners with dyslexia (including references to useful software). As software development is a fast moving area, rather than recommend specific programs here we have included the website addresses for some appropriate providers in Part V so that practitioners can obtain up-to-date information about what is available.

Advocates for the use of ICT emphasise word-processing and the need for keyboarding skills. Word-processing can reduce stress for a learner who is struggling with handwriting. It can also reassure them that their work is as legible as that of peers and that 'content' rather than physical appearance is being judged by teachers/examiners. In addition it can aid composition via its capacity to:

- edit and move sentences/paragraphs in order to present ideas/arguments/stories logically;
- provide templates/scaffolding support for essays, stories, assignments;
- develop vocabulary (substituting alternative words);
- offer a 'spell-check' (although this does not always help pupils and its usefulness needs to be assessed for each learner).

For those with severe motor co-ordination difficulties (many of whom may have dyspraxia) software programs where they can dictate work to the computer (which will then transform it into text) may offer viable alternatives. (Most of these will still take considerable time to establish sufficient voice recognition patterns to operate efficiently and effectively.) References to such software may also be found on the BDA website.

Currently there is still a need for further research into the usefulness of word processing as a means of developing compositional writing skills, according to Connelly et al. (2007), whereas evidence already exists that speed of handwriting is clearly related to compositional skills. Their study showed that unless there is good keyboarding instruction which brings about fast and fluent keyboard input, learners will produce better essays by hand. Earlier, Bennett (2004) suggested that while teachers felt confident about the use of word-processing as a writing tool, very little time was spent on teaching keyboarding skills. In many primary schools we have visited, children are using computers with ease for searching the web for information. All too often, however, they only use word-processing to copy their handwritten stories and essays 'for publication'. (This has replaced 'copy it out in your best handwriting for display', and speed and fluency are not considered.) Christensen and Jones (2000) showed that essay writing could be improved when learners became fluent users of the keyboard. In their study, secondary school learners who were given a good instruction course in keyboarding could type at speed equal to, or better than, their handwriting speed and then produced not only longer essays, but also of better quality than they had done prior to the course. Nevertheless, the debate still continues about whether or not to teach handwriting to learners experiencing great difficulties or to replace this by teaching keyboarding skills and efficient use of a computer for writing. Learners with dyslexia will need to be taught how to organise, store, and retrieve their notes and assignments efficiently because of their organisational and memory difficulties, yet this aspect of word-processing/writing using a computer is often ignored in keyboarding instruction. (All children would benefit from this.) There is no doubt that for many learners with dyslexia proficiency in word-processing has given access to the curriculum and examination success and so should be encouraged and extended.

However, as Dixon and Addy (2004) claim, writing remains the main means of recording information in schools and currently (2011) is still the main medium for formal and external examinations. Legible and fast handwriting remains important and should be well established before learners attend secondary school. This position however may well change in the future. We would argue that fluent handwriting remains particularly important for learners with spelling difficulties, especially those with dyslexia, because it helps establish motor co-ordination and memory. Teaching writing in a multisensory way makes explicit the kinaesthetic (hand/arm movements and 'saying' – or sub-vocalising – a letter name and word), visual (seeing the physical output and using visual memory), and auditory (hearing one's own voice saying the letter or word) linkages thereby establishing the spelling in memory.

A continuous cursive handwriting style therefore helps learners to gain automaticity in both handwriting and spelling. There is no strong evidence as yet that word-processing helps in the same way, although spelling programmes – such as Wordshark or Starspell – can be used to aid spelling and teachers can develop their own activities to enable learners to practise spelling using a computer. The spelling and dictation activities in the Conquering Literacy programme could be carried out using a computer as long as the multisensory routines of 'saying' the spelling and self-checking are carried out. Teachers should use their knowledge of a learner's competence and interest when making a decision about this.

# Teaching Cursive Writing

A range of cursive styles is available and teachers should use the style adopted by the learner's school. We recommend a style that has 'approach' and 'joining' strokes because these lend consistency to the letter shapes – and security to the learner who knows that all letters start on a line, with only a few exceptions where some letters *o,r,v,* and *w* have a mid-point join to avoid confusion with other letters. We have used a style which has loops below the line and also used a closed form of b and p because there is less confusion with u and n. Some teachers would not use a style which has loops in ascenders because these can be confused with the loops in the descenders on the line above.

We would suggest that the 'correct' formation of letters is introduced as an integral part of teaching phonograms within lessons and is used in writing practice, spelling and dictation activities in every lesson (see Part III of the programme). Learning to join letters begins as soon as the second phonogram is introduced so that having learned to form *i* and *t* the learner is accustomed to joining letters to form/spell words: *it*.

## Advantages of Cursive Writing Compared with Print

Cursive writing:

- Aids fluency in writing thereby developing faster speed of writing (helping with spelling and recording ideas quickly – which is important for learners with a poor short-term memory: a more efficient use of time will enable the learner to write more).
- Facilitates left to right movement across the page.
- Leads to consistency in the form of letters, thereby reducing the likelihood of inverting and reversing them.
- Helps with consistent spacing because it is clearer where a word ends and the next one begins.
- Improves legibility.

## Recommended Style

*a b c d e f g h i j k l m n o p q r s t u v w x y z*

Capital letters follow the 'print' style e.g., *A B C* etc. This is slightly sloping forward rather than upright because it aids speed. A software program using this style called Joinit can be found at www.cursivewriting.org and is useful for developing worksheets for handwriting practice.

The method for introducing letter formation is described in Chapter 11 and examples of the cursive letters are given for each phonogram in the programme in Part III.

It may be that handwriting is a specific need for some learners, particularly older learners who may have relative strengths in knowledge of grapheme-phoneme correspondence but whose handwriting is disadvantaging them across the curriculum. These may be learners with dyspraxia or developmental dysgraphia (described below). In this case it may be appropriate to 'teach handwriting' as a very specific element within or in addition to the structured lessons. We would suggest following the recommendations of writers such as Jarman (1979) by teaching letters in groups or 'families' that are related by similarities in formation.

There is often debate about whether or not to use lined paper, and if so, what width the lines should be. Some schools make use of 'writing exercise books' with printed lines above and below the main writing line to provide guidance, and some contain model letters to trace over (although not necessarily in the style required). Letter formation will usually be taught using several media (e.g., sand, wooden letters, markers on flip-chart and then felt tipped pens) before transferring to paper. We would recommend the following practice when transferring to paper in order to produce 'smaller' letters of normal size:

- Providing lined paper (perhaps at first offering a choice of widths so the learner can choose or 'experiment'). Where letter formation is poor, the teacher can draw a faint or dotted pencil line above the writing line to support the development of consistency in the height of letters. This can then be 'faded' over time (fewer dots, or only at the beginning of the line).
- Placing a small cross or dot on the writing line to show where writing begins (the need to do this soon disappears).
- Ensuring that learners join letters together from the beginning, even when not forming words (e.g., producing a line of the same letter: *ppppppppppppppppppp*).
- Encouraging the learner to write neatly and speedily. Dictation exercises can help them to build up speed and legibility of handwriting as well as accuracy of spelling.
- When learners have developed consistent letter formation and spacing of words, encourage them to build up speed using a timer with a target sentence or passage so that they can try to beat their own 'personal best' time. The sentence, 'The quick brown fox jumps over the lazy dog', is often used because it contains every letter

in the alphabet and they can also therefore identify any letters they find problematic. (The practice sentence or phrase should be written 'in structure' if the only handwriting tuition takes place within the programme.)

The other aspects of teaching handwriting as described by Alston and Taylor (1993) should be taken into consideration not just within the normal classroom but also within structured lessons when delivering the programme. They provide examples of appropriate pencil grip for both right- and left-handed learners and also emphasise the importance of positioning the writing paper to best effect. Paper/exercise books should not be placed 'square' onto a desk/table edge, but placed slightly to the right of the midline of a right-handed learner and rotated slightly anti-clockwise so that it is at an angle (in the case of left handed learners the paper should be to the left of the mid-body line and rotated slightly clockwise). This is so that they are not writing *across* their body line which is not only tiring and awkward but also less likely to produce consistently neat writing. Note that there are implications here for seating learners in one-to-one or small group sessions.

## Dyslexia, Dyspraxia, Dysgraphia

The terms 'dyspraxia' (developmental co-ordination disorders or difficulties) and 'dysgraphia' are often found on the assessment reports of learners with dyslexia, particularly those who have handwriting difficulties. The methods proposed in the Conquering Literacy programme are appropriate for those with such a diagnosis. It is likely that more learners with dyslexia could be described as having those conditions but they are undiagnosed. There are some learners who will present handwriting difficulties (dysgraphia) without any of the other difficulties associated with dyslexia. These learners will need a handwriting and motor co-ordination programme, *not* the approach used in Conquering Literacy.

Other forms of specific learning difficulties – such as autistic spectrum conditions and attention deficit disorder (ADHD), as well as dyspraxia – are often associated (co-morbid) with dyslexia. The programme can be used with these learners where they present appropriate difficulties in literacy.

## Handwriting, Self-esteem and Purpose

As stated earlier, many learners presenting handwriting difficulties are not 'motivated' to undertake writing tasks. Many will have been identified as 'reluctant writers' and some may present challenging behaviours and 'avoidance strategies' when faced with a writing task. The challenge for the teacher, therefore, is to justify the importance of learning to write quickly and legibly and to explain that the purpose of practice and routines is to build up new motor and memory programmes in the brain. The learner with dyslexia may have to overcome an emotional barrier in order to improve handwriting: the teacher must provide the necessary support.

## Implications for Practice

- Cursive writing should be taught to learners with literacy difficulties.
- There should be an emphasis on legibility and speed in handwriting as these will aid spelling and compositional skills.
- Using a multisensory approach when teaching handwriting will help to establish motor patterns and memory.
- Teaching good word-processing and keyboard skills to those who can use a keyboard will give them access to alternative forms of recording across the curriculum.
- Learners who are using word-processing should learn to type accurately and quickly (at a speed faster than their handwriting), aiming for at least 19 wpm by age 16.
- Teachers should recognise that writing will often aid recall when revising.
- Teachers need to consider the use of technological aids to support learning and recording of work.

## Summary

The chapter has argued a case for teaching cursive writing to learners with dyslexia who present difficulties in spelling and/or handwriting. Both speed of handwriting and legibility are discussed, with an emphasis on the way in which speed of handwriting can affect spelling and compositional success. Some of the arguments for teaching keyboarding skills or the use of voice-activated software have been explored, but we consider that there is still a need to teach handwriting to school-age learners with dyslexia, although this may be supplemented and supported by the use of ICT and relevant software. For some learners (particularly older, secondary school students) it may be considered more appropriate to teach teaching keyboard skills instead of handwriting. Where this decision is taken it is clear from the research that both accuracy and speed in word processing are essential. This enables learners to concentrate on planning and organising their ideas in producing assignments rather than attending to letter formation. In turn, this can enhance their self-esteem.

# References

Alston, J. (1993) *Assessing and Promoting Writing Skills*. Stafford: NASEN.

Alston, J. and Taylor, J. (1993) *The Handwriting File*. Wisbech: Learning Development Aids.

Barnett, A., Henderson, S. E., Scheib, B. and Scultz, J. (2007) *Detailed Assessment of Speed of Handwriting (DASH)*. London: Pearson.

Bennett, R. (2004) *Using ICT in Primary English Teaching*. Exeter: Learning Matters.

Briggs, D. (1980) 'A study of the influence of handwriting upon grades in examination scripts', *Educational Review*: 185–193.

Christensen, C.A. and Jones, D. (2000) 'Handwriting: an underestimated skill in the development of written language', *Handwriting Today*, 2: 56–69.

Combley, M. (2001) *The Hickey Multisensory Language Course* (3rd edn). London: Whurr.

Connelly, V., Gee, D. and Walsh, E. (2007) 'A comparison of keyboarded and hand-written compositions and the relationship with transcription speed', *British Journal of Educational Psychology,* 77: 479–492.

Cox, A.R. (1972) *Foundations of Literacy*. Cambridge, MA: Educators Publishing Company.

Crivelli, V., Thomson, M. and Anderson, B. (2004) 'Using information and communication technology (ICT) to help dyslexic children and adults'. In Reid, G. and Fawcett, A.J. (eds), *Dyslexia in Context: Research, Policy and Practice*. London: Whurr. pp. 304–322.

DfEE (2001) *Developing Early Writing*. London: DfEE.

Dixon, G. and Addy, L.M. (2004) 'Handwriting and dyspraxia'. In Dixon, G. and Addy, L.M. (eds), *Making Inclusion Work for Children with Dyspraxia*. London: Routledge. pp. 66–80.

Graham, S., Harris, K.R. and Fink, J. (2000) 'Is handwriting causally related to learning to write? Treatment of handwriting problems in beginning readers', *Journal of Educational Psychology*, 92 (4): 620–633.

Jarman, C. (1979) *The Development of Handwriting Skills*. Oxford: Blackwell.

Montgomery, D. (2007) *Spelling, Handwriting and Dyslexia: Overcoming Barriers to Learning*. London: Routledge.

Peters, M.L. (1985) *Spelling: Caught or Taught?* London: Routledge and Kegan Paul.

Reid, G. (2009) *Dyslexia: A Practitioner's Handbook* (4th edn). Oxford: Wiley-Blackwell.

# CHAPTER 7

# DYSLEXIA AND LEARNERS FOR WHOM ENGLISH IS AN ADDITIONAL LANGUAGE

### Chapter Overview

The difficulties associated with identifying dyslexia in learners for whom English is an Additional Language (EAL) has been well documented in the United States since the 1970s but is a more recent area of research in the UK. This chapter considers the implications of research studies from both the USA and the UK for the identification of dyslexia in learners with English as an Additional Language and for intervention. The appropriateness of using structured language programmes with learners with EAL is also discussed.

The US experience has been that in the past multilingual learners were often assumed to have a learning difficulty and placed in remedial education where no learning difficulty actually existed. However, in relation to dyslexia, multilingual learners tended to be under-identified – a situation which was highlighted in the UK by the Commission for Racial Equality (1996). A study undertaken by Deponio et al. (2000) showed that very few teachers tended to consider dyslexia as a cause of literacy difficulties in multilingual learners and this suggests that difficulty in acquiring literacy skills is often inappropriately attributed to EAL factors.

Making decisions about provision for learners with EAL, in terms of the type of support needed and the appropriateness of teaching methods employed, presents a dilemma for many class teachers. Educators need to decide if a learner is underachieving due to a learning difficulty or just needs more time to absorb the culture and gain sufficient exposure to English. For this reason identification may be delayed, as it may take some time to determine if the learner has Special Educational Needs (as defined by the 1981 Education Act) or is experiencing difficulties that are a normal part of second language acquisition and use. The need to make this distinction has been highlighted in recent years by politicians, through legislation, as well as by practitioners in the field, including educational psychologists, language support services, teachers, and bilingual support staff. How this might be achieved is still being debated.

The SEN Code of Practice (DfES, 2001) advises that special care should be taken when identifying and assessing the special educational needs of learners whose first language is not English and that it should be done within the context of 'home, culture and community' (paragraph 5:15). We would concur that knowledge of a learner's culture, home background, and features of the first language is crucial in trying to identify a learning difficulty. The Code points out that a lack of competence in English must not be equated with a learning difficulty. At the same time teachers should not assume that EAL is the only reason for slow progress, as pupils *may* indeed have a learning difficulty, and so their performance in different subjects should be examined. A learner with a specific learning difficulty such as dyslexia will often display an uneven profile across different subjects, performing better in some subjects such as Maths or Science than in English. An uneven profile is usually found 'within' subjects too; learners with dyslexia usually achieve better results in listening and speaking tasks than in those involving reading, spelling, and writing. However, in a multilingual learner such an uneven performance (particularly between language and non-language based subjects) may be attributed to their developing English language skills. The SEN Code also suggests examining the learner's proficiency in all the languages they speak. This could potentially identify dyslexia in their first language thereby enabling literacy difficulties in English to be supported appropriately. However, this is an extremely complex and difficult area because so many of the characteristics of dyslexia can be presented by learners with EAL in the early stages of English Language acquisition. Very few children with EAL, therefore, have a formal identification of dyslexia.

The majority of tests used in the UK have been developed and normed using native English speakers. In learners with EAL English language skills may not have been developed sufficiently to access such tests adequately. For some, the development of the academic language needed can take many years. For example, a study of Bengali children with five years' exposure to English produced low scores generally on a digit span test (see Kelly, 1993). Low scores were also found on several of the subtests of the Dyslexia Screening Test in a class of 8–9 year-old Pakistani children (Kelly, 2002). This suggests that four to five years' exposure to English is insufficient to develop the proficiency needed for standardised tests which use norms that have been developed for a different population.

There are potential problems both in carrying out a psychological assessment and in building up profiles of multilingual learners. While the use of ability tests and discrepancy-based definitions may result in under-identification of dyslexia, equally student profiling could lead to over-identification if cultural factors are not taken into account. Teachers need to consider whether or not a lack of academic success may be due solely to environmental factors (e.g., differences between scripts, teaching methods) rather than to a specific learning difficulty, in understanding learners' lack of progress.

Smythe (2010) suggests that this does not need to be an issue as the label of 'dyslexia' is not important – the teacher just needs to address the difficulty. If they have poor phonological processing then they need training in this area. We would argue that it is more difficult to do this appropriately if the underlying cause is not known. There is an assumption here that multilingual and monolingual students are being taught literacy in the same way but this is not necessarily the case. Students learning English as an Additional Language will usually develop literacy skills in English alongside their oral skills, whereas native speakers will have developed their fluency in spoken English before they start to read and spell. Learners with EAL need an approach to reading that will help to develop their understanding. Iwai (2010) points out that where multilingual learners are in the early stages of learning English, using the bottom-up approach (i.e., concentrating on the decoding of words) exclusively will prevent them from improving in reading, and advocates the use of explicit instruction in meaningful contexts.

However, some multilingual learners might need a structured language programme in addition to their normal EAL teaching and we consider that the Conquering Literacy programme is appropriate for children with EAL who demonstrate the following:

- *A discrepancy between listening comprehension and reading comprehension.* Good listening comprehension skills would indicate that the learner has sufficient understanding of English vocabulary but could be hampered when reading by poor decoding skills or a poor working memory.
- *Persistent phonological deficits despite adequate exposure to English.* If the learner has developed fluency in spoken English to the level of their monolingual peers

but still has problems in phonological processing then the reading difficulty may be due to dyslexia rather than EAL factors.

- *A lack of interest in books – when given the opportunity s/he actively avoids looking at books/reading for pleasure.* A longitudinal study following a class of 4 year-olds (Kelly, 2002) found that children who actively avoided looking at books in the Reception class were most at risk of dyslexia at age 7 and had the lowest reading scores at age 10. A lack of interest in (culturally appropriate) books in young children could be a predictor of later literacy difficulties.

- *Difficulty in acquiring automaticity of basic skills/problems with balance (when asked to multi-task).* A study replicating the work of Fawcett and Nicolson (1991) with Bengali students of secondary age found that 95 per cent of those later identified as having dyslexia had an automaticity deficit in balance when asked to multi-task (Kelly, 2002). In this group balance was not automatic enough to be able to maintain it when the ability to concentrate on the task was removed by a secondary (counting) task. No automaticity deficit in balance was found in 180 (out of 184) of their non-dyslexic peers.

Structured language programmes of the type developed for learners with dyslexia tend to use phonics-based, bottom-up approaches. These will usually start by teaching individual phonemes and then sound blending to build words; when enough phonemes have been introduced they start to build sentences and eventually passages. This approach cannot be used to replace normal EAL teaching, as it is essential that multilingual learners develop a good understanding of everyday (and subject specific) vocabulary, sentence structure, and grammatical features of English within meaningful contexts in order to facilitate comprehension. We do not suggest, therefore, that the Conquering Literacy programme is suitable for all learners with English as an Additional Language. However, where there are concerns about speed of progress in learning to read and write in comparison to their listening and speaking skills, then a teacher may consider using it in addition to the normal everyday EAL teaching provided.

Teachers should try to ascertain, where possible, the underlying cause of the literacy difficulty so that the learner receives appropriate support. In doing so they need to consult and collaborate with people who have a sound knowledge of the cultural background of a student in order to avoid confusing common second language errors with indicators of dyslexia. Parents (or a diagnostic interview in the case of older learners) can also provide important information as they can supply a more complete picture of the learner across a range of situations and settings, including those which do not involve language.

In the rest of this chapter we discuss some of the overlapping characteristics between dyslexia and early stages of English language acquisition and consider the implications for identification and teaching. Examples are taken from a number of different languages. There are some inconsistencies in the research findings from different countries as often they have made different comparisons and so it is difficult to make generalisations from one language to the next. What might be true of one language might not be true of others, which is why it is important that a teacher has knowledge of the first language and its impact on learning English.

## Dyslexia in the First Language (L1)

Accounts of dyslexia in more than one language (polyglot dyslexia) are quite sparse. Salter and Smythe (1997) produced an international book of dyslexia in which 39 accounts of dyslexia world-wide were given, yet none of the authors discussed the incidence of polyglot dyslexia. Studies in this area have tended to concentrate on individual cases rather than large samples and have found that where the first language is more regular (transparent) reading difficulties have not always been evident despite there being literacy difficulties in English. It is argued that reading difficulties such as dyslexia are likely to be identified more frequently in Anglo-Saxon countries because of their lower sound-symbol correspondence. The implication is that the learner may not display the same difficulties in decoding and encoding in their first language as they do in English if sound-symbol correspondence is more consistent and therefore more predictable.

Recent studies have examined reading fluency in transparent languages (such as Italian) and found 'subtle differences' in children at-risk of dyslexia (see Snowling, 2008), suggesting that a phonological deficit exists in the first language (although it may not always be very evident to an untrained eye). In transparent languages there may be more difficulty with encoding than decoding and more errors may be found in writing than in reading. If the first language is more regular than English a multilingual learner who is experiencing literacy difficulties is likely to need particular emphasis on spelling rules and the explicit teaching of irregular words in addition to a phonics-based programme.

## Characteristics of Dyslexia in L1 and English

A number of research studies into the phonological deficit hypothesis now suggest that learners with dyslexia will show phonological deficits in both languages. In a study of Chinese children, Suk-Han Ho and Fong (2005) found that those with dyslexia had similar phonological processing difficulties to those learning in languages that have an alphabetic script. Smythe (2010), however, points out that there are different types of phonological skills and that their relevance is different in different languages. He gives an example of rhyming skills being important for literacy development in English but less important in Hungarian. A child in Hungary will instead need a good knowledge of morphemes and grammar to be a successful reader. It is likely, therefore, that rhyming skills will be poor in Hungarian children regardless of whether they are dyslexic or not. Again, this points to knowledge of the first language being essential both for identifying dyslexia and planning intervention.

Oren and Breznitz (2005) suggest that a defining characteristic is the failure to develop automaticity in English. They found that whilst non-dyslexic bilingual learners were able to develop fluency in the second language, learners with dyslexia were significantly slower and less accurate in processing information in both L1 (Hebrew) and L2 (English) using Event Related Potentials (ERP) to measure brain response. This supported earlier research by one of the authors. Slower, less accurate processing as well as automaticity deficits in basic skills such as balance (when multi-tasking) were found in multilingual learners with dyslexia in a study that profiled over 200 12 year-old Bengali speakers (Kelly, 2002). The same research project found similar difficulties in learners with dyslexia of primary age in a longitudinal study which followed a class of 7–8 year-old Punjabi speakers for four years. A link was found between automaticity deficit in balance when multi-tasking and persistent phonological processing difficulties at age 11. No such difficulties were found in their non-dyslexic peers. Comparing multilingual learners suspected of having dyslexia with non-dyslexic peers in the same language must form part of any assessment.

Multisensory approaches to teaching literacy are particularly appropriate for learners with EAL as they will allow the learner to draw on their strengths (which may be different for different languages) whilst developing weaker areas. Ideas for developing automaticity in reading, spelling, and writing are given in Part III.

## Establishing a Dyslexic Profile

Trying to establish a 'dyslexic profile' in learners of English as an Additional Language using a checklist may lead to 'over identification', particularly if they are still developing English proficiency. In multilingual learners the characteristics that are often associated with dyslexia (such as difficulty in distinguishing differences in vowel sounds, the reversal of letters/words, a poor concept of time, the inability to give day, month, and year of birth, and problems in tracking from left to right) may have causes related to their language and cultural experience and this must be borne in mind when planning and delivering lessons. Such difficulties need examining in light of a learner's previous cultural experiences considering, for example, the strategies that the learner may bring to their reading of English from reading their first language. Multilingual learners may have difficulty acquiring literacy skills in English because of the influence of their first language.

### Implications for Teaching Reading Strategies

Learners who have been taught to read in their first language may struggle in the early stages of acquiring English because of the previous experiences they bring to the task.

For example, for readers of logographic scripts such as Chinese or Japanese (*Kanji*), rote learning is a necessity and they may be unfamiliar with the need to decode (using grapheme-phoneme relationships to tackle new words). If they continue to use the strategies that they apply to L1 in reading in English they are likely to make errors that are similar to those made by learners with dyslexia. Conversely, for learners whose first language is phonically regular, the indirect route (phonological decoding) may be an appropriate strategy. However, an over-reliance on this route will lead to difficulties with irregular English words.

The length of time needed to gain sufficient familiarity with the new language to adopt more efficient strategies will depend on the features of L1. However, as Joshi and Aaron (2006) point out, the degree and development of logographic and alphabetic approaches depends not only upon the nature of the language being used but also on the teaching methods employed to teach reading. Hence appropriate teaching to develop the required skills is essential. The Conquering Literacy programme not only teaches alphabetic principle, decoding and encoding words (non-lexical route) but also strategies for recognising and spelling irregular words (the lexical route) and paying attention to the need to make links with known meanings (the lexical-semantic route) in order to facilitate comprehension. It is suitable therefore for giving intensive additional teaching to learners who have failed to develop appropriate reading strategies despite good quality first teaching.

## The Influence of Script

For some learners, the dissimilarity of the script of L1 and English can lead to confusion in the initial stages of learning to read. If one language has a left-right orientation for reading and the other a right-left orientation (e.g., Urdu), this can lead to tracking difficulties (sometimes associated with dyslexia) and confusion between words such as 'was' and 'saw'. Learners displaying this kind of difficulty will need a lot of practice at tracking letters and words using left to right scanning. Tracking sheets are included in Part V (Resources). Activities such as word searches are also recommended. Words should go from left to right only, to reinforce the correct directionality for reading (not left to right, up and down, or diagonally, as published word searches often do).

## Confusion between Languages

The magnocellular deficit theory discussed in Chapter 1 suggests that dyslexia may be due to a visual processing difficulty, with writing errors such as the transposition of letters and omission of words or word endings as possible indicators. Yet the omission of some words (e.g., definite and indefinite articles) is common in many speakers of Asian languages, as they do not exist in languages such as Urdu, Punjabi, and Thai. The theory also suggests that there may be difficulty discriminating particular sounds due to slow sensory processing; confusion between similar consonants in spelling and reading may be seen (e.g., voiced and unvoiced sounds /d/ and /t/; v/ and /f/; /b/ and /p/; and the nasal sounds /m/ and /n/). However, difficulty in distinguishing between similar sounds is quite common amongst learners with EAL and will often be evident in their written work. For instance, Punjabi speakers often have difficulties producing and distinguishing the plosives p/b, while Gujerati speakers have similar difficulties with the fricatives f/v. Chinese children may use the 'glottal stop', which means that the ends of words will be missing. Thai speakers often confuse the consonants sounds /l/ and /r/, /k/ and /g/, /t/and /d/ in English language learning, as these do not exist in Thai. Instead, the Thai language has sounds that are half way between each pair. This can affect the spelling of many words in English if a phonetic approach is used. It is important not to mistake errors such as these as indicators of dyslexia.

Teaching to overcome these errors is usually part of the normal everyday EAL provision. Learners become more sensitive to the differences between voiced and unvoiced sounds, for example, as they become more proficient in English. For a learner with dyslexia, however, the delivery of a structured programme may need to be adapted to take these confusions into account. It is likely that lessons will need to place more emphasis on spelling rules and the rules of grammar. More visual input will be needed than usual in teaching the spelling of regularly phonic words. Learners with EAL may experience particular difficulty with the Simultaneous Oral Spelling routine (see Chapter 11) as it relies on the ability to listen to a word and analyse the sounds that it contains. A more appropriate routine for them might be the Look, Cover, Spell, Write, Check (LCSWC) routine as there is greater visual input to support the phonological difficulties that are due to L1 interference.

Confusion can also arise where the learner is thinking in L1 and translating to English. An example of this was given by Firman (1997) who noted how a Maltese/English speaker might not access the appropriate language (e.g., in attempting to say the first phoneme of an object when presented with an apple, s/he might think of the Maltese equivalent of apple (*tuffieta*) and retrieve the sound /t/ rather than /a/). The act of translating from English into L1 and back again can also affect the comprehension of texts. Iwai (2010) suggests that in the beginning stages of learning a second or additional language a learner is likely to translate words from English into their first language as they will feel unable to understand what the text is about unless they can understand the meaning of each word, often stopping when they come across unfamiliar vocabulary to look up words in a dictionary. The time that this takes can prevent them from retaining information from the text. Reading comprehension difficulties are sometimes associated with dyslexia, as the learner may have difficulty carrying over information from one sentence to another if long complex sentences are involved due to a limited working memory capacity. Similar difficulties may be found in non-dyslexic multilingual learners with limited English proficiency, making information about the amount of exposure to English vital for understanding the cause of a reading or spelling difficulty. If the level of English proficiency is limited then learners with EAL and dyslexia may need more time to answer questions about the text, shorter passages, more visual props and illustrations to aid meaning, and – importantly – appropriate texts where the context lies within their experience.

## Reading Speed

A slower reading rate in the second language is not uncommon in a multilingual learner. A study of Japanese/Canadian students (Ansaura, 1991) suggested that even where there was no significant difference in the comprehension of English texts the task of decoding longer words and of recognising and integrating the grammatical nature of content words placed a greater cognitive load on the non-native reader, and lengthened the reading times. So, while slower reading speeds in the first language may be due to a phonological deficit indicative of dyslexia, it does not necessarily follow that a slow reading speed in English will be due to dyslexia. More time may be needed to develop English language proficiency. Where concern about the learn-er's progress in literacy has led to additional support, the use of techniques such as recorded reading and paired reading (see Chapter 8) may prove useful in developing reading fluency.

## Labelling Difficulties

Learners with dyslexia have difficulty with rapid naming, even when the stimulus is something very familiar. Rapid naming is included in most dyslexia screening tests. However, labelling difficulties and a slower rate of recall were reported by Klein (1995) as being the normal pattern for multilingual learners. It is reasonable to assume, therefore, that different 'norms' are required for multilingual learners (particularly on timed items) and that these may be different for different languages, or for there to be standardised tests in the first language. Norms are currently being developed for the Dyslexia Screening Test for Hindi speakers (Fawcett, 2010) and are due to be developed for other Indian languages in 2011–12.

In teaching we need to give learners with EAL more time to retrieve vocabulary. For learners with dyslexia a slow processing speed is due to a language learning difficulty, but with multilingual learners it might be a feature of EAL and in that case teachers should try to encourage them to speed up where possible.

## Assessing for Dyslexia in L1

Until recently, research into multilingualism and dyslexia has received little attention compared to studies of monolingual English speaking learners with dyslexia. This was acknowledged in *A Framework for Understanding Dyslexia* (DfES, 2004). A lack of appropriate assessment tools in languages other than English is evidenced by the fact that studies of the identification of dyslexia in multilingual learners have often used American or UK screening tests as part of the assessment procedure. However, there are now a few bilingual tests available. For example, norms were developed in Welsh (Van Daal et al., 2003) as part of the Welsh Dyslexia Project undertaken at the University of Wales and are available to teachers working in Welsh schools. In the USA the Bilingual Verbal Ability Test (Munoz-Sandoval et al., 1998) was developed in 17 languages and has been used in research studies where a discrepancy definition of dyslexia has been adopted or where there has been a need to distinguish between underachievement due to EAL factors or more global learning difficulties. Martin and Brownell (2005) have also developed a test of auditory processing in English and Spanish that may be useful for building profiles.

## Translating Tests from English into L1

A decade ago Peer and Reid (2000) emphasised the importance of developing culture-fair tests and appropriate assessment strategies for identifying dyslexia in multilingual learners. They pointed out that a cultural bias was inherent in both the tests used by educational psychologists and those available to teachers, giving an example from the Wechsler Intelligence Scales for Children (WISC) which asked the child what they should do if they found a wallet in the street – whereas an English child might say 'return it to the owner or hand it in to the police', the response depends on the experiences of the individual concerned and Peer and Reid suggested that in Ireland or Israel the child might say that they should not pick it up as it might explode!

Similarly differences between L1 and English can affect performance on language-based tests due to differing syntax and structure. For example, Martin and Brownell had to abandon one of the subtests in the Spanish version of their test because there are comparatively few compound words in Spanish compared to English. In the UK, tests of phonological processing often include items such as rhyming tasks – where a simple translation is not possible as words that rhyme in English are unlikely to rhyme in a different language. Also tests that involve speed of processing are problematic as the word length may be different, thereby affecting processing speed.

The European Dyslexia Association (2009) estimates that there are 45 million people with dyslexia in Europe alone, yet very few countries, they believe, seem able to meet their needs. There are still many challenges to be faced in ensuring that multilingual learners with dyslexia receive appropriate identification and support. For example, the lack of tests available in languages other than English and the problems of translation often leave teachers unsure whether learners with EAL should be assessed in L1 or L2. Cline and Shamsi (2000) suggest that there is 'no universal answer' to this question. They argue that it cannot be assumed that the learner will be advantaged if they are assessed in L1 as they may rarely use that language for academic purposes. They also propose that the decision must be made based on an evaluation of the learner's exposure to and use of each language.

The Placement Test provided in Part IV is intended to be administered in English in order to make a decision about the appropriate starting point within the Conquering Literacy programme. It should not be translated to screen for literacy difficulties in the first language. The test relates to particular concepts and phonograms that are to be taught using either the accelerated programme or the main programme.

The Conquering Literacy programme includes several aspects which are often missing from structured language programmes that will support the language teaching of multilingual students:

- It explains how the English language works by incorporating a morphological approach.
- It teaches metalanguage through the use of Concept Cards.
- There are exercises included to teach parts of speech, grammatical structures, and the use of tenses.
- Punctuation is explicitly taught.
- The use of 'paired' and 'shared' reading techniques is encouraged to give learners access to whole texts in order to develop comprehension skills.
- Activities for developing the learner's vocabulary and for checking their understanding are suggested.
- There is an emphasis on articulation and the production of English sounds.

## Implications for Practice

- It is important to find out as much as possible about the L1 of a learner and its impact on learning English.
- The amount of exposure the learner has had to English should be considered.
- Progress should be monitored and compared to that of speakers of the same language.
- The learner should continue to receive EAL teaching to the stage where s/he speaks English fluently (i.e., the same level as native English speakers of the same age).
- Literacy support should be in addition to, not a replacement for, EAL teaching.
- Parents should be advised to liaise with teachers and share with them any signs of atypical development in L1.

**Summary** ☐

There are many overlapping characteristics between a learner with dyslexia and the early stages of English language acquisition. This can make the identification of dyslexia in learners with English as an Additional Language particularly difficult. Assessment should be carried out in collaboration with a person who has a sound knowledge of the first language. Learners will continue to need EAL support until their spoken English skills have developed to the level of their monolingual peers. A structured language programme can be used in addition to EAL teaching where there is cause for concern about a learner's rate of literacy acquisition in relation to others who speak the same language and have had a similar exposure to English.

# References

Ansaura, S. (ed.) (1991) 'The science of reading', *Science of Reading*, 35: 1–79. Tokyo: Japnese Reading Association.

Commission for Racial Equality (CRE) (1996) *Special Educational Needs Assessment in Strathclyde: Report of a Formal Investigation.* London: The Commission for Racial Equality.

Cline, T. and Shamsi, T. (2000) *Language Need or Special Need? The Assessment of Learning Difficulties in Literacy of Children Learning English as an Additional Language: A Literature Review*, Research Brief No. 184, University of Luton, Department of Psychology.

Deponio, P., Landon, J., Mullin, K., and Reid, G. (2000) 'An audit of the processes involved in identifying and assessing bilingual learners suspected of being dyslexic: a Scottish study', *Dyslexia,* 6 (1): 29–41.

DfES (2001) *Special Educational Needs Code of Practice.* Annesley, DfES.

DfES (2004) *Delivering Skills for Life: A Framework for Understanding Dyslexia.* London: DfES.

European Dyslexia Association (2009) News Letter, *EDA News*, Vol. 15, No.3, August.

Fawcett, A.J. (2010) Personal communication, 2 August.

Fawcett, A.J. and Nicolson, R.I. (1991) *Automaticity Deficits in Balance for Dyslexic Children,* Report LRG 12/90, Department of Psychology, University of Sheffield.

Firman, C. (1997) 'Dyslexia in Malta'. In Salter, R. and Smythe, I. (eds), *The International Book of Dyslexia*. London: World Dyslexia Network Foundation. pp. 119–123.

Iwai, Y. (2010) 'Re-envisioning reading comprehension for English language learners', *The Internet TESL Journal,* XVI (4).

Joshi, R.M. and Aaron, P.G. (eds) (2006) *Handbook of Orthography and Literacy.* Mahwah, NJ: Lawrence Erlbaum.

Kelly, K. (1993) 'Assessing bilingual pupils with specific learning difficulties'. Unpublished thesis, Manchester Metropolitan University.

Kelly, K. (2002) 'The early detection of dyslexia in bilingual pupils'. PhD thesis, Manchester Metropolitan University.

Klein, D. (1995) 'The neural substrates of bilingual language processing: evidence from positron emission tomography'. In Paradis, M. (ed.), *Aspects of Bilingual Aphasia*. Oxford: Pergamon. pp. 23–26.

Martin, N. and Brownell, R. (2005) *Test of Auditory Processing Skills* (3rd edn). Novato: Academic Therapy.

Munoz-Sandoval, A.F., Commins, J., Criselda, G.A. and Ruef, M.L. (1998) *Bilingual Verbal Ability Test*. Illinois: Riverside Publishing.

Oren, R. and Breznitz, Z. (2005) 'Reading processes in L1 and L2 among dyslexic as compared to regular bilingual readers: behavioural and electrophysiological evidence', *Journal of Neurolinguistics*, 18 (2): 127–151.

Peer, L. and Reid, G. (2000) *Multilingualism, Literacy and Dyslexia*. London: Fulton.

Salter, R. and Smythe, I. (1997) *The International Book of Dyslexia*. London: World Dyslexia Network Foundation.

Smythe, I. (2010) *Multilingualism and Dyslexia*, National Association for Language Development in the Curriculum, July. Available at www.naldic.org.uk/ITTSEAL2/teaching/SLA.cfm

Snowling, M.J. (2008) 'Specific disorders and broader phenotypes: the case of dyslexia', *The Quarterly Journal of Experimental Psychology*, 61 (1): 142–156.

Suk-Han Ho, C. and Fong K. (2005) 'Do Chinese dyslexic children have difficulties learning English as a second language?', *Journal of Psycholinguistic Research*, 34 (6): 603–618.

Van Daal, V., Spencer, L., Cashman, S. and Hoxhallari, L. (2003) *Wales Dyslexia Screening Test*. Bangor: University of Wales.

# PART 2

# CONQUERING LITERACY: A MULTISENSORY PROGRAMME FOR TEACHING LEARNERS WITH DYSLEXIA – TEACHING STRATEGIES

This section of the book provides an introduction to the structured literacy programme Conquering Literacy which has been developed for learners with dyslexia. The rationale for this programme was given in Part I. In Part II we discuss the principles, components, structure, and techniques used in the programme. We also suggest a structure for planning lessons and give brief explanations of each element within a lesson. The emphasis is on developing appropriate strategies to deliver the programme. Techniques draw on the research and theories referred to in Part I so that practitioners can appreciate the rationale for activities and confidently justify them to learners, parents, and other professionals.

Conquering Literacy is similar to other structured, multisensory literacy programmes such as the Hickey Multisensory Language Course (Combley, 2001) and Teaching Reading Though Spelling (TRTS) (Cowdrey, 1984) and several schemes used in the USA. All of these are based on the work of Gillingham and Stillman (1956) and Cox (1972) and we readily acknowledge their influence on the programme we have devised. However, Conquering Literacy is based on more recent research into dyslexia in addition to drawing extensively on our own experience as teachers and as university tutors on courses training specialist teachers and other professionals.

The programme can be used more flexibly than many other structured schemes in order to meet the individual needs of learners. In particular, it does not assume that a learner should always start at the beginning of the programme, and provides an accelerated version (see Part IV). Some activities offer a choice of style of delivery and method (e.g., using Reading Cards). There is some emphasis on putting the learner in control of their own learning. Examples include developing metacognition, using Discovery Learning methods, and involving learners in organisational aspects of the lesson – including producing Reading Cards where they may also choose clue words.

There is much greater emphasis on memory work and speed of retrieval in this programme in order that there is an appreciation of how to foster automaticity. Teaching literacy concepts is given more prominence than in other English schemes to ensure a good foundation for understanding the rules of literacy (e.g., suffixing, syllable division, and spelling rules and choices) and more emphasis is placed on morphology in both reading and spelling. There are also recommendations for developing study skills as an integral part of structured lessons. Practitioners are encouraged to use a variety of reading activities (e.g., paired, shared, recorded reading) and to include some everyday reading in addition to reading 'in structure'. The needs of learners at different ages are considered and practitioners are advised to use age-relevant approaches through the use of games, computer software, and follow-up activities. In addition there are suggestions for using the programme in small group teaching as well as in one-to-one teaching.

## References

Combley, M. (2001) *The Hickey Multisensory Language Course* (3rd edn). London: Whurr.

Cowdrey L. (1984) *Teaching Reading Through Spelling (The Kingston Programme)*. Kingston: Kingston Polytechnic.

Cox, A.R. (1972) *Structures and Techniques: Multisensory Teaching of Basic Language Skills*. Cambridge, MA: Educators Publishing Services.

Gillingham, A. and Stillman, B. (1956) *Remedial Training for Children with Specific Disability in Reading, Spelling and Penmanship* (5th edn). Cambridge, MA: Educators Publishing Services.

# CHAPTER 8

# PRINCIPLES, TEACHING STRATEGIES, AND PROGRAMME STRUCTURE

## Chapter Overview

This chapter explains the principles underlying a structured multisensory literacy programme. It describes the main teaching strategies incorporated within lessons in the Conquering Literacy programme and outlines the rationale for their structure and teaching order.

## Basic Principles

Five basic principles underpin any successful programme for learners with dyslexia. These demand that the programme should be: structured, multisensory, cumulative, based on phonics, and containing opportunities for overlearning in order to develop automaticity and improve recall.

## Structure

Conquering Literacy provides a structured programme, introducing both phonograms and literacy concepts in a particular order. The amount of new learning is strictly controlled so that learners do not encounter too many unfamiliar points in any one lesson. The structure identifies and numbers Teaching Points which should not be construed as the equivalent of a *lesson* as more than one may be introduced in a lesson. Teaching should follow the given order to avoid gaps in a learner's knowledge, skills, and understanding. Practice in reading, writing, and spelling within a lesson is restricted to using only those phonemes and concepts which have already been taught. This is referred to as 'working in structure'. In the early stages of the programme this limits the vocabulary considerably – and also affects the reading and writing opportunities for learners. (Sharing this fact with learners may help them to understand why they will find some 'silly sentences' in their reading and dictation practice.) The positive aspect is that it leads to successful experiences because learners know they will be able to decode anything that is presented to them.

## Multisensory

The rationale for multisensory teaching was provided in the first chapter of this book. Multisensory teaching builds on a learner's strong channels while also developing the weaker ones and will help to develop neural pathways. It involves making clear links between the visual, auditory, kinaesthetic, and tactile senses (VAKT). A 'link' means that two (but preferably three or four) senses should be *simultaneously* engaged in any activity. This means that an activity should include at least two of: seeing something (visual); hearing something related to what is seen (auditory); some form of related movement of muscles, for example speaking or writing (kinaesthetic) and touching or feeling something (tactile). An example is that a student may learn how to spell a polysyllabic word by seeing the word (e.g., 'decoration') first in pencil print, presented by the teacher who also says the word (VA). The learner then looks at the word and repeats it (VAK). The teacher in turn asks the learner to repeat the word and 'clap' to identify its syllables (VAK). The teacher (or learner) then writes over the word using a different coloured pen for each syllable. The learner now looks at and says each syllable separately: dec-or-a-tion (VAK). They then 'spell' the word aloud, one syllable at a time, naming the letters: d-e-c / o-r / a / t-i-o-n (VAK). They should repeat this two or three times and then cover it up, say the word, and then write it – naming each letter as they do so. (Note that this follows the SOS strategy described in Chapter 11.)

## Cumulative

Teaching Points are introduced in a logical sequence of graded steps so that any new point builds on what has previously been taught. There is a progression to the structure in that simpler concepts are taught and learned before more complex concepts are introduced. Practising and building on what learners know leads to more success in learning and boosts their self-confidence.

## Phonics-based

Research into dyslexia, as discussed in Chapters 1 and 3, strongly suggests that intervention for learners with dyslexia should develop their ability to use phonics. Indeed the Rose Report (2006) recommends systematic phonics teaching for *all* beginning readers, referring to the review of research into the use of phonics (Torgeson et al., 2006) which concludes that systematic phonics teaching leads to more successful learning than unsystematic (or no phonics teaching). Systematic phonics teaching involves making the correspondence between sounds (phonemes) and letters (graphemes) explicit and introducing them in a planned and structured sequence.

The Conquering Literacy programme is largely based on synthetic phonics while also acknowledging the fact that 'analytic phonics' has a part to play when using analogy, particularly in spelling (see Milne, 2005).

---

### Synthetic phonics

Learners are presented with individual letter-sound (grapheme-phoneme) correspondences and then required to blend (or synthesise) them into larger units.

---

Examples of synthesis are: blending the phonemes /s/ and /t/ to make the blend /st/; blending /k/ /ă/ /t/ to make the word 'cat'; blending into syllables e.g., /ĕ/ /n/ = 'en' and joining syllables to make words e.g., 'en-act'. This process requires inductive reasoning and knowledge of the structure of language and alphabetic system and help to establish knowledge of the alphabetic principle.

---

### Analytic phonics

Learners are taught to recognise whole words for reading and then analyse the words in order to identify letter-sound (grapheme-phoneme) correspondences.

---

An example of an analytic approach would be to see the word 'cat' and identify the three phonemes /k/ /ă/ /t/. This approach requires a good visual memory and deductive reasoning in addition to knowledge of the alphabetic principle. Hence, it should be seen as a skill to use when some synthetic phonics knowledge is acquired. (Note that using a phonics-based approach does not exclude the use of strategies to teach a 'sight' vocabulary and a whole-word/sight approach to teaching irregular words and 'high frequency' words where appropriate.)

## Overlearning

The need for a programme to involve overlearning, so that each Teaching Point is securely learned before moving on to the next one, is based on the research into memory discussed in Chapter 2. One way of achieving this is to repeat a particular routine or drill until optimal learning is acquired in terms of accuracy and speed. Other appropriate approaches include practising a skill or Teaching Point in a variety of ways (e.g., through games, ICT, worksheets, and different reading activities) to maintain interest and engagement. Sometimes the same skill can be practised using a range of materials (e.g., improving letter formation could involve using a salt tray, sandpaper letters, tracing over using colour, sky-writing, forming letters from plasticine and using handwriting sheets. Overlearning is, of course, embedded within the cumulative structure of the programme.

# Teaching Strategies

This section outlines key strategies which should be incorporated in all lessons and also suggests several optional approaches which can be used within the programme when considered appropriate. (These can also be used in everyday 'quality' teaching.)

## Key Strategies

### i Routines

All lessons involve establishing routines for reading, spelling, writing, and memory work using a direct teaching method. Routines establish security for the learner in that they provide a consistent approach to learning using multisensory techniques. They enable learners to acquire new concepts and information by freeing up memory capacity. Familiarity and consistency facilitate automaticity. The routines are described in Chapter 11.

### ii Guided discovery

Guided discovery methods are used when introducing new Teaching Points, whether phonemes, concepts, spelling rules, or punctuation. Learners are more likely to recall and understand information if they have 'discovered' it for themselves. However, the approach is 'guided' or structured by the teacher in order to support the learner's 'discovery'. Examples of how to use Discovery Learning are provided, particularly in the section on Concept Cards in Chapter 11.

### iii Metacognition

A key feature of the programme is the use of strategies to develop metacognitive awareness (understanding about how they learn), thereby enabling learners to take more control of their own learning and building confidence and self-esteem. Importantly it gives them insights into learning which they can generalise to new situations including those outside their intervention sessions. One approach is to help them develop metalanguage (i.e., the language and vocabulary which facilitate the ability to explain what they are thinking and doing in relation to their learning). Another approach is to offer them a range of ways of learning so that they can determine which of these 'works best' for them in a variety of contexts. They should be encouraged to articulate how they 'learned' a particular Teaching Point or fact.

### iv Revision and review

An important aspect of a cumulative programme is to rehearse/practise what has previously been learned before introducing and then incorporating any new Teaching Point. This might be revision of the Teaching Point that has been most recently introduced, but could also be revision of a concept taught several lessons previously in order to extend and build on it. Revision aids memory, overlearning, automaticity and understanding.

At the end of each lesson the learner is encouraged to 'review' what new learning has occurred, usually prompted by a teacher's questions and using a selected activity, such as the Stimulus Response Routine outlined in Chapter 11.

### v Games

If learning is enjoyable it is more likely to be remembered and to motivate students to want to learn. It is important always to consider *emotional* responses, as very often learners with dyslexia will have experienced failures that will have resulted in emotional barriers to learning. Games can often help to overcome these barriers and re-engage learners. We would suggest that all lessons should normally incorporate at least one age-appropriate game relating to relevant Teaching Points for current or recent lessons. This may be played with the teacher or on the computer. (Note that some students may learn more easily if they can see the whole lesson as a game or a set of games. However, others – particularly those who are older – may prefer not to play a game with the teacher and instead would enjoy using an appropriate computer game.)

### vi Independent learning

All lessons should provide follow-up activities for learners to work on independently in school and/or at home. These will include practising the Reading Packs (and, for older learners, the Spelling Pack and maybe the Concept Card Pack) and may also use worksheets, guided tasks, reading activities, and games. Learners could be directed to use ICT based on a teacher's word lists for spelling in programs such as Wordshark. A variety of software programs can assist story-writing/telling, reading, and spelling. As these often change we would suggest that teachers visit the BDA and other websites which offer literacy games including local authority literacy websites.

## Important Note

While it is fundamental to the structured programme to emphasise direct teaching and teacher support to ensure successful learning, it is equally important to foster independence without putting learners at risk of failure. In part this comes through encouraging them to help organise the activities and materials and providing opportunities for them to demonstrate their understanding and skills as well as by fostering metacognition. Teachers are also encouraged to use other strategies for fostering literacy.

Whilst not exhaustive, the following strategies are particularly recommended.

### i   Self-voice and use of recording

This approach is based on the idea that learning is more effective when material is presented through the learner's own voice rather than a teacher's. In the case of learning to spell, for example, the teacher models the spelling of a word orally. The teacher says the whole word (e.g., said) and the learner repeats it while looking at the word. The learner's voice is recorded. The teacher then models spelling orally, naming the letters (e.g., 's' 'a' 'i' 'd') and the learner repeats the spelling and this too is recorded. The learner's response is played back to the learner who looks at the written word and speaks the letters in unison with the recording and then writes the word from memory, naming the letters as s/he writes. A good quality recorder is needed for this, because some learners may 'mis-spell' or not recall a spelling and any error must be removed so that only a correct response is recorded. This method was developed by Lane (1975) as the ARROW (Aural-Read-Respond-Oral-Write) technique and his research showed it was successful in improving both basic reading and spelling. The 'self-voice' principle can easily be used with today's learners as many mobile phones and other electronic devices owned by the majority of pupils can record speech for later playback. This facility can be used for learners to record their spelling practice in 'self-voice'. Similarly, a learner could record a short section using a webcam and attach it to an e-mail to their home e-dress, again using 'self-voice'.

### ii   Recorded reading

The above approach can be applied to reading where a teacher models reading phrases or sentences which the learner repeats (following a written text) and this is recorded. The process is repeated until a paragraph and then a complete passage or story is built up. The learner replays the recording and reads in unison with his/her recorded voice. This can be used for independent practice in order to improve accuracy.

The technique can also be used to improve reading fluency for a learner who is reading accurately but slowly. In this case, after the first sentence or two the teacher turns down the volume to zero (but leaves it playing) whilst the learner continues to read. At the end of the reading the volume is turned up to see if the learner has 'beaten' the recording while managing to retain accuracy. By listening to the rest of the recording s/he can see how much their speed of reading has improved. This process can be repeated several times if the learner wishes to do so.

### iii   Paired reading

Learners should continue to read more widely than just in structure and will need to recognise that they may need support in this. Paired reading involves the teacher and learner reading in unison until the learner feels confident enough to read alone. S/he can indicate this by giving a pre-arranged signal to the teacher. If s/he falters or makes an error the teacher continues to read, 'fading' when the learner regains confidence. (Sometimes a teacher may start the reading, and the learner will join in when they feeling sufficiently confident.) This technique is usually used at the end of a lesson as it does *not* replace 'reading in structure'.

### iv   Shared reading

This approach can be used successfully within the structured reading part of the lesson, particularly in the early stages of the programme when the words which can be used in structure are very limited. It involves a story containing sentences written in structure (which the learner reads) and words/sentences which are not in structure which the teacher reads. This facilitates the use of stories with more interesting content because it can contain a more extensive vocabulary. An example is provided in Part V (Resources).

### v   Teacher reading

Sometimes a teacher may read a story or 'serial' to the learner as a means of developing listening comprehension and/or to familiarise them with the language of books. This also maintains contact with age appropriate literature – the process and purpose of 'real reading'. Some learners will be stimulated by exposure to texts which have interest levels beyond their chronological age and certainly beyond their reading age!

### vi   Precision teaching

Precision teaching (Lindsley, 1971, 1990) was developed in the 1970s in the USA and introduced into England in the late seventies (Levy and Branwhite, 1987). We recommend a modified form which is designed to improve speed and accuracy when reading words that have been written in structure. It can therefore be incorporated into a lesson as part of the structured reading practice. It is a very successful way of building up a learner's sight vocabulary to an automatic level of rapid naming, leading to improved fluency. Instructions for using this technique and an example are provided in Part III, the Conquering Literacy programme (e.g., Teaching Point 30).

# The Structure of the Conquering Literacy Programme

The programme adopts an integrated approach to teaching reading, writing, and spelling. It presents concepts and phonograms in a logical and structured sequence and also incorporates three other important aspects of literacy acquisition. These are:

- alphabet and dictionary exercises;
- memory work and development;
- study skills.

We have devoted a chapter to each of these aspects, providing a rationale and examples of how to integrate them into structured lessons as well as suggesting how they can be applied to general teaching.

## The Rationale for the Order of Introducing Concepts and Phonograms

Very often there is such a concentration on teaching phonics that the concepts that underpin literacy may be neglected. This programme therefore includes (and starts) with teaching concepts explicitly. This is considered necessary because an assumption that learners have 'picked-up' and internalised these concepts may lead to misunderstandings and the ability to apply them to reading and spelling may not be checked. These concepts are sequenced in relation to their relevance to other learning in the programme. They aid metacognition and provide learners with a vocabulary for talking about literacy and their learning.

Phonograms are introduced in a sequence of simple vowels and consonants which can lead to word-building and generate a large number of words at an early stage. This approach to structuring a multisensory literacy programme was introduced by Gillingham and Stillman (1956), Cox (1972) and Hickey (1977) so it is a well-established method, although there have been some changes to the order of presentation. Conquering Literacy adopts a well-established order for the first five phonograms which can be found in a range of programmes for learners with dyslexia, all of which reflect the work of Cox (1972). However, after the first five phonograms this programme diverges from the sequence used by others and reflects our own experience of teaching and that of many other teachers we have tutored on specialist courses. An example of this is that we introduce 's' blends very early on (although with very young children, discretion can be exercised about their appropriateness). Similarly vowel digraphs have been introduced in an order based on position and spelling choice (i.e., frequency in spelling).

The programme structure also acknowledges the National Primary Strategy for Literacy (DCSF, 2007) and while it does not follow the same order for phonograms as 'Letters and Sounds' (used in Wave 1 teaching) the Conquering Literacy Summary Table in Part III indicates the high frequency words from the strategy including irregular words and shows where they can be introduced. It is therefore compatible with 'Letters and Sounds', but moves at a slower pace. It is vital to remember that Conquering Literacy is designed to be used as an intervention for those learners who have failed to achieve literacy although they have been given normal good 'quality' first teaching (Wave 1) and may even have had small group intervention (e.g., Wave 2 teaching). We would consider, however, that children presenting major difficulties (signs of dyslexia) after receiving good Wave 1 teaching may benefit from this programme without delay so that they revisit learning literacy more slowly and thoroughly and at a pace that meets their individual needs. Slowing down the pace of introducing new information, together with ample opportunities for revision, reinforcement and overlearning, is the 'key' to acquiring literacy skills for learners with dyslexia. For older learners or those with more advanced skills, the Accelerated Programme can be used. This provides a condensed form of the Teaching Points contained in the early stages of the Main Programme, permitting learners to enter the Main Programme at a more advanced stage. A base-line assessment must be carried out to establish current literacy knowledge and skills so that gaps in relation to concepts and phonograms can be filled and prior learning is consolidated and extended.

A table showing the structure/teaching order of the Conquering Literacy programme is given in Part III and a Record Sheet is provided in Part V (Resources). The Accelerated Programme, and its structure in relation to the Main Programme, can be found in Part IV Section A, which also provides details of how to assess those learners for whom the Accelerated Programme is appropriate. A Record Sheet for recording their progress is included.

## Summary

A programme designed for teaching literacy to learners with dyslexia should be structured, multisensory, cumulative, based on synthetic phonics and include opportunities for overlearning. A range of teaching strategies should be used, some of which should be incorporated within all lessons. These include the use of routines and drill, guided discovery, and strategies to develop metacognition. A variety of activities must be used within each lesson in order to motivate learners: the use of games and appropriate computer software is also encouraged.

# References

Cox, A.R. (1972) *Structures and Techniques: Multisensory Teaching of Basic Language Skills*. Cambridge, MA: Educators Publishing Services.

Department for Children, Schools and Families (DCSF) (2007) *Letter and Sounds: Principles and Practice of High Quality Phonics*, Primary National Strategy. London: DCSF.

Gillingham, A. and Stillman, B. (1956) *Remedial Training for Children with Specific Disability in Reading, Spelling and Penmanship* (5th edn). Cambridge, MA: Educators Publishing Services.

Hickey, K. (1977) *The Kathleen Hickey Language Kit*. London: Kathleen Hickey Publications.

Lane, C. (1975) *The A.R.R.O.W. Programme*. Available at www.excellencegateway.org.uk/page.aspx?o=127041

Levy, B. and Branwhite, T. (1987) *The Precision Phonics Programme*. London: NARE.

Lindsley, O.R. (1971) 'From Skinner to precision teaching: the child knows best'. In Jordan, J.B. and Robbins, L.S. (eds), *Let's Try Doing Something Else Kind of Thing*. Arlington, VA: Council for Exceptional Children. pp. 1–11.

Lindsley, O.R. (1990) 'Precision teaching: by teachers for children', *Teaching Exceptional Children*, 22 (3): 10–15.

Milne, D. (2005) *Teaching the Brain to Read*. London: SK Publishing.

Rose, J. (2006) *Independent Review of the Teaching of Early Reading: Final Report*. London: DfES.

Torgeson, C., Brooks, G. and Hall, J. (2006) *A Systematic Review of the Research Literature on the Use of Phonics in the Teaching of Reading and Spelling*, Research Report RR711. London: DfES.

# CHAPTER 9

# LESSON PLANNING

## Chapter Overview

At the heart of good teaching lies good planning. Having a clear and consistent structure to a lesson is particularly important for learners with dyslexia who can approach a lesson with confidence if they can predict the form it will take. It also helps them with organisational skills and, as lessons continue, the use of regular routines reduces memory load. This chapter therefore provides models for planning lessons on a 1:1 basis that follow a consistent format whether the lesson is of one hour or less duration. (Part IV, Section C contains examples of planning for small group teaching.)

The basic plan is for a one hour lesson which can be carried out on a weekly basis, although two or three lessons a week would be preferable for learners with severe dyslexia in order to obtain a faster improvement. (In practice this might mean that a specialist teacher delivers one lesson and for the other one or two lessons would be delivered by a trained teaching assistant (TA).) We also provide plans for an alternative delivery of two half-hour lessons or four fifteen-minute lessons per week, as this is preferred by some schools and certain learners may benefit from short, frequent lessons. In our experience 'poor concentration' should not be used as a reason for short lessons – if a one-hour lesson is planned that includes a number of short, appropriate activities, we have found learners as young as four years are able to concentrate for that length of time.

It is also important to ensure that there is some follow-up to a lesson. This can be:

- homework (which should be in addition to practising the Reading Pack) e.g., a worksheet for independent practice or a game to play with a parent/carer;
- opportunities to work in school with a trained TA on follow-up work, using activities provided by the specialist teacher;
- independent work using ICT as directed by the specialist teacher e.g., reading games, spelling programmes, mind-mapping or story-writing.

As far as possible the specialist teacher should liaise with school staff to see where the skills and strategies acquired during the Conquering Literacy lessons can be applied in different curriculum areas. Similarly school staff can inform a specialist teacher of any particular skill or strategy they would like a learner to use (e.g., a science teacher may provide a list of terms for teaching spelling). Teaching meta-cognition means that when learners are more aware of how they learn best they can apply these strategies throughout the curriculum. The specialist teacher can remind learners they should be doing this by using appropriate questioning techniques, for example 'What do you do when … ?' or 'What do you do so that you don't lose your place in reading/copying?' It is important to use a friendly, supporting tone so that the learner realises this is being done in order to remind them to articulate and use their self-knowledge and does not infer that the teacher is being critical. The same approach can be used to check a learner's generalisation of study skills taught in a specialist lesson (see Chapter 13).

A basic one hour lesson will normally follow the plan shown in Figure 9.1. For each activity we suggest the amount of time to allocate, although this should be adjusted to meet individual needs. Normally a teacher would insert the actual time that a lesson begins and the time when each item should start.

The teacher inserts the detail/resources under each item. The comments column enables a quick note to be made of the learner's response to the item, which then informs the planning for the next lesson.

| Lesson Plan for 1 hour | | |
|---|---|---|
| Name _____ Date _____ | | |
| **New Teaching Point(s)** | | |
| **Time** | **Content/Item** | **Comments** |
| | 1. Alphabet/dictionary (8 mins) | |
| | 2. Memory training (4 mins) | |
| | 3. Revision (5 mins) | |
| | 4. Reading Pack (2 mins) | |
| | 5. Spelling Pack (3 mins) | |
| | 6. New Teaching Point (10 mins)<br>• Discovery Learning<br>• Tracking/relevant exercise<br>• Listening activity<br>• Make new Reading Card<br>• Cursive writing<br>• New Spelling Card<br>• SRR | |
| | 7. Handwriting (3 mins) | |
| | 8. Reading in structure (3 mins) | |
| | 9. Written exercise to practise new learning (3 mins) | |
| | 10. Spelling in structure (3 mins) | |
| | 11. Dictation in structure (5 mins) | |
| | 12. Quick review (2 mins) | |
| | 13. Supported reading (4 mins) | |
| | 14. Game (5 mins) | |

Figure 9.1    *Model for Lesson Plan Lasting One Hour*

## Photocopiable:
*Teaching Literacy to Learners with Dyslexia* © Kathleen Kelly and Sylvia Phillips, 2011 (SAGE)

While a standard lesson should contain all of the above, this is usually built up over about four lessons in order to establish the routines firmly and ensure that the learner understands both the lesson structure and the purpose of each element. (Introducing too many *new* routines in any one lesson could result in memory overload – and consequently the learner will not establish routines and automaticity.) We would suggest a teacher builds up to the standard lesson plan as follows:

| Lesson 1 | Lesson 2 |
|---|---|
| This lesson should introduce the notion of a structured lesson and how the first four lessons 'build up' to what will become the format of most lessons. It should contain:<br><br>• Alphabet/dictionary work.<br>• New Teaching Points (e.g., first six concepts and 'i' or /ī/).<br>• Quick review.<br>• A game. | As Lesson 1 but add:<br><br>• Revision of concepts.<br>• Reading Pack.<br>• Handwriting routine (joining letters/forming words).<br>• Reading in structure.<br><br>(N.B. Learners should understand the purpose of the routines.) |
| **Lesson 3** | **Lesson 4** |
| As Lesson 2 but add:<br><br>• Spelling Pack.<br>• Spelling in structure.<br><br>N. B. These are new routines – plenty of time should be allowed. | This becomes a 'standard' one hour lesson by adding:<br><br>• Memory training.<br>• The new Teaching Point in writing.<br>• Dictation.<br>• 'Everyday reading' by using supported reading. |

Figure 9.2   *Suggestions for 'Building' Up to a One-hour Structured Lesson (N.B. Items correspond to those in Figure 9.1 Lesson Plan)*

## Lesson Content And Rationale

Lesson content reflects the need for learners with dyslexia to follow a structured, cumulative, multisensory, phonics-based programme which includes opportunities for overlearning as described in Chapter 8. It contains the following elements.

### i  Alphabet/dictionary work

It is not only important for learners to appreciate that the 44 sounds identified in the English language are represented by only 26 letters (for reading and spelling) but also that they can recall and name them rapidly and have a secure knowledge of the sequence of alphabetical order. This is because alphabetical order is the most frequently-used system for organising information so it can be accessed readily (e.g., dictionaries, indexes, telephone directories, class registers, books in a library). Chapter 10 discusses how to incorporate this work into lessons.

### ii  Memory training

The aim of this element is to increase the capacity for storing information in working memory and long enough to act on it or store it in long-term memory. The need for this is clear from Chapters 2 and 3. It is therefore important to give learners strategies to do this and suggestions for teaching can be found in Chapter 12.

### iii   Revision of previous learning

A revision exercise should be used to check on a learner's understanding and consolidate their previous learning. Some of the examples in Part III for new Teaching Points can be used as the basis for revision. Revision can take various forms (e.g., games, worksheets, reading a structured story, a listening activity).

### iv   Reading and Spelling Packs

The purpose of these two elements is to develop automaticity through practice and overlearning, as routines may develop new neural pathways which will then improve speed of processing and efficiency of learning. Chapter 11 describes how to make the cards and how to establish routines using the packs.

### v   New Teaching Point

Each lesson will normally include at least one new Teaching Point (concept or phonogram). The methods for introducing new teaching are found in Chapter 11.

### vi   Handwriting

This element is *in addition* to learning how to write any new phonogram in cursive writing when introducing the new Teaching Point. The purpose is to join the new phonogram(s) to others learned previously using cursive handwriting (see Chapter 6). It also provides an opportunity to consider the relative size of letters, spacing between words and the use of punctuation where appropriate. It is a further example of overlearning. The handwriting routine is described in Chapter 11.

### vii   Reading in structure

The purpose of this is to enable learners to apply their knowledge and skills successfully when reading because they are only required to read words which are composed of phonograms they have been explicitly taught. (The reading given to them will move from single words to simple sentences, then to longer passages and stories.) An example of controlling the structure in this way for a learner who has been taught 'i, t, p, n, s' would be to give them the following to read: 'tip', 'sit', 'pin', and/or 'Tip it in'. (A game could be introduced e.g., Word Bingo or Pairs, using this vocabulary and should require the learner to read aloud.)

### viii   Written exercise to practise new learning

Learners should be given an opportunity to reinforce their new learning by undertaking a writing activity, using a worksheet or punctuation exercise or spelling game. Part III contains examples of appropriate activities. (Note that it is important not to use the same activity or worksheet in the following lesson for revision: it can be *similar* but not identical.)

### ix   Spelling in structure

The aim of this element is to enable learners to apply knowledge and skills successfully in spelling. They are only required to spell words which are formed from phonograms already taught. An explanation of how to teach this is given in Chapter 11.

### x   Dictation

This element also involves spelling in structure but is related to learning about note-taking and how to use punctuation in context. It is based on a different routine from that used in single word spelling and involves proofreading and self-checking skills. This routine is explained in Chapter 11 and examples of sentences for dictation are provided in Part III.

### xi   Quick review

The purpose of this is to find out whether the learner has understood the new Teaching Points introduced in this lesson. (Note that this should be learner-led and not interpreted as an opportunity for the teacher to *tell* the learner what s/he *thinks* should have been learned.)

### xii   Everyday reading/supported reading

Each lesson should contain some reading which is out of structure so that learners can retain an interest in and knowledge of literary language and understand that reading is for meaning. This must be supported reading and may, at first, mean that the teacher reads to the learner and then moves to paired or shared reading or uses recorded reading. For older students recorded reading may be the most appropriate form, with a greater use of non-fiction texts including magazines.

### xiii   Game

Games can be used in several places as part of the lesson as suggested earlier. However, we would also suggest using a game as a 'wind-down' at the end of a lesson so that there is an enjoyable final activity.

Games can be incorporated into lessons in order to involve dialogue and reinforce learning in an enjoyable way so that 'learning is fun'. These should always be age appropriate as well as relevant to the learning. It may be better to omit a 'game element' with older learners if an appropriate one cannot be devised. Computer games may be used in many cases.

When working with older secondary/FE students, this aspect and the everyday reading element could be replaced by a short 'advisory session' to support emotional needs and/or offer guidance for managing any curriculum difficulties they may be encountering.

# Teaching Shorter Lessons

## Lesson Planning for Half-hour Lessons

It may be that it is not logistically possible to spend an hour on a lesson. We suggest that two half-hour lessons be substituted (although in some schools the time allocated might be between 30–60 minutes, in which case a teacher must plan the lesson prioritising elements according to a learner's needs but also retain the main routines for consistency and overlearning). A suggested approach is presented below (see Figure 9.3).

| Lesson 1 | Time in minutes | Lesson 2 | Time in minutes |
|---|---|---|---|
| • Alphabet/dictionary | 7 | • Memory work | 3 |
| • Revision | 5 | • Reading Pack | 2 |
| • Reading Pack | 2 | • Spelling Pack | 3 |
| • Spelling Pack | 3 | • Reading in structure | 3 |
| • New Teaching Point | 10 | • Writing exercise | 5 |
| • Handwriting | 3 | • Spelling in structure | 3 |
| | | • Dictation | 5 |
| | | • Review | 2 |
| | | • Game | 4 |

Figure 9.3    *Suggested Items for 2 × 30 Minute Lessons*

(Note that this structure emphasises practising the Reading/Spelling Packs. It is important to ensure that the learner has access to good 'normal' reading experiences, with support outside these lessons.)

## Short, Frequent Lessons (e.g., Four Lessons per Week Each Lasting 15 Minutes)

This approach is *not* appropriate for older learners but it may be used with younger learners where memory is particularly poor or because it is compatible with their school's philosophy and organisation (see Figure 9.4).

It is worth bearing in mind that as intervention usually takes place outside normal classroom/curriculum, learners will often 'lose time' coming to their literacy lesson and returning to their normal teaching group. That time loss will be increased if there are two or four shorter lessons and it is likely to prove more disruptive, not only to their learning but also to that of their peers and other teachers. However, short, frequent,

| Lesson 1 | | Lesson 2 | |
|---|---|---|---|
| | *Time in minutes* | | *Time in minutes* |
| • Alphabet work | 5 | • New Teaching Point | 10 |
| • Memory work | 3 | • Reading in structure | 5 |
| • Revision | 5 | | |
| • Reading Pack | 2 | | |
| **Lesson 3** | | **Lesson 4** | |
| | *Time in minutes* | | *Time in minutes* |
| • Handwriting | 3 | • Reading Pack | 2 |
| • Spelling Pack | 3 | • Spelling Pack | 3 |
| • Writing exercise/game | 5 | • Dictation | 5 |
| • Spelling in structure | 4 | • Game | 5 |

Figure 9.4    *Suggested Items for 4 × 15 Minute Lessons*

fifteen-minute lessons may be useful for younger learners, particularly those with poor memories, and perhaps more compatible with a school's organisation than a one-hour lesson. There is no strong evidence that *length* of lesson is related to learning outcomes.

## Summary

Most one-to-one lessons should be planned to last for one hour although it is possible to teach shorter lessons. All lessons should include several short activities to maintain learners' interest, motivation, and concentration while also reinforcing the main teaching objective. Lessons should include opportunities to learn new Teaching Points while revising and building on previous learning and should incorporate reading, writing and spelling activities, all of which need to be taught and practised using multisensory techniques. The fact that lessons follow a set pattern in addition to the structure in the literacy content raises learners' confidence and self-esteem because they become aware that they will only be expected to know what they have been taught in previous lessons within the programme. A key factor in this, of course, must be that teacher and learner enjoy a good relationship.

## Downloadable Material

For downloadable material for this chapter visit www.sagepub.co.uk/kelly&phillips
Figure 9.1: Model for Lesson Plan Lasting One Hour

# CHAPTER 10

# ALPHABET AND DICTIONARY WORK

## Chapter Overview

Earlier chapters have pointed to the significance of the ability to identify and name the letters of the alphabet for success in both reading and spelling. Learners also need to be able to retrieve letter names *and* order them in alphabetic sequence quickly so as to access information, as stated in Chapter 8. This chapter is concerned both with establishing letter recognition and with teaching alphabetical order. These activities lead to developing the skills for using dictionaries, indexes, and other applications of alphabetical order.

In teaching learners how to sequence the alphabet we use letter *names* because a letter only has one name although it may make several sounds and therefore a learner can have confidence when labelling a letter. Fundamental to identifying letters accurately are the following two principles:

- A letter can be written in a number of different forms e.g., print, cursive, upper case, lower case, and in a variety of fonts and sizes, but it will still retain the same letter name (and sound representations).
- Orientation is a significant feature in identifying letters (particularly in lower case). When teaching the orientation of *all* letters (upper and lower case forms) attention should be paid to the lower case letters which are often confused:

**b /d /p /q : t /f : n / u : m / w**

Whilst what follow below are suggestions about how to incorporate alphabet and dictionary work within structured lessons, most of these activities can be used for teaching whole classes or small groups of all learners. When teaching alphabet work, whether as part of the normal curriculum or in structured lessons, it is important to ensure that learners do not become confused and start to associate capital letters with names and lower case with sounds: they need to realise that a letter, *whatever its form*, has both a name and at least one sound. Similarly, they have to learn that there are five vowels and 21 consonants, but that one of these, 'y', can be used to represent both a vowel and a consonant and is therefore known as a semi-vowel. In the structured programme these concepts are addressed as they arise in the letter order and through the basic routines.

## Using Alphabet Work in Structured Lessons

Normally lessons will start with alphabet work because it offers an opportunity to begin a lesson with 'fun' activities that are multisensory – and particularly involve kinaesthetic and tactile learning – without requiring writing. Wooden letters (or hard plastic) should be used initially for alphabetic work, although small cards with printed letters can be used later or as appropriate with older or more 'advanced' learners.

We would recommend that upper case letters be used at first, especially where learners are having some difficulty with orientation as it is easier to distinguish the letter form. However, where a school has a clear policy of using only lower case, or when working with children who are only familiar with lower case, then of course it will be appropriate to start with lower case letters and to build on their experience. At some point they must be able to work with both and 'match' upper and lower case letters and, in particular, to appreciate that upper and lower case letters have the same name *and* sound(s).

Before deciding what to teach, an informal assessment of a learner's current knowledge should include establishing:

- which letters of the alphabet they can name (use upper and lower case letters);
- whether they know the sounds of the letters (using upper and lower case letters);
- whether they can sequence the letters of the alphabet;
- whether they know the terms 'vowels' and 'consonants'.

This information will indicate where teaching should begin.

If a learner can recognise only a few letters by name then this section of the lesson needs to focus on using games and activities to introduce and reinforce letter and sound recognition rather than sequencing. One approach is to set out the alphabet arc (as described below) leaving a space for letter(s) to be inserted when they have been taught. This will allow the learner to become familiar with seeing the alphabetic sequence without expecting them to know the whole sequence. This method can also be used when introducing the first few letters of the programme. Where a learner can name most letters of the alphabet, but not sequence them accurately or quickly, alphabet work is essential.

## Lesson Planning

Although the introductory lesson will allocate more time to alphabet work (up to 20 minutes) alphabet work should normally last only for 8 or 10 minutes and be taught at a brisk pace. However, further practice could be carried out by a teaching assistant or parent/carer between lessons.

We recommend (as most structured programmes do) that the alphabet is set out in the form of an arc (see Figure 10.1) so that the whole of this arc is within the learner's peripheral vision. This will take up less space than if it is set out in a single line and also leaves space in the middle of the arc/table to use for related activities.

The position of the first and last letters (A and Z) and then the middle letters (M and N) are 'markers' to help the learner set out the full alphabet within the space available,

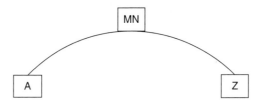

Figure 10.1   *The Alphabet Arc*

placing all letters with their correct orientation. The learner must name the letters aloud as they set them out, so that they are using a multisensory approach, and should say the name (kinaesthetic), hear it (auditory), and link it to the letter shape (visual). Similarly, when they have formed the arc they should go round it in sequence touching each letter and saying its name (and sound if appropriate). The teacher should also ask the learner to 'look carefully and check' so that the principle of self-correction is established.

There are several ways in which the alphabet sequence can be taught to learners who are able to recognise most of the letters of the alphabet. These are, in order of progression of difficulty:

i   Setting out the alphabet A–Z (having put the markers down first).
ii  Setting out the alphabet in reverse order Z–A (after putting out their markers).
iii Taking letters in any order from the box/bag and putting them into their 'correct position' in the arc.
iv  Starting from M and N placing the letters before M and after N in alternate order. (You can also do this by placing the letters after A and before Z.)

(Note that learners should master each of these tasks by laying out the alphabet within one minute before proceeding to the next method.)

Where learners are very slow or hesitant in setting out the arc (perhaps taking three or more minutes to do so), they should concentrate on just setting out the first half (or even quarter) until they can do this in under a minute.

## Activities for Alphabet Work

- Work with the alphabet arc provides an opportunity for overlearning letter recognition. Activities can include:
  - the learner closing their eyes and naming a letter by feeling it and then checking this by looking;
  - the teacher tracing a letter on the learner's back (or back of hand) so they can feel it (subject to the school's policy on touch). The learner then has to name it and remove it from the arc;
  - the learner tracing over the letter formation;
  - the learner touching and naming each letter in sequence rapidly;
  - the learner touching each letter in turn, giving its name and sound.

- Work with the alphabet arc provides opportunities for reinforcing sequencing including:
  - asking the learner which letter comes before/after a selected letter;
  - asking the learner to close their eyes while the teacher removes one or more letters; the learner then looks at the arc to determine the missing letters, saying

their names aloud (this is a good activity to 'reverse roles' so that the learner plays the teacher's role);

o three or four consecutive letters are removed by the teacher and the learner has to replace them in the correct order, naming them as they do so;

o the learner closes their eyes and points to where they think a particular letter is placed in the arc and then opens their eyes and checks;

o the teacher makes a set of cards to practise alphabet sequencing using the arc as a prop (e.g., presented with a card with DE_ on, the learner has to say the names of the first two letters and then name the missing letter). Cards can cover the whole of the alphabet, but be presented randomly. The activity can be made progressively more difficult by omitting the middle and then the first letter;

o learners are asked to 'chunk' letters in pairs as they touch and name them with the stress on the second letter. (e.g., AB', CD', EF', etc.) and then they can do this in threes. (e.g., ABC', DEF') and so on. This activity helps them to understand the concept of stress which they need when considering stress in words (which often changes meaning). It is a useful activity to use when considering accent/stress (see Teaching Point 26 in the programme);

• Putting the alphabet away should be an opportunity to reinforce concepts (such as vowels), letter recognition (names/sounds), and sequencing. Activities include:

o mixing up all the letters and asking the learner to put letters away in alphabetical order;

o the learner putting away a designated letter, and then the one that comes before it, and then the one that comes after it;

o the learner having to look at the arc and put away 'all the letters with' straight edges, or curved edges, or those that are both straight and curved;

o the learner putting away the five vowels, the semi-vowel, and then the consonants.

(Note that learners should be reminded always to *name* the letter aloud as they put them away in the bag or box.)

Activities which do not use wooden letters and the arc can also be used to reinforce both letter recognition and alphabet sequencing (e.g., dot-to-dot alphabet drawings, tracking activities (for single letters, letter sequences, and the whole alphabet in sequence), and games such as alphabet dominoes, pelmanism, and letter Bingo).

# Dictionary Work

Sound knowledge of alphabet sequencing is a prerequisite for dictionary work (as well as accessing any information which is in alphabetical order such as an index or books by author's surname, either in a library or on a reading list).

## Early Stages

- Putting words (written on cards) in alphabetical order using:
  - First letter e.g. it pin sit
    Put the cards under the appropriate letters in the arc, and discuss the order in which they would be found in a dictionary.
  - Second letter e.g., sip snip spit
  - Third letter e.g., spat sped spin

  There is a range of computer programs/games which can be used to practise alphabet sequencing and a large number of free downloads of worksheets on the internet (see the websites in Part V).

- Using the arc, learners should show how to divide it into the four quartiles by leaving a space before the E, M, and S (making the quartiles A-D, E-L, M-R, and S-Z). The reason for this should be explained – that we can expect to find half the words before the middle and half after the middle of a dictionary. When we look at the middle we will find the words beginning with M. If we then split the first section (A-L) into two we will find that words beginning with E are in the middle and if we split the second section (between M and Z) into two halves we will find words beginning with S in the middle. (Teachers should make sure they have chosen a suitable dictionary to illustrate this as some dictionaries differ, particularly those for young children.) It may help learners if the teacher gives a mnemonic for remembering the quartiles e.g. **A**ll **E**lephants **M**ake **S**mells (or **S**quirts).

  Knowing about the quartiles and alphabetical order will help learners locate words easily and quickly when looking them up in a dictionary.

## Activities to Practise Using the Quartiles

i  Given a letter, the learner has to say which quartile it belongs to (they could have a card with either the number of the quartile or the 'marker' letter).
ii  The teacher says a word and the learner has to say which quartile it belongs to.
iii  The learner is asked to sort a set of cards into piles/columns for each quartile.
iv  Given a worksheet with four columns (one for each quartile), the learner is asked to sort word cards under each of these or to write them out under the appropriate column.

Teachers can vary these tasks and in particular present the work in interesting/age appropriate forms (e.g., a worksheet with four goal posts [A-D, E-L, M-R and S-Z] and the letters as 'footballs' – the learner must draw a line from football to correct goal to 'score a goal'). Older learners might use subject specific word lists (even if they cannot read the words unaided).

## Later Stages

Revisit the four quartiles using a dictionary for the following activities:

 i  Learners practise opening a dictionary at the four quartile marker places.
 ii  Given a letter name, the learner has to find the quartile in which it occurs and then find any word beginning with that letter.
 iii  Given a letter, the learner has to count how many 'openings' it takes to find a word beginning with that letter. For example, given the letter 't', they should find the middle (first move), then the third quartile, by halving the second half of the dictionary (second move), and then look between S and Z to see how many moves they need to take to find a word beginning with 't'. This can be repeated as a game or 'challenge' to see how *few moves* they take before they find the given letter.
 iv  The above can be used for blends (adjacent consonants) e.g., 'st' and then clusters e.g., 'scr'.
 v  Learners are asked to find a word that is a guide word (if there is not one in structure then the word chosen should be written on a card or worksheet as the learner may not know the correct spelling). The number of 'moves' or openings is counted and the learner is encouraged to improve on their own performance. (Where a good relationship has already been established between the teacher and the learner this may become a competition between the two.)
 vi  Learners should be taught about the importance of guide words and shown how to use them to locate the correct page for a word. (At this stage they do not need to look for the word itself, just provide the page number.)
 viii  Learners should be given practice in scanning the page to find a word. These could be words in structure or subject specific words perhaps requiring the teacher to say, 'We'll read the definition together' if they are at an early stage of reading.

It is often useful to encourage learners to build up their own personal dictionary using guide words. Also, explicit teaching should show how to apply alphabetic knowledge for using indexes to books, atlases, glossaries, libraries, and Google searches (although the 'quartiles' system does not apply to any of these).

## Other Work Using Alphabet Letters

There are several activities which use the wooden letters to teach or reinforce concepts and skills which are part of the structured programme but not part of the alphabet or dictionary routines. It is often practical to include these activities before putting the letters away.

Examples include:

i   *Onset and rime*
   Letters already taught can be used to create cvc words e.g. pip, nip, sip, tip, by showing '–ip', and the different onsets.
ii  *Long and short vowel sounds*
   After introducing 'i' and 'a' learners are asked to discriminate short sounds by listening to and repeating a word such as 'lip' and touching the appropriate letter, placing a card with a breve symbol on it over that letter to denote the short sound. This routine can be repeated for long vowel sounds using a card with a macron symbol. A variety of words should be used to practise these.
iii *Open and closed syllables*
   The wooden vowels can be used to make and practise open and closed syllables. The learner takes out those vowels already taught in the programme (e.g., 'i', 'a', and 'e') and is asked to use the consonants already taught to make three open syllables and three closed syllables using the breve and macron cards, reading them aloud.
iv  *Syllable division (vc/cv)*
   Practice can be given by the teacher making a two-syllable word (in structure) and asking the learner to place a vowel card (v) over each vowel and a consonant card over each of the two consonants between the vowels. This revises the rule that division comes between the two consonants. The learner physically divides the two syllables, reads each syllable, then pushes the syllable together again and reads the whole word. Examples are:

   kidnap          catkin          napkin          antic          aspic

   Words should be selected carefully to avoid those where a letter occurs twice in a word.

Bearing in mind the time allocated to alphabet-related work, further practice can be carried out between lessons by a teaching assistant or parent/carer using activities such as those listed above, many of which can be adapted for independent learning in the case of older learners.

**Summary**   ☐

This chapter has suggested a range of activities which can be used in 1:1 or small group teaching and also with whole classes to develop knowledge of alphabet sequencing and to teach dictionary skills.

# CHAPTER 11

# INTRODUCING THE NEW TEACHING POINT IN A LESSON

### Chapter Overview

This chapter describes how to introduce new Teaching Points into a lesson, emphasising the introduction of phonograms and literacy concepts. It suggests appropriate techniques and resources for each aspect of a lesson as set out in the lesson plan provided in Chapter 9. It is therefore essential prior reading for the programme in Part III. Each lesson normally introduces a new Teaching Point, although sometimes more than one will be introduced depending upon the learner's understanding and preferred pace of learning.

There are two main types of Teaching Points: *phonograms* (the written symbol(s) representing phonemes) and *concepts*. Teaching about phonograms will also include teaching spelling rules, and teaching about concepts includes the use of punctuation. Both types of Teaching Point can usually be introduced through Discovery Learning.

# Introducing Phonograms – Lesson Plan Item 6

A list of phonograms in the order in which they should be taught is provided at the front of Part III. There are seven stages in introducing phonograms.

## Stage 1 – Identifying the New Phonogram

A phonogram is usually introduced using Discovery Learning based on one of the sensory channels. Examples are:

- *Auditory*
  - Listening: the teacher reads aloud a list of words, asking the learner to identify a common sound in a list of words. The learner repeats each word after the teacher says it so that they *hear* themselves say it and '*feel*' what making the sound is like (e.g., pot, pencil, please, paint, pattern). Initial sounds are used for younger pupils but with older ones the sound could be in any position (e.g., clapping, pencil, steep, rope, puppy).
  - The teacher gives three or four clues to a word, saying one at a time. The learner then has to solve the riddle. For example:
    i an artist uses one;
    ii you can get them in different colours;
    iii you can draw with them;
    iv you can write with them.
  After guessing the word 'pencil' the learner is asked to supply the initial sound.

  - An alternative is that the teacher gives descriptions or definitions of four or five words and the learner has to work out what each one is and identify the common sound. For example:
    i it grows in a garden (plant);
    ii a person who steers an aeroplane (pilot);
    iii a young dog (puppy);
    iv a needle has a sharp? (point);
  The common sound here is /p/.

- *Visual*
  - o Given a set of printed words, the learner is asked to identify a common letter (the learner is not expected to *read* the words). For younger learners the list should be only contain words where the target phonogram is at the beginning, but for older learners it could be in varying positions. For example:
    - i   pen, pot, pull, pin, person;
    - ii  ship, shelter, shin, shot, shell;
    - iii  spent, lips, hamper, help, prance;
    - iv  shelter, dishwasher, slashing, mesh, shining.
  - o The learner looks at a set of pictures, naming the object/picture, and says the common sound.
  - o An advertising slogan using alliteration could be shown or a short sentence in which the target phonogram occurs more frequently than any other: the learner then has to identify the target sound.

- *Tactile*
  - o If the learner can identify most letters of the alphabet already, a wooden letter is presented in a cloth bag and the learner has to identify the target letter and sound.
  - o A number of objects whose names all begin with the same letter are placed in a bag. The learner feels the objects and names them, pulling them out to check if they are right, and then identifies the target sound. (This is an appropriate game for younger children.)

*Note that only one of these approaches should be used to introduce the phonogram.*


## Stage 2 – Pronouncing/Articulating the Sound (Phoneme)

When a learner has 'discovered' the sound being introduced, it is important to ask them to reproduce the sound and 'hear' the sound they make. This helps auditory discrimination which is important in spelling. Chapter 3 outlines how phonemes can be categorised according to how they are produced and where the sound is formed. That chapter also suggests a strategy to help the learner analyse speech production, for although local dialects and accents may affect pronunciation a learner can still be encouraged to 'match' the sound produced by the teacher.

Learners are introduced not to the terminology summarised at the end of Chapter 3 but they are asked to distinguish between voiced and unvoiced sounds (holding a hand to their 'Adam's apple' or throat will help here) and to be aware of the muscle movement (in lips, jaw, and tongue) that is needed to produce particular sounds. A small mirror held to the mouth will further reinforce feedback on pronunciation. This process involves kinaesthetic senses (muscles movement/speech production/putting hand to face/chin), auditory discrimination (self-voice and listening to the teacher's model), and visual senses (observing the position of the mouth and looking at a card with the letter on it or a wooden letter).

An example of this might be when the teacher introduces the voiced 'th' /t̲h̲/ as in 'this'. Learners will often confuse 'th' /t̲h̲' with /v/ (e.g., they may say 'muvver' for 'mother'). It is possible to exaggerate pronunciation by showing more tongue than is necessary in order to minimise confusion. Ask the learner to repeat the set of words below looking in a small mirror, listening for the sound in the beginning position, and to tell you what that sound is. Examples of words would be: this, those, their, they. Ask the learner to tell you how the sound is made and to say what the lips, tongue, or teeth are doing. Then ask whether the mouth is open (with nothing blocking the air) or is something blocking or partly blocking the air (you should expect the answer that the tongue and teeth are partly blocking). Finally ask them to touch their vocal cords and say whether it is voiced or unvoiced and then to tell you whether it is a vowel or a consonant.

## Stage 3 – Consolidating this New Knowledge

Depending on which channel has been used to introduce the phonogram there should be a follow-up using at least one other channel (e.g., if the learner has identified the sound by listening, then the written form of the letter is introduced and the learner is asked to track it, using a tracking sheet, or to find examples on a page of a book or magazine). Similarly, if it was introduced visually, then a 'listening for the 'sound' activity should be used (e.g., Where can you hear the sound /p/ in the following words?) The Beginning, Middle and End strategies described in Part III should be used here. In the case of having introduced the target phonogram through a tactile method, the follow-up should be introduced via the auditory and/or visual approaches described above.

## Stage 4 – Making a Reading Card

At this point a Reading Card should be made (see Figure 11.1), either using ready-cut cards that are commercially available (see Part V: Resources) or white or pale coloured card cut from an A4 sheet (about 7.4 cm by 5.0 cm per card will give 16 per sheet). Different coloured card can be used to distinguish vowels, consonants and blends, but if using white or a single colour these can be differentiated by putting coloured dots in a top corner of the cards.

A card should show the lower case phonogram in print in the middle of the front of the card with a smaller upper case letter printed in the bottom right-hand corner. The reason for this is to provide the learner with the form of the phonogram found in print (i.e., for reading). The upper case letter provides a 'memory prop' that is more consistent in form and direction. This is particularly important when considering letters such as b/d.

On the reverse, print the phoneme within two slashes (e.g., /s/) and a clue word – usually provided by the learner – which is a clear example of the sound being taught (e.g., for 's' choose 'sun' rather than a blend like 'snake'). The learner can then draw a picture of the clue word. It will be useful for the teacher to make a duplicate of the card to retain for future use because learners may 'forget' or lose cards. (As lessons proceed, the Reading Cards will form a Reading Pack which will be used for practice in each lesson as indicated in Chapter 9.)

The learner needs to rehearse the routine for a Reading Card by looking at the phonogram on the front and saying the sound and clue word aloud. They must then turn the card over to check whether they were correct by looking at the picture. (This is a different routine from some other dyslexia language schemes, but one that teachers have found learners to prefer.) However, where a learner chooses to say the clue word and *then* the sound this can be used instead. What is important here is to establish a routine which the learner can use comfortably and quickly as the aim is to establish automaticity through a speedy response.

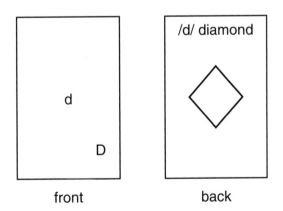

front         back

Figure 11.1 *Reading Card*

## Stage 5 – Cursive Writing of New Letters

At this stage, the learner is shown how to write the letter(s) using cursive writing. This will usually be done in a fairly large form, particularly with young children. One approach is to use a Handwriting Sheet (see Figure 11.2) by dividing a sheet of A4 paper into four boxes and drawing a horizontal line about two thirds of the way down the first three boxes.

## Box 1

The teacher prints the upper case form of the letter with the lower case form next to it. The teacher then demonstrates how to form the letter in cursive writing by starting on the line and tracing over the printed form and adding the joining stroke. Next to this (in the same box) the teacher shows how to form the letter, starting from the line. The learner then says the *sound* and traces over the letter, saying the name of the letter as they write (e.g., for 't' the learner says /t/ then traces over it while saying 't').

## Box 2

The teacher writes the cursive form, drawing attention to the starting point on the line, approach, and joining strokes and the relative size of the letter, including ascenders and descenders where appropriate. The learner writes the cursive letter next to the model, saying the sound and the letter name. (Note that if a learner has a handwriting difficulty, or shows difficulty in copying the letter, further practice can be given using some of the following: a sand or salt tray, a felt board or whiteboard, finger writing on a desk, tracing the letter(s) on corrugated cardboard or in the air (sky-writing), tracing over glitter glue letters, making a letter from plasticine or playdough.)

## Box 3

The top two boxes are covered and the learner is asked to write the letter from memory, saying the sound and then naming the letter aloud as they write.

| Teacher demonstrates. Learner copies. | Learner copies from model. |
|---|---|
| Learner writes from memory. | Learner writes with eyes closed. |

Figure 11.2   *Handwriting Sheet (normally on a sheet of A4)*

**Box 4**

The learner is asked to close their eyes and to write the letter in the last box, saying the sound and the name aloud as before. This is followed by practising on lined paper, giving guidance on spacing. (In the case of older learners, or those with reasonable writing, the 'handwriting' drill can be carried out using wide lined or ordinary lined paper.) The emphasis should be on writing fluently and legibly in order to aid the learner's spelling and compositional skills.

## Stage 6 – Making a Spelling Card

After teaching the cursive form of writing, a Spelling Card is made (see Figure 11.3). This is usually the same size as a Reading Card but will be used horizontally. If using coloured card this should be a different colour from that used for the Reading Cards. On the front of the card the phonogram can be written with the two lines to denote it represents a sound (e.g., /sh/ or /a/). Vowels should have a breve or macron to denote a long or short sound (see the Concept Cards in Part III). On the reverse of the card, it is common practice to draw a vertical line on the left-hand side, about 1 cm wide, to make a margin in which the phonogram is printed as on the front of the card. To the right of the line, the spelling of that sound is written in *cursive script*. As the learner works through the programme other ways of spelling the sound will be taught and added where appropriate. In this way, the learner can begin to appreciate 'spelling choices'. Attention should be drawn to spelling choices in relation to the position of that sound in words, using the terms Beginning, Middle, or End.

Figure 11.3    *Spelling Card*

## Stage 7 – SRR (Stimulus Response Routine)

This stage consolidates the learning from the previous stages in a multisensory routine which requires the learner to make links between the letter name, sound, clue word, and written form (cursive). We have found that learners will better understand the routine if they are given a visual prompt. One way to do this is to draw a large cross labelling the four points as the letter name, sound, clue word, and cursive writing.

Pictures can be inserted at each of these points to indicate a clue about the response to be made e.g., ear (for sound), learner's name/a label (for the letter name), a pen (for writing), and a question mark or magnifying glass (for the clue word). A card of about A5 size is appropriate. An example of an SRR card is given in Part V (Resources).

The routine is established by the teacher providing an example from one of the four areas (a *stimulus*) and the learner giving three responses. An example is:

- Teacher says 'hat' (clue word).
- Learner writes 'h' (cursive writing), says 'h' (letter name), and then says /h/ letter sound.
- The teacher then starts from another point and the learner responds by going 'clockwise' round the diagram from that point.

This routine is repeated until all four starting points have been used. It should be done very quickly to build up automaticity.

## Applying the New Learning

### Handwriting – Lesson Plan Item 7

Having practised the new phonogram, the learner is asked to join the letter to others learned previously, forming words where possible. The teacher models joining letters to build words, 'spelling' them aloud (i.e. naming the letters aloud while writing on paper or a whiteboard). The learner then practises this and is asked to read back the words they have written. As this is an opportunity to improve their handwriting skills, they can practise writing the same words repeatedly (and point to their 'best' example) or write different words using the target letters.

### Reading in Structure – Lesson Plan Item 8

Teachers should compose their own words, sentences, passages and stories, keeping within the structure taught to date. (Some examples of this are provided in Part III.) It is recommended that teachers share the fact that the structure limits what can be written in the early stages of the programme (e.g., by saying that it makes 'silly sentences'). At times the 'Shared Reading Approach' suggested in Chapter 8 can be used to overcome these limitations. It is also important for teachers to be fully aware of the nature of teaching 'in structure'. When, for example, 'i' 't' 'p' 'n' 's' and 'a' have been introduced the words pit, tap, nap, tin, sat, etc. can be used (if the 's' blends have been taught they can be included e.g., snap, spit, spat) *but not* words containing 'ai' as a vowel digraph (for example words like pain, paint, saint, etc.), as the diagraph will not have been introduced. Reading can be at 'word level', which could use Precision Teaching or a game such as Pairs or Bingo. It could also involve reading sentences or short passages. This can be varied by providing sentences on strips of cards that are read and sorted into sequence and then the whole passage or story is read. A similar approach to this would be to match sentences to pictures. Reading in structure enables a learner to read aloud with confidence because no phonogram is introduced in the reading material unless it has already been taught within the programme.

## Putting the New Learning into Writing – Lesson Plan Item 9

This usually involves a worksheet requiring the application of new learning to writing. An example could be a crossword or closure exercise where the missing letters are the new phonogram. An example of an onset-rime exercise which meets this need would be where there is a choice of onset (e.g., sp-, st-, sn-) and the rime is –ap. The learner will first have to blend them in turn (orally) to decide whether they have made a real word or non-word and will then write down the words that are 'real'. This approach can be used with cards, two piece jigsaws etc. where the learner writes out only the real words they have made.

## Spelling in Structure – Lesson Plan Item 10

### Spelling regular words
Normally the SOS (Simultaneous Oral Spelling) is used for regular words as follows:

- Teacher says the target word (e.g., rink) while the learner looks closely at the teacher's mouth.
- Learner repeats this aloud – 'rink'.
- Learner names the letters in word aloud – 'r' 'i' 'n' 'k'.
- Learner writes the word, naming the letters aloud as they do so.
- Learner looks at and reads the word aloud.
- Learner checks the word against a model (proofreading).

### Spelling irregular words
Although words containing the vowel digraph 'ai' are not used in the early stages of the programme the word 'said' might be taught as it is a common key word. The routine used for irregular words is an adapted version of the SOS.

- Teacher shows model of the word and reads it to learner (e.g., 'said').
- Teacher asks the learner to repeat it aloud.
- Teacher asks the learner to highlight the 'tricky bit' (letters which do not conform to a phonically regular structure e.g., 'ai').

- Learner traces over the word, naming each letter aloud (this could be repeated three or four times).
- Learner covers the word. Then says the word. Then names the letters aloud from memory.
- Learner writes the word from memory, naming each letter aloud as they do so. Looks at the whole word 'to check'.
- Learner checks spelling with the model.

(Note that other approaches to teaching spelling of irregular words are considered in Chapter 12, with examples of methods in Part V: Resources.)

## Dictation – Lesson Plan Item 11

If the routine is followed correctly, dictation will provide another opportunity for developing auditory memory skills. Dictation requires additional skills to those necessary for spelling individual words and it is therefore important that new phonograms have been read and written in single words before being embedded in dictation. The length of a dictation passage and mode of dictating should relate to a learner's auditory memory. Dictation passages will usually become longer and more complex as the programme develops. Where appropriate, two syllable (and longer) words should be included when they have been consolidated in reading.

### Routine
An example from the early stages of the programme is:

i Teacher asks learner to look at them as they speak and says the sentence, 'I tip it in'.
ii Learner repeats the sentence aloud, 'I tip it in'.
iii Teacher checks for accuracy. Where the dictated sentence/passage is too long for the learner's working memory it can be further divided (e.g., 'I tip', 'it in').
iv Learner writes the sentence, *not* naming individual letters but saying each word aloud as they start to write it.
v Teacher repeats the sentence and the learner points to each word as said, to check that none have been missed or added.
vi Learner proofreads the sentence (making sure that they look at each word carefully). Teacher uses their discretion whether or not to indicate any errors.
vii Teacher prompts the learner to check their punctuation.
viii Learner reads the sentence aloud. (The teacher should establish 'read back what you have written' as a regular habit so that the learner will read back what they have written in class to make sure it makes sense as well as to check the spelling.)
ix Learner checks their work, word by word, with the model and 'marks' their work (word by word in the case of young learners).
x Misspellings are corrected using the SOS routine.

# Introducing Concept Cards

Some lessons will explicitly teach concepts which can help learners to understand and use the metalanguage and structures of language and literacy. These concepts are reinforced by the use of Concepts of Literacy Cards (hereafter called Concept Cards), which should also be revisited from time to time in order to reinforce a learner's understanding.

The concepts to be taught are listed in the Programme Structure Table in Part III and each is identified as a separate Teaching Point. While we would recommend introducing the concepts in the sequence given, teachers can modify the order (particularly of the first ten concepts) and the pace at which they teach them to meet individual learning needs.

## What is a Concept Card?

A card depicts a symbol or abbreviation representing a concept/aspect of language and literacy. On the reverse side of the card is a definition or information about the concept. Often a Concept Card makes explicit a concept/rule/aspect of literacy which many of us have internalised or 'picked up' as a result of our tacit knowledge of language and literacy – particularly if we have not experienced difficulties in acquiring spoken language and literacy skills.

These cards are 'standard' to the programme and not individually made for learners, so a teacher can prepare a set in advance and use them for any learner. We have found it useful to produce these on coloured card about 10 cm by 7 cm (larger than the Reading and Spelling Cards). This means that eight cards can be made from one A4 sheet of card. Having produced a 'top copy' set these can then be reproduced more easily when necessary. Laminating (using a matt finish material) will prolong their use!

The cards are numbered sequentially in the bottom right-hand corner (a CC number) and a reference is given to the Teaching Point in the Programme Structure Table in the top left-hand corner (a TP number). This is for the teacher's information only. A list of the Concept Cards required can be found in Part III, Table 2, and downloadable materials are available on the website. Suggestions for symbols and definitions are given, but teachers are welcome to devise their own. Definitions should be clear and short where possible.

The purpose of the Concept Cards is to reinforce and review/revise literacy concepts.

## Introducing a Concept

Normally only one concept will be introduced in a lesson, but sometimes (as will be illustrated below) two, three, or even more related concepts may be taught. Teachers can adjust how many concepts they introduce according to the knowledge and understanding presented by a learner.

Sometimes a card will be introduced by showing the symbol and the teacher reading the definition. The concept is then illustrated by examples and activities whereby the learner can demonstrate understanding. We would recommend, however, that concepts should usually be taught using a *guided discovery* process, because although this may take longer, learners will tend to remember and *understand* the concept better if they have been actively engaged in the learning process. Guided discovery usually involves a teacher presenting examples of a concept (either orally or in writing or both) and guiding the learner through 'leading' questions to 'discover' a fact/rule/concept that underpins some aspect of language/literacy. At this point the teacher can then produce a Concept Card to reinforce this learning, explaining clearly the significance of the symbol or abbreviation which encapsulates or serves as a 'reminder' about the concept and then reading the clear, simple definition statement which is on the reverse.

*(Note that there is no expectation that the learner should memorise or recall the definitions and this should be made clear to them. What is important is that they can demonstrate their understanding in practice.)*

## Examples

Two examples of introducing a concept using guided discovery are provided below. They should be seen as offering guidance to teachers who can adapt them appropriately using the principle of 'guided discovery'.

### Introducing base word and suffix (two concepts)

The teacher asks the learner to listen and repeat the following pairs of words (use words in structure)

| | |
|---|---|
| pit | pits |
| tap | taps |
| nip | nips |

and then asks a leading question e.g., 'What was different in each pair?' 'What sound did I add to each of the first words?'

If the learner finds it difficult, each pair should be repeated separately until the answer is /s/. Then the teacher writes the words (on paper or a small whiteboard) and asks the learner to look at the first word in each column, asking, 'Are they complete words themselves?' (Further questions should be asked if the learner is uncertain.) The teacher then tells them they are called *base* words and that, 'A base word is a complete word that makes sense by itself'.

The teacher shows them the relevant Concept Card and explains that there is a symbol on the front to remind them of a concept.

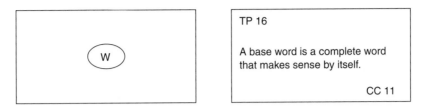

Figure 11.4   *Example of a Concept Card*

The symbol is explained e.g., 'W is used for a word' (already introduced as a concept) 'and it is in a circle here to show it is complete in itself'. The reverse of the card defines or gives information.

At this stage the teacher points to the '*s*' on each word on the paper/board and asks what was added to the word (asking for the *name* of the letter if the learner only gives the sound.). The teacher explains that when we add a letter or group of letters to the end of a word which changes the *meaning* or use of the word, we have added a *suffix*, and states clearly,

> 'A suffix is a letter or letters added to the end of a base word. A suffix changes the meaning of the word and or usage of a word.'

The teacher then explains the symbols used by drawing on the paper/board e.g. (W) as before and add a box to represent a letter or letters. This means the same Card can be used to introduce other suffixes (e.g., –ing, -ly). At this point the Concept Card for a suffix can be shown. The symbol shows the complete word and a box beside it to show some letter(s) added to change its meaning.

Note that in the case of the suffix 's' many learners may be confused and think that a lot of words ending in 's' are examples of a suffix. It is important to clear up any

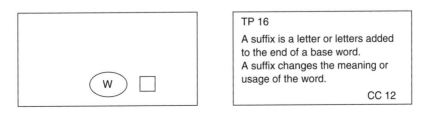

Figure 11.5   *Example of a Concept Card for a Suffix*

potential misunderstanding at this stage by providing examples of words ending in 's' where sometimes the 's' is a suffix and sometimes not, e.g., the words:

<blockquote>
is        lass        nips        laps        taps        us
</blockquote>

These can be written on the whiteboard or card, and the learner told that sometimes 's' is a suffix and sometimes not. The teacher asks which words have a suffix, offering guidance so that if the learner is not sure whether or not the 's' is a suffix, the final 's' can be covered to see if what remains is a complete word. Other written examples can be used if necessary, including words *out of structure* (which the teacher reads to them), for example:

<blockquote>
kiss        pins        focus        sips        spins
</blockquote>

The teacher asks the learner to cover the final 's' and say whether it is a suffix and if it *is* what the base word is. The Suffix Concept Card is shown again, and the learner is told that so far they have learned suffix 's' but later they will learn other suffixes, so the box is left empty.

## Introducing vowels

The concept of vowels is introduced when teaching the first vowel 'i'. Usually the short vowel sound is taught first /ĭ/ and the longer sound /ī/ is introduced later, although for some learners, particularly older ones, it may be appropriate to introduce both in the same lesson. This section deals only with the short sound /ĭ/ which will have been introduced through Discovery Learning as an initial and/or middle sound. The learner is asked whether or not it is an *open* sound i.e., nothing is blocking the air. They should then touch their vocal chords while saying /ĭ/ to see whether or not they can feel vibrations. The teacher tells them that when vibrations occur we say the sound is *voiced*. Open, voiced sounds are called *vowels*.

The teacher then shows them the vowel Concept Card (6), reading the definition, and continues teaching the phonogram for 'i' as in the guidance given earlier in this chapter using the short vowel form. If they wish to, the teacher can introduce the

<table>
<tr>
<td>

V

</td>
<td>

TP 7<br>
Vowel sounds are open with nothing blocking the air and are voiced sounds.<br>
  There is a vowel in every syllable.<br>
CC 6

</td>
</tr>
</table>

Figure 11.6    *Concept Card for a Vowel*

Concept Cards for breve (CC16) and macron (CC17) now rather than later and although one Reading Card can show both /ĭ/ and /ī/ there will have to be two Spelling Cards.

## Reviewing/Revising Literacy Concept Cards

Some concepts need regular review and application. To do this the teacher shows the front of the Concept Card to the learner and asks them what it reminds them about. The teacher then reads the definition/statement on the reverse of the card. (Although learners are not required to repeat or memorise definitions we have found that some do begin to repeat the statement with the teacher – this is all right, but *not* necessary.) Older learners may *choose* to learn the definitions. Using the terms aids metacognition. A Concept Card should be reviewed regularly when first introduced and, after a while, only revisited when appropriate to the main Teaching Point of a lesson or where a learner has made 'a mistake', which could indicate that they have forgotten or not really understood a concept.

## Lesson Planning Based on Teaching Concepts

Some lessons (such as the first one or two) will introduce more than one concept and sometimes a concept may be introduced in the same lesson as a phonogram. However, there will be some occasions when the main focus of the lesson is the introduction of a concept (such as the suffix 's' or a syllable). In this case, using guided Discovery Learning to teach a *concept* becomes Item 6 (the new Teaching Point) of the lesson. Follow-up may involve tracking (if appropriate) and putting the new learning into writing, dictation, structured reading and games, but there will be no new Reading or Spelling Card and no 'Handwriting' as such. Teachers should include as many of the lesson items as are appropriate in order to ensure that the learner has understood the concept.

# Practice and Revision in Lessons

Every lesson should include time to practise the reading and spelling of phonograms using the Reading and Spelling Cards.

## Using the Reading Cards Lesson Plan Item 4

Each time a new phonogram has been introduced the Reading Card is added to the Reading Pack which the learner keeps to practise daily at home and/or school following the same as used routine in the lessons.

### The Reading Pack Routine

  i  Shuffle the cards.
 ii  Learner holds the cards in their hand with the front of card uppermost.
iii  Learner looks at the front, says the sound and clue word (e.g., /p/ pot).
 iv  Learner turns the card to check using the picture. If correct, it is placed on the table. If incorrect, it is placed at the back of the pack.
     (An alternative method is to have two cards – YES and NO – and to place the Reading Card on the appropriate pile, going over the 'No' pile until correct or re-taught.)

The aim is to build automaticity and speed, so using a timer can be useful in the lesson to allow the learner to chart their progress against their 'best personal speed'. (The aim of one second per card may take some time to achieve but this is a good goal.)

## Using the Spelling Cards

A pack of Spelling Cards will also be built up over lessons but not usually taken home for practice. Each lesson, however, contain the Spelling Pack Routine.

### The Spelling Pack Routine

  i  Teacher holds the Spelling Pack face up.
 ii  Teacher says the sound on the front of the first card (e.g., /sp/).
iii  Learner repeats the sound and spells it by naming the letter(s) i.e., the learner's response is /sp/ 's' 'p'.
 iv  Learner says the sound and then names the letter(s) while writing the cursive forms.
  v  Teacher turns over the card so that the learner can check against the model.
 vi  The routine is repeated for each card.

As alternative spellings arise in the structured programme these are added to the appropriate Spelling Card. (Part III shows how and where these are to be added.) The routine has to be adapted so that, for example, on the /k/ Spelling Card step iii in the routine. The learner's response might be /k/ 'c', /k/ 'k', /k/ 'ck' (and others) and similarly will write these in step iv.

*(Note that when the packs become large, cards which represent phonograms which are well-known should be removed and only included from time to time to check they are well established.)*

## Follow-up Activities

Lessons should normally provide a learner with follow-up activities for practice and overlearning. These should be in addition to practising the Reading Pack routine. Some activities may be designed for independent learning (whether undertaken in school or at home) e.g., tracking sheets, alphabet dot-to dot, or other kinds of worksheet; others may involve interaction with peers or an adult (a teaching assistant or parent/carer who wishes to be involved) e.g., games, alphabet arc activities, or shared reading. The use of ICT should be encouraged e.g., for practising spelling using games and word lists as in Wordshark 3 and 4, Nesssy, and Starspell. In this digital age every effort should be made to use ICT for follow–up work, especially if it has not been incorporated in specialist lessons. Learners should be taught how to use ICT in a multisensory way in order to gain maximum benefit.

### Summary

This chapter has described how to deliver the Teaching Points listed in the Conquering Literacy programme, concentrating on introducing them as new learning. Particular attention is paid to the use of guided Discovery Learning in introducing phonograms and concepts. The recommended methods emphasise multisensory learning and the development of automaticity. Practitioners are also reminded of the need for follow-up activities for practice and overlearning. This is, therefore, a key chapter in understanding how to use the activities described in the programme and devise additional tasks and resources which adhere to the underlying principles and strategies of the programme.

# CHAPTER 12

# THE ROLE OF MEMORY IN THE PROGRAMME

## Chapter Overview

This chapter discusses the role of memory in the programme and gives practical examples of strategies and activities that can be included in lessons. The Conquering Literacy programme aims to develop short-term memory skills in two ways:

- Through structure and routines.
- Through direct memory training.

## Structure and Routines

The automaticity deficit theory outlined in Chapter 1 (Nicolson and Fawcett, 2008) points to the need for numerous exposures to a stimulus (e.g., the printed word) before it can be stored in long-term memory and retrieved quickly on demand. The amount of overlearning required for a learner with dyslexia (see the square root rule in Chapter 1) to achieve automaticity is often difficult to attain in the normal everyday teaching of literacy. In the Conquering Literacy programme the development of automatic responses is achieved through the structure of the programme itself (by ensuring sufficient exposure to the material being learned) and the routines built into the lessons (which aim to improve speed of retrieval).

Because each element of the lesson develops automaticity, we recommend that *all* the routines should be included in a lesson of one hour's duration or within two half hour lessons, etc. If some routines are regularly missed out then it is unlikely automaticity will be achieved. Time management is important and the teacher must be careful not to overplan some activities at the expense of others. It is better to include fewer examples and practise all the routines than to include numerous examples and only manage a few of the routines.

The routines themselves are described in the previous chapter. These should be followed precisely as they have been designed to ensure that correct information goes into working memory and is stored in long-term memory. An explanation of why it is necessary to deliver the routines in a particular way is provided in the following two examples, which analyse the spelling and dictation routines in relation to the theory of storage and retrieval described in Chapter 2.

i   In the spelling routine (SOS) the teacher asks the learner to repeat a word before spelling it. This is to check that the learner has heard the word correctly, eliminating auditory discrimination problems and giving the correct stimulus. The learner then spells the word orally, saying the letter names before writing it down, allowing the teacher to check that the learner has analysed the sounds within the word correctly before pen or pencil is put to paper: this therefore avoids incorrect memory traces being built up. If the learner is hesitant or slow to recall the sequence of letters, they can be asked to repeat it several times so that the sequence is verbally rehearsed – thus keeping it in working memory long enough to be written down. The learner then writes down the spelling, naming the letters as they do so. This helps to strengthen the association between letter names and shapes, making more permanent associations within the brain and enabling the storage and retrieval of information to become more automatic. Verbalisation is an important strategy and a key element of all multisensory routines.

ii  The dictation routine also includes verbalisation but in a different way from the spelling routine. Sentences are selected on the basis of an individual learner's working memory capacity. If the learner can only hold four units of information then sentences of three or four words in length will normally be used (with older learners teachers may prefer to break a longer sentence down into chunks of three or four words).

The teacher gives the sentence or phrase and the learner repeats it before writing it. This allows the teacher to check that the learner has heard it correctly and that the sentence is not too long for the learner to hold in their working memory. The learner then writes the sentence down saying each word as they write it, enabling the sentence to be kept on the working memory shelf long enough to be completed (to name each letter as in the spelling routine would cause memory overload). Once the learner has written the sentence down, the teacher repeats the sentence and then asks the learner to check that all the words are there. If some are omitted this suggests that the learner was unable to keep the sentence in their working memory long enough to write it down: a note should be made of this difficulty so that it can be addressed in the memory training sessions. (The next dictated sentence should be broken down into shorter units and possibly rehearsed.) The learner then proofreads the sentence, checking for punctuation and that the spelling looks correct. This gives the learner the opportunity to spot any incorrect spellings for themselves, thus giving them more control over their own learning. The sentence is finally read back and checked against a correct model (on a piece of card or paper). If a spelling error has occurred then the incorrectly spelled word should be practised several times using the spelling routine. This enables a memory trace for the correct spelling to be established and strengthened. If the spelling is left uncorrected then the wrong memory trace may be accessed in future lessons.

Although this routine may appear rather lengthy it is important to adhere to it and not to omit any of the stages, so that the learner has the best chance of success. With practice their speed will improve and they will need fewer reminders of the stages, engaging in them without hesitation and developing fluency and automaticity.

## Memory Training

Memory problems are the most consistently reported area of difficulty in learners with dyslexia. The theory discussed in Chapter 2 suggests that phonological deficits result in limitations in verbal short-term memory, verbal naming, and repetition (see Snowling, 2008). Learners with dyslexia may have a normal memory span for visual information but remember fewer verbal items than expected for their age. Their general level of performance on memory tests has been found to be as good as that of reading-age matched learners but they show impairment when compared with age-matched peers. The average working memory capacity in adults is considered to be seven items (+ or − two) and they can often hold onto information for 15–30 seconds. For learners with dyslexia working memory capacity is reduced as well as the length of time information can be held.

## Improving Working and Long-term Memory

Improving the memory improves motivation. Working memory skills can be developed in learners with dyslexia through teaching strategies to facilitate the holding of information in working memory. Key to this are:

- Metacognition – in this case understanding what it is that helps one to remember/recall information.
- Being actively involved through using different senses.
- Using verbal rehearsal (to keep information in working memory).
- Being given clear and correct information to avoid setting up an incorrect memory trace.
- Strategies based on patterns (e.g., using onset and rime to teach spelling patterns).
- Reducing memory load by 'chunking' information: spelling sequences in two or more chunks, as we do with telephone numbers (e.g., 0111-288-3990).
- Ensuring new knowledge is keyed into previous learning/knowledge.
- Taking into account the 'forgetting curve' or the primary and recency effect mentioned in Chapter 2 in planning activities (i.e., the middle section of a string of information gets lost more easily), present information in shorter chunks and repeat as necessary.
- Using alternative techniques for information that is beyond memory capacity. For examples see Chapter 13 on Study Skills.
- Practice for 'real life' enables the learner to apply the strategies they have learned to classroom and examination situations.

## Memory Training Routines

Two memory training routines should be built into lesson plans. These are outlined below:

i   *Auditory Sequential Memory Routine*

The teacher prepares a set of cards containing letter strings of three to seven letters in length (e.g., AFK). If upper case letters are being used for alphabet work then at first the letter strings should be written in upper case. Memory training usually starts with three letter strings and gradually builds over a period of lessons. For auditory memory training it is better to avoid having letters that rhyme in the same string (e.g., D and E) as this can cause confusion in the early stages.

The teacher reads the letter string on the card, presenting the letters at one second intervals (*note that practice will be needed to get the timing correct – if the teacher repeats the letter silently inside their head this will usually allow about a one second interval*). The learner repeats the letter string (several times if necessary) and then takes the letters out of the alphabet arc (naming them) or writes them in their book (naming them). The learner then checks their answer with the string on the card. If at any point they make a mistake the teacher should ask them to listen again and allow them to rehearse the string as many times as necessary to enable them to place it on the working memory shelf.

ii  *Visual Sequential Memory Routine*

A separate pack of cards is made for visual memory training, using letter strings that have visually distinct letter shapes and avoiding similar letters (e.g., C and G). The teacher gives the learner the card and allows them to take control of the length of time needed to memorise it. When the learner feels confident, the card is given back to the teacher and the learner takes the letters out of the alphabet arc naming them. The letter string is then checked against the model as before. The teacher should discuss with the learner how they memorised the letter string. They may need to be taught strategies such as visualisation (where they close their eyes and imagine it being on a whiteboard), chunking (splitting the string into two or more sections), verbal rehearsal (repeating the string to themselves while looking at the visual representation), or tracing the string on the table with their finger.

If visual memory is a strength, the teacher may question whether it is necessary to include this memory routine. The advantage of still teaching the routine is that it will enable the learner to understand how they can use their strengths to improve their learning.

## Supporting Activities

### Using wooden letters and the alphabet arc

The following activities can be used with the training of both visual and auditory sequential memory. They are in order of difficulty and the learner should be proficient at one level before moving on to the next.
The teacher:

- Gives the learner a sequence of letters in *alphabetical* order, starting with three and gradually building up to seven. Letter strings are presented verbally for auditory memory training and in written form for visual memory training. The learner should take the letters out of the arc immediately after hearing or seeing them.
- Gives a sequence of letters in *alphabetical* order and asks the learner to wait for a short time before taking them out, starting with a time lag of five seconds and gradually building up to 30 seconds.

- Gives a sequence of letters in *reverse* order, starting with three and gradually building up to seven. The learner takes the letters out of the arc in reverse order and rearranges them in alphabetical order. The next step is to present the letters in reverse order and the learner takes them out in alphabetical order. In this activity, the learner must hold the sequence in their working memory while reversing the sequence.
- Gives a sequence of letters in a *jumbled order*, starting with three and gradually building up to seven, and the learner takes them out of the arc in the given order. The next step is to present letters in a jumbled order and the learner takes them out of the arc in alphabetical order. Again the learner has to hold the sequence in their working memory while reordering them.
- Gives an instruction for an action (e.g., close the door, read a sentence, write the date) or asks a question, followed by a sequence of letters, starting with three and gradually building up to seven. The learner must perform the action/answer the question and then take the letters out of the arc in the order they were presented. This is known as putting in a 'distractor'. The learner has to hold on to the sequence while performing an action that may interfere with that information. This simulates everyday experiences in the classroom and provides an opportunity for teaching effective strategies such as verbalisation or visualisation.

## Pencil and paper activities

Sometimes an alphabet activity can be planned that does not involve using the wooden letters. In this case memory training could be done using pencil and paper.

- The same activities are involved as above but the learner writes down the sequence of letters.
- Number sequences or mathematical symbols could be given instead of letters.
- The teacher could demonstrate joining dots together in a particular sequence using a grid of nine dots arranged in three rows of three. The learner must then reproduce the pattern in the same order/direction as was demonstrated. The length and complexity of the pattern are gradually increased (e.g., start with L, Z, M Δ then build up to more complex patterns such as Ŧ Σ Ƕ).
- The learner is asked to remember a sequence of similar letters (e.g., pdp) and write it down.

## Colour sequences

Another alternative to using alphabet letters is the use of colour sequences. These could be used to train memory for patterns in Mathematics (early algebra) – use as appropriate at primary level.

- A sequence of two colours is given and gradually built up to five or six colours. The child is shown the colour sequence on card or told a sequence of colours orally and then asked to make it using unifix bricks.

- A colour sequence is given as above but the child is asked to make it using coloured pegs or paper clips. (This will also help to develop fine motor skills.)
- A colour sequence is given and the child is asked to rehearse the sequence and hold it in their working memory while they colour in circles to recreate the sequence.
- A sequence is given involving shape and colour and the child is asked to make the sequence using geometric shapes or to use pencil and paper to draw and colour the shapes.

### Picture cards

Pictures can be used to develop auditory and visual memory. An example would be to use common street furniture (e.g., a post box, telephone box, supermarket).

- The child is asked to look at a sequence of pictures or listen to a verbal sequence of things they might see going to school. The learner then says 'On the way to school I went past … ', setting out the pictures in the correct order.
- The child is asked to look at a sequence of pictures or listen to a verbal sequence of things they might see going to school. The learner then reverses the order by saying 'On the way home from school I went past … ', setting out the pictures in reverse order. Build up gradually from three pictures to seven pictures.

### Memory games

- Auditory memory games such as 'I went to market … ' can be used to practise the alphabet; extend vocabulary by using categories (e.g., types of birds, etc.).
- Visual memory games such as pelmanism can be used to practise syllables, spelling rules, onset and rime, etc.

### Using instructions

- The teacher gives a sequence of instructions for the learner to carry out, beginning with simple instructions and then building these up in complexity.
- The teacher gives a sequence of actions to be copied or followed, using positional language, left/right, etc.

Many of the strategies being taught in this part of the lesson can be applied in the classroom. One example is the teaching of irregular spellings. Multisensory routines involve a visual, auditory, and tactile/kinaesthetic input to memory, but in differing amounts. In teaching spelling, the teacher can take into account a learner's strengths and difficulties by choosing the approaches that work best for them. If visual memory is stronger than auditory memory then approaches which emphasise visualisation could be considered (e.g., neurolinguistic programming or picture links). If the learner often uses strategies such as 'tracing' to support their working memory in the memory training sessions they may benefit from approaches that ensure strong tactile and kinaesthetic input into memory. For examples of different ways of teaching spelling see Part V (Resources). Strategies for remembering that are developed in the structured lessons can also be applied to learning new material and revising for exams. This is discussed in the next chapter on study skills.

## Summary

In developing literacy skills learners with dyslexia will need a lot more repetition and overlearning than those without dyslexia in order to transfer information into their long-term memory and be able to recall it again quickly. The chapter includes methods for memory training, both auditory sequential and visual sequential, using routines and a range of activities. It emphasises the use of verbalisation (which includes sub-vocalisation) and visualisation. The point is made that many of the strategies used for memory training can be applied in general classroom teaching. Importantly, the chapter suggests ways in which the practitioner can individualise work to build on each learner's strengths to improve their retention and recall.

## References

Nicolson, R.I. and Fawcett, A.J. (2008) 'Learning, cognition and dyslexia'. In Reid, G., Fawcett, A.J., Manis, F. and Siegel, L.S. (eds), *The Sage Handbook of Dyslexia*. London: Sage. pp. 192–211.

Snowling, M. J. (2008) 'Specific disorders and broader phenotypes: The case of dyslexia', *The Quarterly Journal of Experimental Psychology*, 61 (1): 142–156.

# CHAPTER 13

# STUDY SKILLS WITHIN THE PROGRAMME

## Chapter Overview

Literature on study skills often considers that the audience will be students in secondary or further and higher education, but the development of good study skills should start much earlier than this – in the primary school. There are a number of study skills where learners with dyslexia will need support. These include: time management and organisation, memory, reading and writing, note taking, essay planning and exam revision (see the BDA website). This chapter considers how these can be developed through the structured lessons in the programme.

Some aspects can be worked on from the very early stages (for example the fostering of independence and organisational skills) by encouraging learners to set out and organise their equipment, produce their own Record Sheet to record their progress, and so on. Once reading has developed to a stage where learners can manage whole texts then structured reading can be used to develop a range of higher order literacy skills.

# Higher Order Reading Skills

There are three different methods of reading for information and the purpose of the reading task will influence which one is used.

i  *Skimming*

This involves reading the passage quickly to get an overall impression of the content. It is used when the reader needs a general idea of the content or if they have to check if it contains the type of information they want.

ii  *Scanning*

Scanning requires the reader to run their eyes quickly along a line of print or down a page of text to search for information. This is used to find a particular fact or detail.

iii  *Close Reading*

In this an entire passage is read very carefully, thinking about the content. The purpose is to obtain as much information as possible and to understand it fully.

The magnocellular deficit theory proposes that dyslexia may be caused by an impaired magnocellular system which affects the way the eyes move across a page of text. In a reading task the eyes must move very quickly from one letter to the next or one word to the next. The magnocellular system has an important role in controlling these movements or *saccades* (see Stein, 2008). In addition, it is believed that the magnocellular system plays a crucial role in stabilising the eyes during fixations on a word between saccades, keeping them still long enough to recognise the word. The theory suggests that if the eyes are unstable and stray from the letter or word being fixated then the text can appear to blur or move around. The implication is that learners with impaired visual magnocellular systems are likely to find it more difficult to skim the text quickly to get an overall impression of content, to track along sentences scanning for particular information and to engage in close reading, without omitting words or phrases or producing reading errors by mis-sequencing the letters in words. They may benefit from having texts enlarged slightly and double spaced to avoid one line merging into another. Printing the text on pastel-coloured paper may help to reduce the glare that can be produced by black print on white paper (sometimes referred to as Irlen's syndrome, see Irlen, 1991), thus reducing visual distortions.

*Structured passages* can be used to practise and develop higher order reading skills in more than one place in the lesson (e.g., as a revision exercise using a reading passage for the previous Teaching Point or as a reading/writing activity to practise new learning).

Examples of activities are given below.

- Skimming skills can be developed by giving the learner a 'set time' to skim the passage (the time span can be reduced gradually as their skills improve) and then tell the teacher what it is about, draw a picture of the events, or write down five or six key information-carrying words that convey the content of the text. They will need to be taught how to identify key information-carrying words (e.g., looking for capital letters to find the names of people and places).

- Scanning skills can be developed in the early stages of the programme by using a passage to track the new phonogram introduced in that lesson. Later on the teacher can ask the learner to look for and highlight specific information, such as dates, characters, or events.

- Close reading can be encouraged by asking the learner to read the passage carefully and then retell the story, recalling as much detail as they can. (The teacher could have a list of details they want them to recall and the learner scores a point for each one.)

# Reading for Meaning

Structured passages should also be used to develop the ability to read for meaning using 'reading for meaning' techniques that are used for all learners, but always ensuring that these are 'in structure' and employ multisensory approaches. Teaching 'reading for meaning' is particularly important for learners with dyslexia for whom English is an Additional Language. However, many of the activities suggested below are relevant to all learners in establishing good study skills.

## Text Completion

Text completion (closure procedure) encourages learners to read to the end of the sentence to determine an unknown or missing word. Sentences are written 'in structure' with words omitted (e.g., He intends to stop the ___ at ten). The learner is asked to complete the sentence using one of the words the teacher has provided at the top of a worksheet.

## Sequencing

After the learner has read a structured passage, the text is cut up into three or four sections and they are asked to put it in the correct order and then read it back.

## Prediction

The learner reads the first part of a story or passage where the end has been concealed and predicts what will happen next. They must then continue reading to discover the ending given in the text.

## Drawing Inferences from the Text

This involves asking questions where the learner has to infer the answer rather than look for it in the text. For example, they may be asked to infer what the weather is like from the way a character is dressed.

## Table Completion or Construction

After reading the structured passage the learner is asked to look for particular information, for example to list all the foods mentioned in a passage, sort them into fruits and vegetables, and then write them in the correct column in a table on a worksheet.

## Diagram Completion

A partially labelled diagram is given which the learner must complete using information from the structured passage (e.g., a drawing of a treasure map, a diagram of the eye, or a plant).

## Vocabulary

The learner is asked to illustrate given words from the passage to show their meaning, for example:

tiny, big, narrow, **thick** $u^n{}_e v^e n$

Many learners may enjoy bringing their talents to bear on this activity.

## Dictionary or Thesaurus Work

The learner should use a dictionary to check the meaning of any obscure words in a passage. Alternatively they may be asked to substitute words with a similar meaning to given words in a passage using a thesaurus.

Some activities give practice in more than one skill allowing more time to be allocated to the activity on the lesson plan. For example, the time allocated to dictionary skills and structured reading can be combined if the learner is asked to look up some of the words from the passage, as this activity contains two of the elements of a basic lesson. A total of 15 minutes could then be allocated to the task instead of ten minutes for dictionary work and five minutes for structured reading.

# Writing Skills

The skill of note-taking can be developed through the dictation routine which is a key element of the basic lesson. The length of sentences should gradually increase as the learner works through the programme until one or more paragraphs are given. With older learners it may be preferable to give longer sentences than can be held in working memory, breaking them down into shorter phrases, in order to make the task more age appropriate.

Note-making, as opposed to note-taking, involves being able to recognise which are the important points to be noted. These need to be teased out from text or speech that includes many superfluous words. Activities such as highlighting the key information-carrying words in a passage (see revision techniques) in order to make notes are a starting point in developing this skill and can be incorporated into the reading and writing section of the lesson plan. Making notes in a lecture or lesson for revision purposes is a more difficult skill as a learner cannot go back to check they have noted the salient points as they can with a piece of text. Also notes need to be made quickly in a form that will be comprehensible later. A recorded conversation or reading of a passage can be used to practise this skill and the learner asked to jot down the main points. If mind-mapping techniques have been taught (see the next section) then the learner can draw upon those skills to develop their own form of shorthand (including the use of symbols). Identifying and recalling key points for note-making is an activity that can be practised in the slot allocated on the lesson plan for memory training with older learners at the more advanced stages.

## Essay/Assignment Writing

Essay writing is an activity that requires learners to multi-task. The automaticity deficit hypothesis gives an explanation of why learners with dyslexia find it particularly difficult to multi-task. Essay writing involves a number of skills including: sequencing ideas, sentence construction, retrieval of learned spellings, analysis of words (where spelling is insecure), use of punctuation, and correct letter formation including letter joins. These skills are explicitly taught and practised within the programme to enable learners to develop automaticity and to 'free up' enough working memory to create ideas. Proofreading skills are also developed through the dictation routine. This is an important skill in helping learners not only to check that spelling and punctuation are correct but also to make sure the work they have produced makes sense. Often learners with dyslexia will go off the point and produce long rambling sentences or omit part of a sentence, thus making it difficult for a reader to follow. Drafting assignments or essays is particularly important here but learners need to be taught how to do this.

In producing a first draft, many learners employ a range of strategies (some of which will have been taught and some of which they invent) that may not be available to learners with dyslexia. Some learners will use a symbol to indicate something is missing (e.g., the insert symbol '^') or if the phrase omitted is too long to insert they may write it in the margin with an arrow to show where it should go; where a long sentence has been omitted they may write it at the end and use an asterisk to denote its position; if several phrases or sentences are omitted then the asterisks may be numbered, and so on. Many learners, however, and especially those with dyslexia, do not acquire such strategies readily and therefore they must be explicitly taught. This can happen within the structured lessons but must also be practised – for example, as homework.

# Revision Techniques

Learners with dyslexia may need extra help in learning how to revise for tests or examinations. During the delivery of a structured programme teachers have an opportunity to explore with learners which strategies work best for them, so that they can begin to understand the techniques that can be used for revision (metacognition). Some activities that could be tried are as follows.

- Discussing with the learner which words in a passage actually convey the meaning (surprisingly few!). A teacher could ask the learner to read the passage and highlight the key information-carrying or 'recall' words. In the next lesson they could ask that learner to memorise the key 'recall' words using the strategies suggested below and then rewrite the passage. They should then compare it to the original text to make sure that they have not omitted any salient fact. This teaches the learner a technique that can be used for exam revision, as memorising a few key recall words places less demand on their memory than trying to remember a whole page of text.
- Teaching mind-mapping may be useful for learners with good visualisation skills (see Buzan, 2002, 2003, 2006). The teacher may need to support the learner in deciding what to put on the main branches (e.g., characters, plot, scene, ending, etc.) and then ask them to mind-map details from a structured story onto the sub-branches. The learner should be encouraged to use symbols and pictures as memory aids. For example, the word 'character' could be represented by a drawing of a pirate. In a follow-up lesson the learner could be asked to retell the story/passage or rewrite it from the mind-map. This is a technique that can be used later to revise for exams. Several software packages are now available for producing mind-maps on the computer (e.g., Kidspiration 3.0, imindmap 5, visualmind, and SmartDraw). A mind-map is produced for the key points of a topic and reviewed each night before the exam. In the exam, the learner should spend a few minutes highlighting key words for the question and selecting material from mind-maps on this topic, before answering the question or writing the essay. The advantage of this method is that the learner can write down the ideas/facts in the order they generate or

recall them. Then by reviewing the branches and numbering them in a logical order (one for each paragraph) they can produce an answer that is logically sequenced.

- Teaching self-voice techniques (using a recorder). These can be used to learn facts for a test or examination (e.g., chemical symbols, mathematical formulae, multiplication tables). The teacher models the information for the learner who repeats it verbally and their voice is recorded. The learner plays back the recording, listening to their voice (and joining in with it) whilst looking at the written symbol/s and then writes down the information from memory (verbalising as they do so). This technique can be practised in the part of the lesson devoted to memory training.

# Memorisation

The learner should be taught strategies for memorising information. The use of verbal rehearsal, visualisation, and chunking should be taught from the early stages of the programme as discussed in the previous chapter. These techniques can also help learners to memorise key recall words that they can use later to recreate a passage or memorise information on a mind-map for an examination. Other strategies that might be useful are picture association and the use of jingles or mnemonics. If a learner has difficulty remembering a list of five or six key recall words then it may be possible to imagine a board with a picture that incorporates them (e.g., a Christmas tree with objects hung on it that depict the words to be remembered). This is particularly useful for learners with a good visual memory. Alternatively a jingle can be made up that contains the key recall words for those with a good auditory memory.

Mnemonics can be used to help a learner remember difficult spellings including subject specific vocabulary. In this case a phrase is made up where each word represents a letter in the spelling to be memorised (e.g., a mnemonic for the word 'acid' could be <u>a</u>cid <u>c</u>omes <u>i</u>n <u>d</u>rums). Some learners can benefit from writing the mnemonic in a book with an illustration next to it. The first letter of each word in the mnemonic can be highlighted, underlined, or written in a different colour in order to make the spelling stand out.

A variant of the above approach can be used in a process that psychologists refer to as 'reductive coding', which simply means reducing the amount of information by using coding. It can be utilised to remember large amounts of texts for an examination and is particularly helpful for a *seen paper* where learners have the opportunity to write their answer before an exam and memorise it. Using this process a key recall word (or two) can be selected for each paragraph in the essay and then one letter from each key recall word is selected to form a new word (a 'memory jogger'). The learner now only has to remember one word for that examination question. In the exam room they write down the word, each letter triggering the word that it represents, and each of these key recall words in turn triggers a paragraph which will be written in the correct order. For example, the word DIMS might represent key recall words – Definitions, Incidence, Models (of causation), Strategies (for teaching) – in an essay on dyslexia. Practice in using reductive coding can be given using structured passages or the 'out of structure' reading at the end of a lesson.

A number of texts are available on study skills that could prove useful for learners with dyslexia but for specific texts see Hargreaves (2007) and Guy (2008).

## Summary

This chapter proposed that the teaching of study skills should start early in primary schools. It suggests that learners with dyslexia often need specific teaching to acquire appropriate strategies to develop good study skills. Specialist teachers are encouraged to include study skills work in structured, multisensory lessons by using structured passages (see Part III for examples) to develop higher order reading skills. Particular attention is paid to sequencing skills, prediction, the use of a dictionary or thesaurus, highlighting key recall words, mind-mapping key points, and strategies for the drafting of assignments as well as developing note-taking and proofreading skills.

## References

Buzan, T. (2002) *How to Mind Map*. London: Thorsons.

Buzan, T. (2003) *Mind Maps for Kids*. London: Thorsons.

Buzan, T. (2006) *The Buzan Study Skills Book*. London: BBC Active.

Guy, P. (2008) *Study Skills: A Teaching Programme for Students in Schools and Colleges*. London: Sage.

Hargreaves, S. (2007) *Study Skills for Dyslexic Students*. London: Sage.

Irlen, H. (1991) *Reading by the Colours*. New York: Avery.

Stein, J. (2008) 'The neurobiological basis of dyslexia'. In Reid, G., Fawcett, A., Manis, F. and Siegel, L. (eds) *The Sage Handbook of Dyslexia*. London: Sage. pp. 53–76.

## Software

*Imindmap 5,* Buzan, T. – www.thinkbuzan.com

*Kidspiration 3.0*, Inclusive Technology – www.inclusive.co.uk

*SmartDraw,* SmartDraw – www.smartdraw.com

*Visualmind*, Mind Technologies, inc. – www.visual-mind.com

# PART III

# CONQUERING LITERACY – A MULTISENSORY PROGRAMME

This part of the book provides details of the structured, cumulative literacy programme. Part II described the basic principles underpinning the programme including the methods that should be used in all lessons to ensure that multisensory teaching and learning takes place as well as recommendations for planning structured lessons. In addition, it included suggestions for other teaching strategies that could be used.

Part III provides:

- A summary of the programme's structure. This lists the Teaching Points in the sequence in which they should be taught, distinguishing between concepts and phonograms and giving a reference to the page where further information can be found.

    In the case of phonograms, reference is made to the representation of the *sound* on the *reverse* of a Reading Card and on the *front* of a Spelling Card, bearing in mind that there might be two (or more) Spelling Cards for any one letter.

    Table III.1 also shows which 'high frequency' words can be read and spelt when this letter-sound correspondence has been taught. It includes relevant irregular words which should be taught using the methods suggested in Part II, Chapter 11.
- Table III. 2 which lists 40 Literacy Concepts introduced in the programme, cross-referencing these to their positions in the programme structure in Table III.1

(supplying the Teaching Point number). Suggestions are given so that practitioners can make a set of Concept Cards as described in Part II, Chapter 11. However, Part V: (Resources) provides photocopiable sheets for teachers wishing to use them (as Concept Cards can be produced in advance of lessons).

- *Examples* of activities which can be used when delivering the programme. It is important that any practitioner teaching the programme is familiar with the teaching strategies outlined in Part II and also with the format of a structured lesson, as not all the elements of a lesson are included for each Teaching Point in this section. Examples of the format of a Reading Card are given, particularly at the beginning of the programme, in order to help practitioners to become familiar with these. The cursive form is usually provided to remind the practitioner that this is an important aspect of introducing a new phonogram. In nearly every case, we have included a copy of how to write a Spelling Card because both teachers and learners often find this aspect difficult. Spelling is also the area where learners with dyslexia experience greatest difficulty and have to learn to make 'informed' choices. As Spelling Cards are 'added to' throughout the programme, many teachers may find it useful to see illustrations of this cumulative process.

Similarly, examples of structured reading and spelling are provided to reduce some of the practitioner's workload in lesson planning. However, we also hope that practitioners (and learners) may enjoy the freedom to compose their own structured passages for reading and dictation.

*Practitioners are reminded to refer back to Part II, particularly Chapter 11, when planning their teaching and to use Part III appropriately.*

TABLE III:1 – *A Summary of the Main Programme*

| Teaching Point | Page No. | Front of Reading Card | Sound on Reading and Spelling Card(s) | High Frequency Words | Irregular Words |
|---|---|---|---|---|---|
| 1. Symbol | 174 | | | | |
| 2. Sound and // | 174 | | | | |
| 3. Name | 174 | | | | |
| 4. Alphabet | 174 | | | | |
| 5. Beginning, Middle, End | 174 | | | | |
| 6. 'i' | 175 | i | /ĭ/ /ī/ | I | |
| 7. Vowels | 175 | | | | |
| 8. 't' | 177 | t | /t/ | it | |
| 9. Consonants | 177 | | | | |
| 10. Word | 177 | | | | |
| 11. 'p' | 178 | p | /p/ | | |
| 12. 'n' | 179 | n | /n/ | in | |
| 13. 's' | 180 | s | /s/ /z/ | is | |
| 14. Voiced/unvoiced | 180 | | | | |
| 15. 's' blends* st, sp, sn | 182 | st, sp, sn | /st/ /sp/ /sn/ | | |
| 16. Suffix 's' (plurals and verbs) | 184 | | | | |
| 17. Contractions | 185 | | | it's, isn't | |
| 18. Apostrophe | 185 | | | | |
| 19. 'a' | 186 | a | /ă/ /ā/ | a, at, an. as | |
| 20. Long/short vowels | 188 | | | | |
| 21. Breve and macron | 188 | | | | |
| 22. Syllables (counting) | 188 | | | | |
| 23. 'd' | 189 | d | /d/ | dad, said, did, and | said |
| 24. Punctuation: capital letter, full stop, speech marks | 190 | | | | |
| 25. Apostrophe 's' (possessive) | 191 | | | | |
| 26. Accent/stress | 191 | | | | |
| 27. Blends* -nt  -nd | 191 | -nt, -nd/ | /nt/ /nd/ | | |
| 28. Closed syllables vc/vcc | 192 | | | | |
| 29. 'h' | 192 | h | /h/ | had, his, has, this | this |
| 30. 'th' (voiced and unvoiced) | 194 | th | /th/ | this, that | |
| 31. 'e' | 196 | e | /ĕ/ /ē/ | the, then, he, these | she, these |
| 32. Open syllables | 198 | | | | |
| 33. Suffix 'ed' /ĭd/ /t/ just add and doubling rule | 199 | -ed | /ĭd/ /t/ | | |
| 34. 'o' | 202 | o | /ŏ/ /ō/ | not, don't, so, on | do, to, too |

*(Continued)*

*(Continued)*

| Teaching Point | Page No. | Front of Reading Card | Sound on Reading and Spelling Card(s) | High Frequency Words | Irregular Words |
|---|---|---|---|---|---|
| 35. Prefixes: 'in' 'de' | 204 | | | | |
| 36. Punctuation: question and exclamation mark | 204 | | | | |
| 37. 'g' | 205 | g | /g/ | get, dig, got, go, dog | |
| 38. -ng and suffix 'ing' (just add and doubling rules) | 206 | -ng, -ing | /ng/ /ing/ | going | |
| 39. 'm' | 207 | m | /m/ | am, me, him, man | |
| 40. 'c' and prefix 'con' | 209–210 | c | /k/ | can, come, coming | can't, come |
| 41. 'k' | 211 | k | /k/ | | |
| 42. c/k choice at beginning | 213 | | | | |
| 43. sc/sk at beginning | 214 | sc-, sk- | /sk/ | | |
| 44. 'b' | 215 | b | /b/ | be, bed, big | |
| 45. Syllable division vc/cv | 216 | | | | |
| 46. End blends: -sk, -nk, -ct | 217 | -sk, -nk, -ct | /sk/ /nk/ /kt/ | ask, asked | |
| 47. '-ck' and ck/k rules | 218 | -ck | /k/ | back | |
| 48. '-c' (at end) rule | 218 | -c | /k/ | | |
| 49. 'f and '-ff' | 219 | f, -ff | /f/ | of, if, off | of |
| 50. 'l' and '-ll' | 221 | l, -ll | /l/ | last | |
| 51. '-ss' (flossy rule) | 222 | -ss | /s/ | | |
| 52. Suffix 'es' | 222 | -es | /ĭz/ | | |
| 53. Beginning 'l' blends: bl, cl, fl, gl, pl, sl, spl | 222 | bl, pl, cl, fl, gl, sl, spl | /bl/ /pl/ /kl/ /fl/ /gl/ /sl/ /spl/ | | |
| 54. End 'l' blends: -ld, -lf, -lk, -lm, -lp, -lt | 223 | -ld, -lf, -lk, -lp, -lm, -lt | /ld/ /lf/ /lk/ /lp/ /lm//lt/ | | |
| 55. End blend '-ft' | 224 | ft | /ft/ | | |
| 56. '-all' | 225 | -all | /awl/ | all, ball, call | |
| 57. Suffix 'ed' /d/ | 225 | -ed | /d/ | called | |
| 58. 'r' | 226 | r | /r/ | | |
| 59. 'r' blends: pr, dr, br, cr, fr, gr | 227 | pr, dr, br cr, fr, gr | /pr/ /dr/ /br/ /kr/ /fr/ /gr/ | | |
| 60. str, scr, spr | 228 | str, scr, spr | /str/ /skr/ /spr/ | | |
| 61. Prefixes: 'im', 're', 'pre' | 228 | | | | |

| Teaching Point | Page No. | Front of Reading Card | Sound on Reading and Spelling Card(s) | High Frequency Words | Irregular Words |
|---|---|---|---|---|---|
| 62. Beginning blend: 'sm' | 229 | sm | /sm/ | small | |
| 63. End blend: '-mp' | 229 | -mp | /mp/ | | |
| 64. 'u' | 230 | u | /ŭ/  /ū/ | up, but, us, put, pull, mum, must | |
| 65. 'w' | 232 | w | /w/ | we, went, will, with | won't |
| 66. 'wa' as in 'wasp' | 233 | wa- | /wŏ/ | was, want | |
| 67. 'wh' words | 233 | wh- | /w/ | when, what, which, who, where | which, who, where |
| 68. Consonant blends: 'sw' 'tw' | 234 | sw-, tw- | /sw/ /tw/ | two | two |
| 69. Syllable division: vc/v and v/cv | 235 | | | | |
| 70. 'y' (consonant) | 236 | y- | /y/ | yes | |
| 71. 'y' (as a semi-vowel) | 237 | -y | /ĭ/  /ī/ | baby, lady, happy, by, my, why | |
| 72. Suffixes 'ly' and 'ful' adverbs / adjectives | 239 | ly, ful | /lĭ/ /fŭl/ | | |
| 73. Vowel suffix rule: change 'y' to 'i' (babies) | 239 | | | | |
| 74. 'j' | 240 | j | /j/ | just, jump | |
| 75. 'v' | 241 | v | /v/ | have | have |
| 76. 'x' | 242 | x | /ks/ /gz/ | next | |
| 77. Prefixes: 'ex' 'un' 'ab' | 243 | | | | |
| 78. 'qu-' | 244 | qu- | /kw/ | | |
| 79. 'z' | 246 | z | /z/ | | |
| 80. 'sh' | 247 | sh | /sh/ | she, push | |
| 81. 'ch' | 248 | ch | /ch/ | | |
| 82. '-tch' spelling rule 'ch' /tch' | 249 | -tch | /ch/ | much, such, which | much, such, rich, which |
| 83. 'i-e' vowel suffix rule: drop 'e' | 250 | i-e | /ī/ | like, time | |
| 84. 'a-e' | 252 | a-e | /ā/ | came, take, name, made, make, white | |
| 85. 'o-e' | 253 | o-e | /ō/ | home, come, one, whole | come, one, some, move |
| 86. 'u-e' | 254 | u-e | /ū/ | | |
| 87. v-c-e with 'r': 'are' 'ire' 'ore' 'ure' | 255 | are, ire, ore, ure | /er/ /īə/ /ôr/ /ūə/ | | sure |
| 88. 'ee' | 258 | ee | /ē/ | see, been, seen, tree | |
| 89. 'ar' | 260 | ar | /aȓ/ | far, garden | |
| 90. 'ar' (as in 'collar') | 261 | ar | /ə/ | | |

*(Continued)*

*(Continued)*

| Teaching Point | Page No. | Front of Reading Card | Sound on Reading and Spelling Card(s) | High Frequency Words | Irregular Words |
|---|---|---|---|---|---|
| 91. 'or' | 262 | or | /ôr/ | for | |
| 92. 'or' (as in 'doctor') | 263 | or | /ə/ | | |
| 93. 'oo' | 264 | oo | /o͞o/ /o͝o/ | look, took, good | |
| 94. -k /k/ spelling rule -ck /-k | 266 | | | | |
| 95. soft 'c' | 267 | ce | /s/ | once | once |
| 96. soft 'g' | 269 | ge | /j/ | | |
| 97. 'ge' and 'dge' rules | 270 | -ge, -dge | /j/ | | |
| 98. Vowel suffix rule drop 'e': -ce, -ge, -dge | 271 | | | | |
| 99. Prefixes: trans, mis, be | 272 | | | | |
| 100. '-ay' | 272 | -ay | /ā/ | day, may, way, play, away | |
| 101. '-ow' (as in 'snow') | 274 | -ow | /ō/ | own, window | own |
| 102. '-ow' (as in 'cow') | 274 | -ow | /ow/ | | |
| 103. 'er' | 276 | er | /ûr/ | her | |
| 104. 'er' | 276 | er | /ə/ | after, over | |
| 105. Suffix 'er' comparatives/ superlatives | 277 | | | smaller | |
| 106. '-ue' | 278 | -ue | /o͞o/ /ū/ | | |
| 107. Prefixes: post, peri | 280 | | | | |
| 108. 'o' (as in 'won') | 280 | o | /ŭ/ | another, mother, brother, love | |
| 109. '-ie' | 281 | -ie | /ī/ | | |
| 110. 'ea' | 282 | ea | /ē/ | | idea, great |
| 111. 'ea' (as in 'head') | 284 | ea | /ĕ/ | head | great |
| 112. 'ai' | 284 | ai | /ā/ | | |
| 113. 'air' | 285 | air | /êr/ | | |
| 114. 'oa' | 286 | o | /ō/ | | |
| 115. 'igh' | 287 | igh | /ī/ | light | |
| 116. Old wild words | 289 | | | old | |
| 117. Silent letters: 'b', 'g' | 289 | | | | comb, tomb |
| 118. 'oi' | 289 | oi | /oy/ | | |
| 119. 'oy' | 290 | oy | /oy/ | boy | |
| 120. Plural possessives | 291 | | | | |
| 121. 'ou' | 292 | ou | /ow/ | | |
| 122. 'ou' | 293 | ou | /ŭ/ /o͝o/ /o͞o/ | could, should | |
| 123. Final regular syllables: ble/ cle/dle/fle/gle/kle/stle/zle | 293 | | | little | |

| Teaching Point | Page No. | Front of Reading Card | Sound on Reading and Spelling Card(s) | High Frequency Words | Irregular Words |
|---|---|---|---|---|---|
| 124. '-tion' | 295 | -tion | /shn/ | | |
| 125. '-sion' | 296 | -sion | /shn/ /zhn/ | | |
| 126. '-cian' | 297 | -cian | /shn/ | | |
| 127. Silent letters: 'w', 'k' | 297 | | | | |
| 128. 'ir' | 298 | ir | /ûr̂/ | birthday | |
| 129. 'ur' | 299 | ur | /ûr̂/ | | |
| 130. 'or' (as in 'word') | 300 | or | /ûr̂/ | word, work, world | |
| 131. 'au' | 301 | au | /aw/ | | |
| 132. 'aw' | 302 | aw | /aw/ | saw | |
| 133. '-oe' | 303 | -oe | /ō/ | | |
| 134. '-ey' (as in 'grey') | 304 | -ey | /ā/ | | |
| 135. '-ey' (as in 'donkey') | 305 | -ey | /ĭ/ | money | |
| 136. '-ew' | 306 | -ew | /o͞o/ /ū/ | | |
| 137. Irregular 'al' 'el' | 307 | | | | |
| 138. Prefixes: 'mal', 'semi', 'bi' | 308 | | | | |
| 139. Syllable division: cv/vc pattern | 308 | | | | |
| 140. 'ph' | 309 | ph | /f/ | | |
| 141. 'ie' (as in 'brief') | 311 | ie | /ē/ | | |
| 142. 'e-e' and 'ere' | 312 | e-e | /ē/ | these | eyes, were, here, there, where |
| 143. 'ei' (as in 'ceiling') | 312 | ei | /ē/ | | |
| 144. 'ei' (as in 'reindeer') | 313 | ei | /ā/ | | |
| 145. 'ch' | 313 | ch | /k/ /sh/ | | |
| 146. 'eigh' (as in 'sleigh') | 315 | eigh | /ā/ | | |
| 147. 'ear' | 315 | ear | /ēə/ /ûr̂/ | heard, earth | |
| 148. 'a (as in about) | 316 | a | /ə/ | | |
| 149. 'our' | 316 | our | /ə/ | | |
| 150. Suffix 'ous' and 'us' | 318 | ous, us | /ŭs/ | | |
| 151. 'ture' | 318 | ture | /chə/ | | |
| 152. 'eu' | 319 | /ū/ | /ū/ | | |
| 153. 'ui' | 319 | ui | /o͞o/ /ĭ/ | | |
| 154. Prefixes: 'anti', 'ante', 'ad' | 321 | | | | |
| 155. Silent letters ; 'gh', 'gu' | 321 | | | | |
| 156. 'y-e' | 322 | y-e | /ī/ | | |
| 157. '-ough' | 322 | | | | |

* Referred to as 'adjacent consonants' in the Primary National Strategy

Table III.2  *Literacy Concept Cards*

| (Instructions for making and using the Concept Cards are in Chapter 11) | | | |
|---|---|---|---|
| **Concept Card Number** | **Teaching Point (TP)** | **Suggested Front of Card** | **Reverse of Card: Definition/Information** |
| 1 | 1 | Use a road sign or 'Golden Arches' | A **symbol** stands for, or reminds us, of something. |
| 2 | 2 | /44/ | A phoneme is the smallest unit of sound in our language. We use the symbol // round the letter(s) that make a single sound. There are 44 sounds in English. |
| 3 | 3 | N 26 (or learner's name) | Each letter has a name. There are 26 letters in English. |
| 4 | 4 | **ABC ---------XYZ** | The 26 letters are organised in a particular order or sequence called the **alphabet**. |
| 5 | 5 | **B M E** | We use these letters to help us tell where we hear the sounds in words. B stands for Beginning M stands for Middle E stands for End *N.B. teachers can use Initial, Medial, Final I,M,F if they prefer as long as these are used consistently.* |
| 6 | 7 | **v** | Vowel sounds are **open**, with nothing blocking the air, and are **voiced** sounds.  There is a vowel in every syllable. |
| 7 | 9 | **c** | Consonant sounds are usually blocked or partially blocked by the tongue, teeth, or lips. |
| 8 | 10 | **W** | A word is a unit of language which make complete sense. |
| 9 | 14 | (representing vibrations) | Some consonants are voiced (e.g., 'b'), some are unvoiced (e.g., 'p'), and some can be voiced or unvoiced depending on the word (e.g., 's' is unvoiced in 'sun' but voiced in 'is' and 'rose'). |
| 10 | 15 | **/sp/** | Some consonants **blend** together but they make their own sounds. N.B. The National Literacy Strategy uses the term 'adjacent consonants' so teachers may prefer the symbol /cc/.  We do not recommend this as it could be confused with consonant digraph such as 'sh'. |
| 11 | 16 | (W) | A **base word** is itself a word which makes complete sense in itself. It can also be added to in order to form another word. |
| 12 | 16 | (W) □ | A **suffix** is a letter or letters added to the end of a base word. A suffix changes the meaning or usage of a word. |
| 13 | 16 | (W) [S] | Suffix 's' can change a word so that it becomes plural or forms a verb.  (For older learners there could be a reference to third person singular/present tense.) |
| 14 | 18 | **It is = it's** | A **contraction** is a word formed by combining two words. An **apostrophe** is placed to show where a letter (or letters) have been left out (omitted). |

| Concept Card Number | Teaching Point (TP) | Suggested Front of Card | Reverse of Card: definition/information |
|---|---|---|---|
| 15 | 20 | v ▪<br>v ▬▬ | All vowels have two sounds. They can be **short** or **long** vowel sounds. |
| 16 | 21 | ∪ | A **breve** is a symbol to indicate a short vowel sound. |
| 17 | 21 | ▬ | A **macron** is a symbol to indicate a long vowel sound. |
| 18 | 22 | S | A **syllable** is a word or part of a word formed by one opening of the mouth. It usually has one vowel sound in it. |
| 19 | 24 | A | An upper case or capital letter is used:<br>• at the beginning of the first word in a sentence;<br>• for the first letter of a proper name/noun e.g., John, Cardiff, Scotland;<br>• for the first letter of the main words in a title of a book/ story. |
| 20 | 24 | . | A full stop is used:<br>• at the end of a sentence;<br>• to show that a word has been shortened/abbreviated e.g., a.m., Mon. (for Monday). |
| 21 | 24 | " " | Speech marks (quotation marks) are placed round the words spoken by someone. |
| 22 | 24 | , | A comma has many uses. The most common are:<br>• to separate words in a list;<br>• to indicate a pause;<br>• to separate a speaker from the words spoken which are in speech marks e.g., Mark said, "I am going to the park." "I am going there tomorrow," said Ann. |
| 23 | 25 | 's | An apostrophe and 's' are placed after a noun to indicate that something belongs to someone/something. If a noun is singular or itself a plural word such as 'men' add 's' to show possession e.g., Stan's coat, Ann's tin, the children's school. If the noun is plural ending in 's' or a name ending in 's' just add 'e.g. St. James' Park': The dogs' food was placed in the yard (more than one dog).<br>*N.B. It may be appropriate to teach the use of 'its' here as a possessive pronoun but **NOT** to put it on a Concept Card. It does **NOT** have an apostrophe because it is itself a possessive word. When we see 'it's' we should recognise it as a contraction.* |
| 24 | 26 | ´ | Some words or syllables are stressed/accented more than others. We can use the symbol ´ after the letter or syllable that is stressed. e.g., pho´ tograph and photog´raphy. In some cases the use of stress/accent can change a word's meaning e.g., in´valid and inval´id. |
| 25 | 28 | vc<br>vcc | A **closed syllable** ends with at least one consonant. The vowel will be short. |
| 26 | 32 | v ⟶ | An **open syllable** ends with a vowel. |

*(Continued)*

*(Continued)*

| Concept Card Number | Teaching Point (TP) | Suggested Front of Card | Reverse of Card: definition/information |
|---|---|---|---|
| 27 | 33 | ⓦ ed | Vowel suffix – ed pronounced. /ed/ after 'd' or 't' e.g., mended. /d/ after voiced sounds e.g., tailed. /t/ after unvoiced sounds e.g., thumped. |
| 28 | 33 | **cvc + ed = cvcced** | When 'ed' is added to a single syllable word with a **short** vowel the final consonant is doubled e.g., hop/hopped. |
| 29 | 35 | □ ⓦ | A prefix is a syllable placed before a word to change meaning e.g., in/ward, de/compose, con/verse. |
| 30 | 36 | **?** | A direct question is followed by a question mark; e.g., Why? "How much do the oranges cost?" he asked. |
| 31 | 36 | **!** | An exclamation mark is placed at the end of a sentence (or word) to express strong feeling. e.g., Stop! "That's really exciting!" she said. |
| 32 | 38 | **-ing cvc + -ing = cvccing** | Vowel suffix '-ing' shows that something is happening now. When added to a single syllable word with a **short** vowel, the final consonant is doubled e.g., shop/shopping. |
| 33 | 45 | **vc / cv** | When two consonants come between two sounded vowels in a two syllable word, the word usually divides into two syllables between the two consonants. (The accent/stress is usually on the first syllable.) |
| 34 | 52 | **-es** | Suffix '-es' is used for plurals of words ending in '-ss', -'s', and 'x'. |
| 35 | 69 | **v/cv** | Some words have two syllables but the first syllable is open and stressed e.g., sta´men, pu´pil. |
| 36 | 69 | **vc/v** | Some words have two closed syllables but only one consonant between the vowels e.g., satin, panic. These words divide after the consonant (vc/v). |
| 37 | 71 | **y** | The letter 'y' can be a consonant (yes) or a semi-vowel (baby, lady, my, why). |
| 38 | 73 | **-y + s = -ies** | When adding 's' to words ending in 'y' to form a plural, drop the 'y' and add 'ies' e.g., babies. |
| 39 | 83–86 | **-vc** | The final 'e' in vce words is dropped when adding a suffix beginning with a vowel e.g. slope → sloping/sloped, hide → hiding (but hid). Ice/icing/iced. |
| 40 | 139 | **cv/vc** | Usually when two vowels occur together they represent one sound (e.g., read, foil) but in some words **each vowel** represents a sound, one ending in an open syllable and the next beginning a closed syllable. The syllables are divided **between the vowels** (e.g., ru/in) and the first syllable is usually stressed (e.g., di´/alect). |

# THE CONQUERING LITERACY PROGRAMME: EXAMPLES OF ACTIVITIES

This section provides examples of how to deliver the Teaching Points referred to in the grid. It should be read in conjunction with Chapter 11. The number of Teaching Points introduced in a lesson can vary. Sometimes one or more concepts can be introduced with one or more phonograms, particularly in the early stages when working with a learner who has already acquired some literacy skills. At other points in the programme, where there may be more complex concepts or difficult spelling choices, or an area where the learner is experiencing particular difficulty, only one Teaching Point may be introduced – and it may even be that a second lesson is also devoted to the same point in order to ensure mastery and automaticity.

Chapters 9 and 11 provide the framework for a lesson and general information about the variety of forms activities can take. Therefore, the programme outlined in this section does not give a full lesson plan for each Teaching Point but provides a range of examples which can be used.

## Teaching Points 1 and 2

### Symbol and Sound

Introduce the Concept Card for symbol as described in the previous section. Explain that there are 44 sounds in the English language and explore which sounds the learner already knows. Demonstrate how a letter sound is represented using the symbol //. Show Concept Card 2 as advised in Chapter 11.

## Teaching Point 3

### Letter Names

Look at the letters in the learner's name. Discover what they know about each of the letters by discussing them in turn. Ask 'What can you tell me about this letter?' This will enable you to find out if the learner is familiar with the terms 'letter sound', 'letter name', 'lower case', 'upper case', 'capital letter', 'print', 'cursive', etc. Explain that every letter has a letter name. Let the learner discover how many different letters there are in the English language by studying a piece of text or counting the wooden letters. Use Concept Card 3.

## Teaching Point 4

### The Alphabet

Make the learner's name using wooden letters or letters written on separate pieces of card and discuss what the word says. Mix up the letters and ask the learner to sequence them correctly to spell their name. Discuss how the letters must be in the correct sequence. Explain that the letters of the English language also have a sequence called the alphabet. Discuss where the alphabet sequence is used and why. Use Concept Card 4. The teacher can now start to introduce alphabet sequencing into the lessons if the learner is familiar with the early part of the alphabet. If no letters of the alphabet are previously known, then introduce the alphabet alongside the phonemes from the structure as suggested in Chapter 10.

## Teaching Point 5

### Beginning, Middle, End

Ask the learner to look at a cvc word (e.g., cat) and point to the letter at the beginning of the word, then to the letter at the end of the word, and finally to the letter in the middle of the word (do not expect them to be able to recognise the phonograms at this stage). Explain that most words have a beginning, middle, and end. Now ask the learner to listen to some words and tell you which sound they can hear at the beginning of each of the words. Repeat this for end sounds and for middle sounds. Show them a BME sheet (see Part V) and explain that the B stands for beginning, the M for middle, and the E for end. Use Concept Card 5 and explain that BME sheets are used to show where we can hear particular sounds in words.

## Teaching Points 6 and 7

cursive form

### 'i' /ĭ/ and Vowels

*i*

### Reading Card

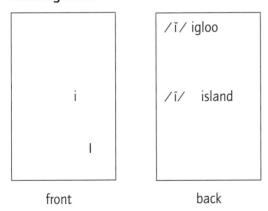

| front | back |

### Introducing the New Teaching Point Using Discovery Learning

The phoneme should be introduced through Discovery Learning. Ask the learner to listen to and *repeat* the following words: igloo, ink, image, ill, insect, imagine. Then ask them to identify the common sound. The Teaching Point should be reinforced through other senses, for example:

• Track the letter, saying the letter, sound/name as it is circled (Tracking Sheet 1 in Part V).
• Use a riddle to identify the clue word on the Reading Card before making it.
• Put three wooden letters in a feely bag and ask the learner to find the letter 'i'.
• Identify the position of the sound in words using a BME sheet.
• Use a mirror to see how the sound is made and to introduce the concept of a *vowel*. Use Concept Card 6.

## Reading Pack Routine

The learner looks at the front of the card and responds with the letter sound and clue word. They turn the card over and self-check by looking at the picture/s drawn on the back. Teacher discretion should be used in deciding when to introduce the long /ī/ sound.

## Writing the Letter

Demonstrate how to form the letter using the handwriting routine and practise joining it to other letters: *iiiiii* . Discuss relative size using handwriting paper if necessary.

## Spelling Card

|  | B | M | E |
|---|---|---|---|
| /ĭ/ | *i* | *i* |  |

## Spelling Pack Routine

The teacher says the sound on the front of the card /ĭ/; the learner repeats it and then gives the letter name. The learner writes it down in their book in the position it can be found in words, saying /ĭ/ 'i' at the beginning, /ĭ/ 'i' in the middle. It may be useful to draw three columns (BME) in the learner's book to begin with.

|  | B | M | E |
|---|---|---|---|
| /ī/ | *i* | *i* |  |

If the long vowel sound has been introduced then a second Spelling Card is made. The learner's response for this card is /ī/ 'i' at the beginning, /ī/ 'i' in the middle.

## Practising the New Learning

Make a pairs game with 12 cards: six with the capital letter 'I' on them and six with the lower case letter 'i' on them. Take turns to turn them over to find pairs.

# Teaching Points 8, 9 and 10

cursive form

## 't' /t/ Consonant and Word

*t*

## Reading Card

| | |
|---|---|
| t | /t/ table |
| T | |
| front | back |

## Introducing the New Teaching Point Using Discovery Learning

Show the learner pictures of objects beginning with the letter 't' e.g., tin, ten, table, torch, telephone, tent, etc. Ask the learner to identify each object and tell you the common sound. Use a mirror to discover how the sound is made in the mouth and introduce the concept of *consonant*. Use Concept Card 7. Track the letter using a tracking sheet, reading book, or magazine. Demonstrate the cursive letter and practise it using a salt tray, a whiteboard, or paint.

## Reading Pack

The new card is added to the Reading Pack. The learner practises all the cards in the pack each lesson, aiming for a speed of one second per card (for automaticity).

## Writing the Letter/s

The learner should practise joining the new letter to the previous one to make a word: *it it it.* Discuss the relative difference in size between the letters 'i' and 't'. Introduce Concept Card 8.

## Spelling Card

|  | B | M | E |
|---|---|---|---|
| /t/ | *t* | *t* | *t* |

## Spelling Pack Routine

The letter 't' can appear in words in the beginning, middle and end positions. The teacher says the sound on the front of the card /t/; the learner repeats it and then gives the letter name. The learner writes it down in their book in the position it can be found in words saying: /t/ 't' at the beginning, /t/ 't' in the middle, and /t/ 't' at the end.

## Practising the New Learning (Auditory)

Ask the learner to identify where they can hear the /t/ sound in the following words: ten, letter, pat, tick, into, satin, tin, beat. As they identify the position they should write the letter in the appropriate box using the BME sheet in Part V.

# Teaching Point 11

cursive form

'p' /p/

*p*

## Discovery Learning

Ask the learner to identify a number of objects (e.g., pen, paper, tape, cap) by touch and give you the common sound /p/. Use a mirror to discover how the sound is formed in the mouth and discuss if it is a vowel or consonant. Track the letter 'p' and practise writing it using the handwriting routine. Ask the learner to choose a clue word for the Reading Card. Make the Reading and Spelling Cards following the instructions in Chapter 11.

## Writing the Letter/s

Practise joining the letter 'p' to previous letters to make the words: *pip, pit, tip.* Use Concept Card 8. Ask the learner to read the words they have written.

## Practising the New Learning

Explore the letter 'p' (lower and upper case) in different fonts, either on the computer or through the use of various magazines. Note how the capital letter 'P' 'stands' on the line, in comparison to a lower case 'p' which 'sits' on the line.

## Stimulus Response Routine (SRR)

Use the SRR described in Chapter 11 to practise linking the letter sound to the letter name, to the clue word, and to the letter shape, using the SRR card/prompt from Part V for each of the letters introduced so far (i, t, p).

# Teaching Point 12

cursive form

'n' /n/                                             *n*

## Discovery Learning

Trace the letter 'n' on the learner's back (or ask them to feel the wooden letter with their eyes closed) and ask them to guess the letter. Ask the learner to listen to pairs of words and tell you which one contains the target sound /n/ (e.g., net/sip; pip/nip; tip/tin). Use a mirror to discover how the sound is formed in the mouth and discuss if the new letter is a vowel or consonant. Using a passage from a reading book or magazine ask the learner to count how many words contain the letter 'n'. Demonstrate how to form the letter in cursive writing using the handwriting routine. Make the Reading and Spelling Cards.

### Writing the Letter/s

Practise joining the letter 'n' to previous letters to make the words: nip, pin, tin.

### Practising the New Learning

Using the wooden letters 'i', 't', 'p', and 'n', ask the learner to make as many words as they can. Then ask them to write each word down, naming the letters as they do so.

### Sentences for Reading and Dictation

Pin it. Tip it in.

### Stimulus Response Routine (SRR)

Use the SRR routine to link the sound /n/ to the letter name, clue word, and letter shape (cursive writing) using the SRR prompt card.

## Teaching Points 13 and 14

cursive form

_ß_

### 's' /s/ Voiced and Unvoiced

### Reading Card

|  |  |
| --- | --- |
|  | /s/ sake |
| s | /z/   pins |
| S |  |
| front | back |

## Introducing the New Teaching Point Using Discovery Learning

Show the learner pictures of: sack, sun, sink, rose, pins, sock, house, bus, nose, etc. Ask them to sort the pictures into two sets. Encourage them to explain what each set of pictures has in common (/s/ or /z/). Use a mirror to discover how the sound is made in the mouth and ask them to put their hand on their throat and feel the difference between the /s/ sound (*unvoiced*) and the /z/ sound (*voiced*) as they name the pictures again. Use Concept Card 9. Track the letter and demonstrate the cursive form using the handwriting routine. Make the Reading and Spelling Cards. *Please note /z/ represents the voiced sound and <u>not</u> the spelling.*

## Reading Card

The new card is added to the Reading Pack. The card will usually have two sounds for 's'.

## Writing the Letter/s

The learner should practise joining the new letter to the previous ones: *sit sip sin.*

## Spelling Cards

| | | B | M | E |
|---|---|---|---|---|
| /s/ | | | | |
| /s/ | | *s* | *s* | *s* |

## Spelling Pack Routine

The teacher gives the sound on the front of the card and the learner repeats it and gives the letter name. The learner writes it in their book in the position it can be heard in words, saying: /s/ 's' at the beginning, /s/ 's' in the middle, and /s/ 's' at the end.

| | | B | M | E |
|---|---|---|---|---|
| /z/ | | | | |
| /z/ | | | *s* | *s* |

The learner's response for /z/ should be /z/ 's' in the middle, /z/ 's' at the end. (Note that /z/ will appear later in all three positions.)

## Spelling Pack

The pack should now contain cards for /ĭ/, /t/, /p/, /n/, /s/, and /z/ (optional).

## Words for Reading and Spelling

Put these words on cards for reading: in, it, is, sit, sip, sin, tip, tin, pin, pip, nit, pit.

These words can also be used for spelling using the SOS routine described in Chapter 11.

## Practising the New Learning

Ask the learner to sort the 'words for reading' into rhyming sets and identify the odd one out. They could also use a visual discrimination exercise here (see Part V).

## Sentences for Dictation

Sip it. Sit in it. It is in.

# Teaching Point 15

cursive form

*st sp sn*

### 's' blends

## Discovery Learning

Use Discovery Learning to introduce the 's' blends through visual, auditory, and tactile/ kinaesthetic channels. Use Concept Card 10 to reinforce understanding of a *blend*. Demonstrate how to join the letters together using the handwriting routine and practise writing the blends using a salt tray, whiteboard, felt markers, etc. Use Tracking Sheet 2 to track the blends. Make a separate Reading and Spelling Card for each blend or 'adjacent consonant'. If a colour-coded system has been used for vowels and consonants in the Reading Pack then a third colour could be used for blends.

## Spelling Card

| | B | M | E |
|---|---|---|---|
| /sp/ | sp | sp | sp |

## Spelling Pack Routine

The blend /sp/ can be hard in words in the beginning, middle, and end positions. The teacher says the sound on the front of the card /sp/ and the learner repeats it and then gives the letter names. The learner writes 'sp' down in their book in the position found in words, saying /sp/ 's' 'p' at the beginning, /sp/ 's' 'p' in the middle, and /sp/ 's' 'p' at the end.

## Writing the Letter/s

Practise joining the blends 'st', 'sp', and 'sn' to previous letters to make the words: snip, spin, spit.

## Words for Reading and Spelling

In, it, is, sit, sip, sin, tip, tin, pin, pip, nit, spit, snip, spin.

## Practising the New Learning

To begin with use the BME sheet to practise identifying the 's' blends in different positions in words. Say a word containing the blend and ask the learner to put a counter or tick, or to write the blend, in the appropriate box. Write the words given orally on a sheet of paper so the learner can 'self check' by first highlighting the blend being practised (e.g., spider, wasp, asp, clasping) and then checking the position of the blend in the written word against the tick, counter, etc. on the BME sheet. Then make a wordsearch containing the 'words for reading' and ask the learner to highlight and read the words as they find them.

### Sentences for Reading and Dictation

Spin it. Snip it.

### SRR

Practise linking the letter sounds /sp/, /st/, and /sn/ to the letter names, clue words, and the written form, using the Stimulus Response Routine (SRR). This routine should be used for each new phoneme and to reinforce any that need further practice.

## Teaching Point 16

### Suffix 's'

The purpose of the Teaching Point is to show that suffix 's' can be used to form plural nouns (e.g., *tins*) or to form third person verbs (e.g., Pip *sips* it).

### Teaching the New Concept

Introduce the concept of 'suffix' using Discovery Learning as suggested earlier (use Concept Cards 11, 12, and 13). This will enable the learner to distinguish between base words that end in the letter 's', such as 'kiss', and base words with suffix 's' added, such as 'pips' (see Chapter 11).

#### Adding the suffix 's' to a noun
Ask the learner to listen to pairs of words and tell you the difference: hat/hats; tin/tins; pin/pins; cup/cups; mat/mats; pen/pens. Discuss how the suffix's' changes the meaning from singular (one) to plural (more than one).

#### Adding the suffix 's' to a verb
Ask the learner to listen to the sentences and identify the verb (doing word): I <u>nip</u> it. Pip <u>snips</u> it. Then look at the suffix 's' in sentences, for example:

- I tip it in/Pip tips it in.
- I spin it/Pip spins it.
- I snip/Pip snips.

Ask the learner to work out what the difference is between the first and second sentence in each pair.

## Writing the Letter/s

Practise writing 's' at the end of the following words:
tin_    pip_    pin_    pit_    nit_.

## Practising Using Suffix 's' with Verbs

Make 12 cards, one for each of the following words: I, Pip, sit, tip, spin, snip, sip, tips, sits, spins, sits, sips. Give the learner the noun/pronoun cards (Pip/I) and ask them to sort them to make ten different sentences, using the verbs correctly, and write them down.

## Words for Reading and Spelling

Sits, sips, tips, tins, pins, pips, nits, pits.

## Sentences for Reading and Dictation

Snip it. Pip sips it. Tip pins in tins. Pip sits in it.

# Teaching Points 17 and 18

## Contractions and Use of Apostrophe

At this stage in the programme it is possible to introduce the use of an apostrophe to denote a contraction in the words 'it's' and 'isn't'. Put an apostrophe on a card and use this with the wooden letters to demonstrate how the second 'i' in '*it is*' is replaced by an apostrophe to form the contraction *it's*. Start to include phrases with contractions in sentences for reading and dictation (e.g., It's a pin tin. It isn't Pip.). Use Concept Card 14.

## Teaching Point 19

cursive form

'a' /ă/ /ā/

### Reading Card

front                    back

### Discovery Learning

Use Discovery Learning to introduce the phoneme through visual, auditory, and tactile/kinaesthetic channels. Use a mirror to discover how the vowel sound is made in the mouth and check if it is voiced or unvoiced.

### Reading Pack

The new card is added to the Reading Pack. The long vowel sound /ā/ is added at the teacher's discretion. Clue words are negotiated with the learner.

### Writing the Letter/s

Practise joining the new letter to previous ones e.g. at, sat, pan, tap.

### Spelling Card

## Spelling Pack Routine

The sound /ă/ can be heard in words in the beginning and middle positions. The teacher says the sound on the front of the card /ă/, the learner repeats it and then gives the letter name. The learner writes it down in their book in the position it can be found in words, saying: /ă/ /'a' at the beginning, /ă/ 'a' in the middle.

(*Note that when 'a' is written at the end of a word it usually makes the sound /ə/ and this is covered later.*)

If the long vowel sound /ā/ is added to the Reading Card, a second Spelling Card is needed.

|       | B | M | E |
|-------|---|---|---|
| /ā/   | a |   |   |

The letter 'a' is only used to represent the long vowel /ā/ at the beginning of words. The learner repeats the sound /ā/ after the teacher, gives the letter name 'a', and writes it in their book, saying /ā/ is 'a' at the beginning (remember that the Spelling Card only represents the 'spelling choices' that have been introduced so far and *others will be added later*).

## Words for Reading and Spelling

At, sap, tan, sat, nap, pan, snap, span, Stan, spat, Nan, pat, Nat, an, as, tap, past.

## Sentences for Reading and Dictation

Pat naps. Stan snaps at Nat. Nan tips it in a pan.

## Practising the New Learning Through a Game

Make a set of onset and rime dominoes to play with the learner using the words for reading, for example:

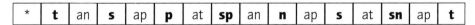

| * | **t** | an | **s** | ap | **p** | at | **sp** | an | **n** | ap | **s** | at | **sn** | ap | **t** |

## SRR

Always remember to use the SRR.

## Teaching Points 20 and 21

### Long and Short Vowels

The terms 'long' and 'short' vowel sounds should be introduced at this point through Discovery Learning. Ask the learner to listen to, repeat after you, and then identify the vowel sound in the words ant, act, can, sad, bat, etc. Give another list of words orally containing the long vowel sound – ape, ale, ache, case, late, tray, etc. Ask the learner to say what is different about the vowel in the second list. Discuss the long vowel sound, forcing more air out of the mouth to produce a 'longer' sound. Use Concept Card 15.

### Practising the New Learning

Take out the wooden letters A and I. Ask the learner to repeat the following words after you and then to touch the correct vowel: ink, ant, apple, insect, add, imp, ill, act. Repeat this exercise with words containing long vowel sounds.

### Breve and Macron

When the learner has grasped the concept of long and short vowel sounds, the symbol for *breve* (Concept Card 16) should be introduced for short vowels and the *macron* (Concept Card 17) for long vowels.

The learner can now practise putting the correct symbol over the wooden letters as they identify the vowel sound in a word. Ask the learner to repeat a word after you (e.g., cat); identify the vowel sound; decide if it is long or short; select the correct symbol and place it over the letter 'a'. Repeat this for words containing the long and short 'i' sound.

## Teaching Point 22

### Concept of 'Syllable'

Ask the learner to explore clapping the beats in the names of students in their class. Encourage them to say what they are doing to a word such as Car-o-line when they clap the beat. What do they notice about each syllable? Each syllable has a vowel and some also have consonants in them. Explore other names to see if they follow the same pattern. Use Concept Card 18.

## Practising the New Learning

Make a worksheet containing pictures on a topic of interest to the learner e.g., sport. Ask the learner to identify each picture, count the number of syllables in each word, and write the number under the picture e.g. tennis(2), golf(1), skating(2), squash(1), basketball(3), swimming(2), paragliding(4) gymnastics(3), canoeing(3).

## Detached Syllables for Spelling (for Older Learners)

Detached syllables can be introduced into the spelling routine for those who need practice at the early stages of the programme using more age appropriate words e.g.

**in**(sect) **tan**(gent) **pan**(demic) **an**(cestor) **san**(itation) **pin**(nacle).

The learner is asked to spell the highlighted syllable only using the SOS routine described in Chapter 11.

# Teaching Points 23 and 24

cursive form

'd' /d/                                                                    *d*

## Discovery Learning

Use a mirror to enable the learner to practise some of the consonants introduced so far. Talk about the position of the tongue behind the teeth and the way that it 'taps' against the back of the teeth as the sound /t/ is produced. Ask the learner to put their hand on their throat as they make the /t/ sound and say if it is voiced or unvoiced. Now ask them to push more air out as they produce the sound and make their voice box vibrate. They should notice that the sound they are now producing is /d/. They have just discovered that /t/ and /d/ are unvoiced and voiced pairs i.e. they are made by the same mouth movement.

Reinforce the new phoneme through visual and tactile/kinaesthetic channels e.g., by tracking the letter, sorting pictures into two sets (those beginning with /t/ and those beginning with /d/), and by practising writing the cursive letter using the handwriting routine. Make a Reading and Spelling Card to add to the packs: /d/ can be heard at the beginning, middle, and end of words.

## Writing the Letter/s

The learner should practise joining the new letter to previous ones to make words: dip, din, dad, sad, pad, Sid.

## Words for Reading and Spelling

Dad, did, dip, Dan, din, sad, pad, didn't.

At this point the learner can be introduced to irregular words because the irregular word 'said' can be made. Show them what is regular and irregular in the word and practise spelling 'said' using the irregular spelling routine (see Chapter 11).

## Sentences for Reading and Dictation

Pat isn't sad.     Dan did dip it in.     "I didn't snap at Sid," said Dad.

Ask the learner to highlight any words in the sentences above that are names of people. Discuss the use of capital letters and full stops. Ask the learner to underline the words in the last sentence that are being spoken. Ask how they know this. Discuss the use of speech marks. Introduce the Concept Cards for capital letters, full stops, comma and speech marks (see Concept Cards 19, 20, 21, and 22).

## Practising the New Learning

Write each of the following words on separate cards: Pat, Sid, Dad, Dan, Nat, Pip, dip, nips, tip, sad, an, past, and, spits, pants, asp, Sis, said, naps, tap, sips, dips, did, didn't, Ann.

Introduce the idea of alliteration orally and ask them to produce some sentences using words beginning with /d/. Then ask the leaner to create sentences or phrases with the given cards using as many of the same sound as possible, for example:

Tap tins. Dad dips Dan. Pat pants past Pip. An ant and an asp. Sad Sid sips and spits.

Then practise inserting punctuation. Pay attention to size of punctuation in writing. Older learners could use subject specific words to give orally some alliterative sentences e.g., magnificent magnesium, smelly sulphur, dangerous dioxin.

# Teaching Point 25

## Apostrophe 's' (Possessive 's')

Introduce the use of apostrophes to denote possession through Discovery Learning. This could be done *orally* first by collecting objects from other learners or teachers and asking the learner to guess which object belongs to whom after giving a clue as to the ownership (e.g., This is Dan's keyring). Demonstrate how to do this in writing. Reinforce this using Concept Card 23. Practise reading phrases by asking the learner to match a person card (e.g., Pat's, Dad's, Pip's, Ann's, Nat's) to an object card (e.g., pad, tip, pan, pips, pit) to make phrases to read: Pat's pan, Dad's tip, Ann's pips, etc. Now ask the learner to insert the missing apostrophe in phrases such as: Pat s sandpit, Nat s pad.

   (Note that this is a good time to show that the word 'its' when used to denote possession – e.g., I don't know its name – does not have an apostrophe, to avoid possible confusion.)

# Teaching Point 26

## Stress/Accent

Introduce the concept of accent and stress first through alphabet work. Ask the learner to go round the alphabet arc naming the letters two at a time (AB´ CD´ EF´) with the accent/stress on the second letter of the pair as in the words: command´, depart´, collate´, combine´, denote´. On another occasion practise putting the accent/stress on the first letter in the pairs A´B C´D E´F G´H etc. as in the words: ro´bot, to´tal, den´tist, lo´go. Accent and stress can also be practised by naming letters of the alphabet in groups of three: A´BC D´EF G´HI J´KL as in the words: guar´dian, el´ephant. Discuss how the position of the accent and stress can affect meaning as in con´tract and contract´; in´valid and inval´id. (Use Concept Card 24.)

# Teaching Point 27

## End Blends

cursive form

*nt    nd*

Although the letters n, t, and d have already been introduced within the programme, the end blends 'nt' and 'nd' should be introduced as separate Teaching Points, particularly for spelling, as the /n/ in words such as 'pant' and 'sand' is very short and is often omitted from words by beginning spellers. These end blends should have their own Reading and Spelling Cards. Spelling and dictation routines can now start to include words with end blends (if appropriate). Concept Card 10 can be used for revision.

## Teaching Point 28

### Closed Syllables

Introduce the learner to closed syllables using Discovery Learning. Present them with a list of words (e.g., sit, and, tip, ant, tin, sip, dad, pant, tint, did) written on individual cards. Ask them to read each word and identify the vowel, writing a 'v' for vowel over the letter. Then ask them how many consonants come after the vowel and mark them 'c' for consonant. The learner should notice that there are two different patterns: vc and vcc. In both cases the vowel is 'closed in' by the consonant/s, making a closed syllable. Explain that closed syllables always have a short vowel sound. Use Concept Card 25.

### Practising the New Learning

Ask the learner to sort the words into two sets (those ending in vc and those ending in vcc). Using the letters introduced so far in the programme challenge them to add three more to each set (e.g., tan/pan/sad; sand/ dint/ stand). Ask the learner to read the words they have made and decide if the vowel sound is long or short. The learner could now be asked to *code* the words by writing the breve over the vowels to denote the short vowel sound.

## Teaching Point 29

cursive form

'h' /h/                                               𝒽

### Discovery Learning

Use Discovery Learning to introduce the phoneme /h/ through visual, auditory, and tactile/kinaesthetic channels. Use a mirror to discover how the /h/ sound is made in the mouth and check if it is voiced or unvoiced. Track the letter 'h' saying the letter sound and name. Demonstrate the cursive letter using the handwriting routine.

## Reading Card

The new card is added to the Reading Pack. Negotiate a clue word with the learner.

## Writing the Letter/s

Practise joining the new letter to previous ones e.g., hat, hid, hand, has, hip.

## Spelling Card

| | | B | M | E |
|---|---|---|---|---|
| /h/ | *h* | | | |

## Spelling Pack Routine

The teacher says the sound /h/, the learner repeats it and gives the letter name. The learner writes it down in the position it can be heard in words saying: /h/ 'h' at the beginning.

## Words for Reading and Spelling

Hit, his, has, had, hand, hip, hat, hid, hint.

## Practising the New Learning (Visual Memory)

Make a coding exercise using a grid similar to the one below containing the letters: i, t, p, n, s, a, d, h, I.

| l | t | n |
|---|---|---|
| s | a | i |
| p | d | h |

Provide the sentence 'I hid a hat in a sandpit' for the learner to decode as follows:

This is a 'new' kind of activity which learners enjoy. There should be sufficient space underneath each shape for the learner to write the corresponding letter using the grid above. Ask them to read back the sentence and then rewrite it in cursive script (if desired) adding the punctuation. Further sentences could be coded and decoded to give more practice with older learners.

## Sentences for Reading and Dictation

It's Dan's hat. Pat hit his hip. "Dad has it," Pip said.

## Teaching Point 30

cursive form

**'th' /th/ and /t̲h̲/'**

*th*

### Reading Card

| | |
|---|---|
| th | /th/ thin |
| | /t̲h̲/ bathe |
| TH | |
| front | back |

### Discovery Learning

The consonant digraph /th/ should be introduced through Discovery Learning using the visual, auditory, and tactile/kinaesthetic channels, e.g., by listening to and identifying the common sound in bath, moth, thick, thistle, thank (unvoiced); and those, then, there, these, them (voiced). Use a mirror to discover how the /th/ sound is made in the mouth and ask the learner to feel their throat as they make the voiced and unvoiced sounds. Revise Concept Card 9. Ask the learner to read the blends introduced so far (st, sp, sn, nd, nt) and to see if they can tell you what is different about /th/. Discuss the difference between a blend and a digraph. Demonstrate how to join the letters 't' and 'h' together using the handwriting routine and practise writing the digraph using a salt tray, etc. Use Tracking Sheet 2 in Part V to track the digraph, naming the letters as the digraph is circled. Make a Reading and Spelling Card for /th/ (a voiced Spelling Card is optional because very few words can be made in structure at this point).

## Writing the Letter/s

Practise joining 'th' to previous letters e.g., that, then, this.

## Spelling Card

## Spelling Pack Routine

The digraph /th/ can be heard in words in the beginning, middle and end positions. The teacher says the sound on the front of the card /th/, the learner repeats it and then gives the letter names. The learner writes it down in their book in the position it can be found in words saying: /th/ 't' 'h' at the beginning, /th/ 't' 'h' in the middle, /th/ 't' 'h' at the end.

If the voiced sound /th/ is added to the Reading Card, a second Spelling Card is needed:

## Words for Reading and Spelling

This, that, thin, path, pith, than.

## Practising the New Learning

Sort the words for reading and spelling into sets of 'voiced' and 'unvoiced'. Practise the words for reading using a simplified precision teaching approach. Enlarge the grid below and ask the learner to read the words left to right:

| his | than | path | that | pith | thin |
|-----|------|------|------|------|------|
| thin | that | this | pith | than | path |
| path | thin | that | than | this | pith |
| that | pith | than | path | thin | this |
| than | this | pith | thin | path | that |
| pith | path | thin | this | that | than |

Continue reading across from left to right and top to bottom until at least 90 per cent accuracy is reached. Start to time the learner and continue reading until their optimal speed has been reached while maintaining accuracy.

## Sentences for Dictation

This is Dad's hat. Dan's hand is thin. 'That's the path,' said Pat.

# Teaching Point 31

cursive form

**'e' /ĕ/ and /ē/'**

*e*

## Reading Card

| | /ĕ/ elf |
|---|---|
| e | /ē/ even |
| E | |
| front | back |

The new card is added to the Reading Pack. The long vowel sound /ē/ is added at the teacher's discretion. Clue words are negotiated with the learner. (Remember to make sure the learner doesn't choose a clue word for /ē/ with 'ea' spelling e.g., eagle.)

## Discovery Learning

Use a mirror to discover how the vowel sound is made in the mouth and check if it is voiced or unvoiced.

## Writing the Letter/s

Practise joining the new letter to previous ones e.g., end, set, pen, nest.

## Spelling Card

| | B | M | E |
|---|---|---|---|
| /ĕ/ | e | e | |

## Spelling Pack Routine

The sound /ĕ/ can be heard in words in the beginning and middle positions.

   If the long vowel sound /ē/ is added to the Reading Card, a second Spelling Card is needed:

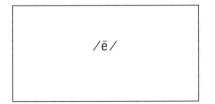

| | B | M | E |
|---|---|---|---|
| /ē/ | e | | |

The letter 'e' is only used to represent the long vowel /ē/ at the beginning of words (apart from words that are open syllables e.g., 'he', 'me', 'we', and 'be'). The learner repeats the sound /ē/ after the teacher, gives the letter name 'e', and writes it in their book saying /ē/ is 'e' at the beginning (remember that the

Spelling Card only represents the 'spelling choices' that have been introduced so far and others will be added later).

## Words for Reading and Spelling

Ten, pet, pen, set, net, test, tent, step, end, spend, Ted, pent, Ned, nest, then, tenth, the, den, depth, tend, hen, spent. (If /ē/ is taught include: he.)

## Practising the New Learning Using a Game

Make a rhyming pairs game using some of the words above.

## Sentences for Reading and Dictation

Dan tends the hens. "That's Ted's pen," snaps Ned. Dad tests the depth.

## Use SRR

# Teaching Point 32

### Open Syllables

Revise long and short vowels sounds and the use of breve and macron (Teaching Points 20 and 21) before introducing open syllables. Using the wooden letters make the word 'hen'. Remind the learner that closed syllables have a short vowel sound. Ask them to code the vowel (using a breve card) and read the word. Remove the letter 'n' to make the word 'he'. The vowel is no longer closed in by a consonant so the syllable is now 'open'. Prompt the learner to work out the vowel sound by saying 'If a closed syllable has a short vowel sound then an open syllable will have a … ?' Alternatively ask them to listen to some words containing a long vowel sound (e.g., he, by, she, we, my, no, be, me, so) and tell you what they have in common (long vowel sound, no final consonant). Produce Concept Card 26 for open syllables.

### Practising the New Learning

Take out wooden letters for the phonemes introduced so far: i, t, p, n, s, a, d, h, e. Ask the learner to make three closed syllables first, then to code them with a breve and read them back (e.g., ĭp, ăd, ĕn) and finally to make three open syllables (e.g., dī, hē, pā) coding them with the macron and read them back. In each case ask them to think of some words that contain those syllables (e.g., pā as in 'paper').

## Detached Syllables for Spelling (for Older Learners)

Detached 'open' syllables can now be introduced into the spelling routine for learners who need practice to use age appropriate words e.g. **di**(verge) **ti**(dal) **pa**(pacy) **a**(gent) **sa**(cred) **na**(tive) **ha**(des) **de**(lete) **di**(morphorous).

The learner is asked to spell 'ta' as in 'table', etc. using the SOS routine.

# Teaching Point 33

cursive form

## Suffix '-ed' /ĭd/ and /t/

*ed*

## Reading Card

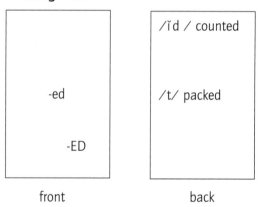

| -ed | /ĭd / counted |
|-----|---------------|
|     | /t/ packed    |
| -ED |               |

front            back

## Discovery Learning

The suffix 'ed' has three different sounds: the first two are taught at this stage and the third sound /d/ is normally added later on in the programme when more words ending in suffix 'ed' /d/ can be generated. However, it can be brought forward and taught here at the teacher's discretion (e.g., the clue word 'sailed'). Introduce the suffix 'ed' through Discovery Learning. This can be done through the auditory channel by asking the learner to listen to pairs of words (e.g., mend/mended, post/posted, count/counted) and tell you the difference between the two words. Alternatively, write a word 'in structure' (such as *test*) on a piece of paper and ask them to read it, then add the suffix 'ed' to make *tested* and see if the learner can work out the new word. Ask how the suffix has changed the meaning of the word. Use Concept Card 27. (Note that at this point you will need to discuss present and past tenses.)

Help the learner to discover the second sound for suffix 'ed' by giving some words *orally* for them to change into the past tense (e.g., net, slip, thank, sprint, clap, flip). Ask them to identify the two sounds that the suffix makes. Track suffix 'ed' in a piece of text. Make the Reading and Spelling Cards for suffix 'ed'. (Note that the second sound for 'ed', /t/, goes on the existing Spelling Card for /t/ as a spelling choice, and below the other choices, because it is a second choice spelling for /t/ at the end of words.)

## Reading Card

A line is written in front of the 'ed' to indicate that it is an end sound. Negotiate clue words with the learner. Check the pronunciation /ĭd/ (some may say /ĕd/) and /t/ to distinguish the voiced and unvoiced forms.

## Spelling Card/s

|  | B | M | E |
|---|---|---|---|
| /ĭd/ |  |  | *ed* |

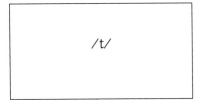

|  | B | M | E |
|---|---|---|---|
| /t/ | *t* | *t* | *t* *ed* |

## Spelling Pack Routine

The teacher says the sound on the front of the card /ĭd/, the learner repeats it and then spells it using letter names: (/ĭd/ suffix 'ed') before writing it in their book. The response for the Spelling Card /t/ is now: /t/ 't' at the beginning, /t/ 't' in the middle, and /t/ 't' or suffix 'ed' at the end. The learner can either give the response orally and then in writing or they can put it directly into writing as long as they name the letters (spelling) as they write.

## Introducing the 'Just Add' and Doubling Rule

Revisit base word patterns by asking the learner to sort the following words into two sets (vc and vcc):

> end   tip   pat   sip   pant   nest   hint   nip   dent   tap   hand   dip

Introduce the 'just add' rule for a vowel suffix: if a word ends in a vcc pattern then you just add the vowel suffix 'ed'. Ask the learner to tell you which of the two sets of words this rule applies to and then to write the words down adding the suffix 'ed'.

Now introduce the doubling rule: if a word ends in a vc pattern then we double the final consonant before adding a vowel suffix (i.e., we must make it into a vcc pattern before we can add the suffix). Write down the word 'tip' and ask the learner if they can work out which consonant can be added to make it into a vcc pattern without changing the sound of the base word (i.e., adding another 'p' to make it tipp+ed) Prompt as necessary so that the learner discovers the 'doubling' rule. This can then be practised as above by writing down the set of 'vc' words and doubling the final consonant before adding the suffix (see Concept Card 28).

## Words for Reading and Spelling

Patted, tended, stepped, tapped, nested, handed, hinted, dipped, tinted, napped, tested.

## Practising the New Learning

Reinforce the concepts of base word and suffix by asking the learner to underline the base words and draw a box round all the suffixes in the following words:

> spends   ended   tents   sped   spits   tested   pits   patted   Ned   sipped   steps   has

Then make a wordsearch using the words for reading above. Give the learner three minutes to find as many words as possible (going from left to right only).

## Sentences for Reading and Dictation

Pat added ten pips. "Ann has ended it," snapped Dan. Dad handed Ned a pad and pen.

### SRR

Practise linking suffix 'ed' by giving the clue word and asking the learner for the sound, letter names, and letter forms.

## Teaching Point 34

cursive form

'o' /ŏ/ and /ō/

*o*

### Reading Card

| | |
|---|---|
| o | /ŏ / orange |
| 0 | /ō/ oval |
| front | back |

### Discovery Learning

Use Discovery Learning to introduce the phonemes through visual, auditory, and tactile/kinaesthetic channels. Use a mirror to discover how the vowel sound is made in the mouth and check if it is voiced or unvoiced. Track the letter 'o' saying the letter sound and name and demonstrate the cursive letter using the handwriting routine. (Note that this is a top joining letter.)

### Reading Card

The long vowel sound /ō/ is added at the teacher's discretion.

### Writing the Letter/s

Practise joining the new letter to previous ones: e.g. top, pond, dot, those.

## Spelling Card

## Spelling Pack Routine

The sound /ŏ/ can be heard in words in the beginning and middle positions. The teacher says the sound on the front of the card /ŏ/, the learner repeats it and then gives the letter name. The learner writes it down in their book in the position it can be found in words saying: /ŏ/ 'o' at the beginning, /ŏ/ 'o' in the middle.

If the long vowel sound /ō/ is added to the Reading Card, a second Spelling Card is needed:

The letter 'o' is used to represent the long vowel /ō/ at the beginning of words and at the end where there is an open syllable e.g. no, so. The learner repeats the sound /ō/ after the teacher, gives the letter name 'o', and writes it in their book saying /ō/ is 'o' at the beginning and /ō/ is 'o' at the end. (Remember that the Spelling Card only represents the 'spelling choices' that have been introduced so far and others will be added later.)

## Words for Reading and Spelling

Top, hot, pod, dot, stop, pond, not, pop, so, no, pot, nod, stopped, topped, dotted, popped, nodded, potted; and irregular words: don't, to, does (if appropriate).

## Practising the New Learning Using a Game – 'Four-in-a Row'

Make a reading game by producing 36 cards containing the words for reading above and some from previous lessons. Set the cards out face up in six rows each of six cards. The game is for two players. Each person has a set of different coloured counters. Players take turns to read a word and when they do so correctly they place a counter on it. The first person to get a row of four counters (across, down, or diagonally) will be the winner, so each player must try to 'block' the other. There are examples of this game in Part V, based on different Teaching Points.

### Sentences for Reading and Dictation

Don't step on the net. 'Sit in the hot spot,' said Ted. Don has stopped, so has Ann.

## Teaching Points 35 and 36

### Prefixes and Punctuation

At this stage in the programme the prefixes 'in' and 'de' can be introduced. Review open and closed syllables (Teaching Points 28 and 32) and code the prefixes using the breve and macron. Ask the learner to read them back to you. Write the prefixes and the base words 'test', 'tend', and 'tent' on pieces of card. Ask the learner to use the prefixes to make new words (e.g., intent, intend, detest). Discuss how the prefix changes the meaning of the word. Use Concept Card 29.

### Words for Reading and Spelling

Intent, intends, depend, detest, indent, instep, insist.

### Practising the New Learning Using a Game

Make a pairs game using 12 pieces of card. Use six cards for the prefixes 'in' and 'de' (each by three) and on the other six write the base words 'tend', 'tent', 'test', 'sect', and the roots 'pend', 'sist'. (A root forms part of a word; roots are common in words of Latin origin.)

Number the prefix cards 1 on the back and the base word/root cards 2. Take turns to turn over two cards (a 1 and 2) to try to make a real word. The winner is the person with the most pairs at the end of the game.

### Sentences for Reading and Dictation

Ask the learner to read the following statements and change them into questions:
Don insists. Dad is intent on it. Dan depends on Pat. Pip detests that top!

Teach the use of question marks and exclamation marks. Try different types of punctuation with the sentence: He intends to stop the test. Discuss how using a question mark or exclamation mark at the end of the sentence changes the way we read it (see Concept Cards 30 and 31).

# Teaching Point 37

'g' /g/

cursive form

*g*

## Discovery Learning

Introduce the phoneme /g/. Demonstrate the cursive form using the handwriting routine. Make the Reading and Spelling card.

## Words for Reading and Spelling

Dig, got, go, snag, hog, dog, gap, ingot; and irregular words: get, gig.

## Practising the New Learning

Look at the letter 'g' written in different fonts, styles etc. e.g., g G g *g* g g G **g** G g *G*.

Look at a page in a magazine and see how many different forms of the letter 'g' can be found.

Ask the learner to circle the words that rhyme:

1. pot    got    dig    get
2. peg    hog    get    dog
3. go     gig    sag    so
4. gag    dog    snag   got

## Sentences for Reading and Dictation

Ann has a peg. Did Ted go to the gig? Ned snags his pants on the dog's tag.

# Teaching Point 38

cursive form

'ng' /ng/                                                          *ng*

## Discovery Learning

Use Discovery Learning to introduce the phoneme /ng/. Use a mirror to discover how this nasal sound is made. Track 'ng' using Tracking Sheet 2 or an extract from a book or newspaper.

## Reading Pack

The new card is added to the Reading Pack showing '-ng'. Clue words are negotiated with the learner (e.g., swing).

## Writing the Letter/s

Practise joining the letters to previous ones: e.g. sting, pang, dong, thing.

## Spelling Pack Routine

The sound /ng/ is usually heard at the end of a base word. The teacher says the sound on the front of the card /ng/, the learner repeats it and then gives the letter names. The learner writes it down in their book in the position it can be found in words saying: /ng/ 'n' 'g' at the end.

## Sufffix 'ing'

Revise the concept of 'suffix' using Concept Card 12. Ask the learner to underline the base word in the following:

  testing        panting        spending        handing        singing        tending

Now ask them to 'box' the suffix 'ing'. Discuss how the suffix changes the verb from present tense (I test/He tests) to present continuous (I am testing/He is testing). Ask the learner to change these sentences into present continuous (and write them down):

He spends it.  Dad hands it to Pat. He sings a song.  Dan pats the dog. He sips it.

Review the 'just add' and 'doubling rule' for a vowel suffix (use Concept Card 32).

## Words for Reading and Spelling

Tipping, sitting, stopping, sending, hopping, sanding, tanning, tinting.

## Practising the New Learning

Make a word search using the following words: song, pang, thing, dong, sing, sipping, tipping, testing, nesting, sanding, sang, hang, dipping, sting.
   Make sure that the words go from left to right. Give the learner three minutes to find as many words as they can. Tell them there are 20 points to be gained – one for each single syllable word and two for words that have a suffix. They must look carefully to gain as many points as possible.

## Sentences for Reading and Dictation

He is singing at the gig. Dan tips Ted's things in the sandpit. Dad is testing the depth.

## SRR

Practise both /ng/ and suffix 'ing', using the Stimulus Response Routine.

# Teaching Point 39

cursive form

'm' /m/

$m$

## Discovery Learning

Use Discovery Learning to introduce the phoneme /m/. Use a mirror to discover how this nasal sound is made. Make sure that the lips stay closed and the mouth does not open or a schwa sound will be introduced. Track 'm' in a piece of text from a magazine, book, or newspaper. Demonstrate the cursive form using the handwriting routine. Make a Reading and Spelling Card.

## Writing the Letter/s

Practise joining the letter to previous ones e.g. man, moth, mend, stem.

## Words for Reading and Spelling

mat, dam, man, map, Tim, Pam, Tom, Meg, hem, mop, dim, mad, Sam, men, ham, them, spam, stem, mopped, mended, mapping, minting, temp, moth, mist.

## Practising the New Learning

Read the words and arrange them in alphabetical order:

a) Sam, man, dim, Tom, hem, Pam.
b) Meg, map, mint, moth, stem, spam.

   Use a snakes and ladders board or a racing track to make a reading or spelling game. Make a pack of cards that contain the words for reading or spelling above. Write a number from 1 to 6 on the back of each card depending on the level of difficulty of the word. The cards replace dice in the game. The player must read or spell the word from the top of the pack in order to move their counter along the number of spaces shown on the card. If a word with a six score is read (or spelt) correctly the player can have another turn. Note that the computer could be used to make a snakes and ladders board that is 7 × 7 instead of the normal 10 × 10 to reduce the length of time the game will take to play.)

## Sentences for Reading and Dictation

Did the man mend it? "Tom detests ham", said Pam. "The mist is thinning!" insists Tim. Sam is mad at Meg.

## Reading Practice

The teacher can compose paragraphs or short stories in structure for the learner to read aloud.

# Teaching Point 40

cursive form

'c' /k/

## Reading Card

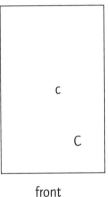

     front            back

## Discovery Learning

Use Discovery Learning to introduce the phoneme /k/'.

## Reading Pack

The new card is added to the Reading Pack. Clue words are negotiated with the learner who then draws the picture. The sound is represented as /k/ on the back of the card.

## Writing the Letter/s

Practise joining the letter to previous ones: e.g. cot, cog, cast, camp.

## Spelling Card

| | | B | M | E |
|---|---|---|---|---|
| /k/ | c | | | |

## Spelling Pack Routine

The letter 'c' can be used to represent the /k/ sound at the beginning of a word. Other spelling choices are taught later. The teacher says the sound on the front of the card /k/ the learner repeats it and then gives the letter name. The learner writes it down saying: /k/ 'c' at the beginning.

## Words for Reading and Spelling

If appropriate, teach the prefix 'con' as in contend, consist, contact.

Can, cat, cap, cot, cod, cog, cost, cast, contend, contest, content, consist. Teach the irregular words 'can't' and 'come' using an irregular spelling routine.

## Practising the New Learning

|     | tent   | tend | test | sist |
| --- | ------ | ---- | ---- | ---- |
| in  | *intent* |      |      |      |
| de  |        |      |      |      |
| con |        |      |      |      |

Ask the learner to complete the grid using the prefixes and base or root words to make as many new words as possible. Check their understanding of the words made.

## Sentences for Reading and Dictation

Introduce tag questions: Dad can cast the net, can't he? Tom has got a cap, hasn't he? Dan is in his cot, isn't he? The cat is Tim's, isn't it? He is content, isn't he? (The use of tag question will need explicit teaching for learners with EAL.)

*Remember to break the sentences down into smaller chunks for dictation if necessary.*

## Teaching Point 41

cursive form

*k*

'k' /k/

### Reading Card

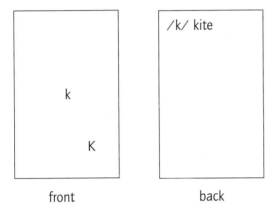

front                     back

### Discovery Learning

Remind the learner of the previous Teaching Point 'c' /k/ through a revision exercise. Using the alphabet arc, ask them if they can find another letter that makes a /k/ sound. Prompt and direct them as necessary to locate the letter 'k'. Track the letter 'k' in a piece of text from a magazine, book, or newspaper. Demonstrate the cursive form using the handwriting routine. Make a Reading Card for 'k' /k/ and add 'k' to the back of the /k/ Spelling Card.

### Writing the Letter/s

Practise joining the letter to previous ones: e.g. kit, king, Kim, kid, Kent.

### Spelling Card

## Spelling Pack Routine

The letter 'k' can also be used to represent the /k/ sound at the beginning of a word. The learner now has two spelling choices for the sound /k/. The teacher says the sound on the front of the card /k/ the learner repeats it and then gives the spelling choices saying /k/ 'c', /k/ 'k' . The learner writes them down in their book in the positions found in words saying: /k/ 'c' at the beginning and /k/ 'k' at the beginning. The middle position could also be introduced *at the teacher's discretion*, but could be left until enough phonemes and syllable division patterns have been introduced to use words with /k/ sound in the middle (e.g., talcum, bacon, balcony, token, spoken).

## Words for Reading and Spelling

Kim, Ken, kit, kin, kid, kip, Kent, kept, kidding, kipping, kids, kitted, kidded.

## Practising the New Learning

Vowels = 2 points. Consonants B to M = 1 point. Consonants N to Z = 3 points.

E.g. Ken = 1+2+3 = 6 points. Ask the learner to read, then score, the following words: Pin, den, kip, kids, spend, Kim, kidding. Then ask them if they can make a word that scores more than 10 points using the letters introduced so far within the programme.

## Sentences for Reading and Dictation

Is Kim in Kent? "Ken is kidding," said Pat. Ken kept the kid in a pen.

(Note that only words containing the letter 'k' to represent /k/ should be used as the rule for c/k spelling choice has not been introduced yet. This should be made clear to the learner before any dictation is given.)

## SRR

Practise linking letter sound /k/, to letter name, to clue word, to letter shape, starting the routine with the clue word so that the learner knows which spelling choice you are focusing on in this lesson.

# Teaching Point 42

## Introduce the Spelling Rule for 'c/k' Choice for /k/

### Discovery Learning

Use Discovery Learning to introduce the spelling rule by asking the learner to sort the following words (on card) into two sets:

can, cast, kin, Ken, kip, cot, kid, Kent, cog, king, cap, cat, kit, cad

Ask the learner to look at the two sets and tell you what they notice about the words (if necessary prompt them to look at the vowel). Try to elicit the answer that all the words starting with the letter 'k' are followed by an 'e' or an 'i'. This is known as the 'Ke /Ki' rule. If they hear the long or short 'e' or 'i' after the /k/ sound then the letter 'k' is used to represent that sound.

### Practising the New Learning Using a Game

Make a game called 'lucky ladders'. Prepare two base boards and a score chart:

| c-n |
|-----|
| k-p |
| k-n |
| c-t |
| k-ng |
| c-st |

| K-nt |
|------|
| k-d |
| c-t |
| k-pt |
| c-p |
| c-st |

| 1 | 2 | 3 | 4 | 5 | 6 |
|---|---|---|---|---|---|
| a | e | i | o | wild | wild |

Each player has a base board containing words written in structure with the vowel missing. Players take turns to roll a dice. The number thrown is checked against the scoreboard. If the player rolls the number 2 then they can write (or place) the letter 'e' on one of the lines to complete a word. The word should then be read back to ensure that it is a real word. *Note that only the vowels 'a', 'e', 'i,' and 'o' are used at this stage as the letter 'u' has not been introduced.* The numbers 5 and 6 are wild and the player can choose the letter they wish to use. The first player to complete all the words in the 'ladder' and read them back correctly is the winner. (A dictionary could be used to check if the spellings are correct if dictionary skills have already been taught.)

With older learners the teacher may wish to practise the c/k choice spelling rule by giving them a worksheet containing words with the first letter missing (e.g., -at, -in, -ip, -ot, -ast, -ing, etc.) for them to complete by writing 'c' or 'k' on the line.

## Words for Reading and Spelling

Cat, can, kid, kip, cast, king, cap, kit, cad, cod, cot, Ken. Compound words can be taught at the teacher's discretion e.g., kidnap, catkin, napkin.

## Sentences for Reading and Dictation

Is Pip a cat? Ken can come with Kim. Has Kim got a napkin? Tom's cat is contented.

# Teaching Point 43

|  | cursive form |
|---|---|
| 'sc' and 'sk' at the Beginning of Words | *sc*   *sk* |

## Discovery Learning

Use Discovery Learning to introduce the phoneme /sk/. Remind the learner that there are two ways of spelling /k/ and ask them how they think /sk/ can be spelled. Track 'sc' and 'sk' using Tracking Sheet 2, or a piece of text from a magazine, book, or newspaper, and demonstrate the cursive form using the handwriting routine.

Reinforce the c/k rule by asking the learner to 'discover' it again using words containing 'sc' and 'sk' blends (e.g., skin, skip, scan, scat, Scot, skit, skid, skim, scam). This usually needs to be taught as a separate Teaching Point as learners will often not generalise the rule without support. Make Reading Cards for 'sc' and 'sk' and negotiate the clue words with the learner. Both cards will have /sk/ on the reverse. Show the learner how to join the letters 'sc' and 'sk' using the handwriting routine.

## Spelling Card

| /sk/ |  |  |
|---|---|---|

|  | B | M | E |
|---|---|---|---|
| /sk/ | *sc* *sk* |  |  |

## Spelling Pack Routine

Only the spelling for /sk/ at the beginning of words is introduced at this stage.

The teacher says the sound on the front of the card /sk/ the learner repeats it and then gives the spelling choices saying /sk/ 's' 'c', /sk/ 's' 'k' . The learner writes them down in their book in the position they can be found in words saying: /sk/'s' 'c' at the beginning, /sk/'s' 'k' at the beginning.

## Practising the New Learning

Ask the learner to build the words and select the correct spelling to write in their book:

 1. sk / sc > ip

 2. sk / sc > an

 3. sk / sc > id

 4. sk / sc > in

 5. sk / sc > ant

 6. sk / sc > it

## Words for Reading and Spelling

Scan, skip, skin, scant, skid, skit, scat, Scot, scads, skep, skint, scanning, skipped, scanned, skidded, skinned; and irregular word 'scent' (at the teacher's discretion).

## Story for Reading and Dictation

Ted is a Scot. He skids in the mist and hits Tom's pet kid. Tom is hopping mad. "The cost is £100," he snaps. Ted is skint so Tom tips him in a skip. Then he tips tins on him. Tom is content, and the kid is OK. Ted isn't!

# Teaching Point 44

'b' /b/

cursive form

*b*

## Discovery Learning

Use Discovery Learning to discover if the sound is voiced or unvoiced. Track 'b'. Demonstrate the cursive form using the handwriting routine. Make a Reading and Spelling Card. The sound /b/ can be heard at the beginning, in the middle (after TP 45), and at the end of words and so the letter 'b' should be written in all three boxes on the back of the Spelling Card.

## Writing the Letter/s

Practise joining the letter to previous ones: e.g. bat, bin, best, bond, hob.

## Words for Reading and Spelling (Select Some)

Ben, big, bag, bid, bad, bet, bat, bin, bam, beg, bit, band, best, banging, bonded, bent, hob, nab, sob, stab, dab, cob, mob, snob, be, bonds, bath.

## Practising the New Learning

1.  Ask the learner to read the following sentences and sort them into 'true' and 'false':

    A hob can get hot. A cob is not a big dog. To be a snob is bad. Big Ben is a man.
    To be contented is to be sad.    A bat can be a pet.    A scam is a band contest.

2.  Scan for words containing the letter 'b' in the story below and underline them.

## Story for Reading and Dictation

Ben has on his best top. He is going to a band contest. At the contest he spots Meg. Ben is not a snob. Ben and Meg get on. The band is not bad and Ben is content.

# Teaching Point 45

### Syllable Division vc/cv

### Discovery Learning

Make the following words (one at a time) with the wooden letters:

kidnap        bandit        catnip        catkin

Give the learner two small cards with a letter 'v' written on them and ask them to place them over the vowels. Ask them to count how many consonants come between the vowels and to place cards with 'c' on them over the consonants. The word has the pattern vccv.

Ask the learner to repeat and clap and say how many syllables are in the word 'kidnap'. Then ask them to separate the syllables in the word by pushing apart the wooden letters. Ask where the consonants have been divided. The learner should notice that they now have a vc-cv pattern. They have worked out the first rule for syllable division – if there are two consonants between the vowels divide the word between them (use Concept Card 33).

## Practising the New Learning

Make a worksheet with the following words:

catnap   basket   napkin   candid   hatpin   insist

Ask the learner to write the letter 'v' over the vowels and the letter 'c' over the consonants between them, then to draw a line between the two consonants to divide the words into two syllables. Ask them to code the vowels with a breve and then read the first syllable, and then the second syllable, and then the whole word. Cut the words in half to make a pairs game.

## Words for Reading and Spelling

Bantam, casket, madman, pendant, bandit, basket, kidnap, napkin, catkin, hobnob.

## Story for Reading and Dictation

Bob the bandit is a bad man. He nabs a bantam hen and hands it to Kim in a basket. "The bantam hen is not big," snaps Kim. "Go!" Kim insists.

# Teaching Point 46

cursive form

*sk nk ct*

## End Blends '-sk' '-nk' '-ct'

Introduce the end blends 'sk', 'nk', and 'ct' through Discovery Learning. Track the blends using Tracking Sheet 2 or text from a magazine or newspaper. The end blends 'nk' and 'ct' should have their own Reading and Spelling Cards, but end blend 'sk' is added to the back of the existing 'sk' Reading and Spelling Cards. An appropriate clue word is chosen to indicate its end position (e.g., mask) on the Reading Card. Words with end blends 'sk' and 'nk' can now be included in spelling and dictation but care should be taken with the end blend 'ct'. In words like 'act' or 'intact' the /t/ sound is part of the base word and so the letter 't' is used. In some words the final /t/ is represented by the letters 'ed' because it is a suffix (usually the past tense of a verb). Revise the suffix 'ed' /t/ as in kicked, picked, ticked. Ask the learner to underline the base word and box the suffix.

## Teaching Point 47

### The 'ck' Rule

### Discovery Learning

Encourage the learner to work out the rule for themselves. Write the following words on pieces of card: sick, pick, tank, task, tick, neck, peck, sank, dock, desk, think, sack. Ask the learner to read the words and then sort them into two sets. Prompt them as necessary by asking what each set of words has in common. They should be able to work out (with support) that when the /k/ sound is heard after a short vowel sound in one syllable words we use 'ck' to close in the vowel, but when it is heard after a consonant as it is with end blends 'sk' or 'nk' there is no letter 'c'. (The letter 'k' uses the other consonant to help close in the vowel.) Let the learner track words ending in 'ck' in a book. Make a new Reading Card for '–ck' /k/ using an appropriate clue word, (e.g., duck) and add 'ck' to the back of the Spelling Card for /k/ in the end position. Words ending in 'ck' can now be used for reading, spelling, and dictation.

If appropriate, the rule for a 'k' ending can also be introduced at this point. Some learners will already know from their knowledge of key words that some words can end in just 'k' (e.g., week, look). In this case they have one syllable, like the words ending in 'ck', but the vowel *sound* is long (usually represented by a vowel digraph). This Teaching Point will need reinforcing later in the programme when vowel digraphs have been introduced and the spelling choices can be practised (see Teaching Point 94).

## Teaching Point 48

### Spelling Rule 'c', 'k', or 'ck' at the End of Words

### Discovery Learning 'c' and 'ck'

Let the learner work out the rule themselves by asking them to sort the following words into two sets:

picnic tactic thick sock aspic pack Nick antic deck speck snack attic

Ask them to read the words and clap the syllables. They should notice that words ending in 'ck' have one syllable but words ending in 'c' have two (or more) syllables.

## Practising the New Learning

Make a work sheet to incorporate the rules introduced for /k/ ending, for example:

Choose the correct ending: c, k, or ck?
1. ban__    2. sa__    3. sin__    4. picni__    5. cas__
6. anti__    7. spe__    8. tacti__    9. pi__    10. thin__

Read the shared story 'Kit's Tip' in Part V. Words ending in 'k' blends (-sk, -nk), 'k', 'c' and 'ck' can now be included in reading and spelling.

# Teaching Point 49

cursive form

'f' and 'ff' /f/

## Reading Cards

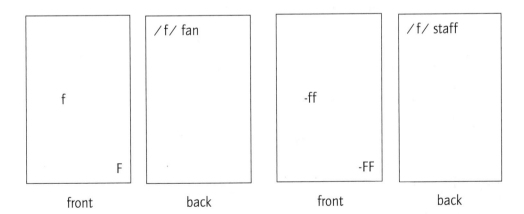

| front | back | front | back |

## Discovery Learning

Introduce /f/ through Discovery Learning. Ask the learner to listen to and repeat words containing /f/ and identify its position in words using a BME sheet. Show the learner some words 'in structure' (e.g., fit, fin, fad, fast, fan, tiff, infect, infant, fantastic, staff, naff, miff, etc.) and ask them which letter/s represent the /f/ sound.

Help the learner to work out the rule: one syllable words with a short vowel sound end in double 'f'. Like the letter 'k' it needs another consonant to help to close in the vowel and give the short sound. Use a mirror to find out how /f/ is made. Track letter 'f' and 'ff' in a piece of text, naming the letters as they circle them. Make separate Reading Cards for 'f' and '-ff'. When showing how to form the letter, tell the learner that this is an example where there could be a pen-lift to cross the letter 'f'.

## Spelling Card

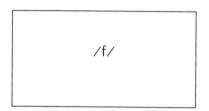

| /f/ | B | M | E |
|-----|---|---|---|
| /f/ | f | f | ff |

## Spelling Pack Routine

The teacher says the sound on the front of the card, /f/, the learner repeats it and then gives the spelling choices saying /f/ 'f', /f/ 'ff' . The learner writes them down in their book in the position they can be found in words saying: /f/'f' at the beginning, /f/'f' in the middle, /f/ 'ff' at the end. (Note: 'f' at the end of words comes after a long vowel sound and can be added to the /f/ card once vowel digraphs have been introduced.)

## Practising the New Learning

Circle the words that rhyme in each row:

|   |       |       |      |      |
|---|-------|-------|------|------|
| 1.| fan   | fin   | tin  | hen  |
| 2.| Ted   | fan   | pan  | sat  |
| 3.| mist  | man   | fist | den  |
| 4.| fit   | stiff | fan  | miff |
| 5.| staff | fad   | fed  | naff |

## Words for Reading and Spelling

Fit, fin, fist, fat, fan, fad, fast, infect, infant, defect, sniff, stiff, staff, naff, miff, off, fantastic. Irregular words 'if' and 'of' can be taught at the teacher's discretion.

## Story for Reading and Dictation

Sniff the cat spots a ham in Meg's picnic basket. He is a fat cat and Meg has not fed him. It is hot and Meg sets off to get a fan. Sniff is fast and nabs the ham. He has the ham and it is fantastic. Meg gets back and is miffed. "Scat, Sniff," snaps Meg and tips the basket. He's not an infant, Meg insists.

## SRR

Practise /f/ starting the routine with the clue word so the learner knows which spelling choice you are focusing on in this lesson.

# Teaching Point 50

cursive form

$l\ ll$

## 'l' and 'll' /l/

### Discovery Learning

Introduce /l/ 'l' and 'll' through Discovery Learning. The rule is the same as 'f' / 'ff'. Use a mirror to discover how /l/ is made. Make two separate Reading Cards but put both spelling choices on the back of the /l/ Spelling Card, writing 'll' in the end position.

## Practising the New Learning

Ask the learner to write the following sentences changing them into the past tense:

Bill skips in the dell.    Nell has a big doll.    Moll fans Meg.    The top fits Len.

## Words for Reading and Spelling

Len, let, lip, list, Bill, tell, pill, dell, sell, doll, till, Nell, dill, still, mill, spill, spell.

## Sentences for Reading and Dictation

Did Bill sell the mill? Has Len still got the list? Can Nell spell 'fantastic'?

## Teaching Point 51

cursive form

### 'ss' and Flossy Rule

### Discovery Learning

Introduce /s/ 'ss' using a BME sheet (as in Teaching Point 49). This is the third 'end spelling' where the final letter is doubled. The learner can be helped to remember the rule by referring to it as the f<u>lossy</u> rule as the word *flossy* contains the letters that are doubled after a short vowel in one syllable words, 'f', 'l', and 's'. Make a Reading Card for /s/ '-ss', and add 'ss' to the back of the /s/ Spelling Card in the end position. Words ending in 'ss' can be introduced now for reading and spelling, keeping to the structure (e.g., miss, pass, moss, less, loss, boss, Bess, hiss, kiss).

## Teaching Point 52

### Suffix 'es'

### Discovery Learning

Revise suffix 's' (Teaching Point 16). Ask the learner to underline the base word and box the suffix in the following words: misses, passes, kisses, hisses, losses, bosses, and then to read back the words. Guide the learner in discovering the rule (with words ending in /s/ we add 'es' to the verb). Ask them to count how many syllables there are in the words. This is another guide to the spelling – if they can hear two syllables it ends in suffix 'es' not suffix 's' (Concept Card 34). Make a Reading Card for Suffix '-es' /iz/ and a Spelling Card for /ĭz/ 'es'.

## Teaching Point 53

### Beginning 'l' Blends

### Discovery Learning

Introduce the 'l' blends through Discovery Learning. Make a Reading and Spelling Card for each blend: (bl, cl, fl, gl, pl, sl, and spl) to add to the Reading and Spelling Packs. Make a word search (using the words for reading) to practise the new learning.

## Words for Reading and Spelling

Black, click, flag, glasses, plank, slip, splat, blink, clocks, flock, sling, gloss, plot.

## Practising the New Learning in Writing

Ask the learner to choose 'ck', 'ff', or 'ss' to complete the following:

   bli--   cla--   sli--   cli--   ble--   flo--   glo--   spe--   gla--   bla--   fle--

## Story for Reading and Dictation

Cliff has his hand in a black sling. He slipped on moss as he stepped on a plank. Cliff's glasses snapped and he hit his hand in the mist.

First ask the learner to track the 'l' blends, underlining the words. Then highlight any that are verbs. Finally, look up 'moss' in a dictionary.

# Teaching Point 54

## End 'l' Blends

### Discovery Learning

Introduce the end blends through Discovery Learning. Include some auditory discrimination exercises e.g. listening for the target sound /lt/ in pairs of words: hilt/ hill; tell /tilt; sell/silt; spilt/ spill; belt/ bell; pet / pelt. Make Reading and Spelling Cards for 'l' blends -ld, -lf, -lk, -lm, -lp, -lt, to add to the packs.

### Practising the New Learning

Ask the learner to match the adjectives to an appropriate noun:

| Adjectives | Nouns |
|---|---|
| hot | belt |
| stiff | scalp |
| black | milk |
| pink | elm |
| big | back |
| slim | neck |

## Words for Reading and Spelling

Held, self, elk, help, helm, belt, milk, scalp, film, kilt, elf, melt, pelted, helped.

## Story for Reading and Dictation

Ken is in a Panda. He spilt hot milk on his lap, and his Panda skidded into a bank. Ken hit his neck as it snapped back. An elf helped him to click the belt. Ken sniffed his "thanks". Ken filmed the elf as he melted into a blanket of mist. He sent it to Nick on his laptop. "Get this," said Ken.

Ask the learner to highlight the nouns in the passage and to read it adding some adjectives *orally* to the nouns (the adjectives can be out of structure).

# Teaching Point 55

cursive form

### End Blend 'ft' /ft/

The end blend 'ft' can be introduced at this point. Make new Reading and Spelling Cards. Practise reading 'ft' blends by asking the learner to use Tracking Sheet 3 to track this sentence and then read it aloud:

Cliff lifts the gift bag and can tell it is a soft doll in a kilt.

## Words for Reading and Spelling

Deft, aft, lift, daft, gift, soft, theft, lifting, softest, sift, sifted, gifted.

## Story for Reading and Dictation

Meg has a big doll. Ben nicks it and tips it in a pit. "That is theft," snaps Meg. Ben thinks Meg is soft. Meg thinks Ben is daft and intends to kick him. Ben gets the doll back and hands it to Meg. Meg thanks him.

Ask the learner to predict what will happen next.

## Teaching Point 56

cursive form

### '– all' (at the End of Words)

The use of 'll' with the vowel 'a' needs introducing separately from the vowels used in Teaching Point 50 as the vowel sound changes from /ă/ to /aw/ when followed by a double 'l'. Make a Reading and Spelling Card for '-all'/aw/. Practise making words ending in 'all' using on-set and rime to make call, tall, ball, stall, hall, gall. These words can be listed on a card to be practised each lesson as part of the Reading Pack. Start introducing words ending in 'all' into spelling and dictation.

## Teaching Point 57

### Suffix 'ed' /d/

The third sound for suffix 'ed' is introduced at this point as it is now possible to make words to practise ed /d/ as in: called, stalled, killed, billed, skinned, milled, spilled, thinned, filled. Add this third sound to the back of the Reading Card for '–ed' with an appropriate clue word. It is the second choice of spelling on the /d/ Spelling Card and goes in the end position. The learner response for Spelling Card /d/ is now /d/ 'd' at the beginning, /d/ 'd' in the middle, and /d/ 'd' and /d/ suffix 'ed' at the end.

### Practising the New Learning

Ask the learner to read and sort the words given for reading and spelling into three sets: (/t/, /d/ /ĭd/).

### Words for Reading and Spelling

Kicked, spilled, mended, tapped, called, milked, gifted, licked, listed, billed, skimmed.

### Story for Reading and Dictation

Cliff called at ten o'clock. "Kim is still in bed," said Dad. "I cannot stop then," said Cliff and set off. "Cliff called," said Dad. "I missed him," said Kim and got mad and kicked the cat. Then Dad got mad and banged a stick on the desk top. Kim stopped. "I'm glad you stopped," said Dad. Kim kissed him and planned to stop getting so mad.

## Teaching Point 58

cursive form

'r' /r/

*r*

### Discovery Learning

Use Discovery Learning to introduce the phoneme /r/. Discover how the phoneme /r/ is articulated. Track 'r' using tracking sheet 1 and demonstrate the cursive form using the handwriting routine. Draw attention to the fact that 'r' has a top joining stroke – it can be a 'tricky' letter and so needs a lot of practice. Make a Reading and Spelling Card. The sound /r/ can be heard at the beginning of words but forms part of a digraph at the end of words, so 'r' is only written in the beginning position on the back of this Spelling Card. (Note that the prefix 'pro' can be introduced at this stage at the teacher's discretion.)

### Writing the Letter/s

Practise joining the letter to previous ones: e.g. rat, rink, rest, rob.

### Words for Reading and Spelling

Rob, rat, rest, rib, rid, rink, risk, rand, red, Rick, rasp, riff, Ross, rap, ran, rag, ripped.

### Practising the New Learning

Ask the learner to read the following sentences and add the punctuation:

has rob a pet rat   rob is at the rink said ross    did it hit his rib
rick sat on a rock  he ripped the red rag        get rid of the rasp  can ross protect him

### Story for Reading and Dictation

Rob has a pet rat called "Pink". Pink has a nest of red rags. Pink had a nap and so Ross banged the nest. "That's a risk!" said Rob. Pink bit Ross and then hid in the rags.

## SRR

Practise linking letter sound /r/ to the letter name, clue word and letter shape, using the Stimulus Response Routine.

# Teaching Point 59

## 'r' Blends at the Beginning

Introduce the 'r' blends through Discovery Learning. Make a Reading and Spelling Card for each blend (br, cr, fr, gr, pr, dr) to add to the Reading and Spelling Packs.

## Words for Reading and Spelling

Fran, pram, prank, bran, grim, cram, gram, prim, dram, prod, frog, frost, drip, crest.

## Practising the New Learning in Writing

Make a word chain starting with one of the words for reading. Ask the learner to change only one letter at a time to make a new word, for example:

Drip ⟶ grip ⟶ grid ⟶ grim ⟶ prim ⟶ pram

See who can make the longest chain and read the words back.

## Story for Reading and Dictation

Ross and Fran go on a picnic. Fran grabs the ham and Ross nabs the milk. The milk spills and drips on Fran's pink top. Fran is grim and prods Ross in the ribs. Fran crams in the ham. "Stop the pranks," spits Fran. "Not a prank," snaps Ross and grabs Fran's hand.

## Developing Comprehension/Study Skills

First ask the learner to think of a good title for the story. Then help them to find and highlight the key information-carrying words. Finally, in the next lesson, ask the learner to retell the story from these key words.

## Teaching Point 60

cursive form

### Consonant Clusters: str, scr, spr

*str, scr, spr*

### Discovery Learning

Introduce the three letter blends through Discovery Learning and add them to the Reading and Spelling Packs. Give practice in discriminating the sounds by asking the learner to listen to a word and hold up a card with the correct blend, or to look at pictures and either write the correct blend or match the correct word (e.g., strap, script, scrap, spring, sprat, sprint, strath, string, stress, strict). The learner should use a dictionary to look up any words they don't know. Start to include three letter blends in spelling and dictation.

## Teaching Point 61

### Prefixes: 'im', 're', and 'pre'

At this stage in the programme the prefixes 'im','re', and 'pre' can be introduced. Review open and closed syllables (Teaching Points 28 and 32) and code the prefixes using the breve and macron. Ask the learner to read them back. Write the prefixes and the base words 'test', 'tend', 'print', 'press', and 'lent' on pieces of card. Ask the learner to use the prefixes to make new real words (e.g., retest, pretend, imprint, relent, reprint, impress). Discuss how the prefix changes the meaning of the word.

### Words for Reading and Spelling

Impress, impend, pretend, resent, rethink, imprint, impact, relent, prefab, prefect.

### Practising the New Learning

Make a pairs game using the new prefixes and base/root words above.

### Sentences for Reading and Dictation

Ask the learner to read the following questions and change them into statements:

Did Rob pretend to be a dog?   Can Ross rethink the task?   Is Dad impressed?

## Teaching Point 62

cursive form

### Consonant Blend 'sm' /sm/

*sm*

### Discovery Learning

Introduce 'sm' /sm/ through Discovery Learning. Use a mirror to enable the learner to discover how the sound is made. The lips should only just open to ensure that the pure sound is made and to prevent a schwa (/ə/ sound). Make a Reading and Spelling Card to add to the packs. Spelling position is beginning (the end and middle position can be added later).

### Words for Reading and Spelling

Small, smack, smell, smock, smelt, smog, smelt, smolt, prism.

### Practising the New Learning

Help the learner to look up unknown words from the list above in a dictionary to check their meaning and ask them to write a sentence using each one of these appropriately or draw a picture to show the meaning.

### Sentences for Reading and Writing Practice

Rob is smelting the glass.

Fran and Rick got lost in the smog.

Fred has a small black rabbit called Meg.

Print the sentences and ask the learner to copy them using a cursive script.

## Teaching Point 63

cursive form

### End Blend '-mp' /mp/

*mp*

Although the letters 'm' and 'p' have already been introduced within the programme the end blend 'mp' /mp/ needs to be introduced as a separate Teaching Point, particularly for spelling, as the /m/ in words such as 'camp' and 'lamp' is often omitted from words by beginning spellers. Make the Reading and Spelling Cards. Spelling and dictation routines can now start to include words with this end blend (if appropriate).

## Words for Reading and Spelling

Damp, camp, stamp, lamp, hemp, ramp, limp, crimp.

## Practising the New Learning

Select two or three of the words for reading and check understanding by asking the learner to say a sentence (orally) that contains the target word.

## Story for Reading and Dictation

Fred, Fran, and Rob go camping. Rob stops at the top of a hill. This is the spot to camp, he thinks. Fran sits on the damp grass and has a drink. Fred has a bag of crisps. Rob has a small glass of milk. Then Fred gets the tents and Fran repacks the milk and snacks. Rob kicks a ball and calls to Fred, "Kick it back." The ball hits Fred's left leg. He drops the tents and limps to a rock to sit. Fred is cross and so is Fran. Rob stamps off in a miff. It is a bad end.

Ask the learner to predict what might happen next.

# Teaching Point 64

cursive form

$\mathcal{u}$

'u' /ŭ/ and /ū /

## Reading Card

| u U | /ŭ/ under /ū/ utensil |
|-----|------------------------|

front                      back

## Discovery Learning

Introduce the phoneme /ŭ/ and ask whether it is voiced or unvoiced. Track the letter 'u' using Tracking Sheet 1, saying the letter sound and name, and demonstrate the cursive letter using the handwriting routine.

## Reading Pack

The new card is added to the Reading Pack. The long vowel sound /ū/ is added at the teacher's discretion but will usually be introduced after Teaching Point 69 (syllable division v/cv and vc/v). Clue words are negotiated with the learner.

## Writing the Letter/s

Practise joining the new letter to previous ones e.g. bun, stump, duck, full.

## Spelling Card

|  | B | M | E |
|---|---|---|---|
| /ŭ/ | $u$ | $u$ |  |

## Spelling Pack Routine

The sound /ŭ/ can be heard at the beginning and in the middle of words. The learner's response is /ŭ/ 'u' at the beginning and /ŭ/'u' in the middle.

## Words for Reading and Spelling

Tub, up, stub, hung, grub, cub, pun, dud, smug, hulk, rung, rub, dump, thump, gulf.

## Practising the New Learning

Ask the learner to read and highlight words with /ŭ/ using the wordsearch in Part V. Track the words from left to right.

### Story Reading and Dictation

Cliff and Rod run to help the man. He has slipped off a rock and into a pond. Cliff jumps into the pond and grabs his top. Rod grabs the man and pulls him to the bank. Cliff hands the man his top and the man thanks them.

## Teaching Point 65

cursive form

'w' /w/

_w_

### Writing the Letter/s

When demonstrating the cursive form, draw attention to the fact that it has a top joining stroke. Practise joining the new letter to previous ones e.g. wet, west, will, web, win.

### Words for Reading and Spelling

Will, went, wind, west, web, wink, with, win, wet, wall; and the irregular word: won't.

### Practising the New Learning

Ask the learner to sort words into alphabetic order e.g., will, went, win, web, wet, wit.

### Story for Reading and Dictation

_The Trip_
Will, Kit, Fred, and Rob got a map. Kit put the map on the top of his desk. "Pick up the pin," said Will, "and stick it in the map". Fred picked up the pin and stuck it in the map. "It is in Kent," said Kit. "That's splendid," said Will. "It is in West Brampton." "My mum went to West Brampton last spring and it is fantastic," said Rob. "Let's get the tent and camp on the sand," he said. "This will be fun. We can run in the sand hills and dig a sand pit. We can pack a picnic and lots of drinks. We can stick windmills in the sand and jump from the rocks. We can …"

Ask the learner to finish the last sentence.

# Teaching Point 66

cursive form

## 'wa' – the Sound /wŏ /

*ₘₐ* (cursive)

### Discovery Learning

Help the learner to discover that when the letter 'w' is followed by the letter 'a' it often says /wŏ/, by looking at and reading the key words 'was' and 'want'. Take the letters 'w' and 'a' out of the alphabet arc and practise making some more /wŏ/ words by adding letters to the end (e.g., wasp, wand, wad). Ask the learner to read the words. Make a Reading and Spelling Card.

### Spelling Card

The learner's response is /wŏ/ 'w' 'a'.

### Practising the New Learning

Revise the syllable division pattern vc/cv and practise reading two syllable words by asking the learner to divide and read the words wallet, wallop, and wastel. Look up 'wastel' in a dictionary or on the web and discuss its meaning. Common 'wa' /wŏ/ words can now be included in reading and dictation.

# Teaching Point 67

cursive form

*ₘₕ* (cursive)

## 'wh' Words

Write some 'wh' words on pieces of card (e.g., when, what, where) for the learner. Ask them to listen to the word as you say it and hold up the one they think is correct. Ask them what they notice about the three words. Help them to discover that these are all question words. Ask the learner to think of some more question words (e.g., which, who). Who, where, and which can be taught *at this stage* of the programme (at the teacher's discretion) as irregular spellings. Make a Reading Card for 'wh' and add it to the back of the Spelling Card for /w/. It is the second choice spelling for /w/ at the beginning of words.

Practise the new learning by asking the learner to re-read the story for Teaching Point 66 and answer the following questions (developing comprehension):

- Who got the map?
- Who stuck in the pin?
- When did Mum go to West Brampton?
- What did Rob think of West Brampton?

# Teaching Point 68

cursive form

*sw tw*

## Consonant Blends 'sw' and 'tw'

## Discovery Learning

Introduce the blends 'sw' and 'tw' through Discovery Learning. Make a Reading and Spelling Card for each to add to the Reading and Spelling Packs.

## Words for Reading and Spelling

Swing, twig, twin, swell, swan, swat, swims, twill, twit, twisted, swap.

## Practising the New Learning

Ask the learner to track the following sentence using Tracking Sheet 3:

Rob can swim in the small pond at the Swiss hut with his twin Ron.

## Sentences for Reading and Dictation

Who can swim? Where can he swim? What is Rob's twin called?

Ask the learner to answer the questions by referring to the sentence they have tracked.

# Teaching Point 69

## Syllable Division v/cv and vc/v

### Discovery Learning

Write the following words on a piece of paper:

motel        token        unit        latent        silent        patent

Ask the learner to write a letter 'v' over the vowels and a letter 'c' over the consonant that comes between the vowels.

Ask them to repeat each word after you and clap to identify how many syllables there are (e.g., in the word 'motel'). Let them discover where the word divides. Repeat this for each of the words above and then ask the learner to draw a line to show where the words divide. They should notice that they now have a v-cv pattern. They have now worked out the rule for the second syllable division pattern – if there is only one consonant between the vowels, divide in front of the consonant. Look at each syllable in turn and identify if they are open or closed. Ask the learner to write the breve symbol over the closed syllables and the macron over the open syllables, to help with pronunciation, before reading the words. Use Concept Card 35.

There are some exceptions to this rule – irregular words that divide after the consonant (e.g., lemon, habit, satin, tepid). In each of these words the first syllable is closed and the vowel sound is short. Make a card for these irregular words and add to it as the learner works through the programme. The card can then be practised for reading and spelling on a regular basis. Use Concept Card 36.

### Practising the New Learning

Make a pairs game using words that follow the vcv pattern above, putting the first syllable on one card and the second on another, using one colour of card for first syllables and a different colour for second syllables The learner has to turn over a first syllable card and a second syllable card and then read them to see if they make a word (refer to Teaching Point 45).

### Sentences for Reading and Dictation

Change these sentences into the future tense:

> Dad goes to the hotel at ten o' clock. Kim has begun to swim. Pam cuts
> up a melon.

## Teaching Point 70

cursive form

### Consonant 'y' /y/

### Discovery Learning

Introduce the consonant 'y'. Track 'y' using Tracking Sheet 1 and demonstrate the
cursive form using the handwriting routine. Make a Reading and Spelling Card ('y' as
a consonant is found at the beginning).

### Writing the Letter/s

Practise joining the new letter to previous ones e.g. yet, yes, yen, yell, yam.

### Words for Reading and Spelling

Yank, yet, yes, yam, yell, yelp, yon, yo-yo; and the irregular word, 'yolk'.

### Practising the New Learning

Ask the learner to sort the words for reading into alphabetical order or make
a rhyming pairs game, using words such as ram/yam, yang/sang, bell/yell, yet/
get, etc.

### Sentences for Reading and Dictation

Dad yells at him to stop. Kim trips and lands on Ted's dog. The dog yelps.
Ben grabs the yam but Bill yanks it from him. "Can Tim get me a yo-yo?" asks Ron.

# Teaching Point 71

## Semi-vowel 'y' /ĭ/ and 'y' /ī/

### Reading Card

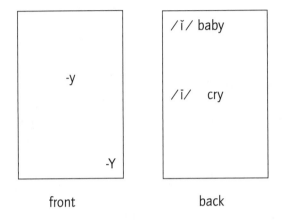

| | |
|---|---|
| -y | /ĭ/ baby |
| | /ī/   cry |
| -Y | |

front                         back

### Discovery Learning

Use Discovery Learning to introduce 'y' /ĭ/ at the end of words (in some regions this may be /ē/). For example, give the learner a set of cards with pictures that contain the /ĭ/ sound in different positions and ask them to sort these according to where they can hear the target sound (beginning, middle, and end). Ask the learner how we spell /ĭ/ at the beginning of a word such as 'ink' and in the middle of a word such as 'tin'. Look at the words baby, lady, happy, nappy, hippy, lumpy. Read these aloud and ask the learner what they notice about the end of the words. Help them to work out the rule: no English word ends in the letter 'i' – the consonant 'y' is used at the end of words to represent a vowel sound and so is known as a semi-vowel (Concept Card 37).

All the words above usually have a short vowel /ĭ/ sound – ask the learner what the long vowel sound is and look at some words ending in 'y' /ī/ (help them to notice that these are usually one syllable words; (e.g., sky or a base word with a prefix e.g., imply).

### Spelling Cards

| | B | M | E |
|---|---|---|---|
| /ĭ/ | i | i | y |

| | B | M | E |
|---|---|---|---|
| /ĭ/ | i | | y |

## Spelling Pack Routine

Add 'y' to the back of the /ĭ/ Spelling Card. The learner's response is /ĭ/ 'i' at the beginning, /ĭ/ 'i' in the middle, and /ĭ/ 'y' at the end. If the long vowel 'y' /ĭ/ is added to the back of the /ĭ/ Spelling Card, the learner's response is /ĭ/ is 'i' at the beginning and /ĭ/ 'y' at the end.

## Words for Reading and Spelling

Nippy, nappy, happy, baby, lady, sloppy, flimsy, floppy, Billy, silly, handy.

Try, cry, by, my, fly, sty, spy, dry, pry, ply, sky, spry, fry, sly, deny, imply, decry, why.

## Practising the New Learning

Illustrate the words to show their meaning e.g., small big (form should reflect meaning).

Slim tiny black sticky happy cry misty fly sloppy.

## Story for Reading and Dictation

Billy has a yak. He is called Tiny. The yak has a pack full of yams. Billy and Tiny pad back to camp but then Tiny stops and will not go. "Don't be silly," yells Billy as he yanks and pulls and stamps in the sand. The yak sets off at a sprint. He passes Billy. "I must try to stop Tiny," he thinks, "I do not want the yams to be tipped in the sand." Billy runs as fast as he can. At last he gets the yams back. "I will fry them with ham and mint," Billy thinks. He is a happy man. (Irregular word: Yak.)

## SRR

Practise 'y' /ĭ/ and 'y' /ĭ/ using the Stimulus Response Routine.

## Teaching Point 72

### Suffixes '-ly' and '-ful'

Write the suffixes 'ly' and 'ful' on pieces of card. Ask the learner to add the suffix 'ly' to the following base words – sad, bad, soft – and to read the words back. Then ask them to give you a sentence orally for each word (e.g., the egg is too soft/he crept softly down the stairs). Discuss how adding the suffix 'ly' changes the use of the word and the adjective (a word that describes a noun) into an adverb (a word that tells you more about the verb). Make a Concept Card for 'adjective' and 'adverb' if you wish.

Use the suffix 'ful' with base words to make restful, sinful, and skilful. Discuss how the suffix 'ful' changes the meaning and the noun (naming word) into an adjective. Note that the suffix 'ful' has only one letter 'l' and the word 'skill' has only one 'l' when the suffix is added. Use a closure exercise to practise putting the new words into sentences.

## Teaching Point 73

### Vowel Suffix Rule: Change 'y' to 'i'

Remind the learner of the rule that no words in English end in the letter 'i' (revisit Teaching Point 71). When a suffix is added to a base word ending in the letter 'y' then it is no longer the last letter in the word and so the vowel sound can be represented by the letter 'i'. The letter 'y' changes to an 'i' and the suffix is added (e.g., 'baby' becomes 'babies'). Help the learner to discover the rule for themselves by giving them the following pairs of words to look at (see Concept Card 38):

Baby/babies, lady/ladies, happy/happiest, snappy/snappiest, happy/happily.

Fly/flies, try/tries, cry/cries, ply/plies, dry/dried, pry/pried.

The exception to this rule is when a vowel suffix starting with 'i' is added to a word ending in 'y' (e.g., babying or babyish). This follows another rule – we do not find a double 'i' in English words. (Note that words which are not of English origin may not obey these rules e.g., ski/skiing.)

Practise the new learning by sorting words according to the rule they follow, using the vowel suffix frame provided in Part V. Making word cards to sort under the columns provides an alternative to writing.

# Teaching Point 74

cursive form

*j*

## 'j' /j/

## Discovery Learning

Ask the learner to listen to and repeat the following words – jet, jam, jury, java, jump, Jane, Jody, Jill, jinx – and identify the common sound. Ask them to track the letter 'j' using Tracking Sheet 1, saying the sound and letter name as they circle it. Practise writing the letter using the handwriting routine and make a new Reading and Spelling Card. The letter is written in the beginning position only on the reverse of the Spelling Card (in English no word ends in the letter 'j'), although it can be written in the middle position in words such as 'inject' or 'reject' and these can be practised at this stage at the teacher's discretion.

## Writing the Letter/s

Practise joining the new letter to previous ones e.g. jam, jest, jump.

## Words for Reading and Spelling

Jet, jam, jag, Jan, Jill, jest, Jock, Jody, Jimmy, jot, Jed, Jack, Jeff, jib, job, jab, jilt, jig.

## Practising the New Learning

Ask the learner to sort the words for reading into common nouns (e.g., jam), proper nouns (e.g., Jill), and verbs (e.g., jot). Discuss which words can be used as a noun and a verb (e.g., jest, jib, jot).

## Story for Reading and Dictation

Jed is a small black pup. He is full of fun. He has a pal, Jack. Jack is a pup, but not as big as Jed. He is Don's best pal and spends long spells with him. Jed and Jack went to the banks of a hill to run and jump. Jack was tugging Jed's leg when Jed spotted a rabbit. Off he ran, dragging Jack with him. Jack let go. The rabbit ran fast and so did the pups. Suddenly the rabbit went up the bank and into its run. Jed tried to get into the run but got stuck. What a jam! Jack gripped Jed's back legs and tugged and tugged. Plop! Jed fell on top of Jack. What a lot of legs! Jed began to yap. Jack began to yap. The rabbit did a jig. What a lot of fun!

# Teaching Point 75

cursive form

'v'  /v/

## Discovery Learning

Ask the learner to look at pictures of the following – van, vest, vehicle, vase, violin – and identify the common sound. Track the letter 'v', asking the learner to say the sound and letter name as they circle it. Use a mirror to discover how the fricative /v/ is made. Ask the learner to put their hand on their throat to discover if it is a voiced or unvoiced sound. Help them to distinguish it from the unvoiced /f/ by feeling the vibrations in their throat. Practise writing 'v' using the handwriting routine and make a new Reading and Spelling Card (v is at the beginning and middle but not at the end). Point out that it has a top joining stroke.

## Writing the Letter/s

Practise joining the new letter to previous ones e.g. van, vet, vast, vim.

## Words for Reading and Spelling

Van, vast, vest, vent, vim, Vicky, David, visit, seven, velum, vamp, Venus.

## Practising the New Learning

Sort the words for reading into alphabetical order. Look up any unknown words in a dictionary.

## Story for Reading and Dictation

David gets up at ten o'clock. He is going to visit Vicky in Devon. It is a long trip and he must get to Devon by half past seven. David begins to panic. He has lost his best vest and his black velvet jacket. He is not lucky. Even the van will not go. Vicky will be mad, he thinks, and runs to get the bus. Will he get to Devon by half past seven?

After reading cut the passage up into separate sentences and ask the learner to put them in their correct order.

## Teaching Point 76

cursive form

'x' /ks/ /gz/

𝒳

### Reading Card

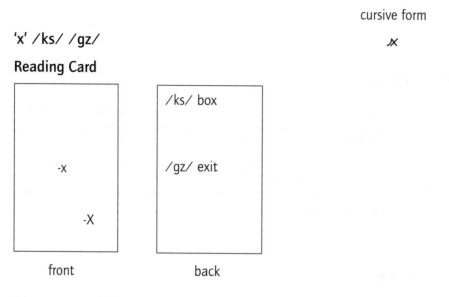

| | |
|---|---|
| -x | /ks/ box |
| -X | /gz/ exit |
| front | back |

### Discovery Learning

Ask the learner to listen to the words containing the /ks/ sound (e.g., box, fox, six, fix, mix, extra, wax, expand) and identify the common sound. Then ask where they can hear the /ks/ sound in the words. Help them to discover how the /ks/ sound is represented by looking at some words written in structure and reading them together. Track the letter 'x' using Tracking Sheet 1, asking the learner to say the sound and letter name as they circle it. The second sound /gz/ (as in exact) is introduced at the teacher's discretion.

### Reading Pack

The new card is added to the Reading Pack. Clue words are negotiated with the learner who then draws the picture. The letter 'x' has three sounds: /ks/ and /gz/ (/z/ as in xylophone can also be added at the teacher's discretion).

### Spelling Card

| | | B | M | E |
|---|---|---|---|---|
| /ks/ | /ks/ | | 𝒳 | 𝒳 |

## Writing the Letter/s

Practise joining the new letter to previous ones e.g. fix, box, six, wax. (In some scripts writing 'x' will require a pen lift.)

## Words for Reading and Spelling

Max, flex, boxes, next, wax, six, mixed, fixed, fox, hex, crux, vex, boxing.

Exam, exit, exist, exhibit, exempt (if appropriate).

Note: a Spelling Card for /gz/ would show 'x' only in the middle position.

## Practising the New Learning

Make a worksheet for the following words and ask the learner to mark the vc/cv syllable division pattern:

| | | | | |
|---|---|---|---|---|
| 1. affix | 2. annex | 3. appendix | 4. context | 5. expand |
| 6. extinct | 7. index | 8. expect | 9. suffix | 10. extra |

Ask the learner how many small words they can find in the following words:

E.g., st<u>and</u>   exist   exact   exam   exit   exhibit   exultant

## Story for Reading and Dictation

Rex and Max put six boxes of presents in Max's van and go to visit Rex's family. It is seven o'clock and Rex's dad is sitting in front of the TV with a drink. His mum is making snacks. "Happy 50th," Max yells. He wants to sit next to Rex's dad but trips on the flex of a lamp and tips the boxes on Dad's lap. His drink spills and drips on his pants. Dad is a bit vexed. Max mops it up and Rex fixes Dad a big drink. All is well in the end!

# Teaching Point 77

## Prefixes: 'ex', 'un' and 'ab'

At this stage in the programme the prefixes 'ex', 'un' and 'ab' can be introduced. Review closed syllables and code the prefixes using the breve. Ask the learner to read them back to you. Write the prefixes and the base words 'sent', 'tend', 'dress', 'press', 'tract' 'fit' and 'duct' on pieces of card. Ask the learner to use the prefixes to make new words (e.g., absent, extend, undress, express, extract, unfit, abduct). Discuss how the prefix changes the meaning of the word. It might be useful to explain prefix meanings referring to their origin – given here in brackets: The prefix 'ab' (Latin), meaning away, off, from; the prefix 'ex' (Latin), meaning out of, from, formerly; and the prefix 'un' (German), meaning not or without (i.e., a negative meaning).

## Words for Reading and Spelling

Abduct, abject, abrupt, absent, abstract, extract, exempt, exit, undo, unpin, unspent.

## Practising the New Learning Through a Game

Play a pelmanism (pairs) game with the cards used to introduce the prefix or make a Snap game using the words for reading above and some from previous lessons.

## Sentences for Reading and Dictation

Kim was abducted by a bandit in a mask. The exit is at the back. Dan is so unfit! Jess undressed the doll and put it in the bath. He is exempt from tax.

# Teaching Point 78

cursive form

**'qu' /kw/**

*qu*

## Reading Card

| front | back |
|---|---|
| qu<br><br>QU | /kw/ quilt |

## Reading Pack

In English the letter 'q' is always followed by the letter 'u' and so 'qu' is written on the front of the Reading Card.

## Writing the Letter/s

Practise joining the new letter to previous ones e.g. quack, quit, quest, quill.

## Spelling Card

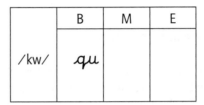

|      | B  | M | E |
|------|-----|---|---|
| /kw/ | qu |   |   |

## Practising the New Learning

Ask the learner to write down a word beginning with 'qu' for each of the following:

i   The noise or sound made by a duck (quack).
ii  The name for a feather made into a pen (quill).
iii The opposite of 'slow' (quick).
iv  The cover for a bed (quilt).
v   To leave or resign a job (quit).

## Story for Reading and Dictation

Vera the duck swims in the pond with six ducklings. Vera is a fat, fluffy, jolly duck and quacks at the babies happily. Suddenly Vera spies a fox in the bush. "That is the bad fox. Quick, quick, swim to me. He is a hungry fox." Danny, the baby duckling, will not swim to his mummy. He swims to the land. "The fox will not get me," he quacks. Danny gets to the bank and jumps in the mud. "This is fun," he thinks. Vera the duck is cross with him but Danny does not want to quit. Just then, the cunning fox jumps up and runs at Danny. "Mummy, Mummy, Mummy. Help me!" Vera flies at the fox to protect Danny from attack. "Run to the pond, Danny. Swim fast." Vera pecks the fox and spits at him, then jumps back in the pond and swims back to the baby ducklings.

## Developing Comprehension and Study Skills

Ask the learner to scan the text and highlight all the words starting with 'qu'. Then ask them to underline all the adjectives in the story. Finally ask the learner to think of a word to describe Danny.

# Teaching Point 79

cursive form

'z'    /z/                                                    ⌀z

## Discovery Learning

Ask the learner to listen to and repeat the following words – zip, zinc, zebra, zombie, zoo – and identify the common sound. Track the letter 'z' using Tracking Sheet 1, asking the learner to say the sound and letter name as they circle it. Use a mirror to discover how to make the /z/ sound. Practise writing 'z' using the handwriting routine and make a new Reading and Spelling Card, adding 'z' to the back of the /z/ Spelling Card in the beginning, middle, and end positions.

## Writing the Letter/s

Practise joining the new letter to previous ones e.g. zip, zest, zap, zonked.

## Words for Reading and Spelling

Zipped, zest, zaps, jazz, Zen, zany, fuzz, zigzag, zenith and zinc, Zulu (irregular).

## Practising the New Learning

Make a worksheet for the following words and ask the learner to mark the vc/cv or v/cv syllable division pattern:

Dizzy  fuzzy  hazy  tizzy  lazy  zero  topaz  jazzy  crazy  zigzag  zany.

Use the breve and macron to code each vowel/semi-vowel and then read the words.

## Sentences for Reading and Dictation

Fran puts the zest of a lemon in the bun mix. The path zigzags across the grass.

Quentin zipped the bag up and slung it on his back. "He is a bit zany," said Vicky.

# Teaching Point 80

cursive form

### Consonant Digraph – 'sh'

### Discovery Learning

Ask the learner to look at some pictures, (e.g., brush, shop, ship, fish, dish, washer, cash, shell) and identify the common sound. Use the BME sheet from Part V and ask them to write 'sh' in the correct box to show where it can be heard in the word. Track the diagraph 'sh' using a book or magazine. Practise writing the digraph in a salt tray. Make a new Reading and Spelling Card for /sh/(beginning, middle, and end positions).

### Words for Reading and Spelling

Shed, ship, shun, shock, shrug, sham, she, rash, wash, gush, wish, cosh, Josh, cashed.

### Practising the New Learning

Ask the learner to choose the correct ending to make a real word and to write this in their book:

1.
sh
- im
- ip
- id

2.
sh
- an
- in
- en

3.
sh
- amp
- ack
- ast

4.
sh
- op
- ap
- ep

### Story for Reading and Dictation

Quentin and his pal Max wanted to go to the shops to get Max a hat. "We will go to the best shop in Wells," said Quentin. "Yes," said Max. "I want a black hat with a big brim." So Quentin and Max went to the end of the block to get the bus. No luck. The bus had crashed on a bend and had to be mended. "Let's run back and ring a cab," said Quentin. When the cab picked them up, "Be quick!" said Max to the cab man. "The shops shut at six." Fred, the cab man, went fast. He sped to Wells but the shops had shut. Max was upset. "I did so want a black hat with a big brim," he said. Quentin was shell-shocked. "Let's try to get a bus back," said Quentin. "The cab cost ten quid and I am skint."

Ask the learner to think of a title for the story.

## Teaching Point 81

### Consonant Digraph –'ch'

cursive form

*ch*

Ask the learner to listen to the following words – chum, rich, chest, lunch, church – and identify the common sound. Track the digraph 'ch' using a book or magazine. Practise writing the digraph in a salt tray or on a whiteboard. Make a new Reading and Spelling Card for /ch/ ('ch' can be found in beginning, middle, and end positions).

### Words for Reading and Spelling

Chest, chin, chap, chop, chill, chink, chimp, champ, chick, chum, chat, choppy, clench, winch.

### Practising the New Learning

Play the 4-in-a Row reading game with the 'sh'/'ch' base board provided in Part V.

### Sentences for Reading and Dictation

Chuck has a chum called Stan. Zack smacks dad on the chin with a chop. Mick chats to Ben. Max has a pet chimp. Len is a boxing champ.

# Teaching Point 82

cursive form

*tch*

## '-tch' and Spelling Rule

### Discovery Learning

Ask the learner to sort the following words into two sets: chick, chest, match, watch, chimp, chilli, hutch, chin, catch, pitch, stitch, champ, latch. Ask them what they notice about the two sets of words. Help them to work out that one set has words that start with 'ch' and the other words that end in 'tch'. Read the words with the learner and ask them what all the words ending in 'tch' have in common (one syllable, a short vowel sound) to help them to discover the spelling rule for /ch/. The end spelling for /ch/ is 'tch' if it comes directly after a short vowel sound. If it comes after another consonant /ch/ is 'ch' (e.g., pinch, bunch). Exceptions to the rule (e.g., rich, such, much, which) will need teaching as sight vocabulary. Make a new Reading Card. Write '–tch' on the front to show that it is an end spelling. Add 'tch' to the back of the /ch/ Spelling Card in the end position.

## Words for Reading and Spelling

Match, catch, fetch, witch, latch, batch, ditch, hitch, patch, hatch, pitch, stitch.

## Practising the New Learning

Ask the learner to track the following sentence using Tracking Sheet 4:

Chuck the chimp can pitch a ball, catch a fish, and match socks.

## Sentences for Reading and Dictation

I am going to the match with Tim. Can Fred catch a big fish? The bandit snatched Kim's handbag. Will the chicks hatch? Stan kicked the ball and it went in the ditch.

Cut each sentence up into words and ask the learner to sequence these to form a sentence from each set of words. Then read each sentence aloud.

## Teaching Point 83

cursive form

'i-e' /ī/

*i-e*

### Reading Card

```
┌─────────────┐   ┌─────────────┐
│             │   │ /ī/ bike    │
│             │   │             │
│             │   │             │
│     i-e     │   │             │
│             │   │             │
│     I-E     │   │             │
│             │   │             │
└─────────────┘   └─────────────┘
    front              back
```

### Reading Pack

The long vowel /ī/ is represented by 'i' consonant 'e' in the middle of words. As several different consonants can be used, a line is drawn between the letter 'i' and the letter 'e' to show this.

### Discovery Learning

Make the following words (one at a time) with the wooden letters: pin, bid, din, strip, trip, kit, fin. Look at the first word 'pin' and ask the learner if the word has a closed or open syllable, and then ask them to place the breve over the word and read it back. Add the letter 'e' to the end of the word to make 'pine'. Explain that 'i-e' is called a digraph because it is two letters making one sound /ī/. This is a split digraph because a consonant comes between the 'i' and the 'e'. Ask them to put the macron over the vowel and read the word. Do this with each of the words above. Show the learner how we write that pattern on the Reading Card. Ask them to track some 'i-e' words in a book or magazine or use Tracking Sheet 4.

At this point the vowel suffix rule for words ending in 'e' can be taught: drop the 'e' when adding a vowel suffix (e.g., 'ing', 'ed, or 'est') (see Concept Card 39).

### Writing the Letter/s

Practise joining to previous letters e.g. ride, mile, wise, pride.

## Spelling Card

Add 'i-e' to the back of the /ī/ Spelling Card, in the middle position

|     | B | M | E |
|-----|---|---|---|
| /ī/ | i | i-e | y |

## Spelling Pack Routine

The teacher says the sound on the front of the card /ī/, the learner repeats it, then writes the spelling choices down in their book in the position they can be found in words saying: /ī/ 'i' at the beginning, /ī/ 'i consonant e' in the middle, /ī/ 'y' at the end.

## Words for Reading and Spelling

Mike, fine, pile, dine, lime, ride, vine, wide, bite, kite, ripe, time, lines, stripe.

## Practising the New Learning

1. Ask the learner to number the words in alphabetical order on the blanks in each column and then write each set in their book:

| hide _____ | pine _____ | spite _____ | kite _____ |
|---|---|---|---|
| bike _____ | tide _____ | bite _____ | dine _____ |
| mine _____ | time _____ | wide _____ | pride _____ |
| pile _____ | dine _____ | ride _____ | pike _____ |

2. Ask them to add the suffix 'ing' and 'ed' to the following base words:

time        file        mine        spike        pile        dine

Finally ask them to write these in the correct column on the vowel suffix frame (Part V) used for Teaching Point 73. All four suffixing rules have now been taught.

## Story for Reading and Dictation

It's ten past nine. Ann packs a picnic. Mike packs his kite. "A bike ride?" asks Mike. Mike's bike is red. Ann's bike is pink. Ann has the picnic on the back of the bike. Mike has the kite in his basket. Ann and Mike ride and ride. "Is it lunch time yet?" Ann asks. Ann and Mike dine. Ann has crab, yams, and ripe melon. Mike has ham, crisps, and tripe. "A drink, Mike? Mine's pink." "Pink? Yuck!" Mike responds. He has a drink of lime and lemon. Back at the bike, Ann has Mike's kite. As the kite rises Mike steps on a brick and trips. Smack!

He sits in the sand, a drink in his hand. Ants in the sand! Ants in his drink! Nine ants hide inside Mike's pants! Mike panics and strikes the ants. The ants bite Mike's hip. Mike is mad. Bad ants, bad! It's a crime. Mike's hip has a red stripe. "Pants Mike!" Ann insists. Stick in hand, Ann bats Mike's pants and puts the insects in the distant sandpit. Ann skips back, Mike's pants intact. Can Mike ride? Ann can sit. Mike can't sit. Mike is sick. Ann and Mike hike!

## Developing Comprehension and Study Skills

Ask the learner to scan the text and highlight what Ann and Mike had for lunch. Ask them to write the words in three boxes headed: meat, vegetables, and fruit.
(Note that the teacher may choose to give only a short section of the story for dictation.)

# Teaching Point 84

cursive form

'a-e'   /ā/                                        *a-e*

## Discovery Learning

Review open and closed syllables and split digraphs from previous lessons. Introduce 'a-e' through Discovery Learning. Make a Reading Card for 'a-e' and add it to the back of the /ā/ Spelling Card in the middle position. The learner's response for the Spelling Card is /ā/ 'a' at the beginning and /ā/ 'a consonant e' in the middle.

## Writing the Letter/s

Practise joining a-e to previous letters e.g. case, flame, late, brake.

## Words for Reading and Spelling

Bale, frame, plane, game, flake, cane, rate, wane, remake, relate, intake, inflate. (Draw attention to the different position of the accent in 'intake' and 'inflate'.)

## Practising the New Learning

Ask the learner to read the following sentences and underline the adjectives:

- Jake insists he has a <u>lime</u> drink.
- The cake has red and pink stripes.
- Jane has a fantastic black dress.
- Mum has baked a tiny cake to give to Jane's baby.
- Mike's pet is a tame rat.
- The bandit is a slim man in a black mask and red cape.
- Dan has a black pen in a plastic case.
- Jade made a fine attempt.

## Story for Reading and Dictation

Jane sat by the lake. She ate a cake and fed a bit to the ducks and drakes. Then she began to dig with a spade. A snake came from the grass and made Jane jump. "Help! Help!" she yelled. Dad came and hit the snake with a cane. The snake hung limply on the end of the cane. Dad flung it in the lake. "I am safe," said Jane. She gave Dad a big hug.

# Teaching Point 85

cursive form

'o-e'   /ō/

*o-e*

## Discovery Learning

Introduce 'o-e' through Discovery Learning. Make a Reading Card for 'o-e' and add 'o-e' to the back of the /ō/ Spelling Card in the middle position. The learner response for the Spelling Card is /ō/ 'o' at the beginning and /ō/ 'o consonant e' in the middle.

## Writing the Letter/s

Practise joining o-e to previous letters e.g. rope, mole, spoke, globe.

## Words for Reading and Spelling

Pole, note, code, mole, rope, wove, globe, decode, hopeful. (Irregular words: some/move).

## Practising the New Learning

Ask the learner to read the following sentences and complete them:

- Bill fell into the hole and …
- Jake broke a plate as he …
- Jane stole a cake from the …
- The black tadpole became a …
- Jade has to take the baby to …

## Story for Reading and Dictation

Mum sent Miss Hope a note. Jake broke a bone in his nose as he fell from a rope into a big hole next to the flats. He came home alone and had to go to the clinic to get it fixed. Mum will send a note when he is well. Jake hopes it will not be long.

# Teaching Point 86

|  | cursive form |
|---|---|
| 'u-e'   /ū/ | u-e |

## Discovery Learning

Introduce 'u-e' through Discovery Learning using visual, auditory, and tactile/kinaesthetic input. Make a Reading Card for 'u-e' and add it to the back of the /ū/ Spelling Card in the middle position. The learner's response for the Spelling Card is /ū/ 'u' at the beginning and /ū/ 'u consonant e' in the middle.

## Writing the Letter/s

Practise joining 'u-e' to previous letters e.g. cute, spume.

## Words for Reading and Spelling

Tube, duke, cute, spume, mule, fuse, rebuke, cube, mute, tune, fume.

(Show the learner that in some 'u-e' words the pronunciation is /$\overline{oo}$/, as in flume, rude, prune, plume, crude, Luke, rule. A Spelling Card for /$\overline{oo}$/ can be made at the teacher's discretion.)

## Practising the New Learning Using a Game

Make a 'Happy Families' rhyming game with the following words: make, rake, take, hake, stake, lake, drake, flake; pole, stole, hole, mole, vole, sole, dole, role; dime, crime, lime, prime, rime, time, grime, slime; cute, mute, impute, jute, repute, refute, commute, tribute. Deal five cards to each player and place the rest face down on the table. Players should take turns picking up a card from the pack (or taking a card from the pile of cards discarded by the other player/s) and must then throw a card away. The first person to get a 'family' of four is the winner. At the end of the game ask the learner to read the cards they have collected.

## Sentences for Reading and Dictation

Can Jake mend the fuse? Luke likes to picnic in the sand dunes. Jade's dress is cute. As the wave hit the rock, the spume shot up. Dad rebuked Jane when she came in late.

# Teaching Point 87

## v-c-e Words with 'r'

The words used for reading and spelling v-c-e words (Teaching Points 83–86) have avoided the consonant 'r' as this letter affects the expected pronunciation. Therefore the use of 'r' with 'i-e', 'a-e', 'o-e', and 'u-e' needs introducing separately. Use the wooden letters to make 'ire', 'are', 'ore' and 'ure', and help the learner to work out how to read them. Make a separate Reading and Spelling Card for each one. In the case of 'ire' (e.g., 'fire') a schwa replaces the 'r'. This is also the case for 'ure' (e.g., 'pure'). In the cases of 'are' and 'ore' the effect of the 'r' is to change the sound of the preceding vowel, as in 'fare' and 'shore'.

## Reading Cards

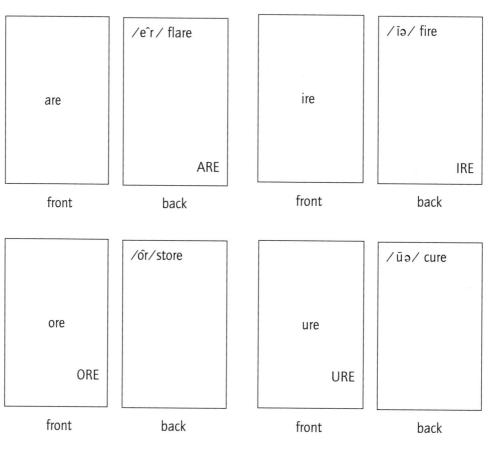

## Spelling Cards

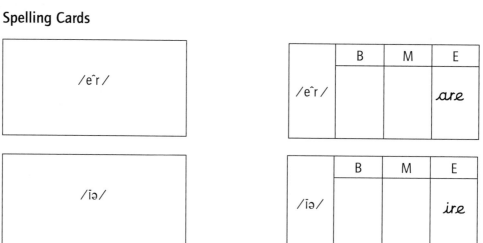

| | B | M | E |
|---|---|---|---|
| /oî/ | | | *ore* |

| | B | M | E |
|---|---|---|---|
| /ūə/ | | | *ure* |

/oî/

/ūə/

## Writing the Letter/s

Practise writing v-c-e words with 'r', e.g. fire, care, store, cure, spire.

## Words for Reading and Spelling

Clare, tire, dare, lore, fire, cure, wire, pure, spore, flare, store, spare, inspire, retire. (Keywords – here, there, were, where, these – can also be taught at this stage.)

## Practising the New Learning

Make a reading game using the words for reading for Teaching Points 83–87. This could be a rhyming pair game, Snap, 4-in-a Row, or a board game where the player has to read a card from their pack if they land on a particular square.

## Story for Reading and Dictation

### The King's Men

"Is it time to attack yet? Is the store complete?" asked Dan the Dane. "Yes, I hope so," said the King. "Jake has plenty of cane and spikes, and a store of stones. The plan is to get close to the enemy, bore a hole, stick in the plastics, make flames and smoke, and attack beside the lake before the men wake." Dan was inspired. He led his tired men to the top of the hill. "Go!" he yelled. He fired a pistol. A man fell and broke his spine. Jake's pole tore a hole in an enemy tent and made a man lame.

A fire flared up and made smoke galore. It lured ten men from the tent. The men inhaled smoke and became ill. Beware! Dan poked his cane into the men until a score of them got sore. "Stop!" the men implored. The enemy stampeded and cascaded into the lake. Can the camp be restored?

Ask the learner to answer the following questions:

- How did the King's men plan to attack the enemy?
- Where did the attack take place?
- What happened to the man who fell?
- How many men got sore from Dan's cane?
- What do you think 'stampeded and cascaded into the lake' means?
- What do you think the King's men felt like as they attacked the enemy?

## Teaching Point 88

cursive form

'ee' /ē/

*ee*

### Reading Card

| | |
|---|---|
| ee<br><br>EE | /ē/ green<br><br>/ē/ tree |
| front | back |

### Discovery Learning

Ask the learner to listen to the following words and identify the common sound: bee, tree, queen, green, week, peel, see. Use a BME sheet and ask them to place a counter to show where they can hear the /ē/ sound in these words. Remind them of how /ē/ is spelt at the beginning of a word and then write some of the words above on the board so they can work out how it is spelt in the middle and end positions. Make a Reading Card for 'ee'. Track words with 'ee' in a book or using Tracking Sheet 4.

## Reading Pack

Two clue words (negotiated with the learner) are written on the back of the Reading Card for /ē/ in the middle and end of words.

## Spelling Card

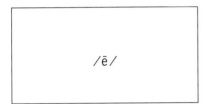

|  | B | M | E |
|---|---|---|---|
| /ē/ | e | ee | ee |

Add 'ee' to the back of the /ē/ Spelling Card in the middle and end positions. The learner response now is /ē/ 'e' at the beginning, /ē/ 'ee' in the middle, and /ē/ 'ee' at the end.

## Writing the Letter/s

Join 'ee' to previous letters e.g. seek, been, meet, green, keep.

## Words for Reading and Spelling

Peel, deep, heel, steel, week, leek, feel, green, jeep, meet, keep, speed, sixteen, coffee.

## Practising the New Learning

Make a closure exercise for the words: see, bee, tree, three, flee, spree – for example:

- A _____ lives in a hive.
- Ben gives _____ sweets to his pal.
- Jake and Jane _____ from the angry bull.

- Ken and Mike _____ a snake in the grass.
- Len sits by the _____ and has his picnic.
- Jade and Kate go on a spending _____.

## Story for Reading and Dictation

Luke lives in a mobile home. It is lime green with a black stripe on the side. The van has five trees next to it that give plenty of shade. Luke has a dog called Spot and three weeks ago Spot ate the plug from Luke's TV while Luke sat drinking a coffee. "Stupid dog," said Luke. "What a mess and the TV is broken. The screen is blank and it is silent. I think I can fix it," said Luke. "I'll put the fuse back in, but Spot is to blame and he will have no bones next week."

# Teaching Points 89 and 90

cursive form

'ar' /aˆr/ /ə /

_ar_

## Reading Card

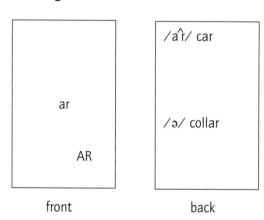

| | |
|---|---|
| ar | /aˆr/ car |
| AR | /ə/ collar |

front          back

## Discovery Learning

Ask the learner to look at pictures of a: car, farm, chart, dart, jar, star, and identify the common sound. Use a BME sheet and ask them to place a counter to show where they can hear the /aˆr/ sound in these words. Ask the learner to repeat the words after you and identify the number of syllables. Write the words on a board or flip chart so they can 'discover' how /aˆr/ is spelt in the middle and end positions. Make a reading card for/aˆr/. Track words with /aˆr/ 'ar' in a book or using Tracking Sheet 4. In the same (or next) lesson the teacher might introduce 'ar' /ə/ by asking the learner to listen to the following words – collar, pillar, nectar, vicar, vinegar – and identifying the common sound. Ask them to clap the syllables in each word. Write the multisyllabic words on the board to help the learner deduce how to read and spell the /ə/ sound at the end of the words.

## Spelling Card/s

Two new Spelling Cards are needed:

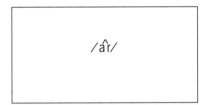

|  | B | M | E |
|---|---|---|---|
| /aˆr/ |  | *ar* | *ar* |

The learner's response is /aˆr/ 'a' 'r' in the middle and /aˆr/ 'a' 'r' at the end.

|  | B | M | E |
|---|---|---|---|
| /ə/ | *a* |  | *ar* |

The learner's response is /ə/ 'a' at the beginning and /ə/ 'a' 'r' at the end.

## Writing the Letter/s

Practise joining 'ar' to previous letters e.g. farm, star, dollar, poplar.

## Words for Reading and Spelling

Card, farm, charmed, darted, star, car, mar, barred, harm, harmful, cart, sparked, lark.

Cheddar, collar, dollar, pillar, nectar, vicar, vinegar, poplar; radar (irregular).

## Practising the New Learning

1. Make a word search for words with 'ar' /âr/. 2. Ask the learner to put the following words in alphabetical order: poplar, solar, polar, molar, dollar. 3. Revisit the syllable division patterns introduced so far and ask the learner to code and read the following: calendar, lunar, Cheddar.

## Story for Reading and Dictation

The hens and the cock slept. The barn was locked up. The sky was dark with no stars. A bad fox came to the barn. The hens woke up and began to panic. "Help, help. The fox will harm us!" the hens clucked. The farm dog woke up and began to bark and snarl. The fox ran off.

## Sentences for Reading and Dictation

Bart pulled up his collar. Dad has a bad molar. Bees collect nectar.

# Teaching Points 91 and 92

cursive form

'or' /ôr/ /ə/

ᴏᴛ

## Reading Card

| | /ôr/ corn |
|---|---|
| or | /ə/ doctor |
| OR | |
| front | back |

## Discovery Learning

Introduce the digraph 'or' in the same way as the previous Teaching Point, using auditory, visual, and tactile/kinaesthetic input.

## Reading Pack

The digraph 'or' can make two different sounds: /ôr/ which can be found in the middle and end positions in one syllable words (e.g., for) and /ə/ which is found at the end of multisyllabic words (e.g. tutor).

## Spelling Card/s

Add 'or' to the back of the ôr Spelling Card:

|        | B | M   | E         |
|--------|---|-----|-----------|
| /ôr/   |   | or  | or<br>ore |

The learner's response is /ôr/ 'o' 'r' in the middle, /ôr/ 'o' 'r' and /ôr/ 'o' 'r' 'e' at the end.
   Add 'or' to the back of the /ə/ Spelling Card:

|        | B | M | E        |
|--------|---|---|----------|
| /ə/    |   |   | ar<br>or |

There are now two spelling choices for /ə/ at the end of words. The learner's response is /ə/ 'a' 'r' and /ə/ 'o' 'r' at the end.

## Writing the Letter/s

Practise joining 'or' to previous letters e.g. fork, cord, doctor, actor.

## Words for Reading and Spelling

Cord, form, born, morning, cork, lord, shorn, torn, cordless, fork, thorn.

Tractor, doctor, factor, actor, reactor, contractor, Hector, victor, sponsor.

## Practising the New Learning

Make a rhyming pairs game using some of the words for reading.

## Story for Reading and Dictation

It is five in the morning and Hector wakes up. It is time to get the tractor and take a bag of corn to feed the pigs. In the barn the big, black pig snorts for his feed. Hector tosses him morsels of corn. The pig scoffs the corn but he is still hungry. He goes to look for acorns. What a greedy pig!

Ask the learner to highlight all the words containing 'or' and then write them into two separate sets: 'or' /ôr/ words and 'or' /ə/ words.

# Teaching Points 93

cursive form

'oo' /ŏo/ / /ōo/

*oo*

## Reading Card

| | |
|---|---|
| | /ŏo/ book |
| oo | |
| | /ōo/ igloo |
| oo | |
| front | back |

## Discovery Learning

Introduce the vowel digraph 'oo' /o͞o/ as in spoon, and 'oo' /o͝o/(or /ŭ/ depending on dialect) as in foot, through auditory, visual, and tactile/kinaesthetic channels. Ask the learner to track 'oo' words in a book or magazine. Make the Reading and Spelling Cards.

## Reading Pack

The vowel digraph 'oo' has a short and long vowel sound. Negotiate a clue word for both sounds.

## Spelling Card/s

Two new Spelling Cards are needed:

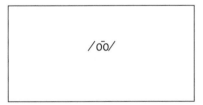

| | B | M | E |
|---|---|---|---|
| /o͞o/ | | oo | oo |

The learner's response is /o͞o/ 'o' 'o' in the middle and /o͞o/ 'o' 'o' at the end.

| | B | M | E |
|---|---|---|---|
| /o͝o/ | | oo | |

The learner's response is /o͝o/ 'o' 'o' in the middle. (Note that if the learner pronounces 'oo' as /ŭ/ then the spelling choice could be added to the back of the /ŭ/ Spelling Card as a second choice spelling in the middle position instead.)

## Writing the Letter/s

Practise joining 'oo' to previous letters e.g. spoon, food, look, hook, boot.

### Words for Reading and Spelling

Hood, soon, tool, food, boo, loop, stool, wool, roof, good, cool, platoon, school.

### Practising the New Learning

Ask the learner to choose the correct prefix and write the words in their book:

re    or    un

tool =    took =    boot =    roof =    hook =

### Story for Reading and Dictation

It was a sunny morning and Luke's Mum and Dad agreed to take him to the zoo. He hadn't been with the school trip as he had been ill. He had been in a sad, gloomy mood for weeks but the prospect of a visit with his Mum and Dad soon made him happy. He put on his best boots and his red woolly hood. It was still cool outside and so Mum packed hot food and drinks. Luke wanted to see the baboons and the white cockatoos. Mum was hoping to see some striped raccoons but all Luke's Dad wanted to see was a baby ape he had seen in a cartoon.

# Teaching Point 94

### -ck/-k Spelling Rule

### Discovery Learning

Ask the learner to read the following words and sort them into two sets: week, sick, pack, lick, seek, peek, kick, mock, reek, rock, duck, spook, crook. Ask them to tell you what they notice about the two sets. Prompt them (if necessary) to work out the rule by asking them how many syllables the words have and if the vowel is short or long. One syllable words with a short vowel sound end in 'ck', while one syllable words with a long vowel sound end in just 'k'. Make a worksheet to practise adding the correct /k/ ending to words. Words ending in 'k' can be included now in spelling and dictation. Add 'k' to the /k/ Spelling Card at the end:

## Spelling Card

|     | B | M | E |
|-----|---|---|---|
| /k/ | c<br>k |   | ck<br>k |

/k/

The learner's response now is /k/ 'c', /k/ 'k' at the beginning and /k/ 'ck', /k/ 'k' at the end.

## Teaching Point 95

cursive form

*ce  ci*

## Soft 'c' Before 'e' and 'i'

## Reading Card

| front | back |
|-------|------|

ce

CE

/s/ centre

/s/ face

## Discovery Learning

Introduce soft 'c' /s/ through Discovery Learning. Use a BME sheet to listen for /s/ in different positions in words. Discuss the spelling choices introduced so far for /s/ ('s' and 'ss'). Remind the learner of the rule for 'c/k' choice: /k/ 'c' is always followed by the vowels 'a', 'o', or 'u' in English words. Write some words on the board that have a soft 'c' in them (e.g., face, cell, ice, city). Read the words aloud and ask the learner what sound the letter 'c' has when it is followed by 'e' or 'i'. Ask them to track 'ce' and 'ci' words in a book or magazine. Make the Reading Card/s. Normally just one Reading Card is made for 'ce' but a second one for 'ci' can be made at the teacher's discretion.

## Reading Pack

Make a Reading Card for soft 'c' by writing 'ce' on the front of the card with two clue words on the back: one for 'ce' /s/ at the beginning of words and one for 'ce' /s/ at the end of words.

## Spelling Card

| | B | M | E |
|---|---|---|---|
| /s/ | ʂ  c | ʂ  c | ʂ  ʂʂ  c |

Soft 'c' is added to the back of the /s/ Spelling Card. The learner's response is /s/ 's' at the begining, /s/ 'c' before 'i' and 'e' at the beginning, /s/ 's' in the middle, /s/ 's', /s/ 'ss', and /s/ 'c' 'e' at the end.

## Writing the Letter/s

Practise joining 'ce' and 'ci' to previous letters e.g. cent, city, face, place.

## Words for Reading and Spelling

Cent, city, cell, cement, censor, civic, mice, space, ice, fence, entrance, replace.

## Practising the New Learning

Vowels = 2 points. Consonants B to M = 1 point. Consonants N to Z = 3 points (e.g., Ken = 1+2+3 = 6 points). Ask the learner to read and then score some of the following words: city, cinema, circus, cell, cement, race, advance, necklace.

## Story for Reading and Dictation

Jake and Jade make a cake. Jake mixes in sugar and Jade adds spice and rice. It is made in a trice. It cooks in the hot oven for a short time and rises well. It looks yummy. Jade cuts a slice and gives it to Jake. Jade thinks the cake tastes nice. Jake takes a bite. "It is fantastic," he states. The kids sell a slice to Mum …. at a price!

(Note that a spelling routine with a strong visual input is needed for learning spellings beginning with 'ce'/'ci'. The 'ce' ending is used after a long vowel sound, whereas 'ss' is used after a short vowel.)

# Teaching Point 96

## Soft 'g' Before 'e' and 'i'

This is a similar rule to soft 'c'. The letter 'g' followed by letters 'a', 'o', or 'u' makes the /g/ sound and where the letter 'g' is followed by the letters 'e' or 'i' it usually says /j/. There are some exceptions. For instance, some old English words such as 'gebur' (a tenant farmer) start with /g/ and some words that have been introduced into English in recent years from other countries (e.g., the Malaysian word "gecko"). Introduce soft 'g' through Discovery Learning and make a new Reading Card with 'ge' on the front. Track words beginning with 'ge' in a book, magazine, or piece of text.

## Spelling Card

The learner's response now is /j/ 'j', /j/ 'g' at the beginning and 'j' /j/ in the middle.

## Words for Reading and Spelling

Gentry, gem, gibe, gelignite, genetic, ginseng, gipsy.

## Practising the New Learning

Put the wooden letters 'c' and 'g' in a feely bag. Ask the learner to identify each letter by touch and tell you the two sounds each letter can make. Ask them to give you a word orally for each of the sounds or to find a picture that represents the particular sound.

### Sentences for Reading and Spelling

Can Garry find the gipsy campsite? Hector has a bag of white gem stones. The bandit had three sticks of gelignite. Molly was born in June.

(Note that words that beginning with 'ge'/'gi' also need a spelling routine with strong visual input as the learner cannot work out the spelling choice ('j' or 'g') from the sounds alone. The teacher may want to target words as they become part of the learner's written vocabulary.)

## Teaching Points 97 and 98

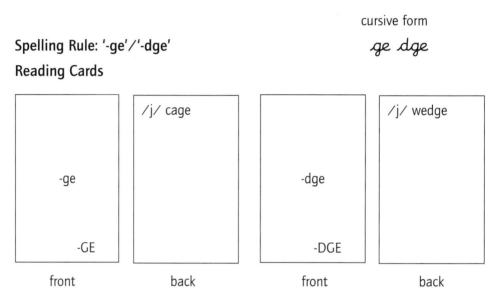

### Spelling Rule: '-ge'/'-dge'

cursive form

*ge dge*

### Reading Cards

| -ge | /j/ cage | -dge | /j/ wedge |
|-----|----------|------|-----------|
| -GE |          | -DGE |           |
| front | back | front | back |

### Discovery Learning

Ask the learner to listen to the following words and identify the common sound: page, nudge, cage, bridge, rage, midge. The rule that no English word ends in the letter 'j' may have already been pointed out when /j/ 'j' was introduced (Teaching Point 74). Ask the learner which letters might be used to make /j/ sound at the end of words (they may suggest 'ge' as this was the last Teaching Point). Write the words for reading on cards and ask them to sort these into two sets. Ask the learner what they notice about each of the sets. Help them to work out the rule: words with a long vowel sound end in '-ge' and multisyllabic words ending with /j/ end in '-ge', but single syllable words with a short vowel sound need an extra letter to close in the vowel and so when the /j/ sound is heard directly after the vowel the word ends in '-dge'.

## Reading Cards

Two new Reading Cards for /j/ at the end of words are made and added to the Reading Pack to be practised daily. Draw a line in front of the letters to show that this is at the end of words only.

## Spelling Card

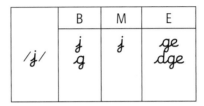

The learner's response is /j/ 'j', /j/ 'g' at the beginning, /j/ 'j' in the middle, and /j/ 'ge', /j/ 'dge' at the end.

## Words for Reading and Spelling

Cage, page, bridge, fudge, wage, huge, judge, rage, fridge, sage, edge, badge.

Point out that words containing 'ar' and 'or' end in '-ge'. Examples are: large, charge, barge, gorge, forge.

## Practising the New Learning

1. Ask the learner to code the following words (vccv or vcv pattern), divide them into syllables, and then read the words:

   image    luggage    cabbage    deluge    village    savage    damage

2. Make a pairs game where the learner has to find two words ending in 'ge' or two ending in 'dge' to make a pair. Ask them to read the words as they turn over the cards.
3. Review the suffix rule: drop 'e' when adding a vowel suffix, by adding 'ing' or 'ed' to judge, page, face, race, rage, lace, edge, damage, fence, cage, bridge, savage. (Other words can be included to practise all four suffixing rules at the teacher's discretion.)

### Story for Reading and Spelling

Jim had to cross the bridge to get to Jed's farm. A flying stone damaged the bonnet of Jim's car. Jim was in a rage. Jed's wife, Jenny, went to the village post office to ring the man at the garage. While the man mended Jim's car, Jenny cooked fish, cabbage, and mash for lunch.

## Teaching Point 99

### Prefixes: trans, mis, be

At this stage in the programme the prefixes 'trans', 'mis', 'be', and 'sub' can be introduced. Review open and closed syllables and code the prefixes using the breve and macron. Ask the learner to read these back to you. Write the prefixes and the base words 'port', 'take', 'fix', 'conduct', 'fit', 'set', 'rate', 'side', and 'form' on pieces of card. Ask the learner to use the prefixes to make new words (e.g., transport, transfix, transform, mistake, misconduct, misfit, beset, berate, beside, subside, subset). Discuss how the prefix changes the meaning of the word; the prefix '*trans*' is Latin meaning across, beyond, from; the prefix '*mis*' is Old English meaning wrongly, badly, unfavourably; the prefix '*be*' is also Old English meaning about, by; the prefix '*sub*' is Latin meaning under, below or within.

## Teaching Point 100

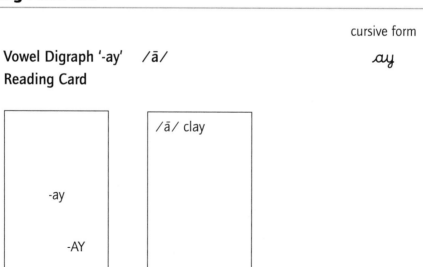

cursive form

*ay*

Vowel Digraph '-ay'    /ā/
Reading Card

| -ay | /ā/ clay |
| :---: | :--- |
| -AY | |

front                back

## Discovery Learning

A BME sheet can be used to listen to words containing the /ā/ sound in different positions. The learner has already been taught how to spell some words with /ā/ at the beginning or in the middle. Help them to discover how to spell it in the end position by looking at words with an 'ay' ending.

## Reading Pack

Make a Reading Card for 'ay' /ā/, drawing a line in front of the letters 'ay' to show that it is found at the end of words.

## Words for Reading and Spelling

Ray, day, May, play, clay, fray, stray, relay, delay, away, jay, pay, hay, stay, spray.

## Spelling Card

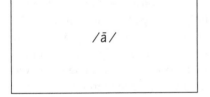

|     | B | M   | E  |
|-----|---|-----|----|
| /ā/ | a | a-e | ay |

## Practising the New Learning

Make a word search using the words for reading. Ask the learner to read and/or spell the words as they highlight them.

## Sentences for Reading and Spelling

Kim has made a clay pot. Dad will pay for the holiday. Vicky took the stray dog home. Ray and Kate will stay with Mum for a week. "My cuff has frayed," said Tim.

## Teaching Points 101 and 102

cursive form

'-ow' /ō/ /ow/

*ow*

### Reading Card

| | |
|---|---|
| -ow<br><br>-OW | /ō/ snow<br><br><br>/ow/ cow |
| front | back |

### Discovery Learning

Introduce 'ow'. A BME sheet can be used to listen to words containing the /ō/ sound in different positions. The learner has already been taught how to spell words with /ō/ at the beginning or in the middle. Help them to discover how to spell it in the end position by looking at the words snow, glow, mow, throw. Make a Reading Card for 'ow'/ō/. In the same (or next) lesson introduce 'ow' /ow/ and add it to the back of the Reading Card. Add 'ow'/ō/ to the back of the /ō/ Spelling Card and make a new Spelling Card for 'ow' /ow/.

### Words for Reading and Spelling

Bow, sow, glow, throw, blow, mow, flow, row, slow, below, grow, show, and own (irregular for spelling). Note the two pronunciations for the words 'bow', and 'sow'. Cow, brow, prow, allow, how, now, bow, clown, town, gown, drown, brown (and owl irregular for spelling).

### Spelling Card/s

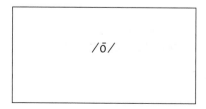

| | | B | M | E |
|---|---|---|---|---|
| /ō/ | | *o* | *o-e* | *ow* |

The learner's response is /ō/ 'o' at the beginning, /ō/ 'o-e' in the middle, and /ō/ 'ow' at the end.

| | B | M | E |
|---|---|---|---|
| /ow/ | | ow | ow |

This is the first choice spelling for /ow/ in the middle or end of words. The learner response is /ow/ 'ow' in the middle and /ow/ 'ow' at the end.

## Practising the New Learning

1. Ask the learner to arrange the following /ō/ words in alphabetical order:

    - glow, mow, snow, blow.
    - slow, tow, show, widow.
    - flow, throw, fellow, elbow.
    - below, crow, grow, barrow.

2. Ask the learner to read the following words and sort them into two sets (/ō/ and /ow/): cow, glow, brow, prow, flow, show, allow, arrow, elbow, how, mellow, now, crown, town.

## Sentences for Reading and Spelling: /ō/

May is playing in the snow. Her face is glowing. Dad has elbow patches on his jacket. Rod took a wheelbarrow full of parsnips to the show.

## Sentences for Reading and Spelling: /ow/

Mum is shopping in town. Kate made a crown from card and brown ink. Dad dresses up as a clown for the party. Jake is playing down in the dell in his dressing gown.

## Teaching Points 103 and 104

'er' /ûr / /ə/

cursive form

*er*

### Reading Card

| er<br><br>ER | /ûr/ table<br><br>/ə/ hammer |
|:---:|:---:|
| front | back |

### Discovery Learning

Ask the learner to listen to and repeat the words herb, kerb, fern, jerk, herd, berth and identify the common sound. Using a BME sheet the learner places a counter to show where they can hear the /ûr/ sound in each word. Write the words on the board so they can work out how /ûr/ is spelt. Make a Reading Card for 'er'. Track words with /ûr/ 'er' in a book or magazine. Teachers can use discretion about using /er/ to replace /ûr/ if appropriate for local accent. In the same (or next) lesson the teacher might introduce 'er' /ə/ by asking the learner to listen to the following words – hammer, number, banner, summer, winter, scatter – and identify the common sound. Write the words on the board so the learner can work out the second choice spelling for /ə/ at the end of the words. Make the Reading Card.

### Spelling Card/s

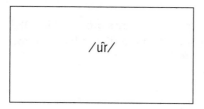

| /ûr/ |
|:---:|

| | B | M | E |
|:---:|:---:|:---:|:---:|
| /ûr/ | | *er* | |

The learner's response is /ûr/ 'er' in the middle.

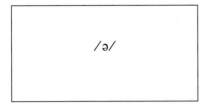

|     | B | M | E |
|-----|---|---|---|
| /ə/ |   |   | *ar* |
|     |   |   | *or* |
|     |   |   | *er* |

The learner's response is /ə/ 'ar' at the end, /ə/ 'or' and /ə/ 'er' at the end.

## Words for Reading and Spelling

Herb, kerb, fern, berth, herd, hammer, summer, winter, manner, miner, finer.

## Practising the New Learning

1.  Ask the learner to put the letters in the correct order to make an 'er' word:

    erbk    berh    mter    kjre    vber    derh    erfn

2.  Ask them how many small words they can find in the following (e.g., <u>task</u> contains 'as' and 'ask'):

    hammer        butler        finger        hanger        banker        ladder        beeper

## Sentences for Reading and Dictation

Kate put the fern in a plant pot. The bin is full of litter. The parrot is on his perch.

# Teaching Point 105

## Suffix 'er': Comparatives and Superlatives

The suffix 'er' can be used to change a verb into a noun (e.g., dock into docker) or to make a comparative adjective (e.g., bigger, smaller, taller, fuller, faster, quicker). Practise this by asking the learner to add the suffix 'er' to base words such as bank, cook, freeze, dock, bake, fast, bathe, brave. In changing words ending in 'e' (e.g., bake to baker, brave to braver bathe to bather) the suffixing rule 'drop e' when adding a vowel suffix is also practised. The learner could be asked to look up the new words in a dictionary to check they have applied the correct suffixing rule.

This is an appropriate point to teach the use of comparatives and superlatives. A multiple choice exercise might be useful to practise comparatives and superlatives. The learner reads the sentences and chooses the correct form of the adjective. Examples are: Jake's cake is bigger/biggest than Jane's cake; Bill's kite was the smaller/smallest of the three.

## Teaching Point 106

'-ue' /ū/ /ōō/

cursive form

*ue*

### Reading Card

| | /ū/ cue |
|---|---|
| -ue | |
| -UE | /ōō/ blue |

front       back

### Discovery Learning

A BME sheet can be used while listening to words containing the /ū/ sound in different positions. The learner has already been taught how to spell words with /ū/ at the beginning or in the middle. Help them to discover how to spell /ū/ in the end position by looking at the words cue, due, statue, subdue, hue, on a board or card. Make a Reading Card for 'ue'/ū/, drawing a line in front ('-ue') to show it comes at the end of words. Add 'ue' to the back of the /ū/ Spelling Card in the end position.

In the same (or next) lesson introduce 'ue' /ōō/ and add it to the back of the 'ue' Reading Card. Add 'ue' to the back of the /ōō/ Spelling Card in the end position.

### Words for Reading and Spelling

Cue, due, statue, argue, hue, subdue, value, revue, rescue, virtue, continue, avenue.

Blue, flue, clue, glue, sue, true.

## Spelling Card/s

| | B | M | E |
|---|---|---|---|
| /ū/ | u | u-e | ue |

The learner's response is /ū/ 'u' at the beginning, /ū/ 'u-e' in the middle, and /ū/ 'ue' at the end.

| | B | M | E |
|---|---|---|---|
| /ōo/ | | oo | ue |
| | | | oo |

The learner's response is: /ōo/ 'oo' in the middle, /ōo/ 'ue' and /ōo/ 'oo' at the end.

## Practising the New Learning

1. Practise adding the vowel suffix 'ed' to the following /ū/ words:

   rescue    argue    subdue    value    continue

   Discuss how the suffix has changed the tense and ask the learner to think of a sentence for each of the new words. (Point out that the final 'e' is dropped to add vowel suffix 'ed'.)

2. Write these sets of words on a card and ask the learner to put the words in the correct order to make sentences:

   a)   green    Blue    and    yellow    make

   b)   glue    with    Stick    paper    the    it    on

   c)   me    Give    a    clue

## Sentences for Reading and Spelling: /ū/

Bill argued with Tom. "It has a value of ten quid," said Jim. I like that hue. Mandy got lost in the hills and Dad got a rescue party to look for her. The statue is made from green glass.

### Sentences for Reading and Spelling: /o͞o/

"It is true," said Ray. Jay likes the blue dress best. A flue is like a pipe and smoke passes up it.

## Teaching Point 107

### Prefixes: Post and Peri

The prefixes 'post' and 'peri' can be introduced at this stage. The prefix 'post' is of Latin origin meaning after or behind. It can be used with the base words script, date, and fix to make postscript, post-date, and post-fix. It can also be used with root words to make postpone, post-mortem, etc. The prefix 'peri' is from the Greek meaning around or about. It can be used with base and root words to make periderm, perinatal, peripatetic, periscope, etc. These can now be introduced into reading and spelling for older learners.

## Teaching Point 108

### Words with 'o' /ŭ/

The second choice spelling for /ŭ/ in the middle of words is the letter 'o'. Introduce o /ŭ/ through Discovery Learning and add it to the back of the 'o' Reading Card and the back of the /ŭ/ Spelling Card in the middle position. As there are relatively few words with this spelling choice you might want to make a card for those which are within the learner's written vocabulary and practise them on a regular basis.

### Words for Reading and Spelling

Won, son, wonder, love, dove, another, brother, mother, woman, glove.

### Practising the New Learning

Copy lists of appropriate words and ask the learner to read aloud the words in each row and underline the 'odd one out', saying this word as they do so:

- son        con        won
- drove       love       dove
- brother     monster    mother
- ponder      wonder     fonder

## Sentences for Reading and Spelling

Sally's gloves are made from pink kid. Ben's brother is sixteen. Jade won the tennis match.

# Teaching Point 109

cursive form

*ie*

## '-ie' /ī/

## Reading Card

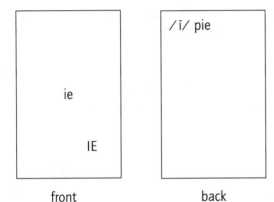

| front | back |
|---|---|

ie

IE

/ī/ pie

front          back

## Discovery Learning

Introduce 'ie' /ī/ using auditory, visual, and tactile/kinaesthetic channels. Make a new Reading Card for 'ie' /ī/ and add 'ie' to the back of the /ī/ Spelling Card as a second choice spelling in the end position.

## Spelling Card

/ī/

|  | B | M | E |
|---|---|---|---|
| /ī/ | i | i-e | y |
|  |  |  | ie |

The learner's response is /ī/ 'i' at the beginning, /ī/ 'i-e' in the middle, /ī/ 'y' and /ī/ 'ie' at the end.

## Words for Reading and Spelling

Tie, pie, lie, vie, die, fie.

## Practising the New Learning

1.  Ask the learner to sort the words for reading into alphabetical order.
2.  Ask them to add the suffixes 'es', 'ed', and 'ing' to the following words to make three new words for each: lie, tie, vie, die. (Note that 'ie' changes to 'y' when adding 'ing'.)

## Sentences for Reading and Dictation

Mum has made a plum pie. Dad went to the shops to get a green and red striped tie. Kate tied the plastic bag to the pram. Jill lied to her brother.

# Teaching Point 110

cursive form

## Vowel Digraph 'ea' /ē/

*ea*

## Reading Card

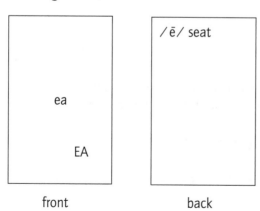

front          back

## Discovery Learning

Introduce 'ea'/ē/ through auditory, visual, and tactile/kinaesthetic channels. Track words with 'ea' in a book or magazine. Make a new Reading Card and add 'ea' to the back of the /ē/ Spelling Card as a second choice spelling in the beginning, middle, and end positions.

## Spelling Card

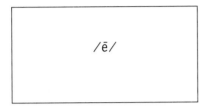

|  | B | M | E |
|---|---|---|---|
| /ē/ | e<br>ea | ee<br>ea | ee<br>ea |

The learner's response is /ē/ 'e' and /ē/ 'ea' at the beginning, /ē/ 'ee' and /ē/ 'ea' in the middle, /ē/ 'ee' and /ē/ 'ea' at the end.

## Words for Reading and Spelling

Bean, tea, plea, pea, sea, lea, seat, meat, pleat, beat, heap, heal, heat, eat steal, read, lead, easy. (Irregular words: great, break, steak.)

## Practising the New Learning Using a Game

Make a rhyming pairs game for the following words: cream/dream, seat/meat, meal/steal, heap/reap, tea/sea, bean/mean, eat/peat, each/peach.

## Story for Reading and Dictation

Peter has a veteran car. It is a two-seater sports car. Peter's car has been kept in good order. He cleans the seats and polishes the body of the car every weekend. His car is dark green with a long bonnet and small boot. It has cream seats, a black hood, and a brass horn. It is Peter's pride and joy and runs well.

## Developing Comprehension and Study Skills

Ask the learner to read the passage and then draw, colour, and label the car. An alternative is to ask them to write an advertisement for selling the car for £10,000.

## Teaching Point 111

### Vowel Digraph 'ea' /ĕ/

The digraph 'ea' has a short vowel sound in words such as 'head' and 'dread' and can be introduced at the same time as the long sound (Teaching Point 110) or as a separate Teaching Point at the teacher's discretion. The short sound /ĕ/ is added to the back of the 'ea' Reading Card as an alternative pronunciation and to the back of the /ĕ/ Spelling Card as a second choice spelling in the middle position. Practise reading and spelling 'ea' /ĕ/ words (e.g., head, thread, feather, bread, dread, spread, weapon, heather, deaf, wealth, health, death, weather). Note also 'read' (past tense) and 'lead' (metal). Make a word search or crossword puzzle using some of these words. Start to include common 'ea' /ĕ/ words in dictation.

## Teaching Point 112

cursive form

### Vowel Digraph 'ai' /ā/

*ai*

### Reading Card

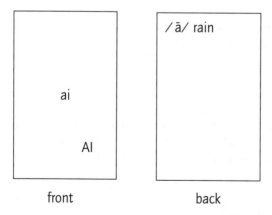

/ā/ rain

ai

AI

front                    back

Make a Reading Card for 'ai' and add 'ai' to the back of the /ā/ Spelling Card as a second choice spelling in the middle position.

## Spelling Card

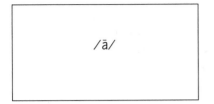

The learner's response is /ā/ 'a' at the beginning, /ā/ 'a-e' and /ā/ 'ai' in the middle, and /ā/ 'ay' at the end.

## Words for Reading and Spelling

Rail, paid, train, faint, brain, gain, plain, Spain, drain, wait mail, sprain, refrains. (Note that in some words e.g., aim, aid, ail, 'ai' is in the beginning position.)

## Practising the New Learning

Add the prefix 're' to the base words gain, pad, main, train and the roots frain. Ask the learner to read these and say a sentence for each one.

## Story for Reading and Dictation

Jack lay in bed. Since coming to Spain for a holiday he had had nothing but bad luck. He had not been for a swim for three days and as soon as the sun began to shine he had slipped on the pool's edge and banged his leg. He was in pain and his leg was throbbing. The doctor said that he had a sprain and had to refrain from swimming for the rest of the holiday. Jack decided to remain in bed for the day and read his train books.

# Teaching Point 113

## 'air' /êr/

The letter 'r' changes the sound of the vowel digraph 'ai' to /êr/ and so needs to be introduced as a separate Teaching Point. However, as there are relatively few words with 'air' the teacher might decide to introduce them as a group (e.g., air, pair, hair, fair, stair, lair, flair, chair, repair). Make a Reading and Spelling Card for 'air' /êr/. Write 'air' on the back of the /êr/ Spelling Card in the end position.

It might be appropriate at this point to work on the homonyms hair/hare, per/pair, flair/flare, stair/stare. Meanings for these should be discussed, the learner should then practise putting them into sentences to attach meaning so they can use them appropriately.

## Teaching Point 114

cursive form

**Vowel Digraph 'oa' /ō/**        *oa*

### Reading Card

| | |
|---|---|
| oa<br><br>OA | /ō/ boat |
| front | back |

Make a new Reading Card and add 'oa' to the back of the /ō/ Spelling Card as a second choice spelling in the middle position.

### Spelling Card

| /ō/ | B | M | E |
|---|---|---|---|
| | *o* | *o-e*<br>*oa* | *ow* |

The learner's response is /ō/ 'o' at the beginning, /ō/ 'o-e' and /ō/ 'oa' in the middle, and /ō/ 'ow' at the end. Note 'oa' can occur at the beginning but only in a very few words (e.g., oats, oast, oath).

## Words for Reading and Spelling

Boat, soap, coat, foal, stoat, loaf, moat, coal, goal, cloak, road, goat, load, groan, roast.

## Practising the New Learning

Ask the learner to put these words in alphabetical order:

- boat, moat, foal, loaf, goat.
- coat, loaf, cloak, load, coal.
- groan, road, goat, roast, goal.

## Sentences for Reading and Dictation

Mum is baking a loaf of bread. Put coal on the fire. The baby foal has just been born. Can the goalkeeper save the day? Scrub it with soap to remove the stain.

# Teaching Point 115

cursive form

*igh*

## Vowel Digraph 'igh' /ī/

## Reading Card

| igh | /ī/ light |
|:---:|:---|
| IGH | |
| front | back |

## Discovery Learning

Introduce 'igh' /ī/. Use a BME sheet to help the learner identify the position of the /ī/ sound in the following words: ice, night, try, fry, item, stile, plight. Revise the different spelling choices introduced so far for /ī/. Write words with 'igh' on a board/card and ask the learner to try to work out which letters make the /ī/ sound. Make a new Reading Card and add 'igh' to the back of the /ī/ Spelling Card as a second choice spelling in the middle position. Words with 'igh' spelling at the end (e.g., high and sigh) can also be taught at the teacher's discretion.

## Spelling Card

| | B | M | E |
|---|---|---|---|
| /ī/ | i | i-e | y |
| | i | -igh | ie |

The learner's response is /ī/ 'i' at the beginning, /ī/ 'i-e' and /ī/ 'igh' in the middle, /ī/ 'y' and /ī/ 'ie' at the end.

## Words for Reading and Spelling

Night, light, might, sight, plight, fight, frightful, sprightly, bright, flight, rightly, tight.

## Practising the New Learning

Using the crossword puzzle in Part V (Resources), ask the learner to read the 'igh' words and then to write a clue for each one. (Alternatively, the teacher could write the clues and give the learner a blank crossword to complete.)

## Story for Reading and Dictation

Sally Lane is my landlady. Last night she was in a plight. At midnight I was woken by a scream. I rushed downstairs to her flat. I switched on the light. Sally was standing on a chair by the bed. Her hair was standing on end and her face was white. She was shaking with fright. "I think something brushed my leg," she whispered. I looked high and low for the culprit. At last I looked under the bed and there was Ginger, my cat. "Here is the culprit," I said. I took Ginger back to my room and, with a sigh, Sally went back to sleep.

## Old, Wild, Kind Words

'Old, wild, kind' words are irregular because the vowel is followed by a consonant making a closed syllable yet the vowel sound is long rather than short. The reading and spelling of these words need to be specifically taught and cards could be made with a list of common 'old, wild, kind' words to be practised regularly (e.g., mild, wild, child; hold, fold, gold, sold, bold, cold; kind, mind, wind, bind, rind, find, hind; host, post, most). Practise adding the prefixes 'un', 're', and 'be' to some of these words to make behold, unwind, unkind, unsold, resold, unfold, refold, repost, remind, behind, etc. Start to include common 'old wild' words in dictation.

## Silent Letters: 'b' in 'mb' and 'g' in 'gn'

Silent letters should be taught at a point where the teacher feels that the learner is ready for them. The teacher may decide to build up a pack of words with silent letters gradually rather than introduce them all at once. Some common words end in a silent 'b' (such as comb and lamb) and the teacher may decide to start with these. Later on the words tomb, bomb, and limb may be added. A visual spelling routine will be needed to teach these words (see Chapter 11 and Part V which contain additional methods for spelling irregular words). Words with a silent 'g' that can be introduced at this stage in the programme are gnu, gnome, and gnash.

cursive form

'oi' /oy/ and 'oy' /oy/

## Reading Cards

| | /oy/ coin | | /oy/ boy |
|---|---|---|---|
| oi | | -oy | |
| OI | | -OY | |
| front | back | front | back |

## Discovery Learning

Introduce 'oi'/oy/ in the middle and 'oy' /oy/ at the end of words through Discovery Learning. At the teacher's discretion words with 'oy' /oy/ in the middle (e.g., voyage) can also be taught and 'oy' can be added to the back of the Spelling Card as a second choice spelling in the middle. Also at the teacher's discretion 'oi' can be added to the beginning position (e.g., oil). However, only a very few words begin with /oy/ (e.g., oyster).

## Spelling Card

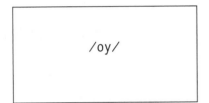

|  | B | M | E |
|---|---|---|---|
| /oy/ |  | *oi* | *oy* |

The learner's response is /oy/ 'oi' in the middle and /oy/ 'oy' at the end.

## Words for Reading and Spelling

Coin, boil, foil, spoil, loin, groin, coil, soil, broil, point, voice, void, join, toil, quoit, oil, ointment.

Roy, boy, toy, joy, ploy, coy, Troy, enjoy, decoy, employ, annoy, joyful.

## Practising the New Learning

1. Ask the learner which of the above 'oi' words for reading can be made from the letters in the following phrases:

   alphabetical order          oriental soup          quaint cottage

2. Ask them to complete these phrases using one of the following adjectives: tall, sharp, gold, plastic, clever.

   - A ____ ploy.
   - A ____ toy.
   - A ____ boy.

- A ____ coin.
- A ____ foil.

## Sentences for Reading and Dictation ('oi')

The soil is very moist. "Do not loiter on the street corner," said Dad. Mum hung five gold coins on the tree. Rob has a very deep voice. The oven was too hot and the cake is spoilt.

## Story for Reading and Dictation ('oi' and 'oy')

A boy, whose name was Roy, crept along the undergrowth. He kept his voice very low as he sang to himself. Suddenly he saw a snake coiled like a spring on the soil where he was going to step. He toyed with the idea of hitting it with a stick to destroy it, in case it attacked him, but then he decided that the best ploy was to stand poised where he was and hope that the reptile avoided him. (Tricky word: *idea.*)

# Teaching Point 120

## Plural Possessives

## Discovery Learning

Introduce the use of the apostrophe to denote the possessive 's' plural through Discovery Learning. This could be done *orally* first (e.g., by showing pictures of the objects to be matched to pictures of different groups of people such as boys, girls, teachers, sailors; e.g., the sailors' boat). Demonstrate how we show possession in writing. Reinforce this using Concept Card 23.

## Practising New Learning

Ask the learner to match a person card (e.g., the boys', the teachers', the footballers') to an object card (e.g., staffroom, manager, cloakroom) to make phrases for reading (e.g., the teachers' staffroom, the footballers' manager, the boys' cloakroom). Then ask the learner to insert the missing apostrophe in sentences such as: The sailors ship sailed away and left them stranded. Plural words and apostrophe 's' should also be taught here (e.g., The children's cloakroom. The women's rest room) so that learners understand the rule about plurals and the use of the apostrophe.

# Teaching Point 121

cursive form

'ou' /ow/

*ou*

## Reading Cards

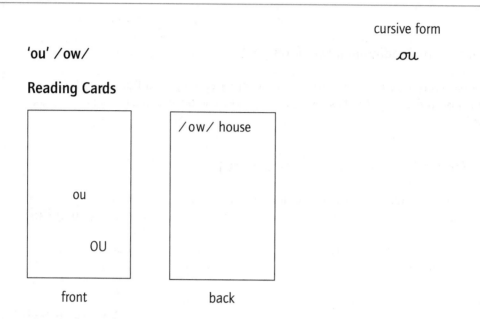

front                    back

## Discovery Learning

Introduce 'ou'/ow/ in the middle position through Discovery Learning using auditory, visual, and tactile/kinaesthetic channels. Add 'ou' to the /ow/ Spelling Card as a second choice spelling in the middle. This can be added to the beginning position at the teacher's discretion.

## Words for Reading and Spelling

House, mouse, count, sound, found, round, bound, mount, pound, out, shout.

## Practising the New Learning

Ask the learner to work out the answers to the following riddles:

- A small rodent (mouse).
- To get on a horse (mount).
- A building to live in (house).
- 100 pence (pound). To reckon up in numbers (count).

## Story for Reading and Dictation: 'ou' /ow/

Ted was a boy scout. He went about the county getting cash for doing odd jobs. It was a cloudy day and he stood outside a house at Number 16, Mount Street. He pounded on the door with his fist. A stout lady in a black top and trousers shouted loudly out of the window. He went around the corner of the house and his mouth fell open as he saw a huge pile of sprouts on the ground. A large hound sniffed around it. "I need to finish peeling them," said the lady, "but a mouse has run into the sprouts." "I can get it out," said Ted. He poked the mound with the tip of his boot. The mouse ran out and in a trice the hound bounded after it. Ted followed at a pace. The hound pounced: so did Ted. He shouted in a loud voice, "I've got it." The lady was so pleased that she gave Ted a five pound note for the scouts' fund.

# Teaching Point 122

## 'ou' /ŭ/ (or /o͝o/) and 'ou' /o͞o/

As there are relatively few words with this spelling choice the teacher might want to make a card for these, starting with words in the learner's written vocabulary and practising them on a regular basis (e.g., could, should, would; country, cousin, touch, young). Use a visual spelling routine and try highlighting the tricky part of each word. Introduce 'ou' /ŭ/ through Discovery Learning and add an appropriate clue word (e.g., 'couple') to the back of the 'ou' Reading Card. Add 'ou' to the back of the /ŭ/ spelling as the third choice for /ŭ/ in the middle.

The digraph 'ou' can also make the sound /o͞o/ (e.g., coupon, toucan, wound, route, soup, cougar). Introduce 'ou' /o͞o/ through Discovery Learning and practise writing 'ou' words by asking the learner to find an adjective to describe each of the previous words. Add /o͞o/ and an appropriate clue word to the back of the 'ou' Reading Card. Add 'ou' to the back of the /o͞o/ Spelling Card as a second choice spelling in the middle. It can also be found in the end position in the key word 'you'. As there are relatively few words with this spelling choice, the teacher might decide to make a card for those within the learner's vocabulary to be practised.

# Teaching Point 123

## Regular Final Syllables – 'le'

Regular final syllables are common word endings that are made by adding the '-le' suffix to a consonant. Take the wooden letters out of the alphabet arc one at a time and add 'le' to find out which consonants can be used to make a regular final syllable. Check by asking the learner to think of and then say a word with that ending. Explain that a vowel sound escapes between the consonants thereby making a syllable. The regular final syllables that can be made are: -ble, -cle, -dle, -fle, -gle, -kle, -ple, -tle, -stle, -zle. (Note the silent 't'.) Write these on a card for reference and practice.

Now ask the learner to choose one of the final syllables to add to each of the following open and closed syllables to make a word:

| Closed syllables | Open Syllables |
| --- | --- |
| an/kle | ca/ble |
| can | tri |
| ap | fa |
| sup | sta |
| pud | ea |

## Words for Reading and Spelling

Candle, wobble, handle, kettle, apple, uncle, puzzle, middle, angle, stable, castle, table.

## Practising the New Learning

Illustrate the following words to show their meaning (e.g., little):

wobble  bubble  steeple  angle  simple  battle  prickle  tangle  dribble

If the letters B to M = 1 point, N to Z = 3 points, and vowels = 2 points, find the value of some of these words: candle, puddle, table, cable, eagle, angle, uncle, treacle, kettle, nettle. Which word scored the most points?

## Sentences for Reading and Spelling

The baby's milk dribbled down his chin. The sum was simple. The triangle has a ninety degree angle. The toddler jumped in the puddle with a splash.

# Teaching Point 124

cursive form

## Suffix 'tion' /shn/

## Reading Card

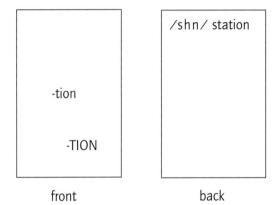

| | /shn/ station |
|---|---|
| -tion | |
| -TION | |

front                back

## Discovery Learning

Introduce 'tion' /shn/ by asking the learner to listen to the following words: fraction, selection, protection, action, option, election. Ask them to use a BME sheet for listening to and identifying the position of the /shn/ sound in the words. Write the words on the board and ask the learner which letters make the /shn/ sound. Track the words with 'tion' in a book or magazine. Make a Reading and Spelling Card for 'tion'.

## Spelling Card

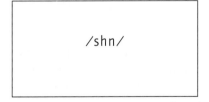

| /shn/ |
|---|
| |

| | | B | M | E |
|---|---|---|---|---|
| /tion/ | | | | *tion* |

The learner's response is /shn/ 'tion' at the end.

## Words for Reading and Spelling

Action, reaction, fraction, friction, station, nation, relation, option, section. Note that question is irregular.

## Practising the New Learning

Demonstrate adding the suffix 'tion' to base words (e.g., inspect = inspection), and ask them to look for a pattern (e.g., drop letter 't' when adding 'tion'). Then ask the learner to add the suffix 'tion' to the following base words:

- detect
- assert
- relate
- invent
- desert
- opt

Also practise adding the regular final syllable 'tion' to open syllables to make nation, station, notion, lotion, and potion.

## Sentences for Reading and Spelling

The dress is on sale at a fraction of the cost. Ben ran to the station to catch the train. The Queen will address the nation.

# Teaching Point 125

### Suffix '-sion' /shn/ /zhn/

Introduce 'sion' /shn/ in the same way as the previous Teaching Point (suffix 'tion') using Discovery Learning. Make a Reading Card for suffix '–sion' using an appropriate clue word (e.g., mansion) and add this to the back of the /shn/ Spelling Card as a second choice spelling in the end position. Practise adding 'sion' to the base words suspense, tense, manse, repulse, convulse, to make suspension, tension, mansion, repulsion, convulsion. Help the learner to work out what happens when you add suffix 'sion' to a base word ending in 'se' (drop the letters 'se'). Give the learner a list of base words (e.g., opt, detect, tense, inspect, manse) and see if they can work out which suffix to add ('tion' or 'sion') by looking at the word ending.

The final syllable 'sion' makes the /zhn/ sound in some words (e.g., television). The Reading Card for 'sion' will therefore have two clue words, one for /shn/ and one for /zhn/. A separate Spelling Card is needed for /zhn/ and 'sion' is written on the back in the end position. Practise reading and spelling words ending in 'sion' /zhn/ (e.g., version, invasion, revision, erosion, elusion, confusion, decision, conclusion, aversion, division).

## Teaching Point 126

### Suffix 'cian' /shn/

Introduce 'cian' through Discovery Learning. Make a Reading Card for suffix '-cian' and add it to the back of the /shn/ Spelling Card as a third choice spelling in the end position. Practise adding suffix 'cian' to the base words magic, logic, politic, electric, music, physic, optic, mathematic, to make the words magician, logician, politician, electrician, musician, physician, optician, mathematician. Help the learner to work out what happens when we add suffix 'cian' to words ending in 'c' (drop the letter 'c').

Practise reading and spelling /shn/ words with all three spelling choices and encourage the learner to identify the base word in order to work out the spelling rule for suffix /shn/. If the base word ends in 't' (or 're') use suffix 'tion'; if it ends in 'se' (or 'de') use suffix 'sion'; and if it ends in 'c' use suffix 'cian'. (Note that suffix 'tion' can be added to words with different endings e.g., in mathematical terms like multiply/multiplication, add/addition.)

## Teaching Point 127

### Silent Letters 'w' and 'k'

Add words beginning with silent 'w' and 'k' to the pack for silent letters. Some common words start with silent 'k' such as know and knee, and the teacher may decide to begin with these. Later, the words knock, knight, kneel, knave, knack may be added. A visual spelling routine will be needed to teach these words (see Part V for examples). A simple mnemonic could be given (e.g., the knock kneed knight). Words with silent 'w' that can be introduced at this stage in the programme are wrist, wrong, wreck, wren, writhe. The teacher might choose to start with words that are within the learner's vocabulary.

# Teaching Point 128

cursive form

'ir' /ûr/                                                   *ir*

## Reading Card

```
┌──────────────┐    ┌──────────────┐
│              │    │ /ûr/ fir     │
│              │    │              │
│              │    │              │
│    ir        │    │              │
│              │    │              │
│        IR    │    │              │
│              │    │              │
└──────────────┘    └──────────────┘
     front               back
```

## Discovery Learning

Introduce 'ir'/ûr/ by asking the learner to listen to 'ir' words (e.g., fir, stir, girl, dirt, first, birth). Use a BME sheet for the learner to discover the position of the /ûr/ sound. Track words with 'ir' in a book or magazine. Make a Reading Card for 'ir' and add 'ir' to the back of the /ûr/ Spelling Card as a second choice middle spelling and a first choice end spelling (only a very few words have 'ir' at /ûr/ the end).

## Spelling Card

|  | B | M | E |
|---|---|---|---|
| /ûr/ |  | *er*<br>*ir* | *ir* |

The learner's response is /ûr/ 'e' 'r' in the middle, /ûr/ 'i' 'r' in the middle, and /ûr/ 'i' 'r' at the end.

## Words for Reading and Spelling

Bird, chirp, girl, stir, first, skirt, sir, firm, squirt, thirsty, shirt, dirt, thirty, third.

## Practising the New Learning

Modified precision teaching: make a worksheet with three columns. In the first column write ten 'ir' words, in the second column write ten 'tion' words, and in the third column write ten 'ow'/ow/ words. Ask the learner to read down the columns, repeating the exercise until at least 90 per cent accuracy has been obtained. Then ask them to read across the columns until 90 per cent accuracy has been obtained. Time the learner and try to improve their reading speed, repeating the exercise as often as necessary until optimum speed has been reached.

## Sentences for Reading and Spelling

Three birds sat in a tree chirping. The girl has a dirty face. Beth squirted lemon into the stir fry. Jill got a blue skirt and top for her birthday. Bill was very thirsty.

# Teaching Point 129

## 'ur' /uîr/

Introduce 'ur' /uîr/ through Discovery Learning in the same way as Teaching Point 128. Pictures could be used (e.g., church, curl, nurse, turnip, purse) as an alternative to listening for the sound in a list of words. Make a Reading Card for 'ur'. Add 'ur' to the back of the /uîr/ Spelling Card as the third choice spelling for /uîr/ in the middle of a word and the second choice spelling for the end of a word.

## Spelling Card

| | B | M | E |
|---|---|---|---|
| /uîr/ | | er<br>ir<br>ur | ir<br>ur |

The learner's response is /ûr/ 'er', /ûr/ 'i'r', /ûr/ /'ur' in the middle, and /ûr/ 'ir' and /ûr/ 'ur' at the end.

## Practising the New Learning

Practise reading and spelling words with 'ur' (e.g., fur, burn, curl, hurt, hurl, burst, incur, turn, spur, surly, blur, church). Play the 4-in-a Row game as in Part V (resources). Make a worksheet with pictures of a church, a girl, a shirt, a skirt, a turnip, and a fern. Ask the learner to look up their spelling in a dictionary and write the words underneath the pictures in order to give them practice at checking spelling choices for /ûr/ in the middle of words.

# Teaching Point 130

### Words With 'or' After 'w' /ûr/

Words in which 'or' comes after the letter 'w' need practising as a separate Teaching Point as the sound changes to /ûr/. Introduce 'or' /ûr/ through Discovery Learning and add it to the back of the 'or' Reading Card. Negotiate and appropriate a clue word with the learner (e.g., world). Spelling choice 'or' is added to the back of the /ûr/ Spelling Card as the fourth choice spelling in the middle position.

## Words for Reading and Spelling

Word, work, worm, worth, world, worse, worst, worker, worthwhile, worship.

## Practising the New Learning

Read the following riddles with the learner (paired reading) and ask them to write down the answer (naming the letters as they write):

- Another name for the earth (world).
- An animal with a long, limbless, segmented body (worm).
- A unit of speech or writing that makes sense (word).
- You do this to earn money (work).
- Very, very, bad compared with others (worst).

Ask the learner to think of a sentence for each of the words they have written in order to practise using them in context or make a closure exercise to practise the words above.

## Sentences for Reading and Dictation

Ben got the worst mark in the class. Bill works in his dad's shop at the weekend. Victor collected worms from his garden to take fishing.

## Teaching Point 131

cursive form

*au*

## Vowel Digraph 'au' /aw/

## Reading Card

| au<br><br>AU | /aw/ sauce |
|---|---|
| front | back |

## Discovery Learning

Introduce 'au' /aw/ by asking the learner to listen to the following words: haunt, taunt, Paul, flaunt, maul, sauce, gaunt. Use a BME sheet for identifying the position of the /aw/ sound in words. Track 'au' words. Make a Reading and Spelling Card for 'au' /aw/.

## Spelling Card

| | B | M | E |
|---|---|---|---|
| /aw/ | | *au* | |

The learner's response is /aw/ 'au' in the middle.

## Words for Reading and Spelling

Paul, Saul, haul, maul, gaunt, flaunts, jaunt, haunt, taunt, sauce, cause, pause, clause, launch, paunch. Irregular words assault, fault, vault at the teacher's discretion.

## Sentences for Reading and Spelling

Paul started to launch the lifeboat. Burt and Paul went on a jaunt to a haunted castle. Bill put mint sauce on his lamb. Haul the rope up.

# Teaching Point 132

cursive form

### Vowel Digraph 'aw' /aw/

*aw*

### Discovery Learning

Introduce 'aw' /aw/ through Discovery Learning. Listen to words with the /aw/ sound in the middle and end positions (e.g., sauce, claw, draw, haunt, straw). Revisit the spelling of the /aw/ sound in the middle of words (Teaching Point 131) and then write some 'aw' words such as draw, jaw, law, claw, saw, raw, flaw, squaw, etc. on the board and ask the learner to work out how the sound is represented at the end of words. Track 'aw' words in a book or magazine. Make a Reading Card for '-aw' and add 'aw' to the back of the /aw/ Spelling Card in the end position.

Words with an 'aw' ending can now be included in reading, spelling, and dictation. There are a few words where 'aw' is found in the beginning or middle positions (e.g., awful, lawyer, awkward). These could be taught at the teacher's discretion. As there are relatively few of them 'aw' is *not* added to the beginning or middle column on the back of the Spelling Card.

# Teaching Point 133

cursive form

## Vowel Digraph '-oe' /ō/

## Reading Card

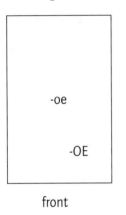

| /ō/ toe |
| --- |

      front                    back

## Discovery Learning

Introduce 'oe' /ō/ through Discovery Learning. Revisit the end spelling for /ō/ already introduced ('ow') (Teaching Point 101) and then write some words with 'oe' on a board/card so the learner can work out the second choice spelling for /ō/ at the end of words. Make a Reading Card for '-oe' and add 'oe' to the back of the /ō/ Spelling Card as second choice end spelling.

## Spelling Card

| /ō/ |
| --- |

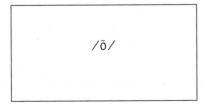

The learner's response is /ō/ 'o' at the beginning, /ō/ 'o-e' in the middle, /ō/ 'oa' in the middle, /ō/ 'ow' at the end and /ō/ 'oe' at the end.

## Words for Reading and Spelling

Toe, doe, foe, oboe, woe, floe, roe, hoe, Joe.

## Practising the New Learning

Ask the learner to choose the correct end spelling for /ō/: 'ow' or 'oe' for the following:

- b--
- tipt--
- s--
- l--
- w--
- d--

They could then check their answers in a dictionary.

## Story for Reading and Spelling

The doe ran swiftly and softly through the woods. Was she still being followed by the foe? She stopped and listened. There was a crackling noise. It was the hunter on tip-toe. Another strange sound, like an oboe, floated on the air. Then a shot rang out. Overcome with woe she fled towards the oncoming ice floe. (Tricky words: 'listened' and key word 'through'.)

## Teaching Point 134

cursive form

### Vowel Digraph 'ey' /ā/

*ey*

Introduce 'ey' /ā/ through Discovery Learning using the following words: grey, they, obey, fey, whey, osprey, survey, prey, convey, purvey. Identify the common sound. Write the words on a board and ask the learner to work out how the /ā/ sound at the end of these words is spelled. Make a Reading Card for '-ey' /ā/ (see Teaching Point 135) and add 'ey' to the back of the /ā/ Spelling Card as the second choice spelling in the end position. Practise looking for words with an 'ay' and 'ey' ending in a dictionary. Start to include 'ey' words in reading and spelling.

## Teaching Point 135

cursive form

*ey*

## Vowel Digraph 'ey' /ĭ/ or /ē/

## Reading Card

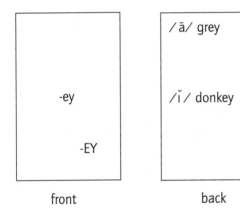

| | |
|---|---|
| -ey | /ā/ grey |
| -EY | /ĭ/ donkey |

front        back

## Discovery Learning

Introduce 'ey' /ĭ/ as in 'donkey'. Add 'ey' /ĭ/ to the back of the '-ey' Reading Card and to the back of the /ĭ/ Spelling Card as the second choice spelling in the end position.

## Spelling Card

| /ĭ/ | | | | |
|---|---|---|---|---|
| | | B | M | E |
| /ĭ/ | | i | i | y ey |

The learner's response is /ĭ/ 'i' at the beginning, /ĭ/ 'i' in the middle, /ĭ/ 'y' at the end and /ĭ/ 'ey' at the end.

## Words for Reading and Spelling

Donkey, monkey, honey, barley, jockey, galley, pulley, spinney.
(Note that the plural form of words ending in 'ey', simply adds 's'.)

## Practising the New Learning

Ask the learner to look at each word for reading and find words that rhyme with:

- money
- parley
- hockey
- valley.

## Sentences for Reading and Dictation

Joe went to watch the hockey match. Five monkeys ran out of the spinney. Jill rode a donkey along the beach. I like honey with my toast. Kate is cooking in the galley.

# Teaching Point 136

cursive form

'ew' /o͞o/ and /ū/                                    *ew*

Introduce 'ew' /o͞o/ as in grew, flew, blew, crew, drew, and 'ew'/ū/ as in spew, few, knew, pew, hew, mew, stew, through Discovery Learning. Make a Reading Card for 'ew' with two clue words on the back, one for /o͞o/ and one for /ū/. Add 'ew' to the back of the /o͞o/ Spelling Card as the second choice spelling in the end position, and to the back of the /ū/ Spelling Card as the second choice spelling in the end position. Incorporate words with an 'ew' ending into dictionary exercises so the learner has to think about possible spelling choices and then check these.

Several homonyms can be introduced at this point (e.g., blue and blew, flew and flue, dew and due, hew and hue, Kew and queue). Put the homonyms into sentences so that the learner attaches meaning to the spelling of the word. Use memory tags: e.g., blew (wind), flew (wings).

## Spelling Card/s

|  | B | M | E |
|---|---|---|---|
| /ū/ | *u* | *u-e* | *ue* *ew* |

The learner response is /ū/ 'u' at the beginning, /ū/ 'u-e' in the middle, /ū/ 'ue' and /ū/ 'ew' at the end.

|  | B | M | E |
|---|---|---|---|
| /ōo/ |  | *oo* | *ue* *ew* *oo* |

The learner response is /ōo/ 'oo' in the middle, /ōo/ 'ue', /ōo/ 'ew' and /ōo/ 'oo' at the end.

# Teaching Point 137

cursive form

*-al -el*

## Suffix 'al' and 'el' /əl/

When the /l/ sound is heard at the end of a word it is usually part of a regular final syllable such as 'ble' in 'table' or 'tle' in 'little'. These have already been taught as a group (Teaching Point 123) and put on a card to be practised regularly. The learner will have started to recognise which consonant sounds can be heard in the final regular syllables -ble, -cle, -dle, -fle, -gle, -kle, -ple, -stle, -tle, and –zle. Where a different consonant is heard with the /l/ sound then the word ends in either the spelling 'al' (as in animal, general, eternal, maternal, oral, naval) or in 'el' (as in tunnel, channel, flannel, jewel, gravel, barrel, squirrel, towel, vowel, travel). Let the learner explore these words to try to identify patterns (e.g., 'el' comes after the letter 'w', double 'n', and double 'r'). Tricky words include mental, hostel, pastel, and petal, as they sound as if they have the final regular syllable 'tle'. These need teaching using a visual spelling routine. Practice will also need to be given in adding the suffix 'al' to base words such as post, magic, dispose, nutrition, front, arrive, to make postal, magical, disposal, nutritional, frontal, arrival.

## Teaching Point 138

### Prefixes: 'mal', 'semi' and 'bi'

The prefixes 'mal', 'semi', and 'bi' can be introduced at this stage. These can be used with base words such as content, form(ed), practice; colon, circle, final, automatic; monthly, polar, and optic (to make malcontent, malformed, malpractice; semicolon, semicircle, semi-final, semiautomatic; bimonthly, bipolar, bioptic). Discuss with the learner how the prefix changes the meaning of the word. (The prefixes are of Latin origin: the prefix '*mal*' meaning ill or badly; the prefix '*semi*' meaning half, partially, or imperfectly; and the prefix '*bi*' meaning double or twice.) These can be introduced into reading and spelling for older learners and others where appropriate.

## Teaching Point 139

### Syllable Division Pattern: cv/vc

### Discovery Learning

Write the following words on a piece of paper:

    triad     diet     triangle     dual     dial     duet

Ask the learner to write a letter 'c' over the consonants and a letter 'v' over the vowels that come between the consonants.

Ask them to repeat and clap to identify how many syllables there are in the word 'triad'. Let them discover where the word divides through clapping 'tri-ad'. Repeat this for each of the words above and then ask the learner to draw a line to show where the words divide.

They should notice that they now have a cv-vc pattern. They have worked out the rule for the fourth syllable division pattern – if there are two vowels that do not form a vowel diagraph then we split the word between the vowels. Look at each syllable in turn and identify if these are open or closed. Ask the learner to write the breve symbol over the closed syllables and the macron over the open syllables – to help with pronunciation – before reading the words. Refer to Concept Card 40.

Many of the words that follow the cv/vc syllable division pattern have what looks like a 'reversed' digraph (e.g., 'ia' instead of 'ai', 'ua' instead of 'au') and the learner will start to realise that these are not digraphs, and that the vowels have to be split for reading. Some words contain what appears to be a digraph but this is not the case (e.g., the word 'ruin' appears to have a digraph like the word 'fruit' but in this case the vowel is split, and the first syllable is 'open' with a long vowel sound). The strategy for these words is – *read as if a digraph but if it does not make sense try splitting it into two separate vowels.*

## Practising the New Learning

Ask the learner to code and divide the syllables in the following words:

| | | | | | |
|---|---|---|---|---|---|
| ruin | poet | diary | violet | triumph | aorta |
| coincide | trial | peony | cruet | violin | video |

## Sentences for Reading and Dictation

The teacher drew a diagram on the board. Mark and Kate sang a duet. The distance across a circle is the diameter. A peony is a flower. Paul plays the violin and piano. (Tricky word: piano).

# Teaching Point 140

cursive form

*ph*

## 'ph' /f/

## Reading Card

| |
|---|
| ph |
| PH |

front

| |
|---|
| /f/ pheasant |

back

Make a Reading Card for 'ph' /f/. Add 'ph' to the back of the /f/ Spelling Card as the second choice spelling at the beginning and middle of words and third choice spelling at the end of words. The 'ph' spelling is found in words of Greek origin. Please note that 'f' as the second choice spelling at the end should have been added to the Spelling Card when teaching vowel digraphs.

## Spelling Card

The learner's response is /f/ 'f', /f/ 'ph' at the beginning, /f/ 'f', /f/ 'ph' in the middle, /f/ 'ff', /f/ 'f' and /f/ 'ph' at the end.

## Words for Reading and Spelling

Photograph, pharmacy, pheasant, phase, philosopher, graph, telephone, phlox, phial, sphere, rephrase, microphone, triumph, cellophane, semaphore, alphabet, orphan, dolphin, phantom. Irregular words are sapphire, morphine, xylophone (but not irregular for 'ph').

## Practising the New Learning

Ask the learner to arrange the following words in alphabetical order:

- sphere, phial, triumph, rephrase, graph.
- pharmacy, semaphore, telephone, sapphire, pheasant.
- phlox, phase, philosopher, photograph, pheasant.

## Sentences for Reading and Dictation

Mum planted some phlox in the garden. He dropped the phial on the floor. The farmer was in the woods shooting pheasants. "Go to the pharmacy with this prescription," Dad said. Philip got a new microphone for the band. Can you rephrase the question?

# Teaching Point 141

cursive form

### Vowel Digraph 'ie' /ē/

*ie*

## Discovery Learning

Ask the learner to repeat the following words and identify the common sound: field, shield, piece, brief, priest. Write these on the board and ask the learner to work out how the /ē/ sound is represented. Track 'ie' words in a book or magazine. Make a Reading Card for 'ie' /ē/ and add 'ie' to the back of the /ē/ Spelling Card as a third choice spelling in the middle position.

## Spelling Card

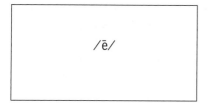

|  | B | M | E |
|---|---|---|---|
| /ē/ | *e* | *ee* | *ee* |
|  |  | *ea* | *ea* |
|  |  | *ie* |  |

The learner's response is /ē/ 'e' at the beginning, /ē/ 'ee' in the middle, /ē/ 'ea' in the middle, /ē/ 'ie' in the middle, /ē/ 'ee' at the end and /ē/ 'ea' at the end.

## Words for Reading and Spelling

Brief, chief, field, shield, fiend, frieze, grief, niece, piece, priest, shield, shriek, siege, thief, yield, relief, grieve, wield, believe.

## Practising the New Learning

1. Make a wordsearch or a rhyming pairs game using some of the words for reading.
2. Make a 'Find the odd-one-out' worksheet using the following sets of words:

   - grief    relief    shriek    pie    piece
   - chief    field    lie    grieve    priest
   - die    tie    vie    lie    brief
   - fiend    niece    tied    shield    wield

### Sentences for Reading and Spelling

Bill has a new baby niece. The sprinter ran across the field. The police chief gave the order. It was a relief to be home. The constable wielded his baton.

## Teaching Point 142

cursive form

'e-e' /ē/

*e-e*

The 'vowel consonant e' (vce) pattern was introduced much earlier in the programme for the vowels 'a', 'i', 'o' and 'u', but has been left until the later stages for vowel 'e' due to the comparatively small number of 'e-e' words. Examples of e-e words are eve, theme, mete, delete, deplete, centipede, compete, extreme, complete, Japanese, Burmese, concrete, discrete, athlete. In addition there are a number of key words with the 'e-e' pattern that may have already been introduced (Teaching Point 87) e.g., were, here, where, there. Please note that these do not follow the 'e-e' = /ē/ pattern.

Make a Reading Card for 'e-e'. Add 'e-e' to the back of the /ē/ Spelling Card as a fourth choice spelling in the middle position.

## Teaching Point 143

cursive form

Vowel Digraph 'ei' /ē/

*ei*

Introduce 'ei' /ē/ through Discovery Learning. Make a Reading Card for 'ei' /ē/ and negotiate a clue word with the learner. Examples of words with 'ei' /ē/ are: ceiling, conceit, deceit, deceive, perceive, preconceive, receive. As there are relatively few words with this spelling choice the teacher may decide to introduce them as a group and write them on a card for the learner to practise reading at regular intervals. Words that are within the learner's written vocabulary can be included in dictation for further practice.

Add 'ei' and a clue word to the back of the /ē/ Spelling Card as the fifth choice spelling in the middle position. Usually this pronunciation/spelling comes after the letter 'c'. The learner might find the following saying helpful:

'i' before 'e' if it rhymes with /ē/, except after 'c' (when 'e' comes before 'i')

# Teaching Point 144

cursive form

## Vowel Digraph 'ei' /ā/

*ei*

Introduce 'ei' /ā/ as in 'rein' through Discovery Learning. Use a BME sheet to listen to words with /ā/ and identify its position. Review the spelling choices for /ā/ introduced so far. Write some examples of words with 'ei' spelling on the board (e.g., vein, veil, beige, reindeer), and ask the learner to work out how the /ā/ sound is represented in those words. Add /ā/ and a clue word to the back of the 'ei' Reading Card. Add 'ei' to the back of the /ā/ Spelling Card as the third choice spelling in the middle position.

Add to the sayings – *'e' before 'i' if it rhymes with 'hay' as in rein.*

# Teaching Point 145

cursive form

## Consonant Digraph 'ch' /k/ and 'ch'/sh/

*ch*

Introduce 'ch' /k/ through Discovery Learning using auditory, visual, and tactile/kinaesthetic channels. Add /k/ and an appropriate clue word (e.g., chemist) to the back of the 'ch' Reading Card. The 'ch' spelling of /k/ is of Greek origin. It is used in beginning, middle, and end positions and many of the words are related to science or music. Add 'ch' to the back of the /k/ Spelling Card as a third choice spelling (beginning and middle) and a fourth choice spelling at the end.

## Spelling Card

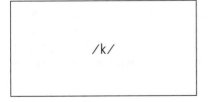

|  | B | M | E |
|---|---|---|---|
| /k/ | *c* | *c* | *ck* |
|  | *k* | *k* | *k* |
|  |  |  | *c* |
|  | *ch* | *ch* | *ch* |

With so many so many spelling choices, shorten the learner's response to /k/ 'c' /k/ 'k', /k/ 'ch' at the beginning, /k/ 'c' /k/ 'k', /k/ 'ch' in the middle, and /k/ 'ck' /k/ 'k', /k/ 'c', /k/ 'ch' at the end.

## Words for Reading and Spelling

Chemist, chronic, ache, chloride, stomach, orchestra, scheme, chaotic, Christmas, school, Christopher, chemical, chemistry, cholera, bronchitis, chord, chorus, echo.

## Practising the New Learning

Ask the learner to illustrate some the following words to show their meaning (e.g., tiny):

orchid     orchestra     Christmas     chemistry     echo     chaotic

or to draw a picture or symbols to represent their meaning.

## Story for Reading and Dictation

One day Christopher woke up feeling glum. He called his mother. "I am not very well," he said. "My throat is sore. I ache all over. I think I have chronic bronchitis or cholera." Mother put a thermometer in Christopher's mouth. His temperature was normal. "You probably have a slight sore throat, but you have no fever. Have a paracetamol for your headache and get up. You can't miss school today. You have orchestra practice, and you are one of the main characters in the Christmas play." Christopher got up, moaning and clutching his stomach. As he left the house, after eating a good breakfast, his mother heard him muttering "Sodium chloride, carbon dioxide … " She knew why Christopher didn't want to go to school. It was all a scheme to miss the chemistry test.

In the same or subsequent lesson introduce 'ch' /sh/ which occurs in words of French origin such as chalet, chiffon, chef, chagrin, charade, champagne, chivalry, chaperone. Add /sh/ and an appropriate clue word to the back of the 'ch' Reading Card. Add 'ch' to the back of the /sh/ Spelling Card as a second choice spelling at the beginning. Practise spelling 'ch' /sh/ words that are within the learner's written vocabulary by including them in dictation.

## Teaching Point 146

cursive form

'eigh' /ā/                                        *eigh*

Introduce 'eigh' through discovery learning. Use a BME sheet to practise listening for words with /ā/ in different positions and review the spelling choices already introduced. Write the words eight, sleigh, weight, freight, eighteen and eighty on the board and ask the learner to work out how the /ā/ sound is represented in these words. Make a Reading Card for 'eigh' and add it to the back of the /ā/ Spelling Card as a second choice spelling at the beginning, a fourth choice spelling in the middle, and a third choice spelling at the end. As there are relatively few words with 'eigh' /ā/ these could be written as a group on a piece of card and practised regularly.

## Teaching Point 147

cursive form

'ear' /ēə/ and /êr/ and /ûr/              *ear*

Introduce 'ear' /ēə/ through Discovery Learning by asking the learner to listen to the following words and identify the common sound: fear, spear, appear, hear, shear, tear, clear, dear. Write the words on the board and ask them to work out how /ēə/ is represented in these words. Use a tracking exercise. Make a Reading and Spelling Card for 'ear' /ēə/. Practise 'ear' words by including them in dictionary exercises or a reading game such as 4-in-a Row.

In the next lesson introduce the short sound for 'ear' /ûr/ as in earl, pearl, earth, earn, early, heard, learn, search, yearn, rehearse. Add /ûr/ and an appropriate clue word to the back of the 'ear' Reading Card. Add 'ear' to the back of the /ûr/ Spelling Card as a first choice spelling at the beginning and a fifth choice spelling in the middle. The learner's response now is /ûr/ 'ear' at the beginning, /ûr/ 'er', /ûr/ 'ir', /ûr / 'ur', /ûr/ 'or' and /ûr/ 'ear' in the middle, and /ûr/ 'ir', /ûr/ 'ur' at the end. Make a word search to practise reading 'ear' /ûr/ words and start to include words from the learner's written vocabulary in dictation. Some 'ear' words are pronounced /êr/ (e.g., bear, pear, wear). These can be learned as a group.

## Teaching Point 148

cursive form

**'a' /ə/ Indeterminate 'a' or Schwa**                    *a*

One syllable words starting with letter 'a' that have been introduced so far (e.g., ant, ask, act) all have the short /ă/ sound. However, in multisyllabic words the 'a' at the beginning of the word often becomes shortened in speech to produce the /ə/ sound (the indeterminate 'a' or schwa, sometimes represented as /uh/). Examples of this are about, arrive, above, alight, aloft, afflict, avail, astound, agenda, appear, assign, abolish, abandon, afflict, associate. The learner should still be able to decode these words for reading but will need to practise them in spelling. This could be done by making a pack of words for practice in spelling games using a race track or a snakes and ladders board and by including them in dictation. It can be added to the back of the 'a' Reading Card and the /ə/ Spelling Card in the beginning position.

## Teaching Point 149

cursive form

**'-our' /ə/**                                            *our*

**Reading Card**

| | / ə / colour |
|---|---|
| -our<br><br>-OUR | |
| front | back |

## Discovery Learning

Introduce 'our' /ə/. Make a Reading Card for '-our' /ə/. Add 'our' to the back of the /ə/ Spelling Card as the fourth choice spelling at the end of words. This is also an indeterminate vowel/schwa sound.

## Spelling Card

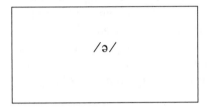

The learner's response is /ə/ 'a' at the beginning and /ə/ 'ar', /ə/ 'or', /ə/ 'er' and /ə/ 'our' at the end.

## Words for Reading and Spelling

Colour, honour, flavour, harbour, glamour, splendour, humour, labour, odour, arbour.

## Practising the New Learning

Place each sentence of the story for reading on separate pieces of card and ask the learner to put these in a logical order.

## Story for Reading and Dictation

Joseph thought it was a great honour to be invited to the banquet. When he arrived he was overcome by the splendour of the occasion. As he walked down the spiral staircase he was able to enjoy the colourful event that was laid out below him. The table decorations were fantastic and the flavour of the food at dinner was exquisite. After the meal, a speech made by the President was full of humour. Joseph could not wait to tell everyone about the glamour of the evening.

(Irregular words: exquisite, everyone.)

## Teaching Point 150

cursive form

### Suffix 'ous' /ŭs/

*ous us*

The suffix 'ous' can be used to change a noun or verb into an adjective (e.g., 'poison' into 'poisonous'). Practise this by asking the learner to add the suffix 'ous' to base words such as joy, murder, nerve, continue, ridicule, desire, grieve, danger. In changing nerve to nervous, continue to continuous and so on, the suffixing rule 'drop e' when adding a vowel suffix is also practised. The learner could be asked to look up the new words in a dictionary in order to check they have applied the suffixing rule correctly. Practise using adjectives with 'ous' ending by asking the learner to match the words above to an appropriate noun (e.g., a murderous look, ridiculous hat, nervous glance).

### 'us' /ŭs/

Introduce 'us' /ŭs/ through Discovery Learning. The 'us' spelling of /ŭs/ is found at the end of a base word (e.g., crocus, minus, plus, cactus, census, citrus, chorus, octopus, fungus, focus, bonus, sinus, Venus, cumulus, onus, stimulus). Give the learner practice at identifying the correct spelling for /ŭs/ by looking at words and underlining the base word ('ous' is added to a base word), e.g., <u>danger</u>ous, <u>cactus</u>, <u>chorus</u>, <u>joy</u>ous, <u>poison</u>ous, <u>minus</u>. This will reinforce the concept of base word and suffix and allow the learner to establish the rule.

## Teaching Point 151

cursive form

### Regular Final Syllables '-ture' /chə / '-sure' /zhə/

*ture sure*

The use of the letter 'r' with u-e was introduced at Teaching Point 87. However, when 'ure' follows the letter 't' the sound changes to /chə/ (e.g., picture, fracture, nature, temperature, adventure, capture, culture, rapture, feature, denture, creature, signature, literature, fixture, lecture, puncture, structure, furniture, vulture, venture, expenditure, scripture, torture, future, ligature, sculpture, rupture, mixture, adventure). Make a Reading and Spelling Card for '-ture'. Give the learner practice at reading words ending in 'ture' through a word search, reading game, or precision teaching (see Teaching Points 30 and 128 for instructions).

Repeat this for '-sure' (and if wished 'jure' /jə/ as in injure and perjure). Point out that 'ure' changes the 's' sound to /zhə/ (e.g., pleasure, measure).

## Teaching Point 152

cursive form

'eu' /ū/

*eu*

Introduce 'eu' /ū/ through Discovery Learning. The sound is heard in the beginning and middle positions but not at the end. Make a Reading Card for 'eu' with an appropriate clue word (e.g., Europe). Add 'eu' to the back of the /ū/ Spelling Card. It is the second choice spelling for /ū/ at the beginning and in the middle. Examples of words with 'eu' /ū/ are neutral, feud, Europe, deuce, eureka, neutron, neurotic, pneumonia, neural, pseudonym, pneumatic. Teach the spelling of words that are within the learner's written vocabulary using a visual spelling routine and start to include these in dictation. (N.B. silent 'p'.)

## Teaching Point 153

cursive form

'ui' /o͞o/ and 'ui' /ĭ/

*ui*

## Reading Card

| front | back |
|---|---|
| ui<br><br>UI | / o͞o/ fruit<br><br>/ĭ/ build |

front                    back

Introduce 'ui' /o͞o/ and 'ui' /ĭ/. Add 'ui' to the back of the /o͞o/ and /ĭ/ Spelling Cards as the second choice spelling in the middle.

## Spelling Cards

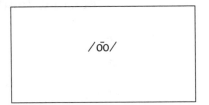

| | B | M | E |
|---|---|---|---|
| /o͞o/ | | oo <br> ui | ue <br> ew <br> oo |

The learner's response is /o͞o/ 'oo' and /o͞o/ 'ui' in the middle, /o͞o/ 'ue', /o͞o/ 'ew' and /o͞o/ 'oo' at the end.

| | B | M | E |
|---|---|---|---|
| /ĭ/ | i | i <br> ui | y <br> ey |

The learner's response is /ĭ/ 'i' at the beginning, /ĭ/ 'i' and /ĭ/ 'ui' in the middle, /ĭ 'y' and /ĭ/ 'ey' at the end.

## Words for Reading and Spelling

Fruit, suit, build, biscuit, cruise, juice, circuit, bruise, nuisance, suitable, sluice, built.

## Practising the New Learning

Ask the learner to sort the words for reading into two sets according to the sound that 'ui' makes and then to write one sentence for each set using as many of the words as possible.

## Sentences for Reading and Dictation

Jim spilled fruit juice down the front of his suit. He tripped and bruised his leg as he ran the last circuit. Mum looked in a travel agent's window for a suitable cruise.

# Teaching Point 154

## Prefixes: 'anti', 'ante', and 'ad'

The prefixes 'anti', 'ante', and 'ad' can be used with base words such as climax, dote, hero, pathetic; chamber, natal, date; here, join, just, to make anticlimax, antidote, anti-hero, antipathetic; antechamber, antenatal, antedate; adhere, adjoin, adjust. Discuss with the learner how the prefix changes the meaning of the word. The prefix *'anti'* is of Greek origin meaning opposite or opposed to; the prefix *'ante'* is Latin meaning before; the prefix *'ad'* is also Latin meaning into or signifying motion towards. They can now be introduced into reading and spelling. (Note that 'anti' is sometimes used as an alternative spelling for *'ante'* in Latin meaning 'before'.)

# Teaching Point 155

cursive form

*gh gu*

## Silent Letters: 'gh' and 'gu'

Ask the learner to listen to the following words and identify the common sound: guess, guide, guard, guest, guitar, disguise, guild, guilt. Write the words on the board and ask them to work out how the /g/ sound is represented in these words. They should notice that the letter 'u' is silent. If the learner looks carefully at the words they may be able to see a pattern. A silent 'u' appears after the letter 'g' in words where 'g' is followed by an 'i' or 'e', but makes the sound /g/ as in 'guide' rather than /j/ as in 'giant'. Practise 'gu' words in reading and spelling.

The letter 'g' can also be followed by a silent letter 'h' as in ghost, ghoul, ghetto, Ghana, ghastly, gherkin, ghee. Most of these are not English words. Ask the learner to look them up in a dictionary or on the web to find their origin and practise their spelling using a visual spelling routine. Make Reading Cards for 'gh' and 'gu'. Add to the /g/ Spelling Card, 'gu' as a second choice at the beginning and 'gh' as a third choice.

## Teaching Point 156

cursive form

'y-e' /ī/

*y-e*

In a small number of words the letter 'y' is used with 'consonant e' to make the long vowel sound /ī/ (e.g., tyre, style, type, rhyme, thyme). The learner should be able to decode these words for reading at this stage but may need to be taught the spelling of this group of words using a visual spelling routine.

## Teaching Point 157

cursive form

'ough'

*ough*

The letters 'ough' can make several different sounds but there are a limited number of words for each. Teach 'ough' as a set of irregular words for reading and spelling, for example:

'ough' /of/ as in  trough, cough.
'ough' /ō/ as in  dough.
'ough' /ow/ as in bough, plough, drought.
'ough' /o͞o/ as in through.
'ough' /ə/ as in thorough, borough.
'ough' /uf/ as in rough, enough, tough.
'ough' /aw/ as in ought, sought, brought, thought.

# PART IV

# ADAPTING THE PROGRAMME

This part of the book is divided into three sections.

## Section A: *The Accelerated Programme*

This section provides an adaptation of the programme for learners who have already acquired several literacy skills and show knowledge of the alphabetic principle. Starting at the very beginning of a structured programme (which most structured literacy programmes recommend) is not always appropriate for them. A Placement Test and diagnostic assessment procedure are included so that a teacher can target any specific intervention necessary at the early stages, but then move to a later stage of the main programme outlined in Part III. The strategies and activities used in the Accelerated Programme are the same as those described in Part III and cross references are made to the Teaching Points in the main programme.

## Section B: *Ideas for Working with Young Children*

This section focuses on strategies and activities which are particularly appropriate when teaching young children (aged 4–6) when early intervention is believed necessary because there are many indicators of dyslexia. However, in England, it may be important to introduce these as support for Wave 1 literacy teaching to prevent failure as there will not be any evidence that very young children have failed to make progress in literacy.

## Section C: *Teaching the Programme to Groups*

Although the main programme has been developed for teaching in a one-to-one situation, in many schools teachers are required to work with small groups (with up to eight learners). This requires careful planning and often poses difficulties for teachers who are uncertain how to meet individual needs within a group. Very few multisensory programmes have been designed for use in groups and the majority do not offer suggestions for practitioners planning to teach in groups. This section considers some of the strategies which can be used for this and offers practical advice for planning, providing three lesson plans as examples each for groups of a different size.

# PART IV: SECTION A

# THE ACCELERATED PROGRAMME

This programme has been developed to enable teachers to plan a structured intervention programme for learners for whom it may be inappropriate to start at the beginning of the main programme because they have mastered many basic literacy skills. The Accelerated Programme is particularly appropriate for secondary school learners and many of those who are at Key Stage 2.

Most writers of structured literacy programmes propose that everyone should start at the beginning of the programme and move through the structure, with the teacher adjusting the pace to suit the learner. They would argue that this ensures that all the important aspects are covered and there are no 'gaps'. Many teachers, however, would consider that to present older learners and those with some literacy skills with a full programme lowers self-esteem, as the lessons will seem too basic and fail to acknowledge a learner's existing skills.

The Accelerated Programme provides a structured approach which is different from the early stages of the Main Programme (outlined in Part III), building on existing literacy knowledge and achievements yet also providing a means of ensuring that all the basic concepts and early reading skills are established.

When learners have successfully completed the Accelerated Programme, they can be moved on to the later stages of the Main Programme.

## Deciding Whether to Use the Accelerated or Main Programme

Teachers will already have carried out a school-based assessment which will have led them to decide that a learner needs a structured multisensory literacy programme. Where this assessment shows a learner has securely developed some skills and knowledge, the issue for teachers is whether or not to teach the whole of the Conquering Literacy programme. A further simple Placement Test should be carried out to establish whether the Accelerated Programme is appropriate. Learners must be able to read and spell all letters by name and sound and be able to read and spell cvc words before starting on the Programme. It may be that they show a few isolated errors in this test, but overall – if they have a good grasp and are fairly confident of their knowledge – they can use the Accelerated Programme. If a *recent* assessment has shown they have already mastered such skills, the Placement Test need not be given.

It is also vital to check on their ability to write using cursive script. If they cannot do so accurately and legibly then this will have to be taught, as letters are not introduced singly in the Accelerated Programme. (In the Main Programme, the cursive form of letters is introduced as part of each new Teaching Point.) Similarly, any articulation problems *and* 'isolated' difficulties should be noted so they can be incorporated into teaching.

## The Accelerated Programme

The Accelerated Programme incorporates all the fundamental concepts of the early stages of the main programme, grouping some together rather than introducing them separately and gradually. It also groups together the initial and final blends which can often pose similar difficulties and introduces these at a faster rate than is the case with the Main Programme.

Some learners may need to work through the whole of the Accelerated Programme (AP) as outlined below but others may only have specific 'gaps' in their knowledge and understanding. If a learner has demonstrated a few difficulties on the Placement Test a teacher may decide to start at the beginning of the Accelerated Programme, but if the learner seems competent and confident in that assessment then a teacher may wish to carry out further assessment using the Conquering Literacy Accelerated Programme Skills Assessment Procedure (CLAPSAP) in order to identify specific strengths and weaknesses and then plan their intervention around targeted Teaching Points, following the sequence shown below.

The CLAPSAP procedure should not be carried out as part of the initial Placement Test because it would involve the learner in a very lengthy assessment procedure. The CLAPSAP concentrates primarily on *spelling* (as this is a major difficulty for older/'more advanced' learners with dyslexia) and the reading of polysyllabic words, particularly word-building using prefixes and suffixes. It is therefore a form of 'screening' to identify a learner's needs in relation to the concepts, blends, and spelling rules of the Accelerated Programme.

# Teaching the Programme

If the CLAPSAP is used, teachers should use the Accelerated Programme Structure Table provided in this section to 'check off' Teaching Points where the learner shows competence in the assessment. However, because the assessment procedure only samples a small number of the concepts and phonograms teachers should ensure that they offer learners the opportunity to use their knowledge and skills through the reading and spelling practice they give. (Where insecure knowledge is found later, then relevant direct teaching should take place.)

The Accelerated Programme structure should be followed in the sequence given, omitting any area which the learner has already mastered. The methods of teaching should follow those provided in the Main Programme in Parts II and III. Each of the Teaching Points (TP) in the Accelerated Programme is cross-referenced to the equivalent TP in the Main Programme so that teachers can find suggestions for teaching. The programme also uses the same Concept Cards described in Part III. The Reading Cards and Spelling Cards will also be the same as in the Main Programme for the particular points taught, but these packs will, of course, not contain the basic phonograms which the learner will already know. Reading, spelling, and dictation practice should be in structure appropriate to the learner's developing knowledge and skills.

This may mean, for example, that if learners show a good knowledge of 'l' blends at the beginning of words (Teaching Point 15) on the CLAPSAP these can be used in structured passages, even if the learner is still being taught the use of the apostrophe (Teaching Point 6). Thus the programme allows the teacher to individualise lessons and follow-up work more flexibly than in the Main Programme. It is particularly important to ensure that materials and activities are also age-appropriate if the Accelerated Programme is to be successful!

The Programme 'accelerates' progress to the Main Programme which learners will join at Teaching Point 83. In addition to the Accelerated Programme Structure Table, this section includes:

- Instructions for giving the Accelerated Programme Placement Test.
- Placement Test materials (which can be photocopied/enlarged to A4 size).
- The Conquering Literacy Accelerated Programme Skills Assessment Procedure (CLAPSAP).
- Instructions with a scoring sheet for teachers' use (photocopiable).
- A Learner Record Sheet to record their progress through the programme.

(Note that all the above photocopiable resources are copyright and for personal use only.)

Table IV.1   *Accelerated Programme Structure Table*

| | Accelerated Programme Teaching Point | Ref. in Main Prog. TP No. | Initial Achievement Checked |
|---|---|---|---|
| 1. | Concept vowels and consonants | 7, 9 | |
| 2. | Concept Beginning, Middle, End | 5 | |
| 3. | Blends sn, st, sp, sm | 15, 62 | |
| 4. | Suffix 's' (plurals and verbs) | 16 | |
| 5. | Contractions | 17 | |
| 6. | Apostrophe for contractions and possessive | 17, 18, 25 | |
| 7. | Use of macron and breve | 21 | |
| 8. | Syllables (open/closed) | 22, 28, 32 | |
| 9. | 'th' and voiced/unvoiced | 14, 30 | |
| 10. | Punctuation (capital letters, full stops, exclamation marks, question marks, speech marks) | 24, 36 | |
| 11. | Accent/stress | 26 | |
| 12. | End blends -nt, -nd. -ft, -mp, -sk, -nk, -ct | 27, 46, 55, 63 | |
| 13 | 'c k' spelling rules: c/k at B, k/ck at E, c at E | 42, 47, 48 | |
| 14. | Beginning blends sc-, sk- | 43 | |
| 15. | 'l' beginning blends bl-, cl-, fl-, gl-, sl-, pl-, spl- | 53 | |
| 16. | 'l' final blends -ld, -lf, -lk, -lm, -ln, -lp, -lt | 54 | |
| 17. | 'r' beginning blends br-, cr-, dr-, fr-, gr-, tr-, pr-, scr-, spr-, str- | 59, 60 | |
| 18. | Suffixes -ed/-ing/doubling rule | 33, 38 | |
| 19. | Syllable division vc/cv, v/cv, vc/v | 45, 69 | |
| 20. | 'Flossy rule' ff/ll/ss | 49, 50, 51 | |
| 21. | Suffix -es | 52 | |
| 22. | 'w' blends: tw/sw | 68 | |
| 23. | 'qu' | 78 | |
| 24. | Prefixes in-, re-, pre-, ex-, un-, de-, mis-, dis-, ab-, im-, con-, in-, trans-, be- | 35, 61, 77, 99 | |
| 25. | 'wa' (wasp) words | 66 | |
| 26. | 'wh' words | 67 | |
| 27. | 'y' (semi-vowel) + suffix rule (change 'y' into 'i') | 71, 73 | |
| 28. | Suffixes 'ly' and 'ful' adjectives and adverbs | 72 | |
| 29. | 'sh'/'ch' (BME) | 80, 81 | |
| 30. | -tch,/ch rule | 82 | |

*Note*: When these have been achieved, the learner should be 'transferred' to the Main Programme in Part III

## Photocopiable:

*Teaching Literacy to Learners with Dyslexia* © Kathleen Kelly and Sylvia Phillips, 2011 (SAGE)

# CONQUERING LITERACY: ACCELERATED PROGRAMME PLACEMENT TEST

This test should be given in cases where an earlier assessment has indicated that the learner would benefit from a multisensory structured literacy programme but has acquired some basic literacy skills. It will indicate the appropriateness of the Accelerated Programme rather than starting the Main Programme from the beginning. (Note that if a *recent* assessment has already covered the items in the Placement Test there is no need to give this test and a decision can be based on learner proficiency in the earlier assessment.)

## Materials

- Test instructions for teacher.
- Test sheet (photocopiable, enlarged to A4, one copy for learner and one for teacher to record results).
- Writing paper/pen for spelling and writing.

## Administration

The test is given in two sessions as indicated in the instructions. It is an individual and untimed procedure. The teacher should make a copy on which to circle any errors. It is also useful to identify any articulation difficulties which might need addressing. The pupil should have a copy of the first sheet.

# Instructions

## (A) Letters and Sounds

**A1** • Ask the learner to read (and say) all the letters of the alphabet by **name** and then to identify the letters by **sound** (short vowels will suffice).
  ○ First ask them to look at Set A (all letters of the alphabet presented randomly in upper case) and ask them to say the names of each letter and then to say the sound of each letter.
  ○ Then ask them to look at Set B (all letters of the alphabet presented randomly in lower case) and ask them to say the name of each letter and then the sound.
 • Take the card from the pupil and give them the writing paper and a pen or pencil.

**A2** • Ask the learner to spell (write) all the letters of the alphabet when given the name.
 • Dictate all 26 letters, randomly, by name.
 • Ask the learner to write both the capital (upper case) and lower case letters. (They can print or use cursive writing.)

**A3** • Ask the learner to spell (write) all the letters of the alphabet when given the sound.
 • Dictate all 26 letters, randomly by sound (using the short vowel sound).
 • Ask the learner to write both the capital (upper case) and lower case letters. (They can print or use cursive writing.)

## (B) Use of Cursive Writing

Ask the learner to write all the letters of the alphabet in cursive writing.

• Check that the learner can write all lower case letters using cursive handwriting. (If not, these should be taught at the beginning of the programme.)

## (C) Single Word Reading of cvc Words

• Provide the learner with a copy of the cvc words and ask them to read them aloud. On your copy, write their response (not simply marking right or wrong, as it is useful to know if, for example, they have difficulties/confusions with certain vowels and/or consonants).

- You should expect at least 20 to be correct before placing the learner on the Accelerated Programme. However, if there is a single consistent error (e.g., confusing 'u' and 'o') then you should teach these points before starting the programme.

## (D) Spelling of cvc Words

- On a **different** occasion, ask the learner to spell the Set D cvc words (unseen) by writing them down. For this, the teacher has the test sheet and dictates the words, saying each word twice only and allowing time for them to write before going on to the next.
- You should expect at least 20 to be correct but if there are only one or two errors teach these before starting the programme.
- Look for consistencies between reading and spelling results to identify particular areas for teaching. (Do any of these point to possible auditory or phonological difficulties that need to be addressed prior to starting the Accelerated Programme?) Place the learner on the Accelerated Programme.

## (E) Interpreting Results

This test/earlier assessment should provide evidence that the learner can:

- Recognise/read all the letters of the alphabet by **name** and sound, in both upper and lower case.
- Spell/write all the letters of the alphabet in both upper and lower case when given the:
  o name
  o sound.
- Read and spell cvc words.

## (F) Placement

- If the learner is successful in most test items, making only isolated errors (e.g., does not know what sound 'x' makes) the Accelerated Programme is still appropriate, but you will need to teach them any points which are 'gaps' in their knowledge from this test, using the relevant guidance from the Main Programme.
- If the learner has shown more advanced literacy knowledge and skills on other occasions, you may decide on further assessment (on a different occasion) using the CLAPSAP, in order to determine which elements of the Accelerated Programme you will then teach as opposed to starting at the beginning.

# CONQUERING LITERACY: PLACEMENT TEST

**Name:** ..................................................... **Class/Form:** ................

## (A) Letters and Sounds

**1.** Say the **name** of each of these letters:

Set A

| | | | | |
|---|---|---|---|---|
| W | G | H | B | X |
| C | N | P | J | A |
| V | L | S | Y | O |
| Z | E | M | I | F |
| R | K | U | T | Q |
| D | | | | |

**2.** Now give the **sound** each of the letters makes.

Set B

**1.** Say the **name** of each of these letters:

| | | | | |
|---|---|---|---|---|
| f | t | k | b | p |
| l | z | u | s | a |
| m | c | i | r | q |
| d | g | z | e | x |
| o | j | w | n | v |
| h | | | | |

**2.** Now give the **sound** each of the letters makes.

## (B) Cursive Writing

Write the letters of the alphabet in cursive writing.

## (C) Single Word Reading of cvc Words

Read the following words:

| | | | | |
|---|---|---|---|---|
| sun | bid | pad | cod | mug |
| fat | hen | top | dim | jot |
| kit | lab | nod | rag | van |
| sip | gap | wet | zip | fox |
| yet | bus | quit | vex | cup |

## (D) Spelling of cvc Words

Spell the following words:

| | | | | |
|---|---|---|---|---|
| yet | sip | kit | fat | sun |
| bus | gap | lab | hen | bid |
| quit | wet | nod | top | pad |
| vex | zip | rag | dim | cod |
| cup | fox | van | jot | mug |

**Photocopiable:**
*Teaching Literacy to Learners with Dyslexia* © Kathleen Kelly and Sylvia Phillips, 2011 (SAGE)

# CONQUERING LITERACY ACCELERATED PROGRAMME SKILLS ASSESSMENT PROCEDURE (CLAPSAP)

This assessment comprises:

Part I:   Dictation (assessing knowledge/use of concepts and blends).
Part II:  Constructing and reading multi-syllabic words (assessing word-building using prefixes, base words, and suffixes).

It can be administered to learners who have demonstrated sufficient literacy skills to suggest that starting at the beginning of the Main Programme would be inappropriate. Its aim is to indicate strengths and difficulties in order to target specific areas for teaching.

## Materials

- Copy of test for the teacher to record results.
- Writing paper and pen/pencil for learner.
- Copy of table of Accelerated Programme structure to record current achievement in areas of the programme.

**Name of student**: ……………………........................ **Form/Class**: …………………

# Part 1: Dictation

There are five items, varying from a single sentence to short passages. (Explain that some may sound 'silly' if you think necessary.) These are written within the structure covered by the Accelerated Programme. Tell the learner what you are going to do so they know the sentences will be broken down into smaller units. Remind them that they should put punctuation marks in where these should be. Allow time for them to write their responses.

Read each sentence as a whole then split it into manageable units for dictation (e.g., a phrase of 2–4 words which you may say **twice** only).

Below each passage is a marking grid showing the particular concepts and blends in the passage. These are Teaching Points in the Accelerated Programme. Where the same Teaching Point appears more than once in a sentence/passage, tick or cross (√ or x) for each occurrence (e.g., if a passage has two sets of speech marks there should be **two** marks: if there are three full stops or three 'st' blends, there should be **three** marks in the appropriate boxes). Be careful not to 'stress' the blends when you dictate but do use normal expression when reading in order to indicate the end of a sentence/question, etc.

## Item 1

*Fran went in the loft with a lamp and got six boxes.*

| fr | nt | ft | th | mp | suffix -es |
|----|----|----|----|----|------------|
|    |    |    |    |    |            |

## Punctuation

| Full stop | Capital letter |
|-----------|----------------|
|           |                |

## Item 2

*Stan spills milk that is "off" and sniffs a strong smell. "It stinks!" he said.*

*(N.B. Here "off" is in inverted commas to help your expression and the learner's comprehension. You should not expect a learner to use speech marks/inverted commas for this word.)*

| st- | sp- | -ii | Suffix 's' | -lk | th (v) | -ff | -nd | sn- | str- | sm- | -nk | Open Syllable 'he' |
|-----|-----|-----|-----------|-----|--------|-----|-----|-----|------|-----|-----|--------------------|
|     |     |     |           |     |        |     |     |     |      |     |     |                    |

## Punctuation

| Full stop | Capital letter | Speech marks | Exclamation mark |
|-----------|----------------|--------------|------------------|
|           |                |              |                  |

## Item 3

*An insect was on Brad's skin and he scratched it until it bled.*
*He felt sick and held his hands up to get help.*

| -ct | /wa/ was | br- | sk- | scr- | -tch | suffix '-ed' | bl- | -lt | -ck | -ld | -nd | suffix 's' | -lp |
|-----|----------|-----|-----|------|------|--------------|-----|-----|-----|-----|-----|-----------|-----|
|     |          |     |     |      |      |              |     |     |     |     |     |           |     |

## Punctuation

| Full stop | Capital letter | Apostrophe (possessive) 's |
|-----------|----------------|----------------------------|
|           |                |                            |

## Item 4

*Alf jumped off a plank in his flip flops into the pond. His twin, Ann, filmed his antic and clapped. Alf pulled Ann into the pond with a splash.*
*"I'm glad I can swim," said Ann.*

| -lf | -mp | suffix –ed | -ff | pl- | -nk | fl- | suffix 's' | th (v) | -nd | tw- | -lm | -ic | cl- |
|-----|-----|-----------|-----|-----|-----|-----|-----------|--------|-----|-----|-----|-----|-----|
|     |     |           |     |     |     |     |           |        |     |     |     |     |     |

| Double rule (before ed) | -ll | th (unv) | spl- | -sh | gl- | sw- |
|---|---|---|---|---|---|---|
|  |  |  |  |  |  |  |

## Punctuation

| Full stop | Capital letter | Comma | Speech marks | Apostrophe contraction |
|---|---|---|---|---|
|  |  |  |  |  |

## Item 5

*In spring, Kim was skipping on the grass when she tripped and fell.*
*Kim's dress was a mess and she was cross. Will mum wash and press it?*

| spr- | -ng | sk- | doubling rule | suffix -ing | gr- | -ss | wh- | -sh | tr- |
|---|---|---|---|---|---|---|---|---|---|
|  |  |  |  |  |  |  |  |  |  |

| suffix -ed | -ll | possessive 's' | dr- | cr- | wash | pr- |
|---|---|---|---|---|---|---|
|  |  |  |  |  |  |  |

## Punctuation

| Capital letters | Full stop | Comma | Apostrophe (possessive) | Question mark |
|---|---|---|---|---|
|  |  |  |  |  |

**Note:** The above procedure has assessed spelling because that is likely to be more problematic for those learners you think should be in the Accelerated Programme. If you have concerns about their ability to **read** particular blends you could present them with the passages in printed form and ask them to read aloud (**on another occasion** – to avoid the fact that they may recall them if you do so immediately after dictation).

Use the Accelerated Programme Record Sheet to record areas from that structure which are areas of apparent knowledge and which may not need explicit teaching (but make sure you 'check' this during lessons by giving activities which require their use).

## Part 2: Word Blending: Reading Multisyllabic Words

This activity presents the learner with a set of cards with base/root words, prefixes and suffixes and the learner is asked to put the base/root word with a prefix and/or suffix to build two and/or three syllable words which they will read aloud to you. (Give a 'practice' example if necessary.)

Copy the words below on to three differently coloured cards to distinguish prefixes, base/root words, and suffixes.

| Prefixes | Base/root words | Suffixes |
|:---:|:---:|:---:|
| dis- | tend | -s |
| ex- | tent | -ed |
| un- | tract | -ing |
| in- | pend | -es |
| de- | box | |
| un- | content | |
| re- | dress | |

(*Note:* Record the words the learner makes and note particularly the prefixes and suffixes used correctly. Remember when presenting reading and dictation practice in your lessons to use those which are already known. This will help to provide more variety and more 'advanced' material for the learner.)

### Photocopiable:
*Teaching Literacy to Learners with Dyslexia* © Kathleen Kelly and Sylvia Phillips, 2011 (SAGE)

# Where Next?

This assessment procedure covers all the main points within the Accelerated Programme. Although we suggest you make Concept Cards for all the concepts in the programme, you do not need to make Reading Cards for blends which are already secure. You may still need to provide Spelling Cards for some choices.

You should look at the Accelerated Programme structure, and – beginning at the start of that programme – teach those concepts and blends where the learner experiences difficulties. The relevant Teaching Point reference is given so you can refer to the Main Programme for ideas on how to present this point.

You can proceed through the Accelerated Programme at a pace that suit the learner's needs, omitting those areas where the learner's knowledge is secure but still presenting relevant reading and dictation practice and using dictionary/research skills to replace the alphabet work in the first stages of the Main Programme (if appropriate).

When the learner has worked through the Accelerated Programme, or at least those parts which they need, you can then move them on to the Main Programme at Teaching Point 83. (If the learner's knowledge of the 'cvce' rule about long vowels is secure, then start at Teaching Point 87.)

Table IV.2   *The Accelerated Programme: Record Sheet*

| Teaching Point in Accelerated Programme | Date Introd. | Date/s Revised | Date Mast'd | Date Checked (√ or x) | Date Re-taught (If Needed) |
|---|---|---|---|---|---|
| 1.   Vowels and consonants | | | | | |
| 2.   **B**eginning, **M**iddle, **E**nd | | | | | |
| 3.   Blends: sn, st, sp, sm | | | | | |
| 4.   Suffix 's' (plural/verbs) | | | | | |
| 5.   Contractions | | | | | |
| 6.   Apostrophe: contractions and possessive | | | | | |
| 7.   Breve and macron | | | | | |
| 8.   Syllables (open/closed) | | | | | |
| 9.   'th' and voiced/unvoiced | | | | | |
| 10.  Punctuation: caps, full stop, speech marks, ! & ? | | | | | |
| 11.  Accent and stress | | | | | |
| 12.  End blends, -nt, -nd, -ft, -mp,-sk, -nk, -ct | | | | | |
| 13.  c/k spelling rules: 'c/k', ck/k, -c | | | | | |
| 14.  sc/sk/scr at beginning | | | | | |
| 15.  'l' blends: bl, cl, fl, gl, sl, pl, spl | | | | | |
| 16.  final 'l' blends: -ld,-lf,-lk,-lm,-ln,-lp,-lt | | | | | |
| 17.  'r' blends: br, cr, dr, fr, gr, tr, pr, scr, spr, str | | | | | |
| 18.  Suffixes 'ed' and 'ing' and doubling rule | | | | | |
| 19.  Syllable division : vc/cv, v/cv, vc/v | | | | | |
| 20.  ff/ll/ss rule | | | | | |
| 21.  Suffix 'es' | | | | | |
| 22.  Blends: dw, tw, sw | | | | | |
| 23.  'qu' | | | | | |
| 24.  Prefixes: in/de/con/im/dis/re/ pre/ex/un/ab/trans/be/mis | | | | | |
| 25.  'wa' as in 'wasp' | | | | | |
| 26.  'wh' words | | | | | |
| 27.  'y' (semi-vowel) and suffix rule: change 'y' to 'i' | | | | | |
| 28.  Suffixes 'ly' and 'ful' adverbs/ adjectives | | | | | |
| 29.  sh/ch | | | | | |
| 30.  – tch and rule ch/tch | | | | | |

*Note*: Rejoin Main Programme at Teaching Point 83

## Photocopiable:

*Teaching Literacy to Learners with Dyslexia* © Kathleen Kelly and Sylvia Phillips, 2011 (SAGE)

# Downloadable Materials

For downloadable materials for this section visit www.sagepub.co.uk/kelly&phillips

Table IV.1 Accelerated Programme Structure Table
Conquering Literacy: Accelerated Programme Placement Test
Conquering Literacy Accelerated Programme Skills Assessment Procedure (CLAPSAP)
Table IV.2 The Accelerated Programme: Record Sheet

# PART IV: SECTION B

# IDEAS FOR WORKING WITH YOUNG CHILDREN

This chapter starts by examining the issues raised by the Rose Report (DCSF, 2009) and the recent review of primary education (Alexander, 2009) in relation to the teaching of young children.

Alexander (2009) argues that primary schools are focusing too much on reading, writing, and numeracy and that the curriculum needs to be broadened to foster independence, creativity, and imagination. The review also suggests that the UK should conform to international practice and formal education should not start before the age of six, instead extending the play-based curriculum of early years teaching to reduce stress in young children. Delaying formal education allows teachers, it is argued, to concentrate on what children 'can do' rather than on what they 'can't do' thus avoiding failure at a very young age, whereas starting too early can make a dent in children's self-confidence.

However, currently many children in the UK start school at age 4 and as the (2009) Rose Report highlighted some will not find the acquisition of literacy skills easy. The difficulties experienced by children with dyslexia usually come to the fore at the start of formal education. Repeated failure often results in low self-esteem and sometimes in a reluctance to attempt tasks – learned self-helplessness. In contrast to the Alexander review, Rose (2006, 2009) has emphasised the importance of high quality phonics teaching in learning to code and encode words so that children learn to read independently as soon as possible. These reviews also recommend monitoring children's progress in literacy carefully so that effective intervention can be put in place earlier, thus narrowing the attainment gap and improving self-confidence. Further, Rose (2009) proposes that those with severe difficulties need specialist support and children with dyslexia will benefit from teaching that is highly structured and systematic. At the same time, the recent move to give teachers more pedagogical flexibility – allowing them to make professional judgements about what constitutes effective teaching and learning – means that more creativity can be brought back into the curriculum. Children can be given more opportunities to learn through play-based activities and more time spent fostering a love of books through informal teaching situations. Young children with dyslexia are more likely to thrive in this kind of environment.

There will still be some, however, who will need a more intensive structured input in order to overcome their difficulties in phonological processing and to develop literacy skills. The Conquering Literacy programme enables specialist teachers to plan and deliver lessons in a more structured and systematic way. Normally we would expect that children under the age of 6 would be supported through good quality first (wave 1) teaching. Sometimes though (particularly if older siblings have dyslexia) additional support may be sought for a child as young as 4 or 5 in developing early literacy skills. In this case the programme will need adapting to take into account the child's current stage of development in relation to the skills underpinning the programme (e.g., a concept of print, phonemic awareness, auditory and visual sequencing, an understanding of sequence). As the Alexander report pointed out, learning through play is crucial for young children and this is built into the approach that we recommend through the use of games.

## Adapting the Programme for Younger Learners

The recommendation that support should be delivered 'little and often' (Rose, 2009) is particularly relevant for young children. The activities suggested below can be delivered in four or five short and frequent lessons of 15 minutes each (see also Chapter 9). If lessons are longer than this but less frequent then these will need to be followed up by the class teacher or a teaching assistant. The examples below show how normal everyday activities can be adapted for use within structured programme.

### Alphabet Activities

Children who have not yet learned many of the letters of the alphabet will not be able to sequence letters to make an alphabet arc. This part of the lesson should be spent playing games to help with letter recognition (e.g., letter Bingo, Snap, pelmanism), using only those letters that have been introduced in the programme to ensure overlearning takes place. Letter recognition can also be reinforced through the use of resources that are commonly available in early years' classrooms, such as alphabet jigsaws, alphabet trays, or tactile letter cards. When introducing a new phonogram to a child you may wish to have the alphabet arc set out in front of you (as described in Chapter 10) so they can see where the letter being introduced fits and become familiar with the whole alphabet even though they are not being asked to sequence it. Feely bags can be used to practise identifying the taught letters by touch. A new phoneme/phonogram can also be reinforced by asking the child to collect objects beginning with a particular sound/ letter and making a table of things that start with this. This can be followed up at home by encouraging parents to help the child to make a scrapbook where each page has a phonogram from the programme at the top and contains pictures starting with the target sound/letter. Alphabet games can also be played at home (see the end of this section).

## Memory Work

Young children may need to be taught about sequence. They may be familiar with the idea of days of the week being in a particular order and might have already been taught a rhyme or singing game to help them to remember it. This experience can be drawn upon to explain that often events will happen in a certain order (as in the school time-table) and that the numbers on pages in a book are in a particular order or sequence – and so are the letters in a word. Sequences can be practised as part of a structured lesson.

For example:

i In practising the following colour sequences the child can learn how to mix paint to make particular colours:

| | | | |
|---|---|---|---|
| • red | white | pink | |
| • red | yellow | orange | |
| • yellow | blue | green | |
| • black | white | grey | |
| • red | blue | purple | |
| • red | blue | yellow | brown |

The colours to be remembered should be presented to the child on a card for them to create, using a peg board or by colouring circles or by actually mixing the first two in a sequence to get the last colour.

ii Colour sequences can also be used to teach the colours of the rainbow. Start with the first three colours (red, orange, yellow) and then gradually build this up to remembering the colours of a rainbow.

iii A visual timetable could be memorised in this part of the lesson so that eventually the child learns what happens on each day of the week.

iv Once the first few phonograms in the programme have been introduced then letter sequences can be practised, but instead of giving a random string of letters use ones that form words from the programme – e.g., i-t (it), i-n (in), i-s (is), s-i-t (sit).

## Developing Reading Skills

Many of the concepts that are involved in phonological awareness training may need to be taught before applying them to letters and words. For instance, the concept of beginning, middle, and end must be taught before asking a child what sound a word begins with. A Beginning Middle End (BME) sheet is provided for this in Part V (Resources). The child is asked to listen to a word such as 'tap' and identify where they can hear the target sound (e.g., /t/) and then to place a counter in the appropriate box on the sheet.

The concept of same and different must also be taught for the child to be able to discriminate between similar sounds. This can be practised using Unifix or coloured cubes before introducing the written form. The child is asked to listen to a sequence of sounds and decide if they are all the same by selecting coloured cubes to represent the sequence.

For example the sequence /p/ /p/ /p/ would be represented by cubes of the same colour:

The sequence /p/ /p/ /t/ would be represented by two different colours:

If three different sounds are given (e.g., /t/ /p/ /n/) then three coloured cubes would be used to represent the sounds.

Eventually words can be analysed. The word 'sip' has three different sounds and so would be represented by three different coloured cubes, but the word 'pip' would be represented with only two different colours, for example:

Once the child understands these concepts then phonograms can be introduced. They can be asked to listen to a word and then write the first letter in the correct box on a BME sheet. Alternatively they may be asked to listen to recorded words while looking at a worksheet containing several pictures of those words (e.g., tent, telephone, teddy, teapot, train, and torch). After each word the recording will be stopped and the child asked to repeat the word, then to write the first letter of the word under the picture on a worksheet while saying the letter sound and name (e.g., /t/ 't'). The letter could be written in pencil for the child to write over in pen or crayon if they are is unable to form letters unaided. Later on the child might be asked to listen to a word such as 'it' or 'sit' and identify how many sounds there are in the word, and then to find the wooden letters that represent the word from a selected few. (Note that young children should have had experience of building words of two or more syllables orally and splitting words into syllables, e.g., clapping the syllables in the names of their friends or using a musical instrument to count syllables, before being asked to split words into phonemes.)

Support can be given to key words and irregular words (whole word recognition) via activities that can help them to focus on the detail so they can discriminate between similar looking words. Word shapes are often used for this and can be produced by drawing round words that are 'in structure' with a pen (e.g., tin and tip) in order to show that they have a different shape and then by matching them to the correct shape on a board. Alternatively they may be asked to find the word that matches a target word from a row of similar words on a worksheet (see Part V for an example).

Helping them to understand that words have meaning can be achieved by using games that include pictures (such as rhyming dominoes or matching pairs) to practise structured reading and whole word recognition.

## Developing Writing Skills

A handwriting routine is described in Chapter 11. This will need adapting for young children so that plenty of practice is given with different mediums before they are asked to write the letter from memory. Letter formation could be demonstrated with roll-a-ball letters or a computer software program and followed up by painting a large form of the letter on an easel or writing it in chalk; then producing the letter in plasticine or playdough before writing a smaller version in wet sand, etc., and finally bringing the letter size down and close to that normally produced in their book by writing it in different colours with pencil crayons, felt-tips, or sensory pens, etc., before writing it on the line in Box 3 of the handwriting sheet.

Children should be encouraged to write for a purpose. This can be difficult within the confines of the early stages of a structured language programme but not impossible. For instance, a young child might be given pictures of a teddy bear, post box, train, telephone, puppet, piggybank, etc. and two shopping lists (one with the letter 't' at the top and the other with the letter 'p'). The child is then asked to put the pictures of the toys on the correct shopping list and to write the appropriate letter next to each picture.

The dictation routine will not be included in lessons until they can write several words in structure. When it is introduced phrases may be preferable to sentences (e.g., 'a pen', 'pips in tins').

## Practising and Reinforcing Learning

Alexander (2009) pointed out that learning in young children is socially mediated and families and peers are important in this process. Games used with the specialist teacher can also be played with peers or taken home to enjoy with family members. A basic game board (such as a snakes and ladders board or a race track) can be used to practise phonological awareness, sight vocabulary, letter formation, etc. For example, to avoid going down a snake the child would have to:

- listen to a word and tell you what sound/letter it starts with;
- write the first letter of a word;
- read a word 'in structure' from a pack of cards;
- give you a rhyming word;
- clap the syllables in a word, or spell a word orally;
- say the alphabet.

Similarly, on a race track if the child lands on a particular coloured square they would have to carry out an activity like those listed above in order to avoid missing a turn. Games can be personalised by having different tasks for each player.

Teachers should also consider sending packs of games and other materials home with children so that these can be practised outside of school. Activities to develop early reading and writing skills – such as making playdough letters, printing their name in paint with sponge letters, and doing name jigsaws, bead threading, alphabet mazes or dot to dots, letter Bingo, alphabet dominoes, etc. – can also be sent home to work on with parents and siblings as a 'homework' activity.

## References

Alexander, R. (2009) *The Cambridge Primary Review*. University of Cambridge: EF Foundation.

Rose, J. (2006) *Independent Review of the Teaching of Early Reading: Final Report*, March. London: DfES.

Rose, J. (2009) *Identifying and Teaching Children and Young People with Dyslexia and Literacy Difficulties*, June. London: DfES.

# PART IV: SECTION C

# TEACHING THE PROGRAMME TO GROUPS

The main programme has been developed for teaching in an intensive one-to-one situation. Teachers seeking accreditation from the British Dyslexia Association (BDA) must currently provide evidence that they can teach a one-to-one multisensory lesson based on a structured, cumulative approach. However, they can also carry out some teaching in a small group (of up to three learners). In schools, specialist lessons for learners with dyslexia may be on a one-to-one basis or in a small group (usually of no more than six although we include a lesson plan for up to eight learners). The purpose of this section is to give practical advice on the planning and teaching of lessons in a small group. Example lesson plans are given at the end of the section.

## Planning the Lesson

It is important that lessons set appropriate objectives to meet the individual needs of the learners in the group. Planning must take into account the level that each learner is functioning at in literacy and should be based on assessment data. This means that it is unlikely that the whole group will be working on the same point from the programme. However, it may be possible to 'pair' learners to undertake activities together while at the same time providing extra support and strategies for particular individuals.

In planning the lesson the teacher must consider how they can organise this in order to enable each learner to have sufficient attention and also how they can ensure that all the activities are fully multisensory. The simplest approach is to have the whole group work on the same element of the lesson but at their particular level. A learner may be paired with one particular student for alphabet or memory work, for example, and with another for reading or spelling activities. Example Lesson Plan 1 is for a group of eight students with dyslexic-type difficulties and shows how sometimes learners may work as a whole group, sometimes in pairs, and at other times in threes. It is planned at three different levels and enables learners to work with others who are at the same level as themselves, sometimes changing partners for different activities to ensure the correct learning objectives are being worked on. At times a new Teaching Point might be the same for the whole group and at others it will be different. In Lesson Plan 2, two of the learners are at a later stage but sometimes need to fill in gaps or revisit insecure aspects from earlier in the programme and so the phonogram 'b' is introduced to the whole group in this example.

Where learners are at very different stages of the programme then the group size should be smaller. In planning the lesson the teacher may sometimes anticipate that one member of the group will need more attention than the rest for a particular activity and may choose to make use of technology to free up enough time to give the right level of attention. An example of this can be found in Lesson Plan 3 (for three students) where one is working on the computer and another with recorded spellings, thereby allowing the teacher to concentrate on one individual for a short period. Self-checking materials are also important and can be used to allow learners to check they have the right letter string in memory work or to mark dictated sentences independently.

## Writing the Lesson Plan

Working with groups of learners is very demanding of a teacher's attention and it is essential to have a plan that enables the teacher to locate the next activity quickly. The plan should be simple, concise, and easy to follow. We would recommend that normally a group lesson plan is only one page in length. Abbreviations might be used, for example for learners' names, the name of an activity or game might be given without a description and routines note where the learner is up to (e.g., a Reading and Spelling Pack) but without stating the routine itself. This is very different from the way most teachers have to work when they are new to delivering structured language programmes. Often they can feel insecure with the routines to begin with and will need to write them on the plan giving as much detail as possible. However, in group teaching too much detail can interfere with lesson flow. Therefore the teacher will need to be experienced in delivering structured lessons, and confident with the multisensory routines and the teaching of concepts *before* they attempt to plan lessons for groups of learners who are at different stages of the programme.

On-going notes should be made of learners' responses to the activities: for example, the time taken to set out the alphabet, letters that were reversed or mis-sequenced, the length of the letter string achieved in memory work, details of any strategies used, time taken for the Reading Pack, and any errors in spelling or dictation. In the example lesson plans at the end of this section a long thin column is provided down the whole page for this purpose. Comments will need to be in note form, but at the end of the lesson the teacher should write a detailed evaluation that will inform planning for the next lesson.

## Delivering the Lesson

In groups of more than three, learners will often be 'paired' for alphabet work with another person who is at a similar stage. In this case they will take turns to set out the wooden letters. This may involve one person setting out the first half of the alphabet and the other the second half (swapping over at the next lesson) or placing the letters in the arc alternately. Strategies can be given to support those individuals who are less secure with the sequence, such as a visual prop (see Lesson Plan 1) where the arc is written on a postcard for reference if required. An activity that is introduced to all the learners, for instance long and short vowel sounds, may be extended with some members of the group (e.g., by introducing the breve and macron symbols) so that individual learning objectives are still met. One advantage of working in pairs is that learners work with each other on activities: tracing letters on each other's back, removing a letter from the arc for the other person to guess, showing their partner a card with a letter string to be remembered and then checking their response, etc. This makes the lessons more manageable and allows the teacher to monitor all the students rather than concentrating on one pair at a time.

The revision exercise will focus on different aspect of the programme and so needs to be managed carefully. Sometimes learners will engage in a similar activity at their own level, as in Lesson Plan 1 where the group work on onset and rime with the wooden letters. In this case the teacher might go round the pairs instructing them which letter to change to make a new word. At other times the group might be working on different activities, as in Lesson Plan 2 where some students are making words with the wooden letters, some are looking up given words in a dictionary, and others are working on a self-checking worksheet for spelling choices. In this example most learners are working independently, allowing the teacher to focus more on the learners using wooden letters as there is no written record to check their work. Similarly, in Lesson Plan 3, two of the group work on different types of worksheets, allowing attention to be given to the picture-sorting activity for suffix 'ed'. It is important to note, however, that learners should still be monitored while they are completing worksheets and the teacher should listen to them in order to check they are verbalising the answers (saying letter names as they circle or write them, reading the words in a wordsearch as they find them, etc.) to ensure that activities are always fully multisensory.

The Reading Pack can be handled in two ways: the pack can be gone through with the whole group starting with the phonograms that everyone has been taught and learners stop participating at the point when the phonograms they have learned have been practised. In this case large cards will be needed (A4 size) so they can easily be seen by everyone. Alternatively, everyone can have their own pack of cards to go through individually with the teacher and short independent activities are provided for the rest of the group to do while waiting for their turn (for example, an alphabet maze or dot-to-dot). The Spelling Pack can also be gone through with the whole group, starting with the spelling choices that everyone has been taught and at the appropriate point some learners stop and wait until the whole group has finished to have their written responses checked. Alternatively the teacher can have three Spelling Packs (one for each pair). The teacher can go round the pairs in turn and while the first pair writes down the response to their Spelling Card the teacher moves on to the second pair, and so on, until all the cards have been used.

The introduction of a new Teaching Point is one of the most difficult parts of the lesson when working with groups at different levels. Activities need to be carefully thought out in order to give the teacher time to direct each of the learners to discover the new Teaching Point for themselves. In Example Lesson Plan 3 one learner is discovering the new phonogram through feeling and identifying objects in a feely bag and then working out the common sound, but the other two learners have activities that involve listening to words. This is managed by asking one learner to listen to recorded words (or to sort pictures) and identify where they can hear the /s/ sound, placing a counter (or picture) in the appropriate box on a BME sheet, while the other learner works with the teacher listening to a list of words such as ring, song, hang, thing, lung, etc. and identifying the common sound /ng/. While two of the learners track the letter/s they have identified, the teacher can return to the one using the BME sheet to remind that learner of the rule for 'll' and 'ff' (covered in previous lessons) and to help them 'discover' how /s/ at the end of words is spelt (the flossy rule) using pre-prepared structured sentences.

Spelling and dictation can be managed in the same manner as the Spelling Pack, going round the group giving one word or sentence at a time to each pair (or individual if there are only three in the group). While one pair writes down their word (or sentence) the teacher moves on to the next pair. As this is fairly time consuming much less can be planned than in one-to-one lessons. For this reason the example lesson plans contain only four or five words for spelling and only one or two sentences for dictation for each pair (or individual). The lesson always ends with a game. Computer games that allow the teacher to enter selected words (e.g., Word Shark) can be used to practise the new learning. The teacher can enter a different list of words for each learner, allowing them to work individually thus avoiding any element of competition (other than competing against their own best performance). However, board games can also be individualised by having a set of cards for each learner (to spell or read) and have the advantage of helping to develop social skills. The teacher should use their personal knowledge of individual learners to plan games and activities that best suit their way of learning.

# Lesson Plan Example 1

**Group:** 3 Children: JB, JC, DP, DH, NB, CM, SR, CJ        **Date:** _____

| | Comments |
|---|---|

**Aims/Objectives:**
Revise phonemes up to /e/, blends, and long vowels vcv, as appropriate. Introduce o /ŏ/ and o-e /ō/.

**Alphabet Activities:**
Set out alphabet arc A to Z, or Z to A (CJ/JB) DH to use cards as prop.
Prepositional language: before, after, middle. Identify vowels.
Long/short vowel sounds. Use of breve and macron (CJ/JB).
Count number of letters in alphabet.

**Memory Training:**
Auditory: letter strings using cards. JC/NB/DP/CM (3) DH/SR (4) CJ/JB (5).
Visual: letter strings using cards. DH/JC/NB/CM (3) SR/DP (4) CJ/JB (5).

**Revision Exercise:**
On set rime: hen, pen, ten, den, (DH/NB/SR/CM). Make cash, lash, rash, crash, (CJ/JB). West, pest, nest, rest (JC/DP): using wooden letters.

**Reading Pack:**
Whole group up to 'e' and up to 'a-e' (CJ/JB).

**Introduce New Teaching Point:**
Feel letter 'o' eyes closed. BME exercise (all) & middle spelling o-e (CJ/JB).

**New Reading/Spelling card:**
'o' orange and 'o-e' mole.

**Cursive Writing:**
Handwriting routine on board. Salt tray: practise 'o'.

**New Teaching Point into Reading:**
Wordsearch for short vowel /ŏ/ and end blends (JC/DP/SR).
Rhyming pairs (DH/NB/CM). Structured Story for o-e (CJ/JB).

**New Teaching Point into Writing:**
Join 'o' to 'n'. Worksheet: illustrate the words 'hot', 'top' 'stop', spots'. Crossword for o-e (CJ/JB).

**Spelling Pack:**

Up to 'o'. Include middle spelling o-e (CJ/JB).

**Spelling Words:**

(1) on, top, dot, hot (DH/NB/CM).

(2) cost, spot, stop, pond (JC/DP/SR).

(3) spoke, stole, pole, choke (CJ/JB). (3 levels).

**Dictation:**

(1) Is it in the pot? (DH/NB/CM).

(2) Did Ted step on the hot tin? (JC/DP/SR).

(3) Mike spotted a mole in a hole at the lake. (CJ/JB). (3 levels).

**Review:**

Make multisensory links using SRR routine.

**Game:**

Syllable pairs: turn over two cards (1st & 2nd syllable) to make a word.

**Evaluation:**

**Comments**

# Lesson Plan Example 2

**Group:** 2 Children: AM, KE, JM, LP, PM, TD

**Date:** _____

| | Comments |
|---|---|

**Aims/Objectives:**
Revise phonograms up to /k/, blends, and long vowels vcv, as appropriate. Introduce b /b/ to whole group and vc/cv syllable division.

**Alphabet Activities:**
In pairs, set out alphabet arc from A to Z, or in four quartiles (AM/KE).
Identify vowels & long/short vowel sounds.
Make three closed syllables. Guess the letter (20 questions).

**Memory Training:**
Auditory: letter strings using cards. JM//LP (3) PM/TD (4) AM/KE (5).
Visual: letter strings using cards. PM/TD (3) JM/LP (4) AM/KE (6).

**Revision Exercise:**
Change final letter: kin, kit, kid, kip (PM/TD). Find: cash, kick, sank, kidnap, in a dictionary (AM/KE). Tutor pack: c/k choice (JM/LP).

**Reading Pack:**
Up to k (whole group) and up to o-e (AM/KE).

**Introduce New Teaching Point:**
Trace letter on back and identify b /b/. Take letter out of arc.
Listen for /b/ in pairs of words: bun/fun, dig/big, said/bed, bit/sit.

**New Reading/Spelling Card:**
'b' clueword: bat.

**Cursive Writing:**
Salt tray: practise 'b'.

**New Teaching Point into Reading:**
Syllable division: bandit, basket, Batman, cannot, hobnob (on board).
Abbreviation: can't for cannot. Shared story for /b/ with different parts.

**New Teaching Point into Writing:**
Join 'b' to 'e'. Crossword puzzle /b/ (3 levels).

**Spelling Pack:**

Up to /b/.

**Spelling Words:**

(1) Ben, bit, bet, bad, bap (PM/TD).
(2) best, bent, stab, bandit, Batman (JM/LP).
(3) bake, bride, bash, shrub, basket (AM/KE). (3 levels).

**Dictation:**

(1) Ben has a pet. (PM/TD).
(2) Did Stan bend it? (JM/LP).
(3) The bandit hit the bank and stole the cash. (AM/KE). (3 levels).

**Review:**

SRR routine for /b/. Syllable division pattern vc/cv. Contraction can't.

**Game:**

Snakes and Ladders Game with packs of Reading Cards (3 levels).

**Evaluation:**

| Comments |
| --- |
| |

# Lesson Plan Example 3

**Names:** FK, JS, TM

**Date:** _____

**Comments**

**Aims/Objectives:**
Revise suffix 'ed' /d/ (FK), g /g/, (JS) and -ll /l/ (TM). Introduce r /r/ (FK), ng /ng/ (JS) and flossy rule (TM).

**Alphabet Activities:**
Set out alphabet A to Z (JS), alternate sides of M (FK), at random (TM).
Rapid naming of letters (All). Alphabet sequence cards (JS).
Dictionary exercise (FK) and sorting words into alphabetical order (TM).

**Memory Training:**
Auditory: 4/5 letter strings using rehearsal (TM/FK), and chunking (JS).
Visual: 4/5 letter strings (JS/TM), 6 letter strings (FK) using visualisation.

**Revision Exercise:**
Figure ground exercise for 'g' (JS). Sort words with 'ed' into three sets: /t/, /d/, /id/ (FK). Change sentences ('ll' words) into past tense (TM).

**Reading Pack:**
Up to g (JS), -ll (TM), 'ed' /d/ (FK).

**Introduce New Teaching Point:**
Identify common sound /ng/ in words, use of mirrors, tracking (JS).
Feely bag /r/, listen for target sound in pairs of words, tracking sheet (FK).
BME sheet /s/ (recorded words), flossy rule, sentence tracking (TM).
Handwriting routine and practice (All).

**New Reading/Spelling Card:**
'ng' /ng/ (JS); r /r/ (FK); and ss /s/ (TM).

**Cursive Writing:**
Salt tray: 'ss' (TM). Whiteboard and pen: 'r' (FK). Glitter glue: 'ng' (JS).

**New Teaching Point into Reading:**
Word search ng /ng/ (JS). Shared story ss /s/(TM). Rhyming pairs r /r/ (FK).

### New Teaching Point into Writing:

Crossword 'ng' (JS). Closure exercise 'ss' (TM). Word chain for 'r' (FK).

### Spelling Pack:

Up to /ng/ (JS), /r/ (FK) and –ss /s/ (TM).

### Spelling Words:

(1) sting, pang, thing, song, gong (JS).
(2) moss, boss, kiss, miss, floss (TM). Spellings on computer.
(3) rink, risk, rand, rest, rasp, Ross (FK). Recorded spellings.

### Dictation:

(1) Hang it on the peg. Dan sang at the gig. (JS). Recorded dictation.
(2) Bess sat on the moss. Can Tess pass the test? (TM).
(3) "Rob is at the rink," said Ross. He ripped the red rag (FK).

### Review:

SRR routine (All) and flossy rule (TM).

### Game:

Off the board spelling game (cards for words with 'ng', 'r' and 'ss').

### Evaluation:

**Comments**

# PART V

# RESOURCES

This part provides a set of photocopiable sheets to support the programme and other useful information. These sheets are examples of the sort of resources that practitioners might make and use. Not all types of activity are included, but the selection provided reflects those areas which practitioners have indicated most useful. Some are designed specifically for use with one Teaching Point (as depicted on the sheet) while others can be used for several Teaching Points (e.g., the Tracking Sheets). We also include copies of the Concept Cards so that these can be prepared in advance of teaching as suggested in Part II Chapter 11. However, teachers can make their own cards using symbols of their choice if they wish.

The websites given at the end of this section suggest sources both for purchasing and for making resources. References are also given to some ICT software together with the website addresses for their respective suppliers.

All of these resources are also available to download from www.sagepub.co.uk/kelly&phillips

Table V.1  *Main Programme Record Sheet*

| Teaching Point | Date Introduced | Date/s Revised | Date Mastered | Date Checked (√ or x) | Date Re-taught (If Necessary) |
|---|---|---|---|---|---|
| 1. Symbol | | | | | |
| 2. Sound and // | | | | | |
| 3. Name | | | | | |
| 4. Alphabet | | | | | |
| 5. Beginning, Middle, End | | | | | |
| 6. 'i' | | | | | |
| 7. Vowels | | | | | |
| 8. 't' | | | | | |
| 9. Consonants | | | | | |
| 10. Word | | | | | |
| 11. 'p' | | | | | |
| 12. 'n' | | | | | |
| 13. 's' | | | | | |
| 14. Voiced/unvoiced | | | | | |
| 15. 's' blends* st, sp, sn | | | | | |
| 16. Suffix 's' (plurals and verbs) | | | | | |
| 17. Contractions | | | | | |
| 18. Apostrophe | | | | | |
| 19. 'a' | | | | | |
| 20. Long/short vowels | | | | | |
| 21. Breve and macron | | | | | |
| 22. Syllables (counting) | | | | | |
| 23. 'd' | | | | | |
| 24. Punctuation: capital letter, full stop, speech marks, comma | | | | | |
| 25. Apostrophe 's' (possessive) | | | | | |
| 26. Accent and stress | | | | | |
| 27. Blends* -nt -nd | | | | | |
| 28. Closed syllables: vc/vcc | | | | | |
| 29. 'h' | | | | | |
| 30. 'th' (voiced and unvoiced) | | | | | |
| 31. 'e' | | | | | |
| 32. Open syllables | | | | | |
| 33. Suffix 'ed' /id/ /t/ just add and doubling rule | | | | | |
| 34. 'o' | | | | | |
| 35. Prefixes: 'in' 'de' | | | | | |

*(Continued)*

Table V.1 *(Continued)*

| Teaching Point | Date Introduced | Date/s Revised | Date Mastered | Date Checked (√ or x) | Date Re-taught (If Necessary) |
|---|---|---|---|---|---|
| 36. Punctuation: question and exclamation mark | | | | | |
| 37. 'g' | | | | | |
| 38. -ng and suffix 'ing' (just add and doubling rules) | | | | | |
| 39. 'm' | | | | | |
| 40. 'c' and prefix 'con' | | | | | |
| 41. 'k' | | | | | |
| 42. c/k choice at beginning | | | | | |
| 43. sc/sk at beginning | | | | | |
| 44. 'b' | | | | | |
| 45. Syllable division vc/cv | | | | | |
| 46. End blends: -sk, -nk, -ct | | | | | |
| 47. '-ck' and ck /k rules | | | | | |
| 48. '-c' (at end) rule | | | | | |
| 49. 'f' and '-ff' | | | | | |
| 50. 'l' and '-ll' | | | | | |
| 51. '-ss' (flossy rule) | | | | | |
| 52. Suffix 'es' | | | | | |
| 53. Beginning 'l' blends: bl, pl, cl, fl, gl, sl, spl | | | | | |
| 54. End 'l' blends: ld, lf, lk, lp, lm, lt | | | | | |
| 55. End blend '-ft' | | | | | |
| 56. '-all' | | | | | |
| 57. Suffix 'ed' /d/ | | | | | |
| 58. 'r' | | | | | |
| 59. 'r' blends: pr, dr, br, cr, fr, gr | | | | | |
| 60. str, scr, spr | | | | | |
| 61. Prefixes: 'im' 're' 'pre' | | | | | |
| 62. Beginning blend: 'sm' | | | | | |
| 63. End blend: '-mp' | | | | | |
| 64. 'u' | | | | | |
| 65. 'w' | | | | | |
| 66. 'wa' as in 'wasp' | | | | | |
| 67. 'wh' words | | | | | |
| 68. Beg. blends: 'sw' 'tw' | | | | | |
| 69. Syllable division: vc/v and v/cv | | | | | |

| Teaching Point | Date Introduced | Date/s Revised | Date Mastered | Date Checked (√ or x) | Date Re-taught (If Necessary) |
|---|---|---|---|---|---|
| 70. 'y' (consonant) | | | | | |
| 71. 'y' (as a semi-vowel) | | | | | |
| 72. Suffixes 'ly' and 'ful' adverbs/adjectives | | | | | |
| 73. Vowel suffix rule: change 'y' to 'i' (babies) | | | | | |
| 74. 'j' | | | | | |
| 75. 'v' | | | | | |
| 76. 'x' | | | | | |
| 77. Prefixes: 'ex' 'un' 'ab' | | | | | |
| 78. 'qu' | | | | | |
| 79. 'z' | | | | | |
| 80. 'sh' | | | | | |
| 81. 'ch' | | | | | |
| 82. '-tch' spelling rule 'ch'/'tch' | | | | | |
| 83. 'i-e' vowel suffix rule: drop 'e' | | | | | |
| 84. 'a-e' | | | | | |
| 85. 'o-e' | | | | | |
| 86. 'u-e' | | | | | |
| 87. v-c-e with 'r': 'are' 'ire', 'ore', 'ure' | | | | | |
| 88. 'ee' | | | | | |
| 89. 'ar' | | | | | |
| 90. 'ar' (as in 'collar') | | | | | |
| 91. 'or' (as in 'fork') | | | | | |
| 92. 'or' (as in 'doctor') | | | | | |
| 93. 'oo' | | | | | |
| 94. –k /k/ spelling rule -ck /'k' | | | | | |
| 95. soft 'c' | | | | | |
| 96. soft 'g' | | | | | |
| 97. 'ge' and 'dge' rules | | | | | |
| 98. Vowel suffix rule drop 'e': ce, ge, dge | | | | | |
| 99. Prefixes: mis, trans, be | | | | | |
| 100. '-ay' | | | | | |
| 101. '-ow' (as in 'snow') | | | | | |
| 102. '-ow' (as in 'cow') | | | | | |
| 103. 'er' (as in 'her') | | | | | |

*(Continued)*

Table V.1 *(Continued)*

| Teaching Point | Date Introduced | Date/s Revised | Date Mastered | Date Checked (√ or x) | Date Re-taught (If Necessary) |
|---|---|---|---|---|---|
| 104. 'er' (as in 'after') | | | | | |
| 105. Suffix 'er' (comparatives and superlatives) | | | | | |
| 106. '-ue' | | | | | |
| 107. Prefixes: post, peri | | | | | |
| 108. 'o' (as in 'won') | | | | | |
| 109. '-ie' | | | | | |
| 110. 'ea' (as in 'sea') | | | | | |
| 111. 'ea' (as in 'head') | | | | | |
| 112. 'ai' | | | | | |
| 113. 'air' | | | | | |
| 114. 'oa' | | | | | |
| 115. 'igh' | | | | | |
| 116. Old wild words | | | | | |
| 117. Silent letters: 'b', 'g' | | | | | |
| 118. 'oi' | | | | | |
| 119. 'oy' | | | | | |
| 120. Plural possessives | | | | | |
| 121. 'ou' (as in 'shout') | | | | | |
| 122. 'ou' (as in 'could') | | | | | |
| 123. Final regular syllables: ble/cle/dle/gle/fle/kle/stle | | | | | |
| 124. '-tion' | | | | | |
| 125. '-sion' | | | | | |
| 126. '-cian' | | | | | |
| 127. Silent letters: 'w', 'k' | | | | | |
| 128. 'ir' | | | | | |
| 129. 'ur' | | | | | |
| 130. 'or' (as in 'word') | | | | | |
| 131. 'au' | | | | | |
| 132. 'aw' | | | | | |
| 133. '-oe' | | | | | |
| 134. '-ey' (as in 'grey') | | | | | |
| 135. '-ey' (as in 'donkey') | | | | | |
| 136. '-ew' | | | | | |

| Teaching Point | Date Introduced | Date/s Revised | Date Mastered | Date Checked (√ or x) | Date Re-taught (If Necessary) |
|---|---|---|---|---|---|
| 137. Irregular 'al' 'el' | | | | | |
| 138. Prefixes: mal, semi, bi | | | | | |
| 139. Syllable division: cv/vc pattern | | | | | |
| 140. 'ph' | | | | | |
| 141. 'ie' (as in 'brief') | | | | | |
| 142. 'e-e' and 'ere' | | | | | |
| 143. 'ei' (as in 'ceiling') | | | | | |
| 144. 'ei' (as in 'reindeer') | | | | | |
| 145. 'ch' (as in 'chemist') | | | | | |
| 146. 'eigh' (as in 'sleigh') | | | | | |
| 147. 'ear' (as in 'fear' and as in 'earth') | | | | | |
| 148. 'a' (as in about) | | | | | |
| 149. 'our' (as in 'colour') | | | | | |
| 148. 'ea' (as in 'break') | | | | | |
| 150. Suffix 'ous' and 'us' | | | | | |
| 151. 'ture' | | | | | |
| 152. 'eu' | | | | | |
| 153. 'ui' | | | | | |
| 154. Prefixes: anti, ante, ad | | | | | |
| 155. Silent 'gh', 'gu' | | | | | |
| 156. 'y-e' | | | | | |
| 157 '-ough' | | | | | |

* Referred to as 'adjacent consonants' in the Primary National Strategy

- Fig V.1    Concept Cards 1–8 Front
- Fig V.2    Concept Cards 1–8 Reverse
- Fig V.3    Concept Cards 9–16 Front
- Fig V.4    Concept Cards 9–16 Reverse
- Fig V.5    Concept Cards 17–24 Front
- Fig V.6    Concept Cards 17–24 Reverse
- Fig V.7    Concept Cards 25–32 Front
- Fig V.8    Concept Cards 25–32 Reverse
- Fig V.9    Concept Cards 33–40 Front
- Fig V.10   Concept Cards 33–40 Reverse

Please note: the cards should be produced 8 to an A4 sheet of card.

## Photocopiable:

*Teaching Literacy to Learners with Dyslexia* © Kathleen Kelly and Sylvia Phillips, 2011 (SAGE)

Figure V.1    *Concept Cards 1–8 Front*

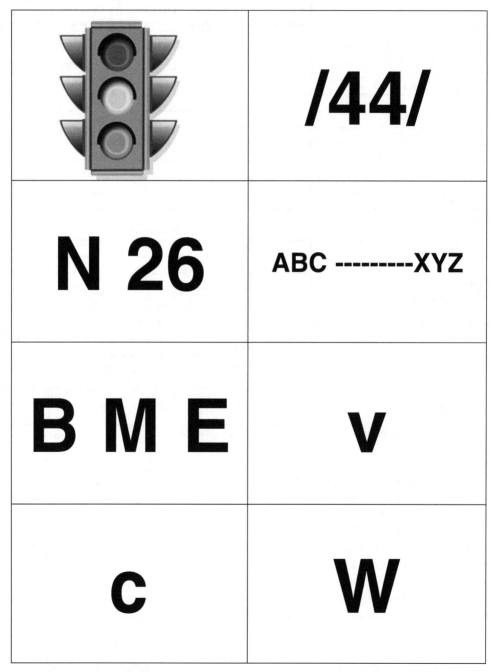

 **Photocopiable:**
*Teaching Literacy to Learners with Dyslexia* © Kathleen Kelly and Sylvia Phillips, 2011 (SAGE)

Figure V.2    *Concept Cards 1–8 Reverse*

| TP2 | TP1 |
|---|---|
| A phoneme is the smallest unit of sound in our language. We use the symbol / / round the letter(s) that make a single sound.<br><br>There are 44 sounds in English.<br><br>CC2 | A **symbol** stands for, or reminds us of something.<br><br>CC1 |
| TP4 | TP3 |
| The 26 letters are organised in a particular order or sequence called the **alphabet**.<br><br>CC4 | Each letter has a name. There are 26 letters in English.<br><br>CC3 |
| TP6 | TP5 |
| Vowel sounds are **open**, with nothing blocking the air and are **voiced** sounds. There is a vowel in every syllable.<br><br>CC6 | We use these letters to help us tell where we hear the sounds in words.<br><br>**B** stands for Beginning<br><br>**M** stands for Middle<br><br>**E** stands for End<br><br>CC5 |
| TP10 | TP9 |
| A word is a unit of language which makes complete sense.<br><br>CC8 | Consonant sounds are usually blocked or partially blocked by the tongue, teeth, or lips.<br><br>CC7 |

**Photocopiable:**
*Teaching Literacy to Learners with Dyslexia* © Kathleen Kelly and Sylvia Phillips, 2011 (SAGE)

Figure V.3   *Concept Cards 9–16 Front*

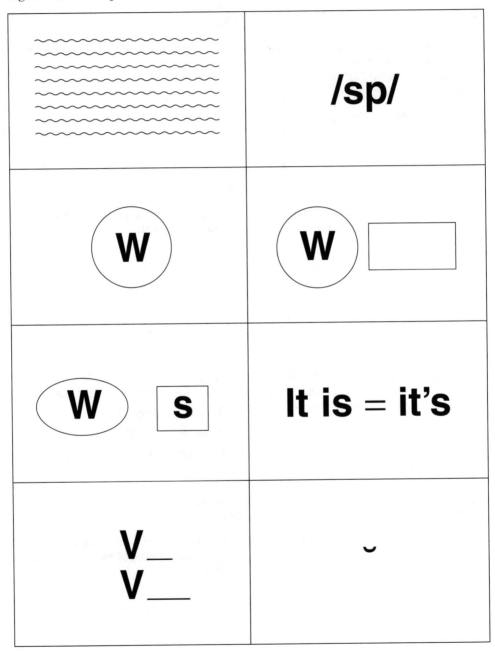

**Photocopiable:**
*Teaching Literacy to Learners with Dyslexia* © Kathleen Kelly and Sylvia Phillips, 2011 (SAGE)

Figure V.4    *Concept Cards 9–16 Reverse*

| TP15<br><br>Some consonants **blend** together but they make their own sounds.<br><br>(N.B. The National Literacy Strategy uses the term 'adjacent consonants' so teachers may prefer the symbol /cc/. We do not recommend this as it could be confused with consonant digraphs such as 'sh'.)<br><br><div align="right">CC10</div> | TP14<br><br>Some consonants are voiced e.g. 'b', some are unvoiced e.g., 'p', and some can be voiced or unvoiced depending on the word, e.g., 's' is unvoiced in 'sun' but voiced in 'is' and 'rose'.<br><br><div align="right">CC9</div> |
|---|---|
| TP16<br><br>A **suffix** is a letter or letters added to the end of a base word.  A suffix changes the meaning or usage of a word.<br><br><div align="right">CC12</div> | TP16<br><br>A **base word** is a word which makes complete sense in itself. It can also be added to in order to form another word.<br><br><div align="right">CC11</div> |
| TP18<br><br>A **contraction** is a word formed by combining two words.  An **apostrophe** is placed to show where a letter (or letters) have been left out (omitted).<br><br><div align="right">CC14</div> | TP16<br><br>Suffix 's' can change a word so that it becomes plural or forms a verb.<br><br><div align="right">CC13</div> |
| TP21<br><br>A **breve** is a symbol to indicate a short vowel sound.<br><br><div align="right">CC16</div> | TP20<br><br>All vowels have two sounds.  They can be **short** or **long** vowel sounds.<br><br><div align="right">CC15</div> |

## Photocopiable:
*Teaching Literacy to Learners with Dyslexia* © Kathleen Kelly and Sylvia Phillips, 2011 (SAGE)

Figure V.5    *Concept Cards 17–24 Front*

| | |
|---|---|
| — | **S** |
| **A** | ● |
| **" "** | **,** |
| **'s** | **'** |

**Photocopiable:**
*Teaching Literacy to Learners with Dyslexia* © Kathleen Kelly and Sylvia Phillips, 2011 (SAGE)

Figure V.6    *Concept Cards 17–24 Reverse*

| TP22<br><br>A **syllable** is a word or part of a word formed by one opening of the mouth. It usually has one vowel sound in it.<br><br><br><br><br>CC18 | TP21<br><br>A **macron** is a symbol to indicate a long vowel sound.<br><br><br><br><br><br>CC17 |
|---|---|
| TP24<br><br>A full stop is used:<br><br>• At the end of a sentence.<br>• to show that a word has been shortened/abbreviated, e.g. a.m., Mon. (for Monday).<br><br><br>CC20 | TP24<br><br>An upper case or capital letter is used:<br><br>• At the beginning of the first word in a sentence.<br>• For the first letter of a proper name/noun e.g., John, Cardiff, Scotland.<br>• For the first letter of the main words in a title of a book/story.<br><br>CC19 |
| TP24<br><br>A comma has many uses.  The most common are:<br><br>• To separate words in a list.<br>• To indicate a pause.<br>• To separate a speaker from the words spoken which are in speech marks, e.g. Mark said, "I am going to the park." "I am going there tomorrow," said Ann.<br><br>CC22 | TP24<br><br>Speech marks (quotation marks) are placed round the words spoken by someone.<br><br><br><br><br><br><br>CC21 |
| TP26<br>Some words or syllables are stressed/accented more than others.  We can use the symbol´ after the letter or syllable that is stressed. (e.g., pho´tograph and photog´raphy).  In some cases the use of stress/accent can change a word's meaning (e.g., in´valid inval´id).<br><br><br>CC24 | TP25<br><br>An apostrophe and 's' are placed after a noun to indicate that something belongs to someone/something. If a noun is singular or itself a plural word (such as 'men') add 's to show possession e.g. Stan's coat, Ann's tin, the children's school. If the noun is plural ending in 's' or a name ending in 's' just add' e.g., St. James' Park, the dogs' food was placed in the yard. (More than one dog.)<br><br>CC23 |

## Photocopiable:

Figure V.7  *Concept Cards 25–32 Front*

| | |
|---|---|
| **vc** <br> **vcc** | **v** → |
| (**W**)   [ **ed** ] | **cvc + ed = <br> cv<u>cc</u>ed** |
| [ ]   (**W**) | **?** |
| **!** | **-ing** <br> **cvc + -ing <br> = cvccing** |

Figure V.8   *Concept Cards 25–32 Reverse*

| TP32<br><br>An **open syllable** ends with a vowel.<br><br><br><br><br>CC26 | TP28<br><br>A **closed syllable** ends with at least one consonant.<br><br>The vowel will be short.<br><br><br>CC25 |
|---|---|
| TP33<br><br>When 'ed' is added to a single syllable word with a **short** vowel the final consonant is doubled e.g., hop/hopped.<br><br><br><br>CC28 | TP33<br><br>Vowel suffix – ed pronounced/ed/ after 'd' or 't', e.g. mended<br><br>/d/ after voiced sounds e.g. tailed<br><br>/t/ after unvoiced sounds e.g. thumped.<br><br>CC27 |
| TP36<br><br>A direct question is followed by a question mark, e.g., Why?<br><br>"How much do the oranges cost?" he asked.<br><br><br>CC30 | TP35<br><br>A prefix is a syllable placed before a word to change the meaning, e.g., in/ward, de/compose, con/verse.<br><br><br><br>CC29 |
| TP38<br><br>Vowel suffix '-ing' shows that something is happening now.  When added to a single syllable word with **short** vowel, the final consonant is doubled (e.g., shop/shopping).<br><br>CC32 | TP36<br><br>An exclamation mark is placed at the end of a sentence (or word) to express strong feeling, e.g., Stop!, "That's really exciting!" she said.<br><br><br>CC31 |

**Photocopiable:**
*Teaching Literacy to Learners with Dyslexia* © Kathleen Kelly and Sylvia Phillips, 2011 (SAGE)

Figure V.9 *Concept Cards 33–40 Front*

| | |
|:---:|:---:|
| **vc/cv** | **-es** |
| **v/cv** | **vc/v** |
| **y** | **y + s = -ies** |
| **-vce** ☐ | **cv/vc** |

**Photocopiable:**
*Teaching Literacy to Learners with Dyslexia* © Kathleen Kelly and Sylvia Phillips, 2011 (SAGE)

Figure V.10    *Concept Cards 33–40 Reverse*

| TP52<br><br>Suffix '-es' is used for plurals of words ending in '-ss', -'s' and 'x'.<br><br><br><br><br><br>CC34 | TP45<br><br>When two consonants come between two sounded vowels in a two syllable word, the word usually divides into two syllables between the two consonants. (The accent/stress is usually on the first syllable.)<br><br><br><br>CC33 |
|---|---|
| TP69<br><br>Some words have two closed syllables but only one consonant between the vowels e.g., satin, panic. These words divide after the consonant (vc/v).<br><br><br><br><br>CC36 | TP69<br><br>Some words have two syllables but the first syllable is open and stressed (e.g., sta′men, pu′pil.)<br><br><br><br><br><br>CC35 |
| TP73<br><br>When adding 's' to words ending in 'y' to form a plural, drop the 'y' and add 'ies' e.g., babies.<br><br><br><br><br><br><br>CC38 | TP71<br><br>The letter 'y' can be a consonant (yes) or a semi-vowel (baby, lady, my, why).<br><br><br><br><br><br><br>CC37 |
| TP139<br><br>Usually when two vowels occur together they represent one sound (e.g., read, foil), but in some words **each vowel** represents a sound, one ending in an open syllable and the next beginning a closed syllable. The syllables are divided **between the vowels** (e.g., ru/in and the first syllable is usually stressed) (e.g., di/alect).<br><br>CC40 | TP 83-86<br><br>The final 'e' in vce words is dropped when adding a suffix beginning with a vowel, e.g., slope sloping/sloped, hide/hiding (but hid), ice′/icing/iced.<br><br><br><br><br><br>CC39 |

## Photocopiable:
*Teaching Literacy to Learners with Dyslexia* © Kathleen Kelly and Sylvia Phillips, 2011 (SAGE)

Figure V.11    *Alphabet Sequencing Cards*

| | | |
|:---:|:---:|:---:|
| **A B -** | **B C -** | **C D -** |
| **D E -** | **E F -** | **G H -** |
| **H I -** | **I J -** | **J K -** |
| **K L -** | **L M -** | **M N -** |
| **N O -** | **O P -** | **P Q -** |
| **Q R -** | **R S -** | **S T -** |
| **T U -** | **V W -** | **X Y -** |

Photocopy the grid above on a sheet of card. Cut up the cards and shuffle them. The learner looks at the first sequence (e.g. N O -), names the first two letters, and gives the name of the missing letter. The learner works through all the cards in the pack. The alphabet arc acts as a prop as they can check if unsure. (N.B. Young children might need the cards enlarging and might only work on the first half of the alphabet or a short section of it.)

## Photocopiable:
*Teaching Literacy to Learners with Dyslexia* © Kathleen Kelly and Sylvia Phillips, 2011 (SAGE)

Use the BME sheet to practise isolating a target sound e.g. /t/ in its beginning, middle or end position. The learner can tick the correct box, place a counter in it, or write the phonogram.

Figure V.12    *BME Sheet*

| B | M | E |
|---|---|---|
|   |   |   |
|   |   |   |
|   |   |   |
|   |   |   |
|   |   |   |
|   |   |   |
|   |   |   |
|   |   |   |
|   |   |   |

Figure V.13    *Tracking Sheet 1*

t  a  d  g  b  t  s  n  a  c  h  d  h  z  e  p  f  i  k

n  g  l  i  s  m  h  a  d  n  b  o  k  s  i  p  r  q  u

v  f  r  c  j  i  t  n  u  e  k  z  m  x  o  y  w  r

a  v  x  g  b  l  w  c  m  j  o  q  r  d  w  n  y  t

b  e  k  j  p  f  h  d  o  s  g  i  w  k  r  f  u  e

x  z  l  n  p  e  c  q  f  h  l  a  r  d  s  j  c  g

t  l  o  p  f  u  b  s  v  d  j  r  w  a  m  v  k  x

i  y  h  l  i  m  o  q  n  s  p  t  u  y  v  c  x  t  z  i

Time: _____                    Date: _____

## Photocopiable:
*Teaching Literacy to Learners with Dyslexia* © Kathleen Kelly and Sylvia Phillips,
2011 (SAGE)

Figure V.14    *Tracking Sheet 2*

| | | | | | | | | | | | |
|---|---|---|---|---|---|---|---|---|---|---|---|
| st | nt | sn | sp | ct | th | sc | nd | sn | sp | ck | th |
| ng | sk | ck | sn | sp | nd | th | sc | nk | ck | sn | st |
| ng | sc | sp | ct | nk | ng | th | sk | sp | sn | nd | nt |
| ck | sk | ng | sc | sp | th | ct | nk | nd | nt | nk | sp |
| st | nk | th | ng | sn | ck | ct | ng | ct | th | sk | ck |
| sp | sn | sc | nk | ck | th | nt | nd | sc | ct | st | ct |
| sp | ck | nk | th | sn | nd | sk | ng | nt | st | ct | sc |

Time: _____          Date: _____

**Photocopiable:**
*Teaching Literacy to Learners with Dyslexia* © Kathleen Kelly and Sylvia Phillips, 2011 (SAGE)

Tracking Sheets 3 and 4 can be used to track whole words in sequence to make sentences. Highlight the words in order for the sentence given (e.g., Rob has a pet rat).

Figure V.15     *Tracking Sheet 3*

Ken     is     he     tells     Cliff     said     a     Scot     the     lifts     Rob     slips     in     pink

milk     the     end     plank     gift     red     tips     doll     thin     Meg     bag     it     held     and

spits     can     swim     tell     tip     thinks     tell     stiff     hot     it     past     mist     is     has

neck     in     damp     a     net     the     soft     hand     mint     black     pond     doll     big

ball     pram     nest     is     rest     a     pet     on     said     at     he     in     Rick     rat     rot     a

blinks     the     rag     missed     kilt     it     Swiss     called     Frank     hut     she     with

swing     call     his     twin     small     cuff     Ron     twill     win     what     twist     me

**Photocopiable:**
*Teaching Literacy to Learners with Dyslexia* © Kathleen Kelly and Sylvia Phillips, 2011 (SAGE)

Figure V.16    *Tracking Sheet 4*

Dad    he    went    is    seen    with    tar    Mike    tells    makes    Chuck    a    big    the

red    chimp    picnic    and    Kim    cake    might    green    can    dart    strong    bike

end    pitch    it    take    me    a    hill    was    ball    in    rope    hike    catch    been

when    has    a    star    cube    pain    rule    sight    fish    hole    flee    mile    and

hen    keep    lake    watch    week    match    car    time    seek    far    Luke    reeds

muddy    pine    weeds    fade    right    farm    socks    lark    night    boat    rain    fade

**Photocopiable:**
*Teaching Literacy to Learners with Dyslexia* © Kathleen Kelly and Sylvia Phillips, 2011 (SAGE)

Figure V.17    *Stimulus Response Routine*

Photocopy the cross below onto a piece of card as a visual prompt.
Pictures or symbols can be used to accompany the words to aid the learner's understanding e.g. ear (for sound), learner's name (for name), pen or pencil (for letter shape), detective with magnifying glass or question mark (for clueword)

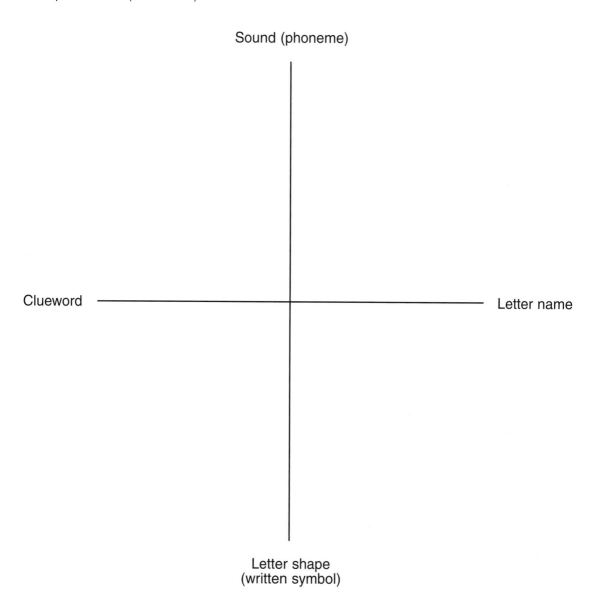

Sound (phoneme)

Clueword ———————————————————————— Letter name

Letter shape<br>(written symbol)

Figure V.18    *Visual Discrimination Exercise*    **TP13**

Ask the learner to highlight or underline the word in each row that matches the target word in the left-hand box.

| **tip** | pit | sip | tin | tip | pin | nip | nit |
|---|---|---|---|---|---|---|---|
| **sit** | sip | pip | sit | pit | tin | tip | sis |
| **pin** | pit | pip | nip | tin | pin | sip | pins |
| **tin** | Pip | tin | tip | pit | tins | pin | sip |
| **pip** | sip | tip | Pip | pit | nip | pip | pin |
| **sip** | tip | sit | sip | pip | nip | pit | is |
| **nip** | Nip | pip | nip | sip | tip | tips | pin |
| **pit** | tip | pin | pip | sip | pit | tin | sit |
| **is** | in | it | sit | is | pip | sip | tin |
| **nit** | tin | pit | tip | sit | sip | nip | nit |

**Photocopiable:**
*Teaching Literacy to Learners with Dyslexia* © Kathleen Kelly and Sylvia Phillips, 2011 (SAGE)

Figure V.19    *Shared Story: Kit's Tip*                                   **TP 48**

| | |
|---|---|
| *Teacher:* | Kit's room is a tip. Dad is cross with him and says he is grounded until it is tidied up. |
| *Learner:* | **Kit sits in his den and sips his drink.** |
| *Teacher:* | Dad is fuming. "You will not go on the picnic with Meg," he warns Kit. |
| *Learner:* | **Kit thinks of a tactic.** |
| *Teacher:* | Dad gets impatient and rants at Kit. Kit runs upstairs and gets on with the task. |
| *Learner:* | **So Dad thinks!** |
| *Teacher:* | Kit sweeps everything together and pushes it under the bed, hiding the mess with the duvet. Then he sees three odd socks next to the door. |
| *Learner:* | **He pops the socks in the bin.** |
| *Teacher:* | Just in time. Dad is on his way in. |
| *Learner:* | **Dad inspects.** |
| *Teacher:* | The room looks tidy and Dad is pleased. |
| *Learner:* | **"Can I go to the picnic?" Kit asks.** |
| *Teacher:* | Dad lets him go. He will be mad when he finds out about Kit's antics. |
| *Learner:* | **Kit can bank on it.** |

**Photocopiable:**

*Teaching Literacy to Learners with Dyslexia* © Kathleen Kelly and Sylvia Phillips, 2011 (SAGE)

Figure V.20   *Wordsearch for /ŭ/*                                    **TP 64**

| d | m | u | m | n | t | u | b | s | t |
|---|---|---|---|---|---|---|---|---|---|
| h | s | c | r | u | m | t | n | u | t |
| m | a | r | u | n | i | p | l | u | m |
| p | u | l | l | i | n | g | s | t | u |
| d | s | m | u | g | b | u | d | l | r |
| t | h | u | d | s | k | c | u | t | h |
| l | r | h | u | g | s | m | h | u | t |
| k | s | d | u | c | k | e | d | e | m |
| d | u | s | k | r | d | u | b | m | d |
| p | t | n | b | u | d | d | i | n | g |
| s | m | u | d | h | p | u | t | n | p |
| i | d | o | s | t | u | b | h | o | d |

## Find the words:

| put | mud | stub | budding |
|-----|-----|------|---------|
| dub | hut | dusk | hugs |
| bud | cut | smug | thuds |
| nut | tub | plum | ducked |
| mum | run | scrum | pulling |

**Photocopiable:**
*Teaching Literacy to Learners with Dyslexia* © Kathleen Kelly and Sylvia Phillips, 2011 (SAGE)

Figure V.21    *Vowel Suffix Frame*                                              **TP 73**

1.  Write the words in the correct column: dinted, hunting, ladies, fried, stopped, filled, cried, funniest, mended, bending, sunniest, slapped, crosses. Use only columns 1–3.

| 'Just Add' Rule | 'Doubling' Rule | Change 'y' to 'i' | Drop 'e' Rule |
|---|---|---|---|
| minted | skipped | babies | |
| sprinted | tipped | tried | |
| | | | |

2.  Add the vowel suffix 'ed' or 'est' to these words (following the suffixing rule) and write them on the frame:

| | | | | | |
|---|---|---|---|---|---|
| tidy | sandy | trip | land | rocky | rest |
| wink | thank | inky | spy | deny | flop |

(N.B. Column 4 can be used at TP 83 and TP 98 to practise the drop 'e' rule.)

Figure V.22   *4-in-a Row Reading Game*                    **TP 81**

| chop | ship | chest | chin | shop | shin |
|------|------|-------|------|------|------|
| dish | chip | rush | chill | shock | chant |
| shell | cosh | chat | wish | chick | fish |
| shrimp | shed | chink | rash | chap | chit |
| bash | chuffed | cash | chomp | flash | chum |
| choppy | chimp | chubby | gush | champ | wash |

**TP 129**

| curl | spurn | purple | incur | return | nursed |
|------|-------|--------|-------|--------|--------|
| burr | lurk | blur | turnip | purse | hurl |
| turned | burly | spurt | hurl | turf | turban |
| curt | turtle | gurgle | burdock | burst | Turkish |
| church | purchase | surly | unfurl | cursed | furlong |
| Burt | burning | lurch | churlish | murmur | hurt |

Players take turns to read a word and place a counter on top of it. The first player to have four counters in a row is the winner.

## Photocopiable:
*Teaching Literacy to Learners with Dyslexia* © Kathleen Kelly and Sylvia Phillips, 2011 (SAGE)

Figure V.23  *Crossword Puzzle 'igh'*  **TP 115**

Write the clues for the crossword:

|  |  |  |  |  |  |  |  | 1. |  |  |  |
|---|---|---|---|---|---|---|---|---|---|---|---|
|  |  |  |  |  |  |  |  | n |  |  |  |
|  |  |  |  |  |  |  | 2. |  |  |  |  |
|  |  |  |  |  |  |  | l | i | g | h | t |
|  |  |  |  | 4. |  |  | g |  |  |  |  |
|  |  |  |  | s |  |  | g |  |  |  |  |
|  |  |  | 3. |  |  |  |  |  |  |  |  |
|  |  |  | f | r | i | g | h | t |  |  |  |
|  |  |  |  |  |  | g |  | t |  |  |  |
|  |  | 6. |  |  |  | h |  |  |  |  |  |
|  |  | r |  |  |  | h |  |  |  |  |  |
|  | 5. |  |  |  |  |  |  |  |  |  |  |
|  | f | i | g | h | t |  |  |  |  |  |  |
|  |  | g |  |  |  |  |  |  |  |  |  |
| 7. |  |  |  |  |  |  |  |  |  |  |  |
| h | i | g | h |  |  |  |  |  |  |  |  |
|  |  | t |  |  |  |  |  |  |  |  |  |

Clues Across:

2.

3.

5.

7.

Clues Down:

1.

4.

6.

**Photocopiable:**
*Teaching Literacy to Learners with Dyslexia* © Kathleen Kelly and Sylvia Phillips, 2011 (SAGE)

Figure V.24   *Additional Strategies for Teaching Irregular Spellings*

Chapter 11 suggested one method for teaching learners how to spell irregular words. There are several others that could be used to replace the one given there and these are listed below.

# Neurolinguistic Programming (NLP)

This method, based on the NLP model, enables learners to develop effective cognitive strategies for spelling. It makes use of visual imagery and may be a particularly suitable method for learners with dyslexia as often visual memory is a strength.

## Procedure

- Write the correct spelling of the target word on card or paper in a large, clear print.
- Hold the card up and to the left of the learner.
- Discuss the visual appearance of the word: the length and shape of the word, any patterns to be seen (e.g., **se**n**se)**, or any words within the word (e.g., Ric**hard**, Indepen**dent)** and then ask the learner to visualise the word in their mind's eye.
- Remove the card and ask the learner to name the letters forwards and backwards. If the learner makes a mistake, ask him/her to look at the card again and point out the notable features of the word.
- Ask the learner to write the word (naming the letters) and then turn card over to check if s/he is correct.

# Look, Cover, Write, Check (LCWC)

This is a very common method for learning irregular words. Normally verbalisation is not included but we believe that this is an important missing element and so have indicated where it should come in the routine.

## Procedure

- Write the correct spelling of the word on card or paper.
- Ask them to look at it carefully – allow about 5–10 seconds – and then cover the word or turn the card over.
- *Ask the learner to spell it out loud using the letter names.* (If s/he makes any mistakes then show the card again.)
- The learner then writes the word down, naming the letters, and checks their spelling against the model.
- If there are any mistakes encourage the learner to look at the card again for a slightly longer period of time and then repeat steps 3 and 4 above.

# Tracing

This method uses kinaesthetic memory (which again may be a strength in learners with dyslexia) to recall the motor movement involved in writing a word. It is a well known method similar to the approach called the Fernald method.

## Procedure

- Use a felt pen to write the target word on card in large letters about 3–5 centimetres high either in print or using a handwriting style familiar to the learner.
- The learner then traces over the letters in the word with their index finger (or pencil) several times, naming the letters.
- The learner writes the word on paper (naming the letters) and checks if it is correct. If a mistake has been made the procedure is repeated until the spelling is correct.

# Mnemonics

This method of provides a way of aiding auditory sequential memory by producing a sentence or phrase where the letter of each word spells out the target word in the correct order. The use of visual clues to support the rhyme or mnemonic is particularly recommended for learners with dyslexia. The more absurd the mnemonic is, the easier it may be to remember. To use this method the learner must be able to isolate and identify the first letter of the words in the mnemonic.

## Procedure

- Write correct spelling of the word on a card and ask the learner to identify the letters in the word.
- Encourage the learner to think of a saying or phrase in which each word starts with a letter in the spelling. These must be in the correct sequential order, e.g. the order of the letters in the word {play} might be remembered by the phrase {People Laughing And Yelling}. If possible use a mnemonic that starts with the word to be learned e.g. girl – 'Girl In Red Lipstick'.
- The learner recites the saying and spells the word, naming the letters.
- If the learner makes a mistake, consider if a different saying should be used.
- Repeat the procedure until the word is correct.

The saying could be written in the learner's book with the first letter of each word highlighted in a different colour, e.g., **S**usan **A**nd **I** **D**ance (for the word 'said' to make it stand out and then a picture drawn next to it is a memory aid. Another useful strategy is to record the saying (and spelling) for the learner to listen to and join in with as s/he looks at the mnemonic in the book).

# Picture Association (Picture Links)

The use of picture association as a technique for remembering information was discussed in Chapter 12 on study skills. It can also be used effectively with some students to teach spellings. The method uses visual imagery and pictures to help the learner to remember the 'tricky' part of the spelling. Learners with dyslexia are often very creative and may enjoy an approach that involves the use drawing and colour as well as imagination.

## Procedure

- Write the target word on a card or piece of paper and highlight the tricky bit of the word (e.g. the silent letter 's' in the word 'island').
- Encourage the learner to think of a picture and phrase that incorporates the spelling. For instance, a common way of teaching the spelling of 'island' is to write the phrase 'an island **is land** surrounded by water' – next to a picture of an island.
- Then ask the learner to write the whole word from memory, naming the letters.
- Check that the learner has transferred the correct spelling into general written work. If a mistake is made then remind him/her of the picture. Ask the learner to recall the phrase and then name the letters in the word before writing it down.

## Words in Words

This method involves visual memory and careful attention to detail in identifying smaller words within a larger word as an aid to correct spelling. The learner must be able to recognise and spell the smaller, simple words in order to use this approach and so a basic level of spelling is required.

## Procedure

- Write the word to be learned on paper or card.
- Ask the learner to scan the word carefully, identify the small words within and underline (or box) them. For example, the word chaperone contains *chap* and *one*; there is a *wed* in Wednesday; and a *bus* in busy.
- Ask the learner to write the word from memory, naming the letters.
- If the learner makes a mistake, repeat the procedure emphasising the tricky bit of the word at step 3, for example, the learner might say 'busy' is 'bus', 'b' – 'u' – 's' and the letter 'y'.

N.B. only select words that *do* contain smaller words within them.

The spelling strategies outlined above are amongst a number of well known methods used by Brooks and Weeks (1999) as part of a DfEE research project into teaching spelling to children with literacy difficulties

## Reference

Brooks P. and Weeks S. (1999) *Individual Styles in Learning to Spell: Improving Spelling in Children with Literacy Difficulties and all Children in Mainstream Schools*. Norwich: HMSO.

 **Photocopiable:**
*Teaching Literacy to Learners with Dyslexia* © Kathleen Kelly and Sylvia Phillips, 2011 (SAGE)

Figure V.25    *Examples of Computer Software*

| | | |
|---|---|---|
| Blend-it | Blending 3-letter words<br>For 5–6 year-olds | HELP Software |
| Brain Booster Study Skills | Study Skills Strategies<br>For 13 years + | Nessy |
| Handwriting for Windows | Convert text to cursive<br>All | Inclusive Technology |
| Inspiration | Visual representation: mind-mapping<br>7–14 year-olds | REM |
| Joinit | A variety of cursive writing scripts also<br>available<br>For teachers/all learners | CCW |
| Nessy Games Player | Reduced version of full programme<br>For 7–14 year-olds | Nessy |
| Starspell | Multisensory spelling<br>For 5–15 year-olds | Inclusive Technology |
| Wordshark 4 | Games for reading and spelling<br>For 5–14 year-olds | Inclusive Technology |

**Web addresses of suppliers:**

| | |
|---|---|
| CCW Cursive Writing | www.cursivewriting.org |
| HELP Educational Games | www.helpgames.co.uk |
| Inclusive Technology | www.inclusive.co.uk |
| Nessy (Net Educational Systems Ltd) | www.nessy.com |
| R-E-M Educational Software | www.r-e-m.co.uk |

Teachers should also refer to the BDA website for reviews of technical aids and software for use with learners with dyslexia which are regularly up-dated: http://www.bdadyslexia.org.uk/

## Photocopiable:
*Teaching Literacy to Learners with Dyslexia* © Kathleen Kelly and Sylvia Phillips, 2011 (SAGE)

Figure V.26    *Useful Addresses for Basic Teaching Resources:*

- www.pacon.com (packs of coloured cards for Reading and Spelling Packs)
- www.craftpacks.co.uk (packs of blank playing cards for Reading and Spelling Packs or for making games)
- www.lakelandeducational.co.uk (wooden letters and alphabet jigsaws)
- www.annarbor.co.uk (high interest-low readability level reading books)
- www.senteacher.org (for making customised worksheets and reading games)
- www.freemind.sourceforge.net (for downloads of free mind-mapping software)

**Downloadable Materials**

For downloadable material for this section visit www.sagepub.co.uk/kelly&phillips

# GLOSSARY

**Accent** In teaching reading accent means the stress/emphasis on one syllable in a word. The accented part of a word (or sentence) is spoken more loudly (or with a higher intonation or for a longer length of time) than the rest of the word (or sentence). The mouth usually opens more widely when accenting a syllable than for the other syllables of a word. An example of 'accent'/'stress' can be seen in distinguishing pho'tograph from photog´raphy where´ is a mark at the end of the accented syllable. (In some modern dictionaries the stress mark precedes the stressed syllable.)

**Affix** A letter or group of letters attached to the beginning or end of a base word or root word, which alters the word's meaning or changes its grammatical form. See also **prefix** and **suffix**.

**Alphabetic principle** The relationship between a phoneme (sound) and the grapheme(s) (letter/s) which represent it.

**Analogy** A resemblance/correspondence between two words /concepts. A reader (or speller) may read/write a word based on recognising some sort of similarity with another word (e.g., may work our how to read or spell 'alarm' based on their knowledge of the word 'farm').

**Analytic phonics** An approach to teaching reading where learners are taught to recognise whole words and then analyse these with constitution units in order to identify letter–sound (grapheme–phoneme) correspondences. See also **synthetic phonics**.

**Articulation**   Production of speech depending on the position of the mouth, lips and teeth. An utterance.

**Attention Deficit (Hyperactivity) Disorder (AD(H)D)**   A developmental, neurological disorder characterised by attention difficulties, impulsive behaviours and distractibility often accompanied by hyperactivity.

**Autistic Spectrum Conditions (ASC) often referred to as ASD (disorders)**   A spectrum of behaviours characterised by difficulties in social interaction, communication, ability to understand 'others' often accompanied by routine/ritualistic behaviours. There is a wide range of such behaviours, so that some may have very limited ability and speech whereas others may be able and articulate. Autistic Spectrum Conditions are often **co-morbid** with dyslexia.

**Autobiographical memory**   An individual's personal recall of events/facts: it often refers to memory of personal history / experiences that evoke emotional responses e.g., the birth of a child.

**Automaticity**   Ability to respond quickly, without attention or 'conscious' effort (thereby allowing effort / thinking to concentrate on comprehension or other aspects of a task).

**Base word**   A word which can stand alone, but to which an affix can be added e.g., 'stable' can become 'unstable'.

**Blend**   Two or more adjacent consonants whose sounds flow together but retain discrete sounds e.g., 'sp' in 'spin' is an initial consonant blend and in 'lisp' is a final consonant blend.

**Bottom-up approaches**   An approach to reading based on recognising or decoding every word. Phonics-based teaching (whether analytic or synthetic) and 'sight-vocabulary' reading are examples of 'bottom-up' approaches. See **top-down**.

**Breve**   A small curved diacritical mark ˘ placed above a written vowel to indicate a short sound e.g. /ă/ in the word 'cat'.

**Cerebellum**   The area of the brain integrating motor skills and balance (providing feedback on the position of the body in space). Neural pathways link the cerebellum to the motor cortex, sending information to the muscles, thereby causing them to move.

**Closed syllable**   A syllable ending with one or more consonants e.g., rab/bit has two closed syllables.

**Cognition**    Processes concerned with knowing, perceiving, and thinking. Cognitive strategies include planning, thinking ahead, checking, evaluating.

**Co-morbidity**    The co-existence of one or more disorders / difficulties in addition to a primary disorder (i.e. co-existence). Some specific learning difficulties are commonly found to 'co-exist' with dyslexia, e.g., autistic spectrum disorders – particularly Asperger's Syndrome, dyspraxia, developmental co-ordination disorder (DCD) and Attention Deficit (Hyperactive) Disorder ADD/ADHD.

**Concept**    As in 'Literary Concept' – a notion, idea or aspect of the features or characteristics of literacy e.g., the concept of a syllable.

**Compound words**    Two words are put together to form a new word e.g., handbag, snowman.

**Decode (in reading)**    To determine the pronunciation of a word by understanding how letters represent sounds.

**Developmental dyslexia**    The characteristics develop naturally during childhood as opposed to being the result of, for example, an illness, accident or trauma as in acquired dyslexia, which might result from a stroke or accident.

**Diacritical marking**    A mark used to 'distinguish' /indicate the pronunciation of a letter or group of letters e.g., a breve or macron above a vowel.

**Digraph**    Two adjacent consonants or two adjacent vowels in a syllable representing a single sound e.g. 'th' in 'this' and 'ai' in 'maid'.

**Discovery teaching**    see **guided discovery teaching**.

**Digit span**    A procedure used to assess short-term and working memory involving presenting a learner orally with a series of single digit numbers given randomly and asking him/her to recall them either in the order presented or in reverse order.

**Double deficit**    A deficit in both phonological awareness and speed of processing/rapid naming.

**Dysgraphia**    Very poor handwriting or the inability to produce the fine motor skills required for handwriting (considered to be a neurological dysfunction).

**Dyspraxia or Developmental Co-ordination Disorders**    Difficulty in controlling muscles and movement which can affect speech and/or balance and motor control.

**Episodic memory** A type of long-term memory of specific experiences (e.g., of places, times, events).

**Event Related Potentials (ERP)** A term referring to a measure of brain response (e.g., a scan) that is directly the result of a thought or perception. The response may be to an internal or external stimulus.

**Grapheme-phoneme correspondence** Making a link between a grapheme (letter or letter cluster) and the phoneme (single speech sound) that it represents.

**Guided discovery teaching** A teaching strategy where new concepts or knowledge are presented in ways which supports learners in 'discovering' or deducing the new Teaching Point.

**Hemisphere** The brain is divided into two parts (left and right hemisphere).

**Irregular word** A word where the spelling contains an unusual (or infrequent) representation of a sound e. g., 'said', 'one'.

**Kinaesthetic** A sensory experience related to movement of muscles and joints of the body.

**Lexicon** A body of word knowledge, either written or spoken – a vocabulary.

**Lexical route** A system which relies on whole word processing.

**Linguistic** Referring to language processing and language structure.

**Linkages (links)** The associations developed in a multisensory language programme between a learner's visual, auditory, kinaesthetic and tactile perceptions.

**Long-term memory** The part of memory to which information is sent for permanent storage. It is seen as having an infinite capacity.

**Macron** A small flat diacritical mark (-) placed above a vowel to represent a long vowel sound e.g. /ā/ in 'acorn'.

**Magnocellular deficit** Difficulty in processing rapid moving information in either the auditory or visual pathways of the magnocellular system of the brain.

**Mastery** Proficiency/competence in a specific skill area: the ability to recall automatically.

**Metacognition**   Consciousness or knowledge of the strategies used to learn a skill or acquire knowledge; an understanding of personal learning process.

**Metalanguage**   Awareness of language and knowledge of the terms and concepts that can be used to analyse language and learning.

**Mind Map**   This is a method of visually recording thoughts and ideas using a diagram which contains words, symbols and pictures to represent those ideas. It shows a central idea with branches containing sub-themes around that main idea which then helps to organise and recall thoughts. It is usually used for planning assignments or exam revision.

**Mnemonics**   A strategy devised to improve memory e.g., chunking, visualising, rhyming, using initial letters in a 'key word' etc.

**Morphology**   How meaningful units are put together to form words (morpheme = a meaningful unit which may be a word in itself e.g., 'find' or a group of letters e.g., '-ing' which when added to a word changes the meaning of that word).

**Multisensory literacy programme**   An approach to teaching literacy that involves the simultaneous use of at least two senses (visual/auditory/kinaesthetic/touch) and teaches listening, speaking, reading, writing and spelling together.

**Neural pathway**   Neurons are cells that make up the nervous system. Neurons are linked to each other (neural pathways) so that they can store and transmit information from one part of the body to another.

**Non-lexical route**   A system which breaks words down into grapheme-phoneme correspondence.

**Nonsense words**   (Also non-words) – a 'word' or grouping of letters which can be decoded phonically (i.e. the graphemes represent particular phonemes) but where the word has no meaning in that language (English).

**Occipital Lobe**   The rear part of the cerebral hemispheres processing visual information.

**Onset**   The initial consonant(s) in a word (e.g., 'c' in cat and 'scr' in scream). See also **rime**.

**Orthography**   The established spelling or representation of words in a written language.

**Phoneme**   An individual unit of sound: the smallest unit of sound in speech.

**Phonemic awareness**   Awareness of the smallest units of sound and the ability to distinguish and manipulate individual sounds in words.

**Phonetics**   The study of sounds in speech in any language including describing them in terms of analysing production (how they are made), and representing them graphically using the International Phonetic Alphabet (IPA).

**Phonics**   The representation of an association between the printed form of letters and the sound(s) they represent.

**Phonogram**   A written symbol representing a phoneme (single unit of sound). It can be called a phonograph.

**Phonological**   Relating to a speaker's knowledge about the sound systems in a language.

**Phonological awareness**   Knowledge of and sensitivity to the phonological properties of words in a language.

**Phonological deficit**   A difficulty in phonological processing e.g. in segmenting or blending sounds or appreciating rhyme.

**Phonology**   The science or knowledge of the sound system of a language both segmental (e.g., phonemes) and non-segmental or supra-segmental (e.g., stress, pitch, volume). The latter is often described as prosodic features.

**Polygenetic**   More than one gene is responsible for a condition e.g., dyslexia.

**Prefix**   A group of letters (forming a syllable) which is added at the beginning of a **base** or **root** word to change its meaning e.g., 'mis' added to 'represent' to make 'misrepresent'.

**Rapid serial naming (or rapid automatic naming)**   A task where an individual is asked to name rapidly a series of printed objects/letters/colours/numbers presented randomly. It tests automaticity and is often used as part of the process of identifying dyslexia.

**Rime**   The written or spoken vowel and final consonant(s) in a word or syllable e.g., 'at' in 'cat' and 'eam' in 'scream'.

**Root**   A word to which affixes can be added, but some 'roots' are morphemes (often of Greek or Latin origin) which cannot stand alone an English word e.g., 'struct' as in destruct/instruct/ instruction.

**Schwa**   An unaccented (indeterminate) vowel whose pronunciation is like /uh/ as the 'a' in about. It is normally represented as /ə/. It is made involuntarily at the end of pronouncing some phonemes e.g., /b/ is often pronounced /buh/ as air escapes when the lips open after forming /b/.

**Segmentation**   Separating a word into units (such as onset and rime, syllables or individual units).

**Semantic**   Referring to the meaning of words.

**Short term memory**   The term short-term memory refers to information presented verbally or visually that is stored for only a very short period of time (seconds).

**Sky writing (air writing)**   The technique of 'writing' a letter or word in the air using the writing hand and arm so that the upper-arm muscles are used to help the writer to establish kinaesthetic traces or memories.

**Square Root Rule**   A rule that gives a rough guide to the number of repetitions (or exposures e.g., to a word) that a learner with dyslexia will need, compared to his /her peers. Multiply the original number of repetitions by its square root to estimate how much revision and repetition that is needed for a learner with dyslexia.

**Suffix**   A group of letters (forming a syllable) which is added at the end of a **base** or **root** word to change its meaning e.g., 's' added to 'house' changes it to a plural form, or to third person singular present tense of a verb; '-ful' changes beauty to beautiful, that is, from a noun to an adjective.

**Syllable**   A spoken or written unit that must have a vowel sound and can include preceding and/or following consonants. It is made by one impulse of the voice.

**Syntax**   The structures of grammar – the system governing how words must be ordered in phrases or sentences.

**Synthetic phonics**   Introducing letter-sound (grapheme-phoneme correspondences) and then blending then/joining them to others to make meaningful units/words. See also **analytic phonics**.

**Top-down approaches**   These refer to teaching reading by emphasising bringing one's own experiences and knowledge to a text in order to extract overall meaning (and establish the idea that the purpose of reading is to extract meaning from a text) before then introducing decoding/word recognition strategies.

**Un-voiced consonant**   A consonant produced with no vocal vibration e.g., /s/ sound in sun.

**Voiced consonant**   A consonant articulated with vocal cords vibrating e.g., /z/ sound of 's' in rose.

**Vowel suffix**   A suffix beginning with a vowel e.g. '-ing' and '-ed'. The addition of this suffix often affects the ending of a **base** or **root** word, particularly where that word ends in a vowel.

**Working memory**   The part of short-term memory that holds on to information long enough to manipulate or use it e.g., as in following an instruction or carrying out a mental calculation.

# AUTHOR INDEX

# SUBJECT INDEX